MENACE

China's Colonization of the Islamic World
&
Uyghur Genocide

Abdulhakim Idris

MENACE
CHINA'S COLONIZATION OF THE
ISLAMIC WORLD & UYGHUR GENOCIDE

First Edition

Center for Uyghur Studies
1101 Pennsylvania Ave NW. Suite 300
Washington, DC 20004
www.uyghurstudy.org

ISBN 978-1-7365414-1-8
Copyright © 2020 Abdulhakim Idris

I dedicate this book to the two most precious women in my life, my mother Habibehan Hajim and my wife Rushan Abbas, and to the two most important men in my life, my father Abdulkarim Hajim and my mentor Muhammedali Akhun Khelpitim.

MR. ABDULHAKIM A IDRIS was born in Hotan city in East Turkistan in 1968. He was educated in Islamic religious studies and Arabic language at the underground Islamic schools (Madrasa) in Hotan before leaving his hometown in 1986 to study Islam in Egypt at Al-Azhar University. After he studied in Cairo, he settled in Munich, Germany, in 1990 as one of the first Uyghurs to seek asylum in Europe. He studied Industrial Management at the Deutsche Angestellten-Akademie (DAA) in Munich.

Mr. Idris is one of the founding members of the East Turkistan Union in Europe established in 1991 in Germany, the first Uyghur organization in Europe. Mr. Idris also co-founded the World Uyghur Youth Congress (WUYC) in 1996 and the East Turkistan National Congress in 1999, and one of the founders of the World Uyghur Congress in 2004. He previously served as Treasury, Vice-Chairman of the Executive Committee, Director of the Refugee Center for the World Uyghur Congress. He was the Treasurer and Chairman of the Executive Committee for the World Uyghur Youth Congress. Additionally, he served as one of the Board of Directors for the Uyghur American Association in Washington DC. In 2017, Mr. Idris and his wife Rushan Abbas founded the non-profit organization Campaign for Uyghurs. He is also the current Inspector General of the World Uyghur Congress (WUC), and the founder and Executive Director of the Center for Uyghur Studies, a Washington D.C.-based think tank.

Mr. Idris has consistently advocated for the Uyghur people's rights and has been a prominent human rights advocate in the Uyghur diaspora. He moved to the United States in 2009 and currently lives in Northern Virginia. He speaks English, German, Arabic, Uyghur, and Turkish.

CONTENTS

INTRODUCTION

"This Time, Danger Comes
from The East"

"They destroyed Islamic culture and civilization and laid waste to Islamic countries. Masjids were turned into stables, the pages of the Holy Book were laid under the feet of animals, valuable works belonging to the Islamic cultural heritage were either burned or thrown into rivers. Millions of people were massacred."

"Mosques were turned into a pigsty, the Koran was seized from houses and burned. 16 thousand 500 mosques were damaged, 8 thousand 500 of them were destroyed. Koranic verses were removed from the walls of the surviving mosques, the minarets were damaged. Millions of people were subjected to genocide."

THE ABOVE TWO EXCERPTS describe the tragedies in two different periods of world history. The first is related to the destruction sowed by the Mongol invasion, an invasion that hit the Khwarezmians for the first time in 1220 and reached its peak in 1258 with the invasion of Baghdad. The other is a summary of the genocide committed by the Chinese Communist Regime in East Turkistan since its invasion in 1949.

With the Battle of Ain Jalut in 1260, the Mamluk army under the command of the Mamluk Sultan Qutuz and one of his amirs Baibars stopped the Mongol expansion, thereby protecting Egypt and other Middle Eastern lands from ravage and keeping some parts of the Islamic civilization intact.

The genocide that started in East Turkistan continues with the economic siege of Pakistan by the sino-colonial regime. This invasion extends from Pakistan to Iran, Egypt, and Africa and even reaches the gates of Europe. This is not an era of invasion with swords and spears or guns and cannons. What we witness today is the realization of the imperialist dream of China, which aims at erasing traces of Islam wherever it can reach, starting from the homeland of Muslim Uyghurs. Nowadays the neo-colonial system forces the doors not with cannons, guns, bombs, or planes but with advanced technologies. Once opened it lures countries into debt traps and seizes their assets.

The main purpose of this study is to ring the alarm bells and warn against sino-colonialism, the damage potential of which is compounded with Xi

Jinping's Chinese Nationalism. The world, especially the Muslim countries, is exposed to 'the danger coming from the east'. The Islamic world is confronted with humanitarian crises in Kashmir, Palestine, Syria, Rohingya, and Yemen. Due to interest-oriented conflicts among superpowers, peoples are massacred and millions have to flee their homeland. There are publications on these issues in both Muslim and western countries. Conducting this study does not mean that tragedies or crises experienced elsewhere should be ignored. The aim is to draw attention to the new dangers that the Islamic world is currently facing, based on the example of East Turkistan.

Ibn al-Athir, a famous Medieval historian, personally met with the people who had gone through the invasion of the Mongols mentioned above and after his extensive research came to the following conclusion: "This invasion is the biggest calamity that human beings have been subjected to since Adam." [1] This calamity affected a vast area covering Asia, the Middle East, and Asia Minor and changed the course of history. The ethnic structure of the Turkic World was completely upended and communities such as Uyghur, Karluk, and Kipchak were displaced. Iraq, the center of science, culture, and administration of the time was ravaged. Thanks to the Mamluks, which stopped the Mongol advance, Egypt and Syria came to the fore as the new center.

The tribes who fled from the Mongols and resettled in Anatolia have changed the ethnic structure there. The influence of the Mongols began to show itself not ' in the field of military and state administration but in every aspect of life. The people subjected to the persecution became more prone to mysticism and the interest in natural sciences declined. [2] The river turned red with the blood of people massacred when two major science centers, Baghdad and Basra, were destroyed. The Islamic world, which once raised names such as Al Biruni, who discovered that the world rotates centuries before Galileo, Ibn Sina (Avicenna), who played a pioneering role in the development of medicine in Europe, and Al-Khawarizmi, one of the pioneers in mathematics, lost its leading role in sciences after the Mongol invasion.

The West started to stand out in science and technology instead of the Islamic World. The consequences of backwardness in technology and science caused by the Mongol invasion have become more evident over the centuries. Western countries, that exploited Africa and the Far East from the 16th to 20th century, first colonized the Muslim communities in those parts of the world. With the collapse of the Ottoman Empire, the territories within its borders were shared by the victorious countries and a new chapter was opened in the colonial oppression in the Islamic world. Some hundred years ago, all Muslim countries were occupied by Britain, France, or other western countries. With the establishment of the Soviet Union after the communist revolution in 1917, the Turkic communities in Central Asia also were put under captivity. The map of the Middle East has been reshaped according to oil reserves.

Humankind's ambition for power has brought Europe to the brink of a second war 20 years after World War I. This war has brought about differing results for Muslim societies. The colonial system in the Islamic world, which was established after World War I and which extended from the Middle East to Africa and Asia, has changed. Under the influence of nationalist movements throughout the world, Muslim states started to gain their independence one by one. Yet, they could not get rid of the dependency on economy and technology and achieve a full-fledged and free state system.

While the Middle East, Africa, and some parts of Asia were witnessing these developments, power struggles among great powers in China and its surrounding region continued until the end of World War II. In 1911 the Chinese empire fell and a republic was established in its place. Led by Mao, the Communist Party, whose seeds were sown under the Soviet influence, established the People's Republic of China (PRC) in 1949. The Cold War period, which started in 1947 between the USA-Europe-England axis and the Soviet Union and its allies, continued until the 1990s.

Although not as much as the Soviet Union, the Maoist-Leninist regime of PRC started to build a new colonial order for itself during the Cold War. Occupying East Turkistan, Tibet, and Inner Mongolia, the communist Chinese regime declared them as its own territory and started to exploit these lands. East Turkistan, the heart of Central Asia and a unique region both geographically and in terms of underground resources, has remained for many years in the position of a gladiator among monsters fighting for his life in a Roman Arena. In 1866, Yakup Beg brought together the Muslim communities there and established a state named Kashgaria, but immediately thereafter the British started to target the new state with their machinations, supporting the armament of the Qing Dynasty through their banks. This armament tipped the military power balance in favor of the Qing Dynasty and the Kashgaria fell as a result. The first East Turkistan Islamic Republic, founded in 1933, collapsed also by the betrayal of the Soviet Union and its extensions in East Turkistan. However, the aspiration of the people of East Turkistan for independence has not died down and in 1944, the second East Turkistan Republic was established.

After the Yalta Conference in 1945, Britain left the decision about the future of East Turkistan to the Soviet Union and the newly established communist China. The Soviet Union in its turn handed over the homeland of the Muslim Uyghurs to the PRC. Sharing the same ideological origins, these two regimes destroyed the new East Turkistan Republic with another plot. The delegation led by Ehmetjan Qasimi, one of the leaders of East Turkistan, was invited to Almaty by the Soviet Union. Since the Soviet Union wanted East Turkistan to be part of the new Chinese Communist Regime, it pressed for Ehmetjan Qasimi and his companions to go to Beijing and accept Mao's terms. However, they did not go to Beijing and eventually disappeared – according to the Soviet Union – in a plane crash. Their disappearance was kept secret from the people of East Turkistan for days.

With the initiative of the Soviet Union, Saifuddin Azizi went to Beijing and had a meeting with Mao and submitted the key to East Turkistan to him. In short, the Soviet Union handed over East Turkistan to China. In 1949, East Turkistan was invaded by the People's Liberation Army (PLA). The economy and agriculture of East Turkestan were handed on a silver platter to the semi-military corps system Bingtuan (Xinjiang Production and Construction Corps - XPCC), which was established in 1954. To support the Bingtuan team hundreds of thousands of Han Chinese were settled in East Turkistan.

When the relations between Mao and the Soviet Union got sour in the following years, millions of people in China, especially the Muslim communities in East Turkistan, were massacred by the communist authoritarian rule. With the Great Leap Forward and Cultural Revolution programs initiated by Mao, the lands of East Turkistan occupied by Mao experienced a huge destruction similar to what was done by the Mongols in Basra in Baghdad. Books were burned, intellectuals were sent behind bars, some were put on trial and executed with medieval inquisition-like trials, while some others were sent to labor camps resembling Stalin's Gulags, by Mao's Red Guards.

After Stalin's death, relations between Nikita Khrushchev, then-Soviet Chairman, and Mao deteriorated further and the Soviets shut the door to the CCP, pushing Mao to look for new support to sustain his rule. Therefore Mao knocked on America's door. The sino-colonial regime, that starved its people, needed international legitimacy. However, as one sage said: "Affection to a hungry beast does not attract its mercy but whets its appetite. Besides, it demands the rent of his tooth and nail." It was US President Richard Nixon and his National Security Adviser and a prominent foreign policy figure Henry Kissinger, who took the first step to pet this monster. As a result of the Kissinger-initiated "ping-pong diplomacy", the way was paved for the removal of the Republic of China (today's Taiwan) from the UN Security Council and its replacement by the People's Republic of China, a move which provided immunity armor for the monster that will grow in the future and take the world in its clutches.

While George H.W. Bush, then-US Ambassador to the UN, was working on "two Chinese formulas", Kissinger waited for Taiwan to be expelled from the UN, and even removed the expressions in favor of Taiwan in the speeches to be delivered on behalf of his government. In parentheses, it should be reminded that the damages caused by the "Realpolitik" doctrine, which Kissinger developed in 1969, were grave enough to send him to court for war crimes. Kissinger's kiss of life at the very moment when the authoritarian Chinese Communist regime was on the verge of collapse, was one of the most important breaking points in world history. The whole world, especially America, started to pay the bill for this step over time.

Kissinger continued to support the CCP regime after Mao through those who replaced him, thereby helping this oppressive regime transform into Frankenstein. America, the heart of capitalism, thus became the biggest ally of China, whose founding philosophy was communism. With the policy of opening up in economy in the 1980s, Beijing turned into a capitalist system that no longer knows any value. This system has two faces. While it warmly welcomed companies coming from the west for investment, it crushed the people with an iron fist in the lands it occupied such as East Turkistan and Tibet. Kissinger saw China as the incarnation of an ancient civilization that has divine ruling principles. [3] However, what he could not or did not want to see was the fact that the regime built during Mao's time destroyed all that historical heritage. In an article published in 1989, Miriam London argued that Kissinger and Nixon failed to see Mao as a brutal dictator, who murdered millions of people to sustain his dark regime. London further emphasized that China experts mushroomed with the wind created by Kissinger created a fictional perception about China in newspaper columns and on TVs. While millions of people died of hunger during the cultural revolution initiated by Mao, these so-called experts claimed that the Chinese people were endowed with the necessary means for happiness and sustenance. Kissinger praised Mao and Prime Minister Zhou Enlai, while the press adorned its pages with illusions about the new China. [4]

With the Tiananmen events of 1989, the Realpolitik had a reality check, showing that it failed and that the Chinese regime would never be a democratic rule respecting universal legal standards. The first student protests against closed regimes such as the Soviet Union and the PRC started in East Turkistan even before Tiananmen in 1985. A march, which took place in 1988, in which tens of thousands of Uyghur students participated, could not get publicity due to the closed-circuit system of that period. One year later in 1989 thousands of students gathered in Tiananmen Square to protest the repressive policies of the government. Among the leaders of these demonstrations was also Örkesh Dölet from East Turkistan, publicly known as Wu'erkaixi. The demonstrations that started on April 15 ended on June 4 with the crackdown of Chinese soldiers with tanks and firearms on the protesters. In the ensuing massacre, thousands of students lost their lives and thousands more wounded. In the subsequent witch hunt, millions were arrested and sent behind bars. No strong objection was heard from Washington, where Kissinger's influence was still felt, against this massacre. Adding insult to injury Kissinger applauded the to- talitarian regime for its massacre. "No government in the world would have tolerated having the main square of its capital occupied for eight weeks by tens of thousands of demonstrators who blocked the area in front of the main government building... A crackdown was therefore inevitable. But its brutality was shocking... Still, China remains too important to U.S. national security to risk the relationship on emotions of the moment." [5]

Along with Kissinger's Realpolitik doctrine, another point that should be rai- sed is the unusual support of Helmut Schmidt, then-German Chancellor, to Mao and his rule. Like Kissinger, he acted on the "need to understand" the CCP, but never saw the egregious human rights violations of the Chinese dictatorial regi- me, thereby playing into the hands of this monstrous mentality. The communist regime was so grateful that it even published a documentary praising the 'colla- borator' Schmidt on its channels. Visiting Beijing after the Tiananmen massacre and meeting with Deng Xiaoping, Schmidt helped China to integrate with the world economy in a way similar to the move of Kissinger when he helped the Communist regime gain legitimacy in 1972. With respect to human rights, Sch- midt took refuge behind the excuse of "non-interference in internal affairs" in support of the authoritarian Beijing regime. If the Sino-colonial Beijing regime is now doing as it pleases in the international arena, it is thanks to Schmidt as much as Kissinger. The economic opportunities created by his "Wandel Durch Handel – change through trade" doctrine paved the way for China to become a trust in a way threatening the world economy.

Beijing lovers are quick to praise the so-called "economic miracle" worked by China. Yet, it should not be forgotten that this so-called success was achieved by the exploitation of millions of people's labor. Another important factor is the fi- nancial and human capital that fled to countries such as Thailand, Malaysia, Ta- iwan, Hong Kong, and Singapore before 1949 and that returned to China with Deng's rise to power. While these companies returned to their homeland and provided the necessary means and incentives to open up the Chinese economy to the world with their capital and experienced staff, the people sent abroad by Deng came back endowed with the West's science and technology.

China's participation in the World Trade Organization (WTO) in 2000 with the support of US President Bill Clinton marked the beginning of a new era in the global economy. A continuation of the opening policy of the 1980s, this development paved the way for China's rapid rise to become second largest economics of the world. Western companies hurried to move their factories to China, especially due to the cheap labor. The fact that the regime remained communist did not prevent them from making huge profits in the savage capitalistic system. In a sense, the Beijing regime was empowered by those companies, that paid 100 dollars per month in China to a worker instead of 2.000 dollars that they have to pay in their own country. Moreover, there are neither workers' rights nor environmental concerns nor international restrictive regulations. As a result, Western countries, America first and foremost, have begun to encounter unemployment and consequently social problems that may lead to social explosions.

On the other hand, the Sinification process by means of the resettlement of Han Chinese and the state-sponsored capitalism carried out through them is also progressing at full throttle in East Turkistan. The transformation of the Chinese economy was accomplished between 2000 and 2012. Thanks to this transformation it became not ' the manufacturing center of foreign brands but built up its own companies and financial institutions. The brains behind this transformation were the Chinese students, to whom western countries opened their doors for the sake of "dialogue" starting from the Kissinger period. They carried every technology and know-how they learned in the West to their own countries, including intelligence and military issues. When countries like America became aware of the dangers of this "information transportation", it was too late. Now, this cruel system flourished and acquired the ability to send shuttles even to the dark side of the moon, bring stones from there, build nuclear weapons and its own planes.

Under the rule of Xi Jinping, who became the President of China in 2012, the Sino-colonial mentality put into effect new economic invasion plans for other countries. As the son of Xi Zhongxun, who was in charge of the North West Region during the Mao era, Xi knows East Turkistan well. Being even more Maoist than Mao he sees himself as China's third greatest leader and wants to complete what his father left unfinished, the painting of East Turkistan in Chinese red. He is also the behind-the-scenes supporter of extreme Chinese nationalism bequeathed by the Red Guards. The desire of Xi not to follow his father's suit, whose policies in the North West region was disliked by Mao and thence fell from grace after a while, was also influential in Xi's being so aggressive. Xi wants Han Chinese, once humiliated by the colonial states and suffered from poverty and hunger, to dominate the world. To this end, he disregards every international rule. American leaders such as Henry Kissinger, Nixon, and Clinton, who paved the way for China's immunity in international organizations such as the UN, are also liable for this.

With the Belt and Road Initiative, announced one year after Xi took the seat, it became apparent that the colonial occupation campaign would follow a two-thronged strategy. The first is the Historical Silk Road Economic Belt, the point of departure of which is East Turkestan under occupation. The second is the 21st Century Maritime Silk Road network to run through the seas. The Digital Silk Road has also been added to this. To be able to put the first strategy into practice, the Muslim Uyghur people in East Turkistan must first be eliminated. The construction in 2014 of concentration camps, inspired by Nazis, was the first step aimed at destroying both Muslim and ethnic identity of the people of East Turkistan, and erasing the traces of Uyghur, Kazakh, and Kyrgyz communities in their homeland.

The second step was the appointment of Chen Quanguo to East Turkistan in 2016. Chen previously ruled Tibet with an iron fist and under his rule the number of camps hiked, reaching 1.200, where each year 1.3 million people are sent. Currently, the inmates of the concentration camps count more than 3 million. The people, who were kept in the concentration camps for a while, were later sent to factories producing for the western giant companies such as Apple, Nike, and Zara for forced labor. While the concentration camps are being portrayed by the Chinese regime to the outside as holiday/education centers, they are being used by CCP for the enslavement of even the most educated people such as academics, doctors, lawyers, religious leaders, and businessmen thanks to whom the wheels of economy turn incessantly.

Although many independent observers, international organizations, and the US government keep saying that the neo-colonial Chinese regime egregiously violates human rights in East Turkistan and enslaves people, big Western big companies deem it "risky" for their economic interests to leave this system. They continue to make huge profits through the bloody labor of millions of Muslims. Companies such as Apple have even started lobbying in the US Congress against a tentative piece of legislation that will impose sanctions on companies benefiting from the forced labor.

As if the enslavement of the people of East Turkistani were not enough, all kinds of crimes similar to those of the Mongols were committed to wipe out the religious and national identity of them. To this end, among others, Han Chinese were resettled in Muslim women's home to share the same bed, children were ripped from their families and placed in orphanages, women were forcibly sterilized, babies were killed in the womb, headscarves of Muslim women were forcibly removed, mosques were razed to the ground, minarets of the mosques left emblematically intact were demolished, boards carrying the names of Allah and Prophet in mosques were replaced with those of Xi and his slogans, and mosques were turned into bars and cafes. The perpetrators of this persecution are Xi, whose motto is "absolutely no mercy," and Chen, who says "round up everyone who should be rounded up." [6]

Pakistan constitutes the most striking example showing that Xi wants to rule everywhere the Sino-colonialist BRI project can reach like he does East Turkistan. With the agreements signed with Pakistan, this country, which has once the potential to lead the Islamic world, became part of the Chinese sphere of influence. It can no longer survive without neo-colonial China. As explained in the relevant section, the system established as part of BRI in this country, where the military has big clout in the civil administration, is the same as Bingtuan in East Turkistan. The Xi rule applied a similar system in the special economic zone built next to the Suez Canal in Egypt. This system has also been imposed on Algeria, where 50 thousand Chinese have been resettled. While building the neo-imperialist system, Xi constantly told the tale of equal development for all countries.

There is one winner in this game: Xi and his sino-colonial communist regime. The airport of Sri Lanka, which was seized when Sri Lanka failed to pay its debt and Yavuz Sultan Selim Suspended Bridge in Istanbul show how the system works. The whole African continent fell captive to China's grip with its 148 billion dollars debt. The sino-colonial system has been built not through economic means. In addition to the genocide in East Turkistan, the Beijing Regime is also destroying the lives of people in other countries to further its sino-colonialist agenda. Rohingya Muslims are a case in point. Because they constitute an obstacle before trade routes through Myanmar, China orchestrated the expulsion and massacre of Rohingya Muslims.

The chaotic situation that has for long dominated the Middle East, in particular, and the Islamic World, in general, has created a great opportunity for the realization of China's colonial ambitions. Thus, the war that has been raging for nearly 40 years in Afghanistan, the instability and turbulence caused by the Arab Spring movements, the ongoing humanitarian tragedies in Yemen and Syria with their ramifications in the economy created an environment conducive to sino-colonialism. There is, in fact, an ongoing occupation of the sino-colonial regime in the Islamic world, a regime, which, under the guise of rushing to the aid of those in economic crisis, wants to take over the economies of those countries to foster its imperialist mentality there. While this cruel regime uses the UN as a shield to forestall the punishment of the atrocities it has committed, it, on the other hand, vetoes sanctions in the UN Security Council against the regimes that it employs as hitmen.

The fact that one country undertakes another country's infrastructure projects such as bridges, roads, and hospitals should, at first sight, be appreciated. However, if we are talking about the Chinese regime, which has built an economic system relying on the exploitation of human labor since day one, we have to think twice. That is because, when the Chinese regime is investing somewhere, it often comes into play during periods of economic crisis. Wherever there is a country in an economic downturn, Chinese companies appear there with no regard to the environment, workers' rights, or other rules. Take Algeria and Tunisia for example. While Algeria, which opened its door wide to the sino-colonial China, received billions of dollars of Chinese investment, Tunisia, which limits the number of foreign workers to be employed to four and stipulates the employment of its nationals, received less than one-tenth of what Algeria got.

In the system established by neo-colonial China, it is always Chinese companies that get the tender, provide financing to the project, work as sub-contractors, carry out all logistics, and at the end operate the facility. Although they seem to have partnered with local companies in some countries, the real power is behind the scenes still in Beijing's hands. In such a system, when the sino-colonial regime invests in a country it makes profits in that market but does not actually contribute to the local economy. For this reason, people took to the streets and protested against China in Kyrgyzstan.

Today this system works in this way in Pakistan, Egypt, Africa, and even in Eastern Europe. With the BRI, the Beijing regime is now knocking on European doors to impose its own system. The system it established in all these countries is actually the same as the one it established in East Turkistan. If neo-colonialist China wants to do away with East Turkistan now, Pakistan and Iran are next in line. What is more dramatic is that all Muslim countries go hand in hand with Xi, who is the arch-enemy of Islam and who throws people into prison to wipe out Islam from their hearts.

Today the danger is coming from the East, a danger which comes in with a smiling face and goes out after enslaving Muslim societies economically.

The approach of the European and other Western countries, which deems China, - a country that destroyed all universal values - as a country whose loss cannot be risked, should be abandoned. The argument that claimed – as championed by Nixon and Schmidt - that if China gets rich economically, it will stop being communist and integrate with the world has now collapsed. This hope is defeated by Beijing's machinations. The sino-colonial system has established its own order, rather than integrating with the world. When the Western countries opened their doors to the Beijing regime for the sake of "integration", the

Introduction

CCP members who entered through those doors carried all kinds of technology and know-how to China and created alternatives to Western rivals: Huawei vs Apple, Baidu vs Google, WeChat vs WhatsApp, Alibaba vs Amazon and Weibo vs Twitter.

Western companies have, on the other hand, become hostages of the neo-imperialist regime. The Digital Silk Road (DSR), established in 2015, was conceived by the neo-colonial China to bring the world into its orbit. Many countries have been incorporated into this system, thereby becoming part of the despotic internet and surveillance network that China has built within its borders. Thus, they handed over all the information on the internet to Beijing with their own hands and became digitally a hostage of that system. World-famous brands such as Apple, Adidas, and Zara have to rely on China's cheap labor to be able to compete with Chinese brands. This workforce consists of Muslim Uyghurs, Kazakhs, and other minority members who are employed as slave labor.

The sino-colonial system established by Xi and his team not ' used its political power in the international arena but also developed new methods to further its agenda. The 'soft power' Confucius Institutes have been transformed into information gathering centers while, on the other hand, they function as the propaganda machine of the regime. All students who are sent by the Chinese regime to study abroad, work like embassy personnel, and collect intelligence for the regime. The "sister city" practice, which was conceived by the West as part of the integration policy, has also been abused by the Chinese regime. While the Chinese sister city does literally nothing to promote its western partner, the western partner becomes the hub for the Beijing government's systematic propaganda.

Advertisement boards in Chinese are hung at public transportation stops in Istanbul, where thousands of Uyghurs live. Advanced technology systems used in the genocide against people in East Turkistan are marketed abroad under the name of "smart cities", whereby the places where these are installed turn into Beijing's satellite. The data collected via back channels created in these advanced technological systems are transferred to China.

The Chinese students who availed themselves of the opportunity provided by Helmut Schmidt's "change through trade" doctrine and came to Europe for "education" put what they learned in every field from automotive to defense industry, from petrochemicals to electronics, from rapid trains to aircraft technology, into practice for the benefit of their own country.

It is a fact that the giant companies that went to China for production also grew their competitors with their own hands. Today, if the Chinese regime is ambitious in high-speed trains, it is thanks to the cooperation with European

19

companies. If the sino-colonial regime has acquired the military technology to establish bases in Africa, the source of this technology should not be sought far away. To understand how neo-imperialist China can deceive the world, it is sufficient to remember the Varyag ship, which passed through the Bosporus in 2001. The Chinese regime bought the aircraft carrier left in 1988 unfinished by the Soviet Union and lied about its intended purpose saying it will be used for touristic purposes as, under the Montreux Agreement, it is not allowed to pass a warship through the Bosporus. It promised millions of tourists and $ 1 billion worth of insurance to Turkey, neither of which was honored. The so-called tourist ship Varyag is now serving as a Chinese warship named Liaoning.

The most powerful thing in the world is knowledge. Whoever holds knowledge dominates the world. China romanticism of some Western leaders such as Kissinger and Schmidt led to the flow of western knowledge to the system created by Beijing and helped China, endowed with this knowledge, invade the world to realize its sino-colonial aspirations. Kissinger's "Realpolitik" and Schmidt's "Change through trade" doctrines collapsed, as, years ago, it became evident that the neo-imperialist Beijing administration had no other goal than exploiting the world. We are now facing a regime that since 2000 'wants to move the world in a direction that will increase its wealth and power. In 2007, former Zambian Minister Guy Scott quoted the Zambian people as saying, "We have encountered bad people before. Whites were bad, Indians were worse, but Chinese are the worst." This saying reflects the true nature of the sino-colonial regime.

Dipak Patel, Zambia's former Trade and Industry Minister, argued that the Chinese sold in the local market replacing local traders. At that time, the Beijing regime even threatened to withdraw investments if nationalist parties defending the interests of their countries win elections. [7] Therefore, Mahatir Mohammed, former Prime Minister of Malaysia, had every right to say no to the BRI order built by Xi Jinping to realize his imperialist dreams. "Everything comes from China for the projects, employees, all materials, and so on. All payments go to China. There is nothing we gain," Mahatir said in an interview with the PBS channel. He pointed out that the Beijing regime is actually the 'winner in these so-called "win-win" projects. [8]

As these realities come to light, leaders, those of the US first and foremost, had to accept that such naive intentions as "Let's integrate China into the world" caused on the contrary dependence on China.

As these realities come to light, leaders, those of the US first and foremost, had to accept that such naive intentions as "Let's integrate China into the world" led on the contrary to dependence on China. In reflection of this disillusionment, a US State Department official noted that if a free 21st century is desired rather than the Chinese century that Xi dreamed of, the long-standing paradigm of 'blind engagement with China' must be abandoned. [9]

In accounting for this "blind paradigm' and the 'greatest failure of American foreign policy since the 1930s' a prominent National Security official emphasized that the US decision-makers ignored the ideology of the Chinese Communist Party and failed to review the key documents published by it, leading to wishful thinking and miscalculation about the nature of the regime. [10]

The humanitarian crisis and the genocide that has been going on in East Turkistan and Tibet for a long time, and the authoritarian regime's latest practices in Hong Kong are eye-opening. Therefore, the timely and relevant warnings of the Speaker of the US House of Representatives Nancy Pelosi should be heeded: " If we hesitate to speak out for human rights in China because of commercial interest, we lose all moral authority to speak out for human rights any place in the world." [11] The new President of the USA Joe Biden's acknowledgment that Uyghurs and other communities have been subjected to genocide at the hands of China's authoritarian regime is also noteworthy in terms of revealing the true nature of the Sino-colonial regime to the world. [12]

It is said that when a mouse wants to eat someone's ear, it whistles into his/her ear so that he/she does not wake up. Today, the world cannot see that while it is lulled to sleep with Chinese tales of "equal development" and "community of common destiny" it is being besieged by China, which dreams of making Beijing the capital of the world. An article titled " China's combative nationalists see a world turning their way" by Chris Buckley, which appeared in the New York Times on December 14, points at how the nationalist mentality of the communist regime views the world. This article contains a picture of a flag hanging on the New York Stock Exchange building in Manhattan, the heart of the American economy, with the phrase "People's Union of America". This picture depicts the imaginary commemoration ceremonies thirty years after the US completely transitioned into the Communist system in 2068. [13] According to this depiction, Manhattan will become a city that resembles the streets of Beijing in 2098. This depiction is a comic strip of China's conquest of the world with fascism fed by the Sino-colonialist Xi and his rule. This article is an indication that all the theses put forward by Henry Kissinger and Helmuth Schmidt about the Sino-colonial China have been brushed aside. The China, which was deliberately nurtured through these two doctrines, is rapidly spreading its authoritarian regime, a strategy which it has put into practice starting from Asia. In other words, this tyrannical monster, which has battened on the love (!) nurtured by the doctrines of Kissinger, Schmidt, and the diplomats who grew up with this doctrine, demands "the rent for teeth and nails" by saying that "having good relations with me is not enough, you must bow to me". The facts explained in detail in the relevant chapters of this book show that the "China would integrate with the world if it got rich" postulate has collapsed, and this naive presumption has served the interests of the Chinese Communist regime.

This work has been written to tell the truth that the Beijing regime's order has surrounded the world and dragged it to destruction and apocalypse in every field, from human rights to the environment, from economy to history, from culture to beliefs. In particular, the danger faced by Muslim countries, that is, the threat of the sino-colonial Chinese regime to the world, was explained. In this context;

This book intends to demonstrate to the extent possible the threat posed by the Sino-colonial Chinese regime both to the world and Muslim countries. The contours of this threat are given in the foreword. In the first chapter, both the origins of colonialism and its emergence in world history, as well as the expansion of modern colonialism, are discussed. The second chapter outlines Chinese imperialist and colonialist ambitions from a historical perspective and sheds light on what China has done to realize them. This chapter is not restricted to the era in which the Chinese Communist Party came to the power but offers a glimpse of the black-stained history of this ancient civilization of Asia. The third chapter examines the war waged by neo-imperialist China against Islam and other beliefs from past to present. For the Sino-colonial Beijing regime adhering to any religion is as dangerous as adhering to Islam. For this reason, they have exerted immense pressure to Sinicize other beliefs such as Christianity, Buddhism, and Taoism. The Chinese Communist regime accepts a religion if it complies with its doctrine. The ensuing chapter recounts how China has ever wanted to occupy East Turkistan, the heart of Central Asia and the homeland of Muslim Uyghurs, Kazakhs, and Kyrgyz, and how the people resisted against it. In the fifth chapter, the Sino-colonial regime's authoritarian leader Xi Jinping's rise to power, and the genocide committed against the Muslim population in East Turkistan in pursuit of China's imperialist ambitions are elaborated upon. This chapter is supported with reports and witness testimonies that reveal how the sino-colonial regime has ever wanted ruthlessly to destroy the Muslim people. Chapters six and seven explain how Bingtuan (Aka the Xinjiang Production and Construction Corps - XPCC), which was established after the 1949 invasion, and the Belt and Road Initiative (BRI) were used for Sino-colonial plans. The remaining chapters show with striking examples how an order was established in the vast geography extending from Asia to Africa and from Turkey to Central Asia to the advantage of Sino-colonialism.

1

The Definition and History of Colonialism

"Just keep in your mind that history is an important science with its many benefits and high goals. Because someone who wants to build religious and world affairs on solid foundations can know and tread the steps of morals of past societies, the lives and struggles of prophets, and the governance and politics of rulers ' by history."
Ibn Khaldun

THE FIRST STEP in understanding the developments happening in the world is, as stated by Ibn Khaldun, one of the founders of social science, to understand the past, that is, to read and analyze history carefully. Whether recent history or the ancient ages are studied, analysts will confront a world largely shaped by empires. These may range from the Macedonian Empire of Alexander the Great to the country of the British 'on which the sun never sets', or to the 'middle kingdom' of China. From another point of view, an empire is a picture in which the concepts of imperialism and colonialism are intertwined.

Conceptual Perspective

The origin of the concept of colonialism or the colonial system, as is found in more recent expressions, is based on the Latin phrase 'colore', which means settlement and cultivation. In other words, the very roots of the words are connected with the expansion of the Roman Empire and the Roman colonies. While colony refers to the territory occupied by the 'mother country', the colonial system, i.e. colonialism means the transformation of this territory through migration and settlement. Of course, this is not the exact definition of the concept of colonialism today. Colonialism is the occupation of a foreign land and then the establishment and implementation of systems to govern this land. [1]

The term imperialism was first used to condemn the military despotism of the French ruler Napoleon. This concept of imperialism is also preferred when expressing a negative connotation for Britain, one of the dominant forces of the 19th century. Although they come from the same origin, the concept of 'imperialism' evokes a more negative meaning than 'empire'. According to Steinmetz, the concept of the empire is the strategy of establishing political control over foreign lands, and for this reason, it does not necessitate the invasion, seizure, or establishment of a new order on this land to protect it from invasion. From this point of view, imperialism is a more comprehensive concept than colonialism. This is because empires can also be used as pawns in global great power games. [2]

Historical Origins of Colonialism

Colonialism took place on the historical stage in every period from Ancient Greece to the Roman Empire. However, the period that tends to spring to mind first concerning the concept of colonialism was when the European countries started to protrude to the distant seas and carry the resources of newly discovered lands back to the main continent. Undoubtedly, the trigger for the establishment of this colonial order was the desire of Europeans to seek new trade routes and obtain new wealth. Crimea, the cities of Istanbul in Turkey, the port of Alexandria in Egypt, and the Beirut port in Lebanon remained as important centers for trade until new sea routes for trade were discovered. For the Europeans on the trade route from East to West, the desire to dominate the Mediterranean formed the basis of the struggle between Venetian and Genoese sailors. Commodities coming from far Asia to these ports via the 'spice route' or Silk Road were distributed to Europe, especially by the Venetians. Other European countries, contrary to this domination of Venice and the Genoese in the Mediterranean, plunged onward into new quests. At this point, having control of the coasts along the Atlantic Ocean gave the Spanish and Portuguese the opportunity to move more independently and quickly on explorations. [3]

The starting point of the "Age of Discovery", or, more accurately, the new era of European colonialism, came with the Portuguese sailors' arrival in Ceuta, which is located across the Strait of Gibraltar in North Africa, and its seizure in 1415. This small region next to Morocco was later captured by the Spanish and remained under their control until the present day. Following the steps of the Portuguese, the Spanish sent ships to the high seas. In 1492, Christopher Columbus, who wanted to reach India and China by sea, first arrived in the Bahamas in the west and there laid the first foundations of Spanish colonialism in the distant seas. Competition between Spain and Portugal continued with the discovery and capture of new lands in Asia, America, and Africa. [4]

The importance of the Mediterranean in maritime trade continued until the 17th century. Until the discovery of the Americas and new sea routes, the Mediterranean was accepted as the hub of trade. However, with the arrival of the early colonists, who sailed to distant seas under the sponsorship of kings, new lands caused the center of the economy to shift from the Mediterranean to the Atlantic region. These discoveries also caused radical changes in Europe, starting with Portugal and Spain. Although the economic conditions of the continent initially gave Portugal an economic advantage with the resources it obtained from its discovered lands, in the gold trade which followed, Europe's inability to provide the necessary supply to new places, that is, to develop trade in a balanced way, forced Portugal to take a step back after a while. There had been a similar effect in Spain. The economic superiority passed to the Netherlands, England, and France. Many new products which included coffee, tobacco, chocolate, tea, and potatoes, appeared before Europeans for the first time. [5]

Reflections of Old Period Colonialism

With Great Britain, France, and the Netherlands in the colonial order, a great competition began between the European countries. Apart from America and Asia, by the 18th century, they set their eyes on the African continent and began to exploit it. The underground treasures on the continent, particularly gold and diamonds, whet the appetites of the Europeans. Gold obtained from the Americas and the African continent was transformed into bullion, replacing the barter system with a monetary one. Joint-stock companies became as effective as states. The East India Company, whose foundations were laid in the Netherlands, also set an example for England and France. The French India Company and the British East India companies were also established. In a sense, the companies utilized by the Chinese Communist Party as a bridge to dominate the world in our era, are present-day footprints of the East India Company.

While occupying the new places that they discovered, the European kings claimed that they acted legitimately by using religious and legal terms to justify themselves politically and morally. While occupying those lands, they claimed that they were there to assume the role of civilizing the peoples they defined as 'barbarians' or 'savages'. For this reason, they took the clergy along with them everywhere they went. The local people never easily accepted these invasions and thereby "forced the conquerors" to provide 'illumination' by their resistance of the colonial forces. Colonial states also carried out infrastructure work in some regions and also provided some medical treatments and new technologies. [6]

Another issue that must be mentioned here is that colonial states enslaved the people of the lands they occupied. France alone enslaved 5 million 300 thousand African people from the African continent and transferred these enslaved peoples first to the island of Haiti and then to other French colonies. [7] According to the data of the Trans-Atlantic Slave Trade, a total of 12.5 million Africans were enslaved and sent to other countries by ship. [8] This situation is similar to China's gathering of the people of East Turkistan first into concentration camps, action that has been followed by then sending these people to factories in the inner regions of China to work as slaves.

Philosophical Basis of Colonialism

The foundations of colonialism were set by the famous Scottish philosopher Adam Smith. This approach, called mercantilism, is based on the idea that a country's wealth is measured by the amount of gold and silver it possesses. Indeed, this had an effect on the pursuit of gold and silver by colonialist countries ranging from Spain and England to the Netherlands. According to this theory, exploited countries have value as long as they have an economic benefit to the exploiters. Otherwise, these lands are useless. The exploiting countries must extract raw materials from the countries they colonize to create a balance in favor of their economies and this trade must be monopolistic. [9] In other words, the traces of this economic philosophy can easily be seen today when we consider China's activities in Africa.

From the perspective of political philosophy, there is an intellectual division as to whether new-era imperialism is shaped by economic forces or military forces. It would be incomplete to say that ' the economy ensures efficacy, but it will also be so incomplete to say that ' political and military purposes have been sole motivators. Among British liberal economists, John Atkinson Hobson is the intellectual pioneer of economic imperialism in this debate. Hobson pointed out that the interests of those who held the capital were the trigger of the colonial system, although impulses such as patriotism and the spirit of adventure influenced the continuation of colonial ideals in the respective nations. The fact that these structures, which held the economy in England and Europe, controlled production and also maintained a monopoly on income distribution, caused the need to seek new markets in foreign countries. Joseph Alois Schumpeter, one of the leading economists of the 20th century, pointed out that there are three important factors based on the colonial approach in his work entitled "Sociology of Imperialism". According to the first of these, there is a persistent tendency in the imperialists towards war and occupation, leading to useless expansions. The second factor is that this situation is not created by an inborn desire for humans. Different people groups have gone through difficulties to protect generations. In this process, societies were divided into two groups of people and warriors. The warriors continued to fight to maintain their existence. The third point to be examined was that wars and the pursuit of new places were maintained under the leadership of the individuals who benefited most from them and by the internal interests of the ruling classes. Schumpeter believed that, as capitalist societies developed, the influence of these factors would decrease and imperialism would be thrown away. From his point of view, the development of capitalism depends on peace and free trade, and colonialism should have no place in this system. [10] However, Schumpeter was wrong at this point. Although the colonialist era has ascended and the occupied countries referenced have gained their superficial independence, new actors are still on the scene, especially with the development of technology. Colonialism has changed its dimensions.

Colonialism's Path to World Wars

France had long been the most important actor in the colonial system. France engaged in colonialism activities in many parts of the new world, from India to North America and Africa. Traces of French culture in today's Canada date back to colonialism in the 1700s. France's biggest rival on this stage was the British. The British were at least as active as the French in seizing resources both on the American continent and in Asia and cultivating the means to meet their imperialist goals there. The end of the 18th century and the 19th century are the periods when France began to lag behind England. Those were the days when Britain began to establish its 'empire on which the sun never sets'. The British colonial system was now dominant in many places from New Zealand to South Africa and the American continent. During the same period, Spain and Portugal were largely unable to protect their rank in the league of colonialist struggle. With the development of maritime transport, hundreds of thousands of people from Europe migrated to the American continent and became the first pioneers of today's societies there.

By the 1900s, there were now new actors in the colonialist system, which was established by traditional empires, started by Portugal and continued by Britain. The Americans, who founded their state on the lands that were exploited for a period, and states such as Russia, Germany, Belgium, and Italy also took action to get their slice of this pie. Since there was no place left to 'explore' in Africa, America, or Asia, the competition grew over the existing places. Although the British Empire managed to maintain its position against its successors with superiority in production, trade, international finance and its effective naval power, the struggle over smaller areas increased. Wars and diplomatic maneuvers intensified. Britain, which carried out the first industrial revolution, strengthened its empire on which the sun never sets' through the advantages gained through this period. Technologies that were developed with the second industrial revolution facilitated the moves of other colonial countries that just entered the scene. This, in turn, opened a new curtain on imperialism and colonialism. [11]

After the First World War, which started in 1914 and lasted for 4 years, following the collapse of the Ottoman Empire, victorious nations shared the lands stretching from the Middle East to North Africa under the name of colonialism. Britain's imperialist activities from the Middle East to Africa and India continued with the encouragement of the British victory in the war. After the revolution in 1917, Russia declared its sovereignty in Central Asia. While French colonialism's influence in Africa continued, a new colonial doctrine emerged in the 1930s. The 'axis powers', formed by the Germans, Italians, and Japanese, developed new and aggressive colonialist tendencies. These countries, claiming that the current Western system was beginning to lose power, wanted the world to be shared again, based on racial superiority, high birth rates, and excessive productivity. Japan set its slogan as "Asia for Asians" and began expanding its empire in the Pacific region. The Italians attempted to reoccupy Africa, and these steps became the first stages of the process that led the world to the second World War. Germany's invasion of Poland on September 1st, 1939 started World War II. 65 million people lost their lives in the 6-year war. Following the war, Russia, Britain, and America divided the world based on the distribution of powers among themselves at the conference held in Yalta in 1945.

By the end of the Second World War, a new colonial period emerged in contrast to what had been started 500 years ago. Nations from India to African countries and Asian states had started to declare their independence from the colonial powers. During this period, which is also known as the post-colonial period, the influence of European colonists on the local populations began to partially decrease. Each country began to transition towards an order in which they would determine their own administrations. A bipolar order was established in world politics, with the Atlantic front led by America in the West, and the Warsaw Pact led by Russia in the East. Some of the countries that gained their independence during the Cold War preferred to approach the Atlantic coast and some preferred to ally themselves with Russia. In the 1990s, with the dissolution of the Soviet bloc, the balance of power in the international arena changed once again. Even though the colonial countries politically withdrew from the countries they occupied, they still continued to maintain their economic existence in these countries. Today, almost all of the companies managing underground resources in Africa have their headquarters in the capitals of western countries. Likewise, the Central Asian countries, which gained their independence in the 1990s, continued to remain as satellite states of Russia economically and politically.

Post-Cold War Neo-Colonialism and Globalization

The period when the Soviet Union collapsed is a time in history when a new concept started to emerge in every aspect, from the economical to sociological and political. The fall of the Berlin Wall, according to some, was now a sign that borders were beginning to disappear. The world would inevitably become globalized, that is, globalization would prevail. According to those that disagree with this view, globalization is another name for the new stage of capitalist exploitation. Some said that the world societies would take a new shape from now on, while some believed that nothing would change. [12] Although globalization is a recent concept, the history of the colonial system was also that of the process of laying the foundations of capitalist globalization. A sailor from Europe reaching the American continent and transporting resources from there to the home continent was going beyond existing political borders and creating a new ecosystem. From this point of view, the globalization process and the colonization process of third world countries have continued side by side, balanced on the axis of capitalism. The movement of mercantilism initiated by Adam Smith, the founding father of capitalism, also constitutes the philosophical basis of this method. According to this idea, a global division of labor and the world market is needed for companies to profit and to maintain an earning system. There is a system of core country, a semi-peripheral country, and a peripheral country in the table drawn by the American sociologist Immanuel Wallerstein. According to this system, there is a hierarchical structure aligned from the periphery to the center. In this global economic order, inequality is based on the seizure of the economic values produced in the periphery and the semi-periphery by the core country. [13] This means the establishment of a system that will continuously feed the economic leadership goal of its central government in its sphere of influence extending to Africa, just as China has done in East Turkistan, which was occupied and defined as an autonomous region today by China. East Turkistan meets the projection of the semi-periphery and Africa is the projection of the periphery.

Today, there are four pillars of the capitalist order. China, which had thrown communism, its founding philosophy, into the dusty leaves of history by shouting "count me in" has also been thrown into the mix. The four pillars are labor, production, marketing, and capital. The success of this four-pillar system is based on simple logic: how cheaply goods are produced and how much profit can be made. [14] What those who believe that "the world is globalized to the point now that societies have to change", do not see or do not want to see is the fact that capitalism is getting stronger with globalization. The breakdown of borders has not always affected societies for the better. It also has a negative effect in terms of the gap between the development of the welfare level in a significant part of the colonial countries in the neo-colonial system and the economic development in the neo-imperialist countries. Kings, which the Spanish sailors railed against, have been replaced by heads of state today. To ensure that capitalism is successful, every stage in the chain from production to reaching the end consumer must be further accelerated. Therefore, the capitalist system needs political accelerants. [15]

Effects of the New Colonialism

The new global trend that started in the 1990s led to fundamental changes in capitalism and therefore world politics. The transformation from state-sponsored economies to an economic system in which large companies functioned as the locomotives to drive economic development had begun. The new economic order, which is defined as the "new world order" in politics, had moved to a new stage with financial regulations, waves of new technological inventions, the spread of the internet, greater communication strategies, and cheaper logistics parallel with technological developments. [16] But not all of these dizzying developments were entirely beneficial to the countries that were weaker both economically and politically. The endless hunger of capitalism had made the governments of less powerful countries vulnerable to corruption. This made the economies of these countries dependent on countries such as the United States, Britain, and, recently, China. In short, the order of exploitation was not changed and the African countries have continued to be where resources are exploited and workers are employed for free. One of the most striking examples of this situation is that of Ghana, the leading country in cocoa bean production, which has almost no share in chocolate production. This is because the raw cocoa beans are sent to Belgium. The colonial state turns them into chocolate and further increases its economic wealth with the resulting value. Here, from a different point of view, we can see the reflection of the famous sociologist Ibn Khaldun's phrase: "geography is destiny".

The history of globalization is also the history of capitalism, which is consequently the history of the colonial system. Dizzying advances in technology are transforming the world into a seemingly smaller place. The distances have shrunk and the transfer of information occurs with incredible speed. [17] This increasing competition has pushed both governments and companies, which have a voice in politics and economy as well, to search for how to produce cheaper goods. As David Harvey, known for his work entitled *Spaces of Global Capitalism*, stated "the compelling laws of competition have pushed capitalists to relocate their production in more advantageous places". [18]

China, and some other countries which possess a supply of cheap labor, have turned out to be the most profitable countries in this relocation. Factories in many countries from America to Europe and Turkey have been moved to the territories of the red regime since 2000. The Communist Party of China has developed a new hybrid administration and established a system of 'state capitalism'. We see that the cost of this relocation emerges as a major blow to local production in the countries which outsource production. Domestic manufacturers have become unable to survive when competing against these countries, starting with China and extending to Vietnam and Bangladesh. As can be seen in the examples of Turkey and Egypt, factories are destroyed and shopping malls have been built in their place. What we see in these shopping malls are stores with brands whose products were produced cheaply abroad. Another example worth reflecting on is that, together with the change in labor, working for lower wages in stylish environments in shopping malls became more attractive to many laborers than working in a factory. A major influence of the new era of global capitalism has been seen in the cultural sphere. Brands and fashions coming out of the West have reached the most remote points of the world.

Technological System of Colonialist Exploitation

The developments in the technology sector and particularly of mobile phones and mobile technologies are now shaping the cultural and social life of the new era. Now we see the colonial system, which began with ships opening to the High Seas, with its new face of 'corporate imperialism'. From the lessons that are given in schools to the taxi cabs we take on the way home, a new life is being shaped by giant technology companies.

The world is, on the one hand, living in a state of constant communicative status, but on the other hand, it has become open and vulnerable to being affected and damaged at the same rate. Enveloped countries and technology companies, acting with the philosophy that "knowledge is power" and "if you have the power, you rule the world", have established a surveillance system that monitors every moment of people's lives. An upper stage of technological capitalism is now surveillance colonialism. Surveillance capitalism constantly imposes various impositions on people, from mobile phone messages, video calls, messages shared on social media, to global positioning systems that work voluntarily or without consent. The ethical debate that began when the internet was first invented has already been forgotten, and humanity, which has benefited from technology has also been its biggest victim. On the one hand, although it facilitates human life, these technological steps that shape the future can be used in dangerous dimensions. As is clearly expressed in the coming chapters of this work through the example of the Chinese Communist Dictate's genocide against Tibetans and Uyghurs in East Turkistan, one of the most important means of destroying a population is the colonial system that operates based on technology and surveillance.

China, whose political system is communism and economic system is capitalism, and which established the brutal colonial order of the new era, is now a new player on the scene of globalized modern life where western brands and lifestyles are at the forefront. Aiming to become the factory of the world in the 2000s, the Beijing administration made remarkable advances in technology and said 'count me in' in the game of global capitalism. This allows them to serve as an alternative to the West with the aim of becoming the ruler of the world in this new era. The Chinese regime, which has not weakened the production of countries, is somehow knocking on every door, establishing a presence from cinema to mobile phone production and television. The influence of 'state capitalism' as developed against the West by China, which has established an unimaginable repressive order with its advanced technology-based surveillance systems in East Turkistan, can be clearly seen in world politics.

2

China's Desire for Global Domination

"Because of the lack of harmony between the beggars and the people, because of the Chinese people's cunning and craft and intrigues, and because the younger and the elder brothers chose to take counsel against one another and bring discord between beggars and people, they brought the old realm of the Turkic people to dissolution and brought destruction on its lawful khagans. The sons of the nobles became the bondsmen of the Chinese people, their unsullied daughters became its slaves." (1)
Bilge Kagan

"HOW WOULD YOU briefly describe the People's Republic of China?" If asked, is almost impossible to summarize 4 thousand years of 'neo-imperialist' history. Particularly because we see a system that started with the communist idea in 1949 and then suddenly decided to open up to the world and adopt an idea of "I am now in favor of a free-market economy, in short, I am a capitalist." It is a combination of systems containing a capitalist stance against foreigners, a communist attitude to its people, and a cruel colonial behavior against occupied regions such as East Turkistan, Tibet, and Inner Mongolia. In her famous horror novel, British author Mary Shelly tells the story of the young chemist Victor creating a monster in order to realize his dream of creating a human. There is no single description of the beast in this novel, it is generally called by adjectives such as 'creature', 'demon', 'failure', 'wretch', and 'it'. Taking its place in the horror literature as Frankenstein, this monster, which is a combination of elements that would not come together in a normal world, is now the definition of killing and destruction. If one looks at what fits this definition today, there is no doubt that the Chinese Communist Party, which is both communist, capitalist, dictatorial and colonial and which erodes by targeting the vulnerabilities of the countries through deception, will be first to come to mind. So it is the neo-colonialist, the Frankenstein of the modern world. The description in the Bilge Kagan inscription of the Gokturk inscriptions tells that China was no different in the past.

Brief Overview of Chinese History

The First Dynasties

The first evidence of Chinese civilization, which has a history of thousands of years, including the ancient ages, was found in a cave 40 kilometers away from Beijing in 1921 by the Swedish paleontologist J. G Anderson. Among the evidence estimated to belong to ancient times, isolated skulls, bones, and teeth belonging to 40 people were identified, along with a fossil recorded as 'Peking Man'. According to today's knowledge, the period when agricultural activities began was in the 5000s BC. [2]

According to early legends in Chinese history, the state in the traditional sense started with the establishment of the Xia dynasty by a named Yu in 2000 BC. This dynasty features heavily in the written sources that have been found. The dynasty which followed and helped to shape Chinese civilization was the Shang Dynasty. The last emperor of this administration, Zhou, showed a complete tyrannical rule by using cruel methods such as killing those who criticized him, cutting the hearts of ministers who objected to his opinionsinto slices for examination, and burning his opponents on grills in the most painful way. His cruelty had led to the end of himself and his empire. On Chinese soil, another dynasty acceded in 1028 BC. This dynasty took its name from its king that overthrew the Shang; its name was the Zhou dynasty. [3] With the end of the Zhou dynasty in 481 BC, the "WarLords" period (Warring States period), which would last for about 2 centuries, began. [4]

This period came to an end gradually with the dominance of the weak by the superior, and the Qin dynasty established its rule over all lands. Qin became the first emperor of the Qin dynasty in 221 BC, but as being the shortest enthroned dynasty in Chinese history, the rule of the Qin dynasty lasted 14 years. With the accession of Lui Bang to the throne, the Han Dynasty achieved an imperial period that would last about 4 centuries. After the fall of the Han Dynasty, an unstable period started. In 581, the Sui dynasty domineered and ensured territorial integrity. Following this rule, which lasted for about 40 years, the Tang Dynasty took control and ruled China for 3 centuries. In 907, this dynasty collapsed, and after a chaotic period of 53 years, the Song dynasty came to power. This administration ended with his defeat after protracted battles with the Mongols. The famous Mongol ruler Genghis Khan captured Beijing in 1215 and took all the northern lands under his rule. [5]

In 1254, Genghis Khan's grandson Kublai Khan took the throne and adopted the Chinese system rather than choosing to fight the Chinese. Kublai later identified himself as Yuan and became the first non-Chinese but founder of the dynasty that ruled there. Following Kublai Khan's death in 1294, the Yuan Dynasty also came to end, and the Ming dynasty took over. The Chinese-descended Ming dynasty, which took control of the country after the Mongols, ruled for 276 years. The Manchu nation, which lives in the northern parts of the historical Chinese Great Wall today, began to seize power by passing over the wall as of 1618. The Manchus stated that they were the true heirs of China and took the name of Qing. They captured Taiwan, the last place in the hands of the Ming Dynasty, in 1660, and established their rule over the whole country.

The Qing Dynasty's Invasion of Tibet, East Turkistan and Mongolia

The Manchus are the second 'foreign' power in China to take over the empire after Kublai Khan. Although they make up 1 percent of the population, like the Mongols, they have held the administration in their hands for centuries. [6] The emperors of the Qing dynasty also initiated an invasion campaign against the regions in western China. In particular, the territory of Tibet, present-day East Turkistan, and Mongolia was occupied by the Qing. The section about East Turkistan will be discussed in more detail in the following chapters. However, the Dzungar Khanate - a kingdom established by the peoples of Mongolian origin and other communities living there, known as the Çungar Khanate in Turkish sources - which ruled in the area of today's Mongolia and East Turkistan, even for a short time, put a great obstacle to the Qing Empire during the expansion of China. Their battle with the Manchus continued for decades. The Qing Empire first took over the Tibet region and made years of preparation to advance towards the East Turkistan region. Just after finishing the preparations, they took action and destroyed the Dzungar Khanate with the advantage of an epidemic disease that broke out at that time. The next step was Inner Mongolia. In 1760, they incorporated these lands into the empire. [7]

According to historical sources, the Tibetan Empire, which dates back to the 7th century, had always been one of the regions that the Chinese aimed to conquer, due to its ideal geographical location opening to the west and lands such as East Turkistan. Tibet was occupied by the Qing Empire in 1720. When the imperial order disappeared after the revolution in 1911, Tibet declared its independence. Wanting to turn this situation into an advantageous one, Tibet's leading prominent chose the 14th Dalai Lama in 1938. Tibetans started a search for support from abroad, from America and other countries, and in 1950, Communist Party soldiers occupied Lhasa, and thus the Dalai Lama went abroad. The Communist Party declared this land as the Tibetan Autonomous Region. Hundreds of thousands of Tibetans died during the period of the CCP's so-called great leap forward program. Six thousand monasteries were destroyed during the cultural revolution. [8] As mentioned earlier, the occupation and genocide policy towards East Turkistan will be discussed in more detail in the relevant chapter.

At this point, it is necessary to remind that the basis of today's claim by the Chinese regime that East Turkistan, Tibet, and Inner Mongolia belonged to China for thousands of years dates back to this period. Although they destroyed the Qing or Manchu dynasty and superseded them, they continued to use the legacy left by them for their colonial ambitions. Even the fact that Qing, who occupied the lands of East Turkistan, called this land "Xinjiang", meaning "new Territory", is the simplest proof that that region did not belong to the Chinese in history. [9]

The Period of Humiliation

While the Qing Empire expanded its territory, it also became the target of European merchants who reached Asia by sea. The 'golden period' ended because stability had not been achieved in the regions such as East Turkistan, Mongolia, and Tibet that it occupied for a long time. The Qing Dynasty lost its former power due to the negative effects of European merchants on the country's economy, the rapid population growth, poverty, corruption of local rulers and military rulers. British-based companies that invaded India and produced opium there began to sell this product to China, which had a population of 400 million at that time. The British East India Company, which also sold cotton along with opium, bought tea, silk, and porcelain from China in the first period of commercial relations. However, the increasing demand for opium strengthened the British hand economically and opium was sold to China for silver. Following this problem, the administration took action to stop opium sales and officially banned this product. Opium continued to be sold illegally in the market, and even an imperial official named Lin Zexu came to Canton, the entry point of opium into the country, in order to solve this problem. Applying pressure to British companies for the sale of opium, Lin also wrote a letter to Queen Victoria of England, informing her that he would not permit British companies and the navy to import this illegal substance into their lands. In the letter, he said that if the British did not comply with the prohibitions, he would block the sale of tea, porcelain, and other healthcare products in China. As expected, Britain did not accept this solution, and a month later in 1839, the events which are now known as the 'Opium Wars' began. [10]

China's naval power was by the British Navy, and the British attacked the Canton and Tianjin regions. The Empire agreed to give Hong Kong away to the

British in 1841 to ensure peace. However, after failing to find a solution despite extended negotiations, the British again attacked and advanced to Shanghai and captured Nanjing, the historical capital of the Ming Dynasty. After the loss of this historic city, the Qing Empire agreed to the treaty, and the British gained control of four additional ports along with Hong Kong. Other Western countries, emboldened by Britain's acts, had also benefited from this weakness in China. The Americans obtained advantages such as an agreement to establish hospitals and churches for Protestant missionaries, and France received the advantage of an extradition agreement. These developments revealed that China had lost its sovereignty in its own country. [11]

But these concessions and this frustration in the face of Western countries' triumphs led to internal revolts. The most famous of these revolts was the Taiping Rebellion, which lasted 14 years. It began in 1850 and lasted until 1864. Western countries helped China fight this rebellion, and on the other hand, forced China to agree to a second agreement. So, the Empire was once again humiliated. [12] The second time the Qing Empire was 'humiliated' was during the period when it faced the Japanese. In the battles between China and Japan, the soldiers of Emperor Cixi, who built a 'marble ship' instead of strengthening China's naval power, suffered a heavy defeat. Moreover, this defeat of a thousand-year-old empire by a state that emerged long after it once again basted China's traditional honor. For this reason, this period is known as the 'second humiliation' period in Chinese history. [13]

Republican Revolution

These successive defeats marked the end of the Qing Dynasty. The two-year Boxer Rebellion, which started in 1898, is one of the keystones that ended the Manchu period. The imperial system ended as a result of the pressures from both 'revolutionaries' and outside forces. [14] With the end of the imperial era, the foundations of the republican era began to be laid in China. Here, there is no doubt that the name Sun Yat-sen is key among those who laid the way for the revolution. Born to a poor farming family and playing a role in laying the foundations of the revolution while living abroad, Sun secretly established the Revive Chinese Society movement. After China's defeat by the Japanese army, he arrived in Hong Kong but was captured here. After a short time in prison, he took refuge in England. Sun, who pioneered the establishment of revolutionary cells against the Chinese imperial order in western countries during his stay abroad, took over the United League (Tongmenghui) established in Tokyo in 1905. But because he did not find what he expected in these organizations, he returned to the west again and continued his organizational work there. By 1911, demonstrations spread all over China and eventually the imperial administration collapsed completely. Organizations led by Sun from abroad had also achieved success. Sun, who was the first president of the new republican regime, agreed with Yuan Shikai, one of the former ministers of the empire, to continue the revolution, and had Shikai take over the newly formed Nationalist Party. [15]

Guomindang and the Founding of the Communist Party

Chen Duxiu, one of the leading figures, embarked on various pursuits after the West had left them in the lurch against the Japanese. On the other hand, Li Dazhao, who was educated in Japan, returned to Beijing and started to work as an assistant editor at a newspaper that supported the reforms. Li later met Chen when he was appointed as the head of Peking University's library. During this period, another revolutionary, Mao Zedong, was hired by Li at the library. As one of the revolutionaries who had been disappointed by the West, Mao had been influenced by the revolution in the Soviet Union. He started investigating Marxism with his friend Chen. A delegation from the International Communist League then came to Beijing and gave training on Marxism. In 1921, the Communist Party of China was founded. However, although he did not attend the establishment meeting out of fear at the time, Chen was chosen as party secretary. [16] Liao Zhongki, who was expected to succeed Guomindang Party leader Sun Yat-Sen after his death in 1925, was assassinated. Allegations had been raised that his ultranationalist and possible rival Chiang Kai-shek was responsible for his death. Chiang strengthened his position by marrying Sun Yat-sen's widowed sister. After he became head of the party, he began to expand the regions under his rule, when there was no one around to rival him. [17]

Under the leadership of Chiang, Guomindang had turned into a military dictatorship. Chiang said in his statement in 1930 that China was not yet ready for democracy and quickly suppressed the communist uprising staged by Li Lisan. However, Guomindang did not achieve the success it wanted in the guerrilla war initiated by Mao in mountainous areas in the interior of China. In 1934, Chiang started a major siege operation against Mao. Mao, who wanted to escape from this siege, attempted an expedition to get rid of it. This escape attempt is known as the 'Long March' in history. Of the 90 thousand soldiers, 20 thousand were able to continue this long expedition. But at that time, with Japan's invasion of the Manchuria region, both sides declared a truce and began to fight against the Japanese. The Japanese first formed a puppet government called Manchukuo and began to invade the rest of China in 1937. Thousands of people had been killed in Nanjing, but the size of the land did not allow the Japanese to take all the regions. [18]

America entered the war in the Pacific when the Japanese bombed Pearl Harbor in 1941. Chiang immediately began to cooperate with the Americans. There were some steps including the construction of new airports and the establishment of hospitals for cooperation. The German attack on the Russians at that time led to the failure of Communist Party members in China to get the support they expected from Russia. Additionally, their attacks against the Japanese in the north further provoked the Japanese and caused them to destroy the entire population in many places. Mao saw that liberation would depend on increasing the number of Communist Party members and started a 2-year program. In this cleanup program, those who did not comply with the party program were removed and replaced with new members. Leninist-Maoist training was given in schools established in secret. Mao began to see himself as an equal to both Marx and Lenin. This period of cleanup is also when attempts at brainwashing were intensified. Members who met in groups were involved in processes such as adopting Mao's doctrines, and admitting their own mistakes against the party. The cleanup period also offered Mao the opportunity to purge a large number of people from the party. [19]

Guomindang and the Communist Party began to take part in the war more effectively together with both America's war against Japan and Russia's attack on the Japanese in the Manchuria region after repelling the Nazis. Mao's ability to lead his party members into the war in a more disciplined manner gave him an advantage. So much so that America, the defender of capitalism, accepted the Mao administration as more reliable. However, Chiang Kai-shek participated in talks on behalf of China at the Yalta Conference as a result of the war. [20] After World War II, Communist Party members resumed guerrilla warfare tactics and began to prevail over Guomindang. In November 1948, the Communists defeated Chiang Kai-shek's troops in the Battle of Huai-Hai, which lasted until January 1949. After Guomindang was defeated, the Communist Party seized Beijing and then took control of important cities such as Nanjing and Shanghai. Mao declared the foundation of the People's Republic of China in Beijing on October 1, 1949. [21]

The Foundation of the People's Republic of China and its Aftermath

The steps taken by the Communist Party under the leadership of Mao to make China an Iron Curtain country, led to political and economic fluctuations in the country. According to Rossabi Morris's definition; "Changes are sometimes predictable and sometimes sudden. The period of rapid transition had been very harsh and difficult to understand." [22] Although the motivation for protection against foreign threats is effective, it created disappointments in other parts of society, ranging from the struggle within the party to the intellectuals. A transition towards a purely Marxist-Leninist-Maoist development doctrine had begun while realistic approaches to economics were abandoned. This transition was not easy for the people and due to military and police pressure, demonstrations, and sudden policy changes, the Chinese people could not achieve the stability that they had expected. One of the first acts of the communist regime was to ensure continued dominance in territories such as Inner Mongolia, Tibet, and East Turkistan, which were occupied during the Qing Dynasty. In 1947, China sent troops to Inner Mongolia to prevent independence movements. Right after sending the troops, China made Ulanhu, a puppet ruler, party representative of the region and declared this territory as the Inner Mongolia Autonomous Region. To comfort the people there, they made promises that they would never fulfill. These included such assurance as the protection of their cultural heritage, languages, and religion. [23] The effects of the Sinicization process in those regions have continued to the present day.

The Great Leap Forward

After coming to power, Mao made his first official visit to the Soviet Union. He did not get what he desired from the Soviets when he came knocking on the Soviet Union's door with great expectations in December 1949. Mao asked the Soviet Union for support in invading Taiwan and defeating Chiang Kai-shek but received an answer that he would be supported in his economic matters. Moreover, Soviet influence in East Turkistan, Mongolia, and Manchuria further angered the Communist Party administration. Mao did not achieve his dream of invading Taiwan and taking complete control there. USA-led countries that sent military support to South Korea in the Korean War, which began in 1950, repelled North Korea. America gave a clear warning by sending its navy to the region that would not allow the Communists to invade Taiwan. Supporting North Korea in this war put China in an even more difficult position. [24] Military losses together with the economic destruction caused the isolation of the Communist Party from the world. After that, Mao initiated the great leap forward program for China's economic development. However, 36 million Chinese people living in a major economic and poverty crisis died due to hunger and absence. [25] As an additional matter, North Korea was still being patronized by China during that time. The mentor of the North Korean dictators, who kept an eye on Beijing about politics and international relations since the Korean War, for economic, technological, and even political issues is still China today. This informal humanitarian program of the communist regime, which once starved its people under the name of the great leap forward program, is still ongoing in North Korea. The way to prevent North Korea from being a risk to the international public can be achieved again through Beijing. China's moves to protect North Korea at the UN are also indicative of the unbreakable ties between the two countries.

After the failure of the Great Leap Forward Program, Lui Shaoqi, one of the prominent figures of the Communist Party, and Deng Xiaoping, who would later reopen China to the world, began to search for ways to return to the original plan regarding the economy. Mao had to accept the idea of modernizing instead of the leap forward program, which he considered a source of pride for a while. The modernists led by Lui closed inefficient large farmer cooperatives and paved the way for producers to obtain larger places for themselves, and allowed the products to be sold by them. In other words, the Maoist regime had compulsorily begun to reduce the influence of the state in the economy. On the other hand, developments in the region had started to create new barriers in front of China. In addition to America's attack on Vietnam, the Soviet Union announced that it regarded the Chinese Communists as "radical" and that they could not adapt to the "world order" and started to condemn them. As a result of the fact that the dispute between the two states of the same ideological origin became insurmountable, the Soviets withdrew all technical support teams. After the complete rupture of relations between the two neighboring countries, Mao faced a different version of the 'period of humiliation' experienced after the First World War. He had no contact with any country that has a say in the world. To be effective in foreign policy, he established connections with authoritarian administrations in the Middle East and Africa. [26]

One of the Greatest Catastrophic Periods
in World History: The Cultural Revolution

Mao and his team, who had been isolated in foreign policy, started a new project to strengthen their administration. This time they chose the name 'Cultural Revolution'. In this revolution that began in 1966, especially young people were put at the forefront of disastrous policies. During the 10-year Revolution, millions of people experienced one of the greatest disasters in the history of the world. Young people who targeted everyone and everything, including culture, religious beliefs, and knowledge of the past called themselves 'red guards'. During this so-called Cultural Revolution, which Mao also used as an opportunity to destroy his opponents, party officials, teachers, intellectuals, and writers were targeted with the label of 'foreigner/outsider'. The Red Guards ransacked the homes of anyone 'suspicious of bourgeois inclination' and destroyed books

and works of art. Groups that confiscated all public transportation came together at Mao's rallies. They even went so far as to seize the Ministry of Foreign
Affairs and try to manage China's foreign policy. [27]

Millions of teachers, civil servants, and administrators had been kicked out
of their positions, those who showed any interest in other cultures were attacked, and anyone who tried to resist had been beaten, thrown into dungeons,
or sent to 'training camps', which we see examples of today in East Turkistan.
Opera stars, singers, and academics had been forced to clean toilets. Even all
Chinese books not mentioning Mao were burned. Universities and colleges had
been closed for years on the grounds that they propped up the 'elite class'. When
they began to reopen, they were converted into inspection areas. In addition,
high school graduates in big cities were tasked with being 'productive labor
in the countryside' in order to prevent young people from 'losing their roots'.
These individuals would later form the core of the organization called XPCC,
or Bingtuan, China's largest semi-state-owned company. By the 1970s, about
17 million young people were sent to rural areas under this program. Even as
the Red Guards were sent to the rural areas, the disaster continued. All but Mao
were targeted as suspects. Even though Lui Shaoqi was considered Mao's natural heir, he was eliminated by Mao's order after being labeled as 'right-wing'
because he wanted to fix the economy. Deng Xiaoping, who would launch the
policy of opening to foreign countries in 1979, was publicly humiliated, abused,
and even his son was permanently disabled. [28]

The greatest damage of this so-called Cultural Revolution had also been seen
in lands such as East Turkistan, Tibet, and Mongolia. Uyghurs, Mongols, and
Tibetans, who wanted to protect their traditional family ties and morals, languages, religions, were humiliated, insulted by the Red Guards, and exiled from
their homeland to other places. All kinds of torture had been carried out in the
name of destroying family values and human dignity. By 1971, China decided
to take another sharp turn to combat the desperation and loneliness brought out
by their foreign policy. Chinese officials invited the American table tennis team
to Beijing. The delegations also began talks to bring together Mao and then-US
President Nixon. The two leaders met in the autumn of 1972, and the meeting
did not produce the expected outcome for both sides. China's biggest gain had
been the right to replace Taiwan at the United Nations. [29] After this step, the
Beijing government started to restore its relations with the western world.

Economic Expansion in the Post-Mao Period / Black Cat – White Cat
After Mao's death, there was a big fight over who would take over from him. A
group, which called itself the gang of four (Mao Zedong's last wife Jiang Qing,

The other members were Zhang Chunqiao, Yao Wenyuan, and Wang Hongwen) opposed modernization and outward expansion. Groups led by them took to the streets, demanding a more radical system of communist rule, and an even more radical system than that seen under Mao's regime. Hua Guofeng, who was a nobody during Mao's reign, became the favorite candidate of radicals and quickly moved to grab power. As soon as he took the seat, his first job was to arrest all of the leaders of the radical gang of four. [30] But, Deng Xiaoping and his supporters, who advocated leap forward and outward expansion in the economy, rendered Hua Guofeng dysfunctional. In 1978, Deng took over the administration and started to take steps that ensure the development of China's economy today. Deng, who pondered the philosophy of Marxism during his time in France, considered 'pragmatism' as indispensable for China to take its place among other states. The famous unforgettable quote of "It doesn't matter whether a cat is black or white, as long as it catches mice." by Deng was the touchstone of Deng's policies. Looking at the paradigm of the economic leap forward at that time, the impact of the wealthy and educated people who had previously fled China should also be taken into account. Before 1949's A significant number of wealthy and educated people had left the country and settled in countries such as Taiwan, Malaysia, Singapore, and Japan after the efforts of the Chinese Communist Party to nationalize everything and to equalize people without considering if they were rich or poor. These people, who had grown their capital and became even richer in exile, were contacted by Deng and his regime. They were informed about China's new economic model and they were promised to run their business comfortably when they returned to their own country. Since Deng also lived abroad for a while and returned, these people he met trusted Deng's word and brought both their capital and manpower back to China. Another notable project of Deng, who was a Marxist of words but a capitalist of deeds, was sending of Chinese young people abroad to study under the name of the student exchange program. When Deng brought up this idea, some opposed. However, according to the information contained in various sources, Deng had shown himself as an example to those who oppose sending young people abroad and convinced them. The contribution of these young people to the creation of executive human resources that serve in all areas of the Chinese administration, from politics to technology, but also establish systems like the West, is great. After the 1980s, with the acceleration of the transition to a free-market system, China turned into the factory of the world and had learned to utilize the advantages of cheap labor and the size of its production potential. Beijing, which still rules its people under the communist style of governance, had shown itself to be the most cunning capitalist in the world.

The Tiananmen Massacre

During The Deng period, while the economy continued its expansion to the outer world, the increase in inflation and corruption in the public services triggered a public reaction. Deng and his Regime, on the other hand, began to act more oppressively against these public reactions. In May 1989, thousands of people, mostly young people, gathered for a demonstration in Tiananmen Square in the capital city of Beijing in a way to remind them of the May 4 Movement. The slogan of 'be an officer, then be rich' had been gradually circulated as a rumor. Although the demonstrators were never involved in the violence, the Beijing Regime perceived this move as a 'threat'. On June 4, the government drove tanks against the crowd in the square. Thousands of students and demonstrators died in the massacre that the world remembers with a symbolic picture showing a demonstrator standing in front of a tank. The incident was written as the 'Beijing massacre' in the history books. The pressure of the government was not ' limited by the square, but thousands of people were arrested and executed, and intellectuals were re-targeted, just as the Red Guards did. In the continuation of these events, pressures increased in Tibet, East Turkistan, and Inner Mongolia. [31] The Tiananmen protests were proved to be one of the turning points in China's history. Because after this event, people's expectations of being a democratic country with the effect of outward economic expansion were destroyed. No matter how much expansion is made against the outside world, the Chinese Communist regime has shown that it will rule its people and occupied territories with an iron fist.

Chinese Style of Administration:
Iron Fist the Inside Velvet Glove Outside

The Chinese Communist Party started to put its stamp on human history as a capitalist-communist and despotic regime. One of the most dramatic examples of this was the 1989 Tiananmen Square protests in which they crushed students with tanks, and the other was the genocide they practiced in East Turkistan. Thanks to the capital power provided by economic growth, China domineered many administrations to itself by using its money in international relations. The Beijing government is now using its thousands of years of political accumulation to dominate the world through 'soft power' tactics.

Spending Annually 10 Billion USD for Propaganda

'Arrival of Train At La Ciotat', which was watched by 25 people at the Grand Café in Paris On December 28, 1895, is known as the first film in the history of cinema. Shot by the Lumiere Brothers, this film formed one of the cornerstones of show business. Cinema, which has developed over the years, has become both entertainment and an effective means of delivering news to people from time to time. Exactly 125 years after the Lumiere Brothers' Show, those who flock into movie theaters today or watch a movie on their tablet and phone or TV, definitely see the name of a Chinese company as a 'sponsor' whenever they start watching a movie. Zengfu Pictures is one of them. When Apple presented its latest film, Greyhound, which was produced for the online Cinema channel Apple TV, Zengfu Pictures was seen in credits and titles. It is noteworthy that Zengfu, a Chinese film company, is among the supporters in this film, which tells the story of an American navy warship guarding merchant ships while crossing the Atlantic Ocean during World War II. Zengfu Pictures is just one of the companies the Chinese Communist Party has used for spreading Chinese propaganda to the world.

The Australian Strategic Policy Institute, which became more visible with its reports on forced labor, concentration camps, and similar practices by the Chinese government regarding Uyghurs in East Turkistan, also examined how the Beijing government had influenced other countries for propaganda purposes. This Australian example has highlighted what tactics have been practiced. According to the report entitled "Mind your tongue", the Chinese Communist Party (CCP) spends 10 billion dollars a year on international propaganda. These expenditures have aimed to strengthen the positive image of China and shape the programs of other governments to be in line with the commercial long and short-term goals of the Beijing government. Activities such as student exchange programs, opening Confucian classes in public schools and universities, and taking journalists to China for free trips are carried out in line with these propaganda aims. These activities do not immediately raise any apparent problems. [32]

Divide and Rule Tactic

The ambitions of the Chinese authorities exceed this limit of formality. As is the case in Australia, heavy censorship is applied in the media channels and broadcasts of which Beijing Management is a partner. There is even pressure applied to embassies and consulates to postpone events that would damage the image of the Communist Party by threatening with withdrawing their advertising and sponsorship support. The Chinese Communist Party was again the best practitioner of "playing one brother against another" or "Poniarding Policy" as it is defined in expressions of Bilge Khagan, one of the Gokturk Khagan. According to ASPI's report, the Beijing government defines those who oppose its policies as 'enemies' and has exploited internal divisions and strife among them. [33]

The Center for Strategic and International Studies (CSIS), one of the leading think-tanks based in America, had also discussed in detail how China manipulated public opinion in Australia. In the report, the Beijing government's intervention in Australia's politics via extraordinary donations was examined under the title of "China's trap of influence Australia course". A prominent politician was expelled from parliament for blaming the Chinese media for the South China Maritime Policy and warning his president, who had ties to the Communist Party of China, of government oversight. Following this, the impact of China on universities in Australia initiated discussion. The storm that began in politics spilled over into Australian Chinese society and many prominent names became involved in the situation. With the support of the parties in parliament, the prime minister removed China's technology companies Huawei and ZTE from the country's 5G network. The Communist Party responded to this step by reducing coal imports from Australia. [34] Considering the relations of the countries, which remained silent on the genocide carried out by the Beijing regime towards the Uyghurs and other Muslim communities in East Turkistan, and the pressure targeting the people of Inner Mongolia and Tibet, it was observed that "operation of influence" tactics similar to those used on Australia wereused by China in these countries. Again, in another report prepared by CSIS, these tactics by China were highlighted. According to the report, the modus operandi of the Communist Party in Australia to target politicians is to buy political influence with money, to seize the elite, and to control the diaspora communities. On the other hand, China has used "soft power" in the case of Japan. In other words, methods such as public diplomacy, cultural diplomacy, bilateral exchange were used. Concurrently, also chose to oppress in secret, coercive and by more corrupt forms of influence. While tactics to organize joint conferences and seminars were used effectively, the Confucius Institute has also been a vitally important tool for the Chinese regime to achieve its aims. China also targeted the Japanese diaspora in the country. Hostage diplomacy was a tactic used by Beijing without hesitation when the above-mentioned tactics did not work. By this precedent, China arrested dozens of Japanese by using the Anti-Espionage law issued in 2014. [35]

One of the most important tools used by the Chinese Communist Party in the sense of 'soft power' is Confucius Institutes, as mentioned earlier. Although Mao tried to erase traces of the historic figure of Confucius himself because he considered himself superior to him, the image of Confucius has now been turned into one of Beijing's critical weapons. Since 2004, more than 500 Confucius Institutes have been established in 140 countries, some of which are under state universities. More than 1000 Confucian departments have been opened in schools outside of universities. Celebration events for the Chinese New Year were also organized to introduce their own culture to other countries. The most comprehensive of these celebrations were held in 2010 and 2000 events were held in 140 countries with government sponsorship. State-sponsored media outlets broadcasting in foreign languages had also been strengthened. For example, it is aimed to increase the number of Xinhua news offices in foreign countries to 200 this year. China Global Television Network has 6 channels broadcasting in different languages. [36] While the Beijing administration expanded its hegemony over the world with rapid growth in the economy since the 2000s, the language used in diplomacy has also changed significantly. Like the predator approaching without frightening its prey, China had developed new arguments to prevent a loss of its positive image, which would prevent it from implementing its secret agenda. The most prominent of these are: "multipolarity", "multilateralism", "democratization of international relations", "peaceful development", "peaceful rise", "harmonious world". [37] These arguments clearly illustrate the contradiction of the communist-capitalist hybrid authoritarian regime, which does not tolerate dissenting voices in its own country, ruled its country with an iron fist, the work of an oppressive communist mentality, which has no practice for democratic rule.

A Devil Approaches from the Right, aka, the Red Bribe!

The Chinese administration, on the one hand, spends billions of dollars on marketing, and on the other hand, tries to buy politicians in Western countries with money. Politicians in America, the biggest rival economically, are its primary target. While working with public relations and lobbying firms for this purpose, it hires former politicians and public officials. It is important to note the assessment of Frank Wolf, former co-chair of the US Congressional Human Rights Commission, who spoke on the subject to The Daily Beast and said: "Nobody could represent the Russian government in the 1980s, but now you find a lot of lobbying for the Chinese government. I find that shocking." [38]

The most remarkable developments in this regard have occurred in Australia. A legal investigation was launched against Shaquett Moselmane, a representative of the Australian Labor Party because the country's policy was manipulated by China. In the same way, Sam Dastyari, who was considered a bright future politician for a period, was discredited due to his donor relations with China. [39] He has worked to increase Chinese influence in politics not in America and Australia but also in Europe. For example, pro-Chinese attitudes have gradually turned into a mainstream political trend in the Czech Republic. President Zeman recently appointed Ye Jianming, former head of CEFC China Energy Company, as chief adviser on relations with Beijing. [40]

In its report, the Hoover Institute, affiliated with Stanford University, one of the world's leading universities, examined China's influence in various countries and revealed how politicians come under the influence of the Beijing government with money. Accordingly, the Beijing government is trying to hide its party-state practices through state-funded research centers, media, universities, and exchange programs in democratic countries. Depending on the dramatic growth in its economy, China attempts to penetrate state institutions to increase and protect its interests abroad. For example, the Canadian Intelligence Service found in 2010 that two politicians were under China's control. The Chinese administration donated $1 million to the fund bearing the surname of Prime Minister Trudeau in Canada in 2016. In 2017, it was reported in the press that two senators established a private company to advise China's investments. It has been determined that high-profile politicians with high profiles in New Zealand, including former party leaders and councilors, serve on the boards of directors of Chinese banks. [41]

Is it Nations United with China (C-UN) or The United Nations (UN)?

Establishment of the UN and China's Membership

The foundations of the United Nations organization were laid during the Second World War. 26 states came together under the leadership of the President of the United States of America Franklin D. Roosevelt on January 1, 1942, in order to oppose the Axis Powers including Germany and Japan, and started the foundation works of the United Nations (UN). On October 24, 1945, an agreement on the establishment of the UN was signed in San Francisco with the participation of 50 countries and many organizations. Following the establishment, the United States, Britain, the Soviet Union, France, and China became permanent members of the Security Council with the joint signatures of 45 members. The influence of the four victorious countries, as well as its position and influence in the Asia Pacific region, brought China this chance to become a permanent member of the Security Council. Today the UN has 193 members and five main bodies. These are the General Assembly, the Security Council, the Economic and Social Council, the Secretariat, and the International Court of Justice. The sixth body, the UN Trusteeship Council, which was established at the beginning has not been active since 1994. But it should be noted here that the People's Republic of China was represented by today's Taiwan at the UN until 1971. Until that time, the official name of Taiwan was the Republic of China. As stated before, Mao, who met with the American President Nixon within the scope of the outward expansion policy that started in the 1970s, demanded that the Chinese Communist Party be represented in the UN instead of Taiwan, and this demand became possible with the approval of the UK. Since then, the People's Republic of China (PRC) has been a permanent member of the UN Security Council, i.e. it has the veto power.

The Security Council played a supporting role during the bipolar Cold War between Russia and America. The council's influence on international politics began to increase after the fall of the Berlin Wall in the 1990s. The organization issued 511 resolutions from 1990 to 2011. As part of these resolutions, the UN imposed sanctions on countries such as Iraq, Rwanda, North Korea, and Iran and intervened directly and indirectly in many crisis areas from the former Yugoslavia to Haiti. [42]

Protecting Authoritarianism

In the new millennium, when the Chinese economy started to grow rapidly, the Beijing government increased its intervention in Security Council resolutions on issues related to other countries. Today, decisions on countries, which are often associated with poverty, dictatorship, and corruption, have all been vetoed because they are contrary to the economic interests of the Beijing administration. In these decisions, the Chinese government has shown that it prioritizes its interests over international universal values. China has an effective position especially with its economy, population power, and size in military spending. As Joel Wuthnow put it, "The power of veto is important for the implementation of China's negative agenda." The Beijing Government always holds the "veto card" because the volume of trade between China and the repressive regimes that Western countries want to impose sanctions on is greater than the total trade volume between other veto holder countries and these regimes. [43] After gaining Permanent Membership status in 1971, the PRC did not have much influence on UN resolutions until the 1990s. This situation continued in the same way in the 1990s. China vetoed no resolutions from 1980 to 1989. After the end of the Cold War, China began to increase its influence in the Security Council. However, due to the Tiananmen events in 1989, the PRC adopted an approach in which western principles were tried to be observed, albeit partially, but on the other hand, flexibility was also granted. Between 1990 and 1999, the PRC approved 598 of 642 UN resolutions and vetoed 2 of them. It abstained from the abstention vote 42 times. From the 2000s, PRC began to leverage its influence on the Security Council even more. The most important examples of this are the embargo on North Korea, nuclear weapons sanctions on Iran, the events in Sudan and political pressure on Burma, the events on the axis of Libya and Syria. [44] The Chinese administration, which supported imposing sanctions on Libya during the events of the Arab Spring that began in 2010, vetoed the sanctions when it came to Syria. PRC supported the pressure on Gaddafi to protect 40 thousand Chinese citizens in Libya. The idea of taking the same position as the African League in this veto is also effective. As for Syria, China vetoed the embargoes proposed in 2011 and 2012, wanting not to confront them due to the Arab League's ambivalence. In recent years, China has agreed with Russia on 13 of its 16 veto rights. The Beijing government, which has been using its veto right 10 times to prevent the actions against Syria since 2011, used its veto right for the UN's decisions against Myanmar in 2007, Zimbabwe in 2008, and Venezuela in 2019. [45]

Trojans in UN Agencies

The Beijing Administration's influence on the UN increased even more after Xi Jinping became the President of China. China is the second country after America to provide the most financial assistance to both the overall UN budget and the peacekeeping budget. In return for this money, the PRC wants its word to be heard more in the UN. The unit that the Beijing government provides the most financial support is the UN's Department of Political Relations. Since there are no intelligence services within the UN or there is no employee in charge of following the political developments in the countries where the UN has representative offices, China tests whether this department can play a role in the developments in places such as Myanmar, North Korea, Sri Lanka. An indication of China's growing interest in the UN's relationship with political issues is the appointment of a Chinese official to the Department for the first time in 2015. One year later, a second Chinese man started working in the same department. In 2017, the political relations department opened an office in Shanghai to establish relations with the Shanghai Cooperation Organization. As it is stated by Jeffrey Feltman, UN Secretary-General for Political Affairs, "China's influence on peace and security issues within the UN is growing, it is inevitable. It may be difficult to stop this, but by ending the gap created by America, we can stop China from developing its system of governance on issues such as the core values and human rights contained in the creation of the UN." [46]

Another indicator of the PRC's influence in the UN is the increase in the number of Chinese leaders at UN-affiliated institutions. Of the 15 agencies, 4 are managed by the Chinese. These are the Food and Agriculture Organization, International Communication Association, UN Industrial Development Organization, and International Civil Aviation Organization. Since 2007, the Economic and Social Affairs Secretariat has been led by Chinese diplomats and this allows Beijing to shape the UN's development programs to be in line with their interests. China applies the Belt and Road Initiative (BRI), which it uses to dominate the world economically and politically, also to the UN Sustainable

Development Goals (SDG). The Chinese Head of the Department of Economic and Social Affairs, Lui Zhenmin, promotes that the BRI is well-suited for development goals. While China is pouring money into the organization, it also enjoys being privy to criticism of human rights in return for this money. China, a country renowned for its theft in the field of property rights, tried to put its candidate Wang Binying at the head of the "World Intellectual Property Organization (WIPO)", just as the fox wanted to be the guardian of the coop. But this attempt was blocked at the last moment with the US taking a stand. But given that the heads of 5 more UN-affiliated agencies will change soon, it is now time for someone to tell Xi Jinping to stop. [47]

China on the Human Rights Commission

In the history of the UN, the step that will be referred to as a black mark on the universal values and human rights that constitute the raison d'être of the organization is the election of China to the UN Human Rights Commission once again. China, one of the countries that gained the right to be represented in the Human Rights Commission in the UN for three years, maintained its membership position, although it received fewer votes than the previous election. According to The Guardian newspaper, the Beijing government, which won the support of 180 countries in the 2016 elections, was supported by 139 countries this time. This, in turn, is a notable indicator of the influence of authoritarian regimes in the UN, which is a center for resolving human rights issues. Another example of China's influence on the commission is Jiang Duan, who represents China in the advisory group that will serve the Human Rights Commission in Geneva until March 2021. [48] In recent years, China has moved itself to a more active position rather than showing a defensive stance in the UN Human Rights Council. There are two main objectives in this change, which is clearly seen by the fact that China has a member in the Advisory Group. The first is to prevent future criticism against China, and the second is to support approaches that oppose outside intervention on human rights, transparency, and accountability. The Beijing government has long held this point of view, but actively implementing them began during Xi's reign. [49] The basis of the new discourse developed by the Communist Party is the idea that "if there are human rights violations somewhere, no one should interfere from outside, that country should solve that problem itself". For example, in the statements titled "Supporting Common Benefits on Human Rights" discussed in the meetings in June 2017 and March 2018, it was noted that the countries' independence should be emphasized by conducting silent dialogue and cooperation instead of investigating and taking action on human rights violations. [50] However, this method conflicts with the UN's Responsibility to Protect (R2P) regulations used in Libya to make decisions against the Gaddafi administration. R2P gives the international community the right to intervene if the administration in a country is insufficient concerning human rights. But Beijing does not want the genocide committed in East Turkistan to be investigated, so instead of R2P, it wants to cover up its crimes by asking the Human Rights Commission to meet with the relevant country behind closed doors.

For many years, the leaders of the PRC have wanted to use the 'socialist policy of the Chinese character' to intervene on international problems. In particular, China, where one party has the authoritarian rule, contrary to human rights norms, applies this policy. As Ted Piccone, who examined the process in the UN Human Rights Commission, points out in his findings, the Beijing administration does not merely advocate for its own management model with its economic leverage, which has increased its power worldwide. It also targets the international human rights system and its long-term practices, the participation of civil society, and independent monitoring mechanisms. [51]

The Neo-Red Guard – Beijing's Military Targets

One of the projects China is trying to implement without attracting the attention of the international community is to increase cooperation on military issues, especially with countries with which it has developed bilateral economic relations. The effectiveness of the People's Liberation Army (PLA) is increasing in the geography starting from Asia and extending to the Middle East. The fact that the communist dictator constantly increases China's armament capacity while telling the world tales about the growth of prosperity, democracy in international relations, and walking towards common goals is another indication that it dominates the world with military and economic power, not peace.

The report, in which the American Ministry of Defense examined the PRC, reveals the incredible dimensions of the military capacity of the Beijing government. China has 350 warships along with submarines, 130 of which are large surface combatants. The U.S. Navy's combat strength is 293 as of the end of this year. Beijing has 250 land-launched ballistic and cruise missiles with a range ranging from 500 to 5,500 kilometers. In parallel with Xi's desire to become the ruler of the world, the PLA has embarked on a new 30-year modernization process. [52] The communist regime conducts the 'Military-Civil Fusion' (MCF) development program, which will integrate economic, social, and security strategies to prepare China as a refreshed power for future periods. In connection with the MCF, a modernization program has also been launched, which will start this year and end in 2035. The goal is to transform the 'army of the people' PLA into the 'army of the world by 2049. [53]

Establishment of Military Bases in BRI Countries

The Communist Party is already increasing the role of the PLA in foreign relations. On the other hand, many military exercises have been held with other countries in recent years. China, which extends from Asia to Africa and Europe in an economic sense with BRI, does the same thing in the military field with the PLA. Apart from the military base currently located in Djibouti, China plans to establish bases in other countries to carry out naval, land, and air military operations. The countries where these bases will be located also show that BRI is not 'economic but also it is based on military expansion. Countries, where China wants to establish military bases are Myanmar, Thailand, Singapore, Indonesia, Pakistan, Sri Lanka, United Arab Emirates, Kenya, Seychelles, Tanzania, Angola, and Tajikistan. [54]

As part of the Communist Party's new configuration of foreign military relations, PLA commanders visited their interlocutors in more than 40 countries. China has also established defense and security consultations as well as working meetings with 17 neighboring countries. These mechanisms are also being built with countries in Africa, Latin America, the Caribbean, and the Pacific regions. [55] These steps are taken to defend Beijing's expanding global interests and to implement its foreign policy goals within the framework of "Great Power Diplomacy in the New Age". As part of the activities outside the scope of the war, the People's Liberation Army Naval (PLAN) ships visited the Middle East, Europe, Africa, South Asia, Southeast Asia, and Latin American countries in 2008. The purpose of these visits is to protect China's interests outside the South Asian sea and to protect China's military marine communication network. [56]

Three-Way Warfare and Military Investment in Sophisticated Technologies

The PLA, the neo-Red Guard of the Communist Party, has been implementing the concept of 'three-way warfare' since 2003, namely the Psychological Operation – the War of Public Opinion – the War of law. As part of the psychological operation, China uses propaganda, deception, threats, and coercion to influence the opponent's decision-making process, while also conducting this operation to prevent counter-operations against itself. In the context of the war of public opinion, China ensures the dissemination of information targeting local and international audiences in order to direct and influence international public opinion. In the field of law, local and international legal rules are used to support these operations. The PRC acts with a method that uses military and civilian elements together to turn the PLA into a worldwide power. By utilizing a system called Military-Civil Fusion (MCF), Chinese companies are encouraged to invest more in the military field, while the aim is to buy, adapt, and renew foreign technology in the military field. With the unification of MCF in this approach called IDAR (Introduce, Digest, Absorb, and Re-Innovate), the distinction between civilian and military uses is hidden. Here, the biggest risk for western countries and companies is that they contribute to China's growing military capabilities without being aware of foreign strategic technology and expertise, that is, raising their enemies with their own hands. [57]

This method, which dates back to Mao, was accelerated by an outward expansion process that began in 1979. Chinese scientists work at foreign universities specialized in relevant fields to bring technologies from other countries to their own lands and to implement the redevelopment methodology. Beijing's goal is to become the world's powerhouse in scientific and technological innovation. Another notable feature of the MCF is to make various additions and interventions to infrastructure projects to be used for military purposes. Civil companies and military institutions aim to work in harmony with this program. The most effective use of both MCF and IDAR are issues directly related to the PLA. Every technology developed by private companies, from unmanned aerial vehicles to artificial intelligence, is made even more sophisticated so that the neo-red guard PLA can benefit from these technologies. The Central Commission for the Development of Military-Civil Fusion, headed by Xi himself, oversees this process. The seven largest state-sponsored MCF funds allocated a budget of $ 56.9 billion in 2018 to encourage civil-military cooperation. Thousand Talents Plan has been put into effect to find human resources. In 2018 alone, 60 thousand people were recruited in fields such as artificial intelligence, biochemistry, quantum communication, integrated electricity, developed metals, and similar fields. Chinese students have been encouraged to study critical technology not ' within the country but also abroad. So much so that this situation caught the attention of the US Department of Defense, and the following assessment was made in the annual report: "Chinese science and engineering students have mastered technologies that later became critical for military systems and over time have reached unintentional violations of US export control laws." Neo-Red Guard PLA has sponsored the training of more than 2,500 military engineers abroad since 2007. For this reason, the progress made by the PLA on sensitive military technologies has been deemed risky by some experts and various restrictions have been demanded. [58]

China is Watching the World!

"Big Brother is watching you" is one of the iconic phrases of the novel 1984, a popular word which tells about how a dictatorial state turns people's lives into hell by completely surrounding them with advanced technology, and while doing so, how it frightens and intimidates people with lies. While George Orwell is writing his cult novel, the foundations of another dictatorial regime are laid in another corner of the world. The People's Republic of China, founded by dictator Mao, had undergone 'metamorphosis' in the 1980s and begun to turn into a semi-communist, semi-capitalist monster. He transformed East Turkistan into a laboratory/prison with online walls where he experimented with advanced technological products. In a Frontline Documentary Program of the American PBS Channel, it is explained that the artificial intelligence technologies developed by China, have reached dangerous dimensions.

Investments in advanced technology are at the top of the list of areas that the Chinese Communist regime attaches most importance to. Knowing the communist monster regime's appetite for technology, both Chinese and western companies explain their discoveries to the Beijing administration and, with their approval, test these technologies in regions such as East Turkistan. According to a compilation of the documentary published by Frontline on the website of the Campaign For Uyghurs, there are 1,200 technology companies in East Turkistan alone. According to the statements of relevant individuals from technology companies, the Integrated Joint Operations Platform (IJOP) system has been established in these regions. Billions of data are transmitted to this platform from each channel and these data are analyzed. These data include footage from security cameras at every corner, face-scanning systems for ID control, and data from private applications downloaded to phones by government pressure. The data are evaluated together with the data collected by the Han Chinese in the field. Thus, if a strained expression on the face of any person walking on the street is suspicious, that person can be stopped and interrogated by the police immediately. The producers of the program give this warning: "The ideological conflict of this century will be between Chinese-style authoritarian regimes and the shaky liberal democracy of the west. People shouldn't just think of it as a local incident in East Turkistan. This is a situation that will affect human rights and democracy around the world." [59] The technological persecution of Uyghurs will be discussed in detail in the relevant chapter.

Today, the most discussed issue in the field of technology and security in western countries is whether artificial intelligence (AI) and Big Data will be used by authoritarian regimes such as China to reshape the international order with economic effects. Some experts think that China cannot yet collect data on people outside of its own country's borders and turn it into a threat. However, the fact that the technologies developed by Chinese companies are not applied locally but also exported to other countries is a sign that the world will encounter this reality soon. Because the "New Generation Artificial Intelligence Development Plan (AIDP)" and "Made in China 2025" documents published by the Beijing government in 2017 show the importance attached by the leaders of the Communist regime to AI. The spending plan of two regional administrations for artificial intelligence is $ 14.7 billion. The Beijing government and its affiliates closely monitor all publications and news about AI in western countries, especially in America. In 2018, one of the Politburo meetings under the chairmanship of Xi was dedicated to artificial intelligence. At this meeting, Xi warned that "Pay attention to our shortcomings on this issue and make sure that critical and fundamental technologies on AI are firmly grasped and in our hands." Although the communist regime tells the world about its "concerns" (!) about the artificial intelligence arms races, the leaders of the regime believe that the use of AI in the military field is inevitable and pursues it. Zeng Yi, chief executive of China's third-largest defense industry company, said the following remarkable statement at a conference held in 2018: "In the future, people will not be on the battlefields" Beijing's goal is the further expansion of fully automatic weapons by 2025. [60]

On the other hand, the Chinese government sells drones to Middle Eastern countries, mainly the United Arab Emirates and Saudi Arabia. For example; the Ziyan company sold the Blowfish A2 model to the United Arab Emirates and started negotiations with Saudi Arabia and Pakistan to sell the same model to these countries. These high-tech drones can hit the target with high accuracy in more complex combat environments. These unmanned aerial vehicles can be equipped with weapons according to the demand of the buyer countries. One step beyond this is the use of artificial intelligence as a decision-maker. It is known that Chinese military officials have been thinking about this for a long time and are working on all kinds of alternative technologies. They admit how they use artificial intelligence technologies in East Turkistan in the following sentences: "We use big data and artificial intelligence in East Turkistan. We use technologies that track and identify all movements in the local area, including smart city systems. We have a facial scanning system." A company called SenseTime, which builds virtual prisons for Uyghurs, also sells this technology to countries in Latin America, Africa, and Asia. According to Gregory C. Allen's findings, the Chinese Ministry of National Defense recently established two new research centers on artificial intelligence. These new R&D centers, established under the National Defense Technology Innovation Institute (NIIDT), are the Unmanned Systems Research Center (USRC) led by Yan Ye and the Artificial Intelligence Research Center (AIRC) led by Dai Huadong. These two R&D centers, which are currently among the fastest-growing organizations, continue to recruit new engineers to their staff. In the long term, their goal is to bypass the development process and have a stronger and more powerful position than Western countries, especially America. [61] Another point that should be focused on regarding artificial intelligence is its development in Mobile Communication Technology. In the 5G process, the new phase of telecommunications infrastructure services, safety concerns lie beneath the attitude of America and other countries to the Chinese Huawei company. The economy to be triggered by 5G on the one hand, concerns about espionage, and the huge investments of the Chinese Communist Regime on the other hand will play a critical role in future competition.

Is Covid-19 A Biological Weapon or A New Tool for Colonization?

Dr. Li Wengliang, a doctor who was working in Wuhan, China, wrote to an online chat group on December 30, 2019, and warned them that 7 people died of an "unknown disease" in his hospital. Li told this chat group with his colleagues that he was also "quarantined in the emergency room". "Is Sars coming back?" one of Li's colleagues asked him and reminded him of previous epidemics in which 800 people died. The USA-based New York Times newspaper reports that this doctor, who tried to warn the world, was questioned by the hospital administration on the same night and that they asked him why he shared this information. According to the report, three days later, the police also took testimony from Li for 'illegal behavior'. [62] At the time these lines were written, the epidemic, identified as Covid-19, infected over 105 million people worldwide and claimed the lives of more than over 2.3 million people. More than 26 million people in America were infected by this virus, and 462 thousand of them died because of the virus. At the time of this writing, the daily number of cases is around 52 thousand in the United States. [63]

The coronavirus outbreak started almost a year ago. From March 2020, this disease, which suddenly brought the world to the brink of disaster, has opened a new page in the history of the world. However, the developments that have emerged since the day Dr. Li warned us have brought up the issue of whether this disease is a new type of biological weapon. Experts on the subject will undoubtedly examine the evaluation of this disease, called Covid-19, within the scope of a biological weapon. But the mistakes of the Chinese Communist Regime in the spread of the disease are making humanity pay a new price in this century. As always, the CCP demonstrated its character of being an authoritarian and repressive state in this regard. Firstly, Dr. Li, who announced the disease, was questioned and he soon became a victim of this horrible disease. Afterward, information about the disease was hidden from the public for a while, to protect the so-called "Chinese Honor". Although symptoms were first reported in November, Beijing has hidden the disease from the world public for weeks. When the epidemic started to be seen in other countries, the Beijing administration, which was desperate, had to inform the World Health Organization about the incident. The World Health Organization, which patted the back of China throughout the entire process, also showed the beadledom of "celebrating the PRC because of its superior struggle", although the Beijing administration did not take the precautions regarding the virus that caused the death of millions of people. It is a great contradiction for China, who have not given reliable information about the virus from the beginning, to explain that a few thousand people died in a country where more than 1 billion people live. The announcement that tens of people lost their lives in East Turkistan, where more than 20 million people live, also strengthens the suspicions that the PRC is manipulating the information.

The American administration expressed China's irresponsibility at every opportunity and believes that this virus was developed in Chinese laboratories. "There is substantial evidence that this virus came from a laboratory in Wuhan," Former Secretary of State Mike Pompeo said in a television program. "The best experts consider the virus to be man-made. I also see no reason not to believe this view," he said. Pompeo's statements naturally drew the reaction of Chinese authorities. [64]

A determination that Covid-19 is considered as a biological weapon has not been scientifically and definitively confirmed to date. But this does not mean that the communist regime has no interest in biological weapons. When we look at Beijing's biological weapons history, it will be seen that China suffered great losses especially by the Japanese during World War II. For this reason, China is one of the countries that signed the Biological and Toxic Weapons Convention signed in Geneva in 1952 and 1984. Although China has signed these declarations, strong doubts have been expressed about China's efforts for developing biological weapons. In 2005, the American State Department issued a statement saying that China had developed biological weapons intended for attack and had violated the Geneva Convention. This determination was also included in the ministry's reports of 2010, 2012, and 2014. According to the Ministry's reports, biological weapons research is being conducted at the Institute of Military Medical Sciences Microbiology of the Chinese Ministry of Defense and Epidemiology and the Lanzhou Institute of Biological Development. The Beijing government stated that these facilities are ' intended to develop vaccines. Continuous attention is drawn to China's biological weapon development potential in articles published in Western scientific journals. The following findings in an article are worrying the world public opinion: "China has an advanced ability to deploy and distribute aerosolized biological weapons. Such advanced capabilities have the potential to infect too many people because aerosolized diseases are the most contagious species" [65]

One of the perspectives that helps to understand these seemingly complex events is that "if you are looking for the perpetrator of an incident, first look at who benefited most from that event". Although no concrete evidence has been put forward to date, one of the first names that will come to everyone's mind when asked who benefited most from the chaotic situation caused by coronavirus is undoubtedly the Beijing regime. So much so that in international circles, the term 'mask diplomacy' is not a description invented for nothing. PRC, which hid the deadly virus for days so that its "reputation" would not be harmed, but let it spread around the world, tried to develop its own diplomatic relations with the masks it sent under the name of humanitarian aid like the killer taking the first seat in the funeral of his victim. This is just like the drug couriers distributing food and aid in areas of the drug mafia-dominated Latin America to increase love for their bosses.

In China, many institutions and organizations from private companies to municipalities have sent aid to 150 countries and four international organizations, with the guidance of the government. Video consulting services were provided to 170 countries and health teams were sent to 30 countries. Thank you messages were sent to President Xi throughout the places where help was sent. Also, Huawei, which is the most popular telecommunications company in China and trying to dominate investments in 5G technology in the world, tried to fix his negative image created by being on the blacklist of the United States through donations. The same company helped Canada to lobby for the release of former Financial Affairs Coordinator Meng Wanzhou. The government of Beijing promoted its own institutions while giving help like an advertisement. Especially with the improvement it has made in the military field, it sent medical support to 20 countries with military personnel and demonstrated its overseas operation power. It is also seen here that the communist regime wants to use America's decision to withdraw its support to the World Health Organization in its favor. [66]

The Beijing government and its media outlets turned channels such as Twitter and Facebook into a propaganda war tool during the pandemic when people locked in their homes and followed developments on social media. Stanford University Freeman Spogli Institute for International Studies examined Twitter messages of 11 Chinese media outlets broadcasting in English between January 18 and May 30. Each message posted by these accounts, which have a total of 42.2 million followers, was interacted with an average of 269 times. Social media accounts were immediately activated according to the events in countries such as Japan, Korea, Italy, and Canada, which were selected as targets. For example, when a virus is detected in a member of Shincheonji, one of Korea's leading religious organizations, China's aid to South Korea has been on the agenda immediately on social media. Masks sent by the same company to Canada, where the former Huawei executive is under arrest, have also been advertised on social media. Aid was provided to countries such as Pakistan and Serbia, which took part in the Belt and Road Initiative, and shows were organized on the internet. [67] However, it bears reminding once again that the Chinese Communist regime, which put Uyghurs on trains in East Turkistan and sent them to work to factories in the interior regions, despite the Covid-19 epidemic, has shown its unscrupulousness by using a deadly disease to show the world how 'humane' and 'globally responsible' it is.

On the other hand, the virus epidemic that originated in China and paralyzed the world has damaged the economies of the countries. In the latest report titled 'Economic Outlook of the World' prepared by the International Monetary Fund (IMF), it was emphasized that although the countries reactivated their economic activities in May and June, the expected recovery was not reached due to acceleration of the spread of the virus. The exception here is the recovery in the Chinese economy. It has been stated that the recovery of countries other than the PRC will take a long time. There are signs of recovery in global trade, but China, the country that has managed to suffer the least damage from the virus, has an effect on this increase. [68]

First Lend, Then Enslave – The Sino-Colonial System

100 Years of a Marathon Effort to Rule the World!

"If allowed to continue in its current form, could lead to a loss of personal freedom for Western civilization. It really is that much of an existential question." John Mauldin, the founder of Mauldin Economics, begins with this warning in his article titled" China's grand plan to take over the world" published in Forbes. In the 2000s, when China was admitted to the World Trade Organization, no one thought about today's picture, Mauldin said, getting rid of this process is no longer easy, given the economic and legal confusion. [69]

China's economy was very weak, stagnant, centrally controlled, and isolated from inefficient policies and the global economy when Deng Xiaoping launched his outward expansion program in 1979 nearly 40 years ago. Since China started implementing free-market reforms, it has accelerated its economic growth. With a 9.5 percent growth in 2018, it has once again been the largest economy in history, continuing its sustainable expansion. With this economic growth, China is moving towards reaching its goal of becoming the leader of the world. President Xi Jinping declared that they will reach the goal of "Rejuvenation of the Chinese Nation" by 2049, that is, until the 100th anniversary of the founding of the communist chinese republic, both by growing economically and by rejoining Taiwan. While doing this, he developed a new concept. With this term expressed as "socialism in the character of China", China moves towards its aims, sometimes as a capitalist and sometimes as a totalitarian regime, whatever turns China on. The philosophical origin of these dreams of sovereignty is based on the tradition of communist ideology, which dates back to Karl Marx. The key point here is that Xi thinks he is the leader to see this goal achieved, and indeed, he sees this goal as an indispensable fate. [70]

There is increasing evidence that the Sino-colonial rule is indeed aiming to be a global power and perhaps to achieve global superiority over future generations. Here, steps are taken to establish a new world order in which China can compete on its own. In his speech at the Party Congress in 2017, Xi Jinping emphasized a China "that is standing up, getting rich and stronger" and that it will be the leader of the world by 2049. Xi and the Communist Party believe that for this aim, the world order must change. When the statements of Beijing spokespersons are examined, Liza Tobin, an expert on China, draws the following picture: "The USA and its allies system will be replaced by a China-based global partnership network. The world will see China's authoritarian vision rather than a western democracy." The Beijing Regime strives in pursuit of "building a new global economic order centered in China" for an international relations order in which it supported repressive regimes instead of applying pressure to them. [71] The process that started with China's membership to World Trade in 2001, continued with China's assuming the task of "saving the global economy" in the economic crisis in 2008, and in this period, China became the second-largest economy by surpassing Japan and thus reached the final stage. In other words, this is the stage of becoming the leader of global trade and investment and opening a new episode in the colonial order that started in the 15th century. The goal of becoming a world leader in the economy that will enable joining into this episode is about to be caught by the PRC. The IMF's 2020 World Economic Outlook October report predicts that the global economy will shrink by 4 percent this year. Among the developed countries, China is the ' state that is expected to increase its growth rate this year. While China is expected to grow 1.9 percent, it is estimated that America will shrink 4.3 percent, Japan 5.3 percent, Germany 6 percent, and India 10.3 percent. [72] To ensure the realization of the Sino-Colonialism goals of the PRC, which wants to be the ruler of the world in the economy, project networks from East Turkistan to Africa are being developed and countries are connected to the Communist Party economically and politically.

China in Africa: Aid - > Investment - > Neo-slavery

China, the world's second-largest economy, is also the country most in need of waste fossils, underground wealth, and alternative energy resources. There is nothing more natural than the communist dictate, which makes a $400 billion deal with the Islamic Republic of Iran while hating Islam and even which walks all over its founding philosophy and calling it the "Chinese Version of Socialism" to maintain the leadership in the economy, to set sights on Africa. The CCP's interest in Africa dates back to the Mao era. During the Great Leap Forward and the Cultural Revolution, seen as the two catastrophic periods in Asian history, in a period when China's own people were crushed and starved to death, China, for the aim of not being isolated from the world, provided aid in the field of health and agriculture to the African countries that have not yet completed their democratization processes and not gained their full independence and also developed some infrastructure projects for this region. After the outward expansion policy that started in 1979, China changed its previous support methods and used the China Export and Import Bank and China Development Bank to fund the projects while continuing to provide aid. In the new millennium, after China joined the World Trade Organization, there has been a serious increase in investments in Africa. While the Foreign Direct Investment (FDI) amount of China in Africa was 75 million dollars in 2000, this figure reached 2.9 billion dollars in 2015. [73] The FDI reached $4.1 billion and $5.3 billion respectively in 2017 and 2018 when Xi Jinping declared China's "second spring" and the Party Congress was held. [74]

For the Beijing government, the importance of this continent is summarized under three headings. The first is the supply of raw materials needed to sustain the growth of the world's second-largest economy. 90 percent of the world's cobalt and platinum are sourced here. Half of the demand for gold, a third of manganese, and 35 percent of uranium are also met from Africa. 75 percent of cobalt, which is one of the critical items of electronic equipment production from mobile phones to computers, is obtained from these soils. For this reason, mining and petroleum are in the first place in terms of investment in China. Other than these, Chinese companies have investments in Africa in every field from infrastructure investments to food production. Since these companies are state-owned, they have the advantage over their competitors in terms of obtaining cheap financing. The second title is undoubtedly political motivation. The Red Administration takes the countries in the continent as its supporter in order to expand its steps towards dominating the global world. The most obvious examples of this are African countries whose names can be seen under the UN voting or statements supporting China. On the other hand, China has the opportunity to increase military cooperation along with economic cooperation. The last title is that developing countries offer important opportunities to developed countries. China, therefore, wants to take advantage of the growing importance of Africa in the future and its ability to be a growing market. [75]

When analyzed in terms of economic policy, it is seen that the Communist dictate turned the investment need of African countries into an opportunity in their favor. This attitude of the Beijing government towards African countries has signs of how it will treat the rest of the world as it equates its power with the United States. For this reason, the activities of the Beijing Administration in Africa mean neo-colonial, that is, re-exploitation of African people and their natural structure. "Whites were bad, Indians were terrible, but China is the worst among them" is the summary of what happened. [76]

Numerous examples of the destruction of the Sino-colonial system on the African continent are included in the records. Among them, one of the most notable examples occurred in South Sudan. China National Oil Company has irresponsibly destroyed the environment during oil works in the region. These works caused the birth of children with disabilities, destruction of fertile lands, poisoning of livestock, and pollution of rivers. China's destruction of nature in the same geography, in the North Upper Nile, harms the indigenous Dinka Padang communities in South Sudan. China does not use its own technology when running projects on the continent. At the same time, it transports its own citizens as workers to these regions. In other words, China's contribution to Africa's employment and economy is controversial. For example, the amount of the Standard Gauge Railway Project to be built between Djibouti, Ethiopia, and Kenya is 4.5 billion dollars. From an external perspective, this can be considered a large and important investment. But 'the devil is hidden in details.' One of the biggest financial resources of the project is China Export-Import Bank. The wagons to be used on the railroad tracks are made in China and the Chinese Civil Engineering and Construction Company will do the project. In other words, the Beijing administration takes the money from his one pocket and puts it in his other pocket. [77] While the number of Chinese working in Africa 20 years ago was 46,800, the number of Chinese sent to projects on the continent increased approximately 5 times as a result of Beijing's increase in investments on the continent after the economic crisis in 2008. As of 2018, 201,570 Chinese work in Africa. Again, in the same period, the amount of income obtained by Chinese construction companies from Africa is around 1 billion dollars. These companies made $48 billion by the end of 2018. [78] This is another proof that the Communist party sees Africa not as a place of development, but simply as a place to make money. A significant part of these huge projects is part of the Belt and Road Initiative, which will be described in detail in the following chapter. But big projects mean big debt. It is called 'debt diplomacy', a term which the world's most ruthless state capitalism brings to the economy.

Results of the Fulfillment of the Phrase "The Borrower Also Takes Orders"

According to rumors, the Crimean Khagan Giray asked to borrow money from Sultan Suleiman. And Suleiman replied to this request by ordering his minister "Give him the money, whoever borrows today will take orders tomorrow". However, it is possible to see the most striking examples of the reflection of this word in international relations today when we look at the leaders begging at the doors of China. The communist dictatorship enacted a law to suppress the anti-democracy demonstrations that started this year in Hong Kong and to rule Hong Kong by despotism like they do in the mainland. And 53 members of the UN had supported this regulation. When these 53 countries are examined, it is seen that 40 of them are the countries involved in the Belt and Road Initiative. Authoritarian regimes such as Syria, Saudi Arabia, and North Korea, which are not included in the BRI but have political and economic relations with China, also supported the Communist dictatorship in this regard. [79]

Sri Lanka is one of the most notable countries that the Beijing government has thrown into a debt trap. When the government, which wanted to rebuild the infrastructure that was destroyed after the civil war in Sri Lanka, sought a debt, it came up with China "providing money easily and cheaply." But this easy and cheap money later caused trouble for the country. Unable to overcome economic difficulties, Sri Lanka transferred its control of Hambantota Port to China in 2017 when it could not pay its supposedly low debts. [80] To put it in words like it is comm' used in Turkey, 'usurers' have arrived and seized the property. The vigilance of the PRC here is this: Unlike the International Monetary Fund (IMF) and World Bank loans, China asks the country's natural resources with the highest long-term value as collateral while providing this country with money. The reason China flopped down on the Hambantota port is that it is located in a geostrategic location that opens East Asia to the Indian Ocean. For economically weak countries, China's target is mines, airports, and other resources. China has done the same thing not in remote Asian and African countries but also at the gates to Europe. [81]

Communist dictatorship imposes a new system of enslavement on the world. It was China that came from the other side of the world to the aid of Greece, which needed money to heal the wounds of the economic crisis it had experienced. A Chinese company bought the Port of Piraeus for $436 million. Thus, the communist and authoritarian regime became a neighbor of European countries. Here, as mentioned earlier, there are two goals. Keeping its own domestic economy alive and strengthening its diplomatic effectiveness. As it is stated in Chellaney's findings, the sino-colonial administration gave the message that "it corrected historical injustice" after taking Hong Kong from the British in 1997. But the Sri Lankan example shows that Beijing is building new Hong Kong-like colonies in its own way. [82] Likewise, Laos, which has been in an economic crisis for some time and has difficulty repaying its debts to Chinese state banks, fell victim to the Red Dragon. A report was published stating that the control of most of the national electricity network in the country had to be left to a Chinese company. According to the information contained in the report, under the electricity grid shareholding agreement signed between the state-owned Électricité du Laos (EDL) and China Southern Power Grid Co. on September 1, the Électricité du Laos will transfer majority control of Transmission Company Limited to China. [83] Kenya's high debts from China have put the risk of Mombasa port in this country becoming a second Sri Lanka. Today, many countries from Argentina to Namibia have fallen into the debt trap of the Red government. And these countries have been subjected to bitter prescriptions to pay off their debts, and these countries have been asked to sacrifice their precious assets. The debt trap diplomacy of the PRC once again justified the Bilge Khagan and revealed how they deceived humanity. Saying that he wanted to bring China back to its youth in the 100th anniversary of the communist revolution, what Xi really wanted to do was to acquire the natural resources, namely "fresh blood", that they will need while dominating the world by seizing the mines of small independent countries. Another example of this situation is Djibouti, which is one of the small but strategic countries of Africa. Djibouti had to lease the place that China needed for the construction of its military base on the continent, to the Communist dictatorship for $20 million annually. [84]

The African continent, exploited by European countries for centuries, is also the biggest victim of China's debt trap. Today, the number of borrowings of African countries to China is 1076. The total debt amount has reached 148 billion dollars. Africa, which owed 129 million dollars in 2000, had the highest debt in 2016 with 29.4 billion dollars. The amount of debt borrowed in 2018 is 8.9 billion dollars. When these debts are analyzed by sectors, the transportation sector ranks first with 44.2 billion dollars. The energy sector comes second with a debt of 37 billion dollars and the mining sector comes third with a debt of 18.6 billion dollars. The largest indebted country is Angola with $ 43.2 billion. Angola is followed by Ethiopia with $ 13.7 billion and Zambia with $ 9.7 billion. [85] So this picture is the most striking result of Beijing's 'sino-colonialism' policies.

China's Games in the Middle East

After World War I, Britain and America were the number one allies of the Arabs in the Middle East, where Western countries were setting their eyes on the oil reserves of the region. A new player appears on this bloody chessboard made of oil. China is now one of the largest oil consumers in the world with its production economy that has accelerated after the 2000s. Countries in the Middle East and the Gulf region are solving China's energy problem arising from the biggest impasse in the way of continuing economic growth.

As Christian Le Miere, an energy expert at the American-based Atlantic Council, highlighted in his article, Beijing now ranks first in the list of oil exports of Gulf countries. China imports 72 percent of its oil consumption. In 2019, Beijing's oil imports from Saudi Arabia increased by 47 percent, and daily oil imports increased to 1.6 billion barrels. That figure is 16.5 percent of China's imports. Iraq is the third-largest supplier, selling 1.01 million oil a day to the Red Dragon. Oman sells 630 thousand, Kuwait 430 thousand, Iran 310 thousand, and UAE 280 thousand tons of barrels to China. In total, 40 percent of China's oil needs are met from the Gulf. China supplies not oil but also a significant part of its natural gas needs from the Middle East. The Chinese Communist regime, which already supplies 20 percent of its natural gas consumption from Qatar, expects an additional 10 percent increase over the next 20 years. [86] This semi-communist, semi-capitalist, that is, crucial regime, which transforms its foreign trade relationship into a strategic relationship with the presidency of Xi and which wants to take an active role in the developments in the Middle East, also aims at involving in military and security fields. The Chinese government has signed cooperation agreements with 15 Middle Eastern states to date. These agreements aim to provide security in the Arab Sea and the Gulf of Aden within the scope of combating piracy and maritime. In the report titled "China's Big Game in the Middle East" prepared by the European Council on Foreign Relations ECFR, it is emphasized that Beijing is one of the important players in the region. Camille Lons, who is the editor of the report, warns that "If it is thought that the rise of China in the region is intensifying geopolitical rivalry in the immediate vicinity of Europe, European politicians should take this country into account in their moves towards the Middle East." The BRI will increase its influence in the Middle East as it stretches from Asia to Europe. Taking lessons from the negative image created by oil and security issues, the first thing to come to mind when talking about the West and Middle East, Beijing government emphasizes issues such as economy, infrastructure investments, and increasing mutual trade in its long-term reports for the Middle East. But on the other hand, it should also be noted that China established its first military base in foreign countries in Djibouti, which is immediately located in a critical geographical location between the Middle East and Africa. [87] China again leads the countries that benefit the most from the curiosity to build giant construction and infrastructure projects in the Middle East countries. Qatar's Lusail Stadium built for the 2022 World Football Cup, the Yanbu Refinery in Saudi Arabia, the high-speed train between Jeddah and Mecca are some of the remarkable projects, according to the researcher Jonathan Fulton's article. Chinese companies also play an active role in the reconstruction of Iraq, Yemen, and Syria. [88]

Another importance of the Middle East, which is critical for China due to its being an energy center and its strategic location, is that this region is an economic corridor to Europe. For example, 60 percent of China's trade to Europe and African countries passes through UAE. On the other side of the coin, we see the expectation of Saudi Arabia to increase its dominance in maritime over the region while tolerating the increase of Beijing's dominance in the Red Sea. Other countries also want to gain a greater share of BRI and strengthen economically and politically. For example; the UAE, demanding control of the Horn of Africa region, wants to make giant port projects with China. The Gulf countries' willingness to invest in the CPEC project in Pakistan, which has turned into Beijing's backyard today, is a fact that should not be ignored. The democracy of taking shelter under the wings of Beijing, which has the veto right in the UN Security Council on the one hand, while doing business with the Chinese Communist regime, on the other hand, is an important advantage for the Middle Eastern countries that are not yet developed. [89] The Gulf countries now see China as a strategic partner, granting concessions to companies from China in oil fields while also providing them with military equipment. According to the news published in The Economist magazine in February, the main weapon imported by the Gulf countries from China is unmanned aerial vehicles. These unmanned aerial vehicles, equipped with weapons, are used to destroy specific targets. For example, the UAE killed one of the Houthi leaders with these drones. [90] On the one hand, the Gulf Countries that use China's technologies in the arms race, on the other hand, surrender to Beijing's "soft power". The fact that Mandarin is taught in 60 schools in the UAE is one of the dramatic examples of the UAE making overtures to China. [91] One move ahead for these overtures is, which one can understand from the marches sung by Arab children, that the Emirate of Dubai organized celebratory events for the foundation anniversary of the irreligious Communist regime.

3

China's War Against Islam

"We do not allow young people to go to the mosque. But it's okay if they're 65 or older. We report those who do not obey this rule to the police station in the village. Then they are sent to a concentration camp." (1)

THIS WAS FIRST published in a Radio Free Asia news report, and offers a clear picture of the oppression that the People's Republic of China (PRC) has perpetrated against the Muslims. In the same publication, it was reported that young people who went to the mosque in East Turkestan, were reported to the police station, and then were sent to the camps after being captured by the police forces of the Communist regime. (2) Beijing government officials claim at all press conferences that everyone in their country is respectful to religious beliefs. However, according to the reports coming from there, what actually happened is the exact opposite of these statements. Neither Muslims nor members of any other religion are allowed to fulfill the requirements of their faith in this geographical region ruled by the Communist Party, which adopts the philosophy that "believing in religion is a disease" as its motto. This regime, which claims to be respectful to religion in its public statements, has damaged 16,500 mosques in East Turkestan thus far in practice and has destroyed half of them. As if this was not enough, the status of these historical places of worship as mosques has been removed as physical characteristics are altered. The minarets of the mosques were destroyed, and the crescents were thrown on the ground. Masjids, which reflect historical beauty, are turned into tea gardens and restaurants for tourists.

Another indication of the communist regime's disrespect for religion is that women with headscarves who are taken to concentration camps, are forced to remove their headscarves. The mentality that collects and discards copies of the Qur'an from houses and destroys mosques, of course, will not allow young people to pray. Parents who teach these young people how to pray, fast, or read the Qur'an are subjected to torture in concentration camps just because they raise their children religiously. Those who have been to other Muslims majority countries to study the Islamic religion have been deported and sent back to China following the agreement between China and those governments. The Chinese Communist regime threw Uyghurs Muslims into prisons following their deportation to China. Those who perform fasting during the Ramadan as part of their worship, which is the second of the five pillars of Islam, have been subjected to what is in effect, a witch hunt. Charitable people, who collected aid for the construction and expenses of their places of worship, were caught and taken away by the police. In addition to all of this, government officials visited imams in their homes and forced them to eat pork, which is forbidden by the religion of Islam. If a Muslim asks what kind the meat the official bought from, such questions is considered as a "radical" act and legal action can be taken against him or her. The system operates to collect copies of the Qur'an from mosques, and then replace them with books describing the faithless doctrines of Chinese socialism. The verses and hadiths on the walls of the mosques have been dismantled and thrown on the ground, and Xi Jinping's words are hung on the walls instead. The PRC's respect for religious beliefs is so completely lacking that during Ramadan, a dinner with alcohol was organized in a mosque that was turned into a restaurant, and a dance show was allowed to be held there and this event was subsequently published on social media. Social media users who insult religion have been slapped on their backs in this country where any person who objected to Communist doctrines is sent to prison. The authotratian mentality, which has carried out all these actions, has also managed to silence many Muslim countries with the sino-colonial system it has built.

The Chinese Communist Party and The PRC's Viewpoints on Religion

The communist revolution that took place in Russia in 1917 had both political and economic effects in Asian countries. Those who carried out the Russian revolution accepted Marxism as the basic ideology, which denied the necessity of both religious beliefs and religious institutions. Therefore, religions and religious structures have come under great pressure. Behind the idea of adapting Marxist thought to their own interests is the pragmatism of the use of anti-religious movements as a lever by which the new revolutionary elites can hold ruling power. China is one of the countries that has adopted Marxism and its

Soviet Union version, Leninism, in the establishment of the new authoritarian order. Many countries that gained their independence after colonialism, from the Middle East to Africa and Latin America, have acted with the same ideology and logic. The country that has preserved the Marxist-Leninist political philosophy until today is China. [3] Based on this political philosophy, Mao and his comrades founded the Chinese Communist Party (CCP) in 1921. by conditions that led to the development of the Marxist idea, had not really existed for Mao or his comrades to adopt anti-religious ideology. As Thosnchev emphasized in his work Religion and Communism in Modern China, the thought system pioneered by Karl Marx is based on anti-capitalism. But when the CCP was founded, capitalism, industry, and trade were not yet fully developed in China. The words and phrases found in the papers and writings of Mao, who saw himself as a Marxist leader and spoke passionately on this subject, aimed to manipulate the minds of the crowds he dragged after him, and they had no historical, political or economic background in reality. They were brought forth for the purpose of creating a wave of excitement. [4] Mao copied the thoughts of Karl Marx to maintain his authoritarian order. He acted relentlessly in complete rejection of religious or traditional beliefs, by behaving like a student who is becoming a master. Claiming that he destroyed the imperial order and was the representative of the people in power, Mao established a system in which his words would be heard while establishing this ruling order from the very beginning. Although the constitution of both the communist party and China contained basic principles that were essentially for a show at the beginning, all rulers kept their eyes on Mao. Like any authoritarian leader, Mao has somehow pacified the names around him that would be potential alternatives to him over time. This characteristic of Mao is seen in Xi Jinping today. Just as Mao saw himself as Marx's most important heir, Xi likewise claims to be the late founder and promoter of Marxist ideology. This motivation is central to the thinking that underlies the Chinese concept of socialism. This motivation stems from the fact that Xi sees himself above everything else and even above the Chinese Constitution.

As mentioned in the previous chapters, the management system in the PRC today is that of a hybrid administration. In other words, this regime is communist, on the one hand, capitalist on the other, and this is in the interests of the ruling elite. When examined in terms of political philosophy, as Tsonchev put it, the system in China is just a hollow "communist regime" and consists of propaganda of authoritarian rule. [5] There is no statement about "religion" or "creator" in the founding declaration of the Chinese Communist Party, which has rejected religion since its establishment. [6] Since Mao, the founder of the party, considered believing in any religion as the choice of backward people, he wanted his party and party members to adopt 'the ideology he founded as a 'belief'. Because authoritarian regimes established by rulers like Mao, who says he is Marxist, develop new rhetoric and ask their members to worship the trilogy of "party, leader, and ideology". [7] Wild Swans, by the author of the book Three Daughters of China, explains that this worship was transformed into a new religion, and Mao was trying to create a "society without its own thoughts" to pave the way for his deification. [8] CCP members are prohibited from believing in any religion. If a member is found to be a member of a religious belief or religious organization, he or she can be expelled from the party. Although this ban is ' for members, families of members also apply self-censorship towards themselves regarding religious belief. [9] Anti-religious propaganda consistently used to lecture the young people starting from first grade in the Chinese education system shaped within the framework of communist-atheist ideology. Students are taught that believing in a religion is a "feudal superstition".

Freedom is on Paper

In the Constitution of the People's Republic of China (PRC), it is stated that the Chinese State respects 'freedom to believe' in any religion. But this freedom to believe does not mean that religious worship will be comfortably performed. Likewise, the Chinese Constitution guarantees that nobody will be discriminated against because of their religious beliefs. It is noted that normal religious worship can be performed "as long as they do not disturb the public order, do not affect people's health or do not interfere with the state education system". When looking from outside, there seems to be no problem with this perspective. However, when the country in question is the People's Republic of China and its communist and atheist party leaders, everything can be included in the definition of "disrupting public order", which is placed subjectively in the constitution. [10] Articles on which the Chinese constitution defines religious freedom are interpreted by the Communist party as follows: "People who believe in a religion are free. People who do not believe in any religion and are 'against' believing in religion are also free. People have the freedom to change their religion." [11] Just like the trap in the phrase of religious worship disrupting public order, the Communist Party Regime has ensured methods to protect their authoritarian rule between the lines. When these items are examined carefully, the statement "those against religion are free" also has a meaning that can protect the attackers when those who are against religion are likely to attack the believers. But the same freedom is not designed to protect believers in the face of an attack. [12] On the other hand, although the Chinese Communist regime claimed that it came to power by destroying the imperial tradition, they did not completely break with the traditional imperialist administrative system. This is because the Chinese version of communism has always been shaped alongside Confucian philosophy. Like Confucian philosophy, the CCP has promoted the concepts of education, self-development, and secular ritualism, which ' the party would accept, and at the same time made strict obedience to the state as a basic requirement. [13] One of the purposes of Sino-Colonial China in popularizing the Confucius Institutes as a "soft power" everywhere from Asia to the American continent is to adopt this approach to other societies. One of the critical steps taken by Xi, who sees himself as China's greatest leader after Mao, to expand his hegemony, is to instruct the "Chinese interpretation" of every thought and belief. Just as in the "Chinese version of socialism" logic, a 5-year plan was prepared in 2018 for the interpretation of Islam, Protestantism, Catholicism, Buddhism, and Taoism under the communist doctrine and China's goal of controlling the world. [14] Naturally, anyone who opposed this idea was deemed to have opposed the state, and this pressure has been exerted on a wide audience from East Turkistan to Tibet and on Christian churches in various regions.

Repression of Tibetan Buddhism

The Communist Party, the absolute ruler of the PRC, always looks at other religious and religious practices with an approach from the imperial era. Tsonchnev describes this approach as "sometimes with open hostility, sometimes with an iron fist in a velvet glove." [15] The Beijing Government, displaying "open hostility" to Uyghur Muslims in East Turkistan, gradually crushes other Muslim communities and members of other religions under its despotic regime. An example of this is the increasing pressure on Hui Muslims in recent years. A similar situation applies to Buddhism. In China, where it is estimated that between 185 and 250 million Buddhists live today, the government is tolerant of Buddhism and Daoism with its own rules and transformations, but when it comes to Tibetan Buddhists, the attitude changes 180 degrees. More than 3 million people living in the Tibet Autonomous Region practice various forms of Buddhism. The Dalai Lama is both the religious and political leader of Tibet and has been fighting for the full independence of its people from abroad since March 1959. Tibetan monks have been organizing non-violent demonstrations against the pressure of the central Chinese government in the region. The Beijing government, which wants to make this region completely Chinese, immigrates Han Chinese to that region just like in East Turkistan. This causes tension between the two communities. The Tibetan people, who lost thousands of monasteries and many Buddhist monks during the Cultural Revolution in

1966, did not give up their struggle for freedom. High-tech surveillance systems established with the aim of destroying Uyghur Muslims are also being installed in Buddhist temples today. [16]

Acting on the logic of "the best Buddhist is the one who does not break my word", the Beijing Government started to transfer the management of the temples of the Tibetan people to the party representatives it sent there. Larung Gar in Sichuan Province, one of the world's largest Buddhist study centers, is one of the most painful examples of this. Party representatives destroyed almost half of this center in 2019, turning 6 thousand priests out. Tibet's leading Buddhists and opinion leaders have been asked to reject their religious and political leader, the Dalai Lama. Not satisfied with this, the central government eliminated the child who was seen as the successor of the Dalai Lama and believed to be the "Panchen Lama" by the Tibetan People and showed the beadledom of proposing another person instead of him. [17]

Christianity

The periods when Christianity first spread in China are after Buddhism. The first spread of Christianity here came with the pioneers among the first Christians who went to Far Asia immediately after the death of Jesus. The second wave was Nestorianism starting from about the seventh century. Members of the Christian religion also came to China during the Mongol-Yuan Dynasty, Ming and Qing Dynasties. Finally, the periods of most intense groups of missionaries arriving were during the 1800s. Christians were also affected by the persecution occurring during the Cultural Revolution, in which Mao tried to destroy all religions. All the churches were closed, the holy books were destroyed, and Christians were tortured in attempts to force them to renounce their religion. [18]

The end of the disastrous Cultural Revolution and the launch of the Beijing government's outward expansion program paved the way for the re-growth of Christianity in China. The estimated figures are that there are over 100 million Christians in China. Both government-approved churches, independent churches, and unregistered institutions exist in China. Repression similar to that towards Muslims and members of other religions have been increasingly applied against Christians in recent times. What should not be forgotten here is that a significant number of non-Catholic churches in China refused to enroll in the Religious Affairs Bureau, established by the Beijing government to control religions. Churches that do not accept security cameras and similar applications to protect the identity and privacy of their members are therefore recognized as "unregistered" churches. In a report published by the organization China Aid, it is pointed out that the Chinese Communist Party established a system that would directly control religion with the new decisions taken by the Central Committee in its meeting in 2018 and in which President Xi determined a new roadmap to make China sovereign in the world. According to the information in the report, more than 1 million Christians were investigated in 2018. Likewise, the number of arrests increased by 35 percent, and the number of those sent to prison increased by 44 percent. During the same period, 50 thousand people were abused. [19] During these repressions, the symbols of Christianity in China were also damaged. Wang Yi, a prominent pastor of Early Rain Covenant Church, was sentenced to 9 years in prison after being arrested. The church headed by Yi, like many other churches, refused to establish security systems in their own spaces and to register with the Religious Affairs Bureau. Just because a church is registered in China does not mean that it acts freely. The communist regime puts pressure on these churches to 'reduce their relations with the West'. Churches have been ordered to play anthems of communism instead of their Christian hymns. Because the Beijing government does not want these churches, which it cannot fully control, it has even begun to award those who denounce these 'unregistered churches'. [20] In some sources, it is revealed that some churches that did not register with the state were not allowed to function again and were closed after they were identified. For example, a church with 1800 members was closed in Beijing. [21]

Vatican-China Agreement

Although news, reports, and books have been published about the pressure on Christians, arrests, and even attempts to change Christianity in China, the Vatican, the heart of the Catholic world, has made an agreement with China, which is one of the most striking events of the last period. This agreement, approved by Pope Francis, brings to mind the 12th Pius, who turned a blind eye to the Holocaust occurring during World War II and even handed over the Jewish people who took refuge in churches to the Nazis. Hitler reached an agreement with the Vatican in 1933 which allowed him to develop his domination in Germany, and as a result, he dissolved Catholic political organizations and trade unions that would oppose him. The Papacy's cooperation with the Nazis continued after the war, and many prominent Nazis escaped by the support of the Vatican. The world community has been shocked yet again by the cooperation between an authoritarian government and the Papacy. The Vatican concluded a secret agreement with China in 2018. This agreement was confirmed by the Vatican's Foreign Minister, Cardinal Pietro Parolin. Parolin noted that the papacy is trying to open up ways of dialogue with China. Many fractions, especially America, objected to this attempt of the Papacy. America's objection to the agreement almost turned into a diplomatic crisis, and Former Secretary of State Mike Pompeo's request for a visit was rejected by Pope Francis in contrast to previous traditions. Pompeo made a statement and called the Vatican to condemn the oppression of China against religious and ethnic minorities, including Catholics. Pompeo noted that the issue should not be considered as a problem between America and China, but rather about opposing a totalitarian rule. [22] Although the Chinese communist regime has made an agreement with the Pope behind closed doors, it also continues to increase its pressure on Catholics. According to an article by Shen Hua from the Voice of America, Xu Yonghai, one of the church leaders in Beijing, stated that since 2014, the pressure against both registered and unregistered churches has increased. Mr. Zang from the Yunnan region, on the other hand, evaluated the Vatican's agreement as a "betrayal of God". [23]

Torture of Falun Gong Members and Organ Trafficking

Members of the Falon Gong movement, founded by Li Hongzhi in the early 1990s, are another faith community that has come under pressure from the Chinese Communist regime. This movement originated in the late stages of the 'qigong' movement, which practices energy exercises and regular breathing in China. Falun Gong combined the 'qigong' exercises with moral philosophy. The members of this group introduce themselves as part of the school of Buddhism, although they have borrowed the principles of the development of morality and virtue from Taoism. Falun Gong, which became rapidly widespread after its establishment, was banned by the Beijing regime in 1999. Since then, members following this teaching have been subjected to inhumane treatment, such as arrest, torture, and murder for the purpose of organ trafficking. According to the reports of the International Tribunal, which researches organ trafficking, many people in prisons in China were killed for organ trafficking in 2019. [24] Among those who were killed for organ trafficking, a large percentage were imprisoned for being members of Falun Gong.

Historical Process of China's Persecution of Muslims

The introduction of Islam into Chinese territory dates back to the 7th century. In the periods following the first encounter with Muslim merchants, they took a key position in China's trade. Relations between Muslim states and China developed as trade-indexed until the 12th century. A large number of Muslims settled in China. Muslim communities that assumed mercenary duties during the Yuan-Mongol Dynasty also experienced no pressure or problems during the Ming period. Starting from the period of the Manchur-Qing, when "nationalist" feelings were high, pressures against Muslims started to intensify during the 17th century. The first attempt to assimilate Sinicization or Sinification took place during these years. The freedom of Muslims was restricted, and newly arrived Muslim immigrants were forced to settle in the lands along the western border occupied by the Qing. In the following years, as a result of the invasion of the Qing emperors towards the west, many regions where Muslims lived were captured. [25]

Today, although the PRC's anti-Islamism, which has imposed genocide on Muslim Uyghur and other Turkish communities in East Turkistan, is directly evaluated concerning the Communist doctrine, historically it is based on Han nationalism during the Manchu-Qing dynasty. As it is noted by Haiyun Ma, who authored the work "Anti-Islamic Movements in China" at the Hudson Institute, the empire expanded westward and Han Chinese were forced to migrate to the regions where Hui Muslims lived. In the continuation of these migrations, the ideology of nationalism developed among the Han Chinese, and the Han Confucian opinion leaders began to denounce Islam and Muslims. In parallel with the strengthening of the reputation of the Han Chinese in the empire, the practice of religious duties of Muslims in daily life was tried to be marginalized. This situation is seen in the reflection of the anti-Hui opposition of the Confucian language and geography scientist Gu Yanwu, who lived in the 1600s. Shandong Governor Chen Shiguan, who had a similar view to Gu and also lived in the 17th century, saw Islam as a "threat" and attacked Qing rulers who viewed other Muslims with tolerance. Another Han Confucian, Wei Shu, wanted Muslims to be forcibly expelled from China. [26]

The 18th century in China was a period in which attempts were made to fully control the regions where Muslims lived and resistances against these attempts were observed. The Yunnan region, one of the regions where Muslims lived, is one of the furthest points that the Qing Dynasty tried to control in the southwest. Kunming, the largest city in the region, was one of the important commercial centers at that time. The central administration did not intervene here much until the reign of Emperor Yongzheng and this region was administered through governors. Another reason why the region is important for Chinese emperors is the copper mines in the region. The vitality of the economy caused a large number of people to migrate there. But over time, the balance between the Han Chinese and other societies had deteriorated. The tension that emerged with the abolition of the general governorship system by the emperors turned into bloody events. After the massacre in which 8 thousand Muslims were killed in 1856, the region was in complete chaos. The central government, on the other hand, prioritized keeping the copper mines safe and to prevent the intervention of neighboring countries. [27] After the collapse of the empire in 1911, in the years when the republic was first established, Muslim peoples were regarded as equal like other societies. Although Han Chinese nationalism continued to rise until the Communist Party came to power, there were fewer attacks against Muslims during this period. [28]

Transformation of Mosques Into Pig Sties

During the Cultural Revolution, some of the most disgraceful acts carried out by the Communist Party led by Mao involved the suffering of Muslims. Throughout the cultural revolution that started in 1966, having a Muslim identity was considered a crime. During this so-called revolution; copies of the Quran were burned, mosques were damaged, places of worship were turned into pig pens, religious scholars were forced to eat pork in front of the community, and all kinds of insults, persecution, and torture were applied to people to force them to give up their beliefs. As a result of Mao's view of religious beliefs as superstition, Muslim societies were subjected to great persecution. [29] Those who wanted to protect their belief in Islam were tortured, imprisoned and some were killed. At that time, when learning about religion was considered a major crime, all books on Islam were banned, except for the Quran. Since the cultural revolution aims to heathenize people and destroy their spiritual values, the culture of respect for mother and father, one of the main pillars of Islam, was intended to be eliminated. Students were given instructions to insult and humiliate their parents in front of everyone. Due to policy changes that started in the 1980s following Mao's death, there has been a slight decrease in the oppression against the Muslims in China. Compared to previous periods, China gained a relatively short period of religious freedom in this period. The efforts of the Chinese regime during the period reflected that they considered the Soviet Union's invasion of Afghanistan as a strategic threat, and so they attempted to attract Muslim countries through international relations which also contributed to the increase of these freedoms. [30]

Beijing Takes Advantage of the 9/11 Attacks

The terrorist attack on the twin towers in New York, the financial heart of America, on September 11, 2001, was one of the turning points for the Muslim communities in China, especially East Turkistan. While the communist regime preferred to use the "separatist" label to criminalize Muslim societies until that date, it saw this attack on America as an opportunity to carry out its own repressive methods in new ways. The Uyghurs, the largest Muslim community in China, have always been considered a threat to the Beijing government that must be destroyed. For many years, every step Muslim Uyghurs took to protect their language and religion had been viewed as separatist action and as problems stemming from the influence of foreigners. The repercussions of the aircraft crashing into the Twin Towers in this country have become a new reason for the added persecution of the Muslim Uyghurs. For this reason, the Chinese Communist regime was the first to adopt America's "war against terror" argument. China, almost louder than the United States, claimed that there were al-Qaeda-linked organizations in its country. The Beijing government has launched a movement that will eliminate anyone who opposes it within the scope of the war on terror as if it found this unexpected opportunity. In the following chapters of this study, it will be explained in detail how this so-called war turned into a genocide. [31]

Islamophobia in Social Media

The point to be emphasized here is that there is an increase in the news against Muslims in China, just as it has been observed in various media outlets in the West. Given the Beijing government's control over almost all of the media, content such as global terrorism, violence and war have been deliberately embedded in broadcasts about Islam. As a result, fear and hatred against Uyghurs and Muslims became widespread. [32] With the increase in internet use, the mentality on online platforms that sees Islam as a threat in China has also been strengthened. Anti-Islamism became widespread, especially on the microblogging site Sino Webio and the messaging program WeChat. While the fake news that was produced spread immediately on social media, the state did not take any measures to combat it in this regard. Retired researcher Xi Wuyi, the advisor to the Chinese Ministry of Commerce, is one of the prominent names connected with this decision. Xi Wuyi intensely shared posts targeting Islam on Webio. The contents shared by Xi Wuyi, who posts more than 9 thousand 244 times, also include directly insulting elements. Social media managers also often share these content on their own personal pages. Content creators boast about having affiliation with the Chinese Communist Party. The fact that no measures have been taken to date is a sign that these hateful people are protected by the state. [33] The PRC regime has targeted not Uyghurs and other Muslims but also Muslims in general in recent years. For example, an imam who was selected as an "exemplary cleric" and assigned to the Gansu region in 2015 was arrested because there was an Uyghur student among the students he lectured. A bookseller, who has a bookstore in Beijing and has been working in the Haidan region for more than 10 years, was also arrested in East Turkistan and sent to a concentration camp because he sells "Islamic" works. [34] The demolition of the minarets and domes of the great mosque near the city of Linxia, a place where Muslims care in China, the similar destructions in Inner Mongolia, Henan, Ningxia, the closure of mosques in Yunnan province, and other examples are just a few of the steps taken by President Xi to destroy Islam after came to power. Xi's main goal is to interpret and change the religion of Islam in his own way.

The Ever-Existent Pressure on Believers

The oppression and persecution of members of other religions, especially Muslims in China, has continued unabated. In the annual "Freedom of Religion Report" prepared by the US Department of State, it was emphasized that people were tortured, imprisoned, insulted, and forced to adopt the communist doctrine because of their beliefs. The communist party regime takes refuge behind the excuse of "fighting against separatism, extremism in religion and terrorism", which is used to criminalize Muslims and is defined as a triple threat. It was stated in this report that Uyghur and Kazakh Muslims were abducted and deported to concentration camps, forced to renounce their religion in these camps, women were forcibly sterilized, babies are murdered and taken from their mother's womb without the consent of their mother, Muslim girls were forced to marry Chinese atheists, and children whose parents were sent to concentration camps were placed in orphanages of the communist regime. It is also stated in this report that the life of Muslims has been turned into a virtual dungeon with advanced technologies such as security cameras installed everywhere, phone applications, face-scanning systems that enable them to be followed at every stage. Children under the age of 18 are prohibited from learning religion, and it is compulsory to learn about atheism in schools. In schools, religious education, and any initiative that can evoke it is not allowed. Communist Party police officers carry out practices targeting religious leaders to distance the people from Islam. Scholars and opinion leaders are arrested, imprisoned, and tortured. The bodies of those tortured in prisons and camps are also used for organ trafficking. [35]

Initiative for The Sinicization of Islam

The PRC, which has based its foundation philosophy entirely on being anti-religion, tells the world that they provide everyone the freedom to have religious belief as stated in the constitution in order to get the support of its own public opinion and to reduce the negative reactions from the international community. While the Beijing government puts out the message that "everyone can believe in whatever they want", they are concurrently rapidly reducing the visibility of religion in daily life. As stated before, here the Chinese Communist Party also aims to reshape religious beliefs in parallel with the spread of the rhetoric of "you can believe but not worship".

Communist Chinese regime intends to change all major religions while creating its own ruling legacy. President Xi gave the first indication of this in 2015, by bringing the "Sinification of Islam" to the agenda. After a long preparation period, at the beginning of 2019, the Chinese authorities aimed to sinificate Islam in 5 years. In the news published on January 4 in Global Times, which is under the guidance of Beijing, it was announced that a meeting was held with the participation of Muslim representatives. According to the news, it was discussed how to harmonize Islam with Chinese norms at this meeting and an official made a statement that "It is important for the Muslim community to improve their political stance and to follow the party leadership". Moreover, this meeting was held a few days after three mosques were raided and more than 40 people were arrested in Yunnan province, where Muslims are the majority. According to David Stroup from the University of Oklahoma, who evaluated the meeting to the German broadcaster DW, Beijing's goal is to control religion in all areas. This control covers a wide area up to determining the content of the weekly sermons of imams. According to the point emphasized by academic Hauyin Ma, here the aim is to cut the relations of Muslims living there with other Islamic countries and to isolate them. [36] President Xi also mentioned this issue at the meeting where the East Turkistan issue was discussed and he said "We must continue to Sinification of Islam to maintain the healthy development of religion." [37]

Communist Doctrine Training for Imams

As part of this forced change program, the Beijing government demands that imams working in mosques receive permanent political education. According to the information given by an imam from Qinghai province to the Bitterwinter broadcasting regime, these training cover Chinese history and Chinese policies and last about 10 days. At the end of the training, everyone gets their certificate after writing an article. The following words of the Imam reveal how communist doctrine was injected into Islam: "I have many certificates. The government carries out brainwashing activities through professors. They want us to tell the community what is taught in education in the mosque. "On the other hand, imams are closely followed by state officials and if they do not express their doctrines in sermons, they are punished. An imam, who works in Sanmenxia, Henan Region, conveys that they should advertise the Chinese Communist Party ideology and tell their congregation that they should obey the party's committees, by saying "Every day we have to say Communist Party is beautiful." [38] The following words of another serving religious official also outline what the CCP wants to do: "The CCP is atheist and if we try to resist it, we will be arrested and persecuted as counter-revolutionaries. The government instills Communist Party beliefs in believers. They are asking people to believe in the party rather than their own religions. " [39]

Modern-Day Destruction of Mosques

The religion of the people living in any city can be understood from the places of worship in this city. Despite this widely accepted understanding, the PRC's destruction of the visibility of places of worship is an indication that it cannot tolerate anything other than belief in the party. As a result of this intolerance, with the program of Sinification of Islam, the government demolished the minarets and domes of mosques and replaced them with the raised eaves with green tiles that are common in Chinese architecture. Thus, the architectural link with other Islamic countries was broken. The deletion of Arabic letters is also among the applications in this scope. A Chinese flag was hung on each mosque, and government propaganda was written on the walls of the mosques. In these writings in the mosques, the laws of the Chinese Communist regime on religion were praised, socialism was promoted, and the Chinese culture was praised. [40] The verses and hadiths written in Arabic letters adorning the walls in all mosques in Islamic countries were seen as dangerous and erased by the Chinese Government. Instead, Xi's words were embroidered on the walls. Libraries in mosques were revised, the Quran and other religious books were removed, ' books containing Xi and party propaganda were placed. [41]

The Banning of the Practices of Islamic Religion In Daily Life

Banning Muslim Uyghurs from praying, as cited at the beginning of this chapter, is just one of the steps in China to curb Muslim worship. As stated in the news of Radio Free Asia, Muslims are not allowed to fulfill the requirements of their faith, especially in East Turkestan. Here, the main argument of the Communist regime, as discussed earlier, is the excuse that worship disrupts public order. However, the oppression of Muslims is seen everywhere, not in East Turkistan. For example, in Yunnan, where Hui Muslims were the majority and where the oldest traces of Islam in China were once located, the management of Minzu University removed "halal menus" in student canteens, especially during Ramadan, to prevent the preparation of meals for suhoor. The university administration has gone a step further and banned teachers and students from covering their heads. [42] One of the steps taken by the Chinese Communist regime to control Muslims is about Hajj. This year, Beijing's authoritarian regime introduced new rules on Hajj. It has been announced that no names approved by the Chinese Islamic Union, which is affiliated with the United Front Work

Department, which is tasked with controlling religious groups in the govern-ment, can go on pilgrimage. The unit in question is the unit established by the regime in contact with other Muslim communities around the world, and its purpose is to make the Chinese Communist regime look cute. Under the new rules, it is forbidden to go independently to Saudi Arabia for the pilgrimage. Those who want to go on pilgrimage will be trained for 'citizenship and condu-ct' by the Union and will learn how to act in their talks with other groups when they arrive at Holy Sites. [43]

In China, the Muslim community is now aware that they cannot easily per-form their daily worship. One of the breaking points for them was the publicati-on of images showing the shattering of the golden dome of the mosque in Gaz-huang City on social media. In an article written by Gerry Shin and published in the Washington Post newspaper, it was stated that traditional clothes bearing the sign of Islam will no longer be featured on television channels in China. In this cultural revolution, practices such as the prohibition of the Quran and the imprisonment of those who sell the framed versions of the Prophet's hadiths are at the door. Communist propaganda slogans are now everywhere, not in state institutions but also in mosques, which are regarded as a "public space". The central government almost says to the Muslims there, 'you shall worship me before Allah.' Under the new rules, party members were prohibited from going on pilgrimage, even if they were members of the Hui community. Public employees should never go to places of worship, even businessmen should take off their caps when meeting with government officials. A victim who met with Shin expressed the following concerns: "We are afraid that a major action will be launched against Muslims. Because similar events have occurred in China's past. They boil us like they boil the frogs slowly." [44] In Gansu, which was one of the most important points of the Silk Road for a period and was located on the route carrying Muslim Merchants to China, all Arabic plates were removed be-cause they evoke Islam. Signs reading 'halal' have been destroyed in restaurants. The quota of the schools teaching the religion of Islam was limited and their capacities were reduced by 90 percent. [45] Local governments in Hebei province issued the "Notice of Comprehensive Examination of Arab Symbols and Reli-gious Elements in Public Spaces" and accordingly it was decided to destroy all Arabic symbols in public places. Halal food is prohibited in school canteens in Hebei, as in the Yunnan region.

Attempt to Rewrite the Qur'an

One of the main features of the Holy Book of the Islamic religion, the Qur'an, is that it has preserved its originality from the Golden Age of Islam to the present day. In the Quran, the 9th verse of the Surah al-Hijr says: "It is certainly We Who have revealed the Reminder, and it is certainly We Who will preserve it." Tabari, one of the tafsir scholars, explains this verse as follows: "We will definitely prote- ct the Quran and prevent an expression, a mistake that does not exist in it, from interfering with it or a deficiency in its decrees, rules, and fards." In light of this verse, all Muslims have protected the Quran from the time of the Prophet until today. [46] While it is clear that the Quran has preserved its original form until to- day, one of the targets of the Chinese Communist regime, which wants to comp- letely erase the traces of Islam in its own land, was the Holy Book of Muslims. The Xi administration, which wanted to sinificate Islam, attempted to rewrite the Quran. New decisions were taken on November 2019, at the conference held by the Committee for Ethnic and Religious Affairs of the National Committee of the Chinese People's Political Consultative Conference, which oversees ethnic and religious issues in China, about the Sinicization of religions such as Islam and Christianity. According to the news in various media organizations, it was decided to "rewrite the holy books such as the Holy Quran and the Bible in a way that "these religious systems would be in accordance with the characteristics of China." The committee noted that the Bible should not contain anything against the ideology of the Communist Party after rewriting it. Farid Hafez of the Geo- rgetown University Bridge Institute, one of the leading universities in America, made the following assessment on this subject: "In the context of a totalitarian politics, we are faced with an iron-fisted government in China to enforce its own order." [47] No explanation has been made to deny these allegations.

Sino-colonial Influence on The Islamic World

The main reason why the PRC does not hesitate from the international public opinion while applying all kinds of pressure from Sinification the religion of Islam and banning the worship of Muslims to rewriting the Quran, against the religion of Islam, is the silence of the Islamic countries. The Organization of Islamic Cooperation (OIC), the roof organization of Muslim countries, failed to meet what was expected from the organization. This passive attitude of the OIC shows the influence of the 'sino-colonialism' order established by the Chinese Communist regime.

In historical retrospect, China's official relations with the OIC were first es- tablished in 1974. The Beijing government, which periodically supports some of the decisions taken by the OIC, started negotiations with the organization on human rights and terrorism-related issues to get the support of the OIC on the "war on terrorism" argument, which is declared by itself, using the Septem- ber 11 attacks as an excuse. The Chinese government invited the OIC members to the region after the events that took place in East Turkistan in 2009 and the pressure against the Uyghurs and told them its perspective as "we are fighting separatism". OIC representatives also expressed their "condemnation against separatism". The mentioned condemnation brings to mind the colonialist era when colonial governors repeated what the central government said. The fact that the organization uses the same expressions as the Beijing government is one of the signs that China, the founder of the world's new neo-colonial system, has been able to force the organization to make similar statements in terms of economy and politics. As the rate of surrender to the colonial mind-set increases, the voices of systems that have become slaves to this economic power become more muted. The OIC member states, which are part of the "Belt and Road Initiative", which is the showcase of the new economic and political invasion plan of the Chinese communist regime extending from the Muslim countries to the west, are under the control of the red regime. The impact of Sino-colonialism on Muslim countries has clearly surfaced in developments in international public opinion.

The Founding Principles of the OIC Compromised by Sino-Colonialism

Repressive practices against Muslim societies in China started to increase in 2017 and have become the agenda of all human rights organizations since 2018. At that time, the foreign ministers of the OIC member countries gathering in Abu Dhabi in March of 2019 were expected to make a statement against China. After all, an organization whose name begins with Islam was naturally expected to con-demn the persecution of Muslims. But instead of condemning neo-colonial Chi-na, the OIC both praised China and decided to increase cooperation with it. The organization, by denying its founding philosophy, has surrendered to this neither communist nor capitalist, sino-colonial mindset, which demolished mosques, dis-mantled Muslim crescents from tombs, handed the remains of their relatives bu-ried by people and said, "Take this to your house, I will tell you where to bury it", collected prayer rugs from houses, confiscated the Qurans, and turned millions of people's lives into dungeons. In other words, the OIC has turned its back on the article "protecting the rights, dignity, religion, and culture of Muslim communi-ties and minorities in non-member states", which is one of its founding goals.

Farida Deif, the Canadian director of the International Human Rights Or-ganization, questions are just in place: "How could the OIC make such an em-barrassing decision? Have countries like Turkey, which has condemned the harassment of Uyghurs in recent months, agreed? Has Saudi Arabia changed the scale? Did China send two dozen delegations there to lobby, as reported to us?" Deif noted that the OIC's decision to cooperate with Beijing has damaged its founding principles and sent a dangerous message to other countries. This attitude means stabbing not ' Uyghurs but also Muslims in other countries in the back. What is even more ironic is that Saudi Arabia, which runs the organization's secretariat, and the United Arab Emirates, the place where this meeting was held, are classified as 'sensitive countries' by the Chinese Communist regime as Muslim Uyghurs are linked abroad and are therefore considered dangerous. [48] Another remarkable point is that the message published one month before this meeting on the social media account of the organization expressed concern over the oppression against Muslims and the reports prepared by human rights organizations. However, experts believe that China's financial and diplomatic pressure has affected the OIC to take this stance. Because Muslim countries are an important part of the Belt and Road Initiative that Beijing has developed to dominate the world. [49] After this Foreign Ministers meeting in March, Chinese President Xi Jinping sent a message to the OIC's 14th Plenary Session, which took place in early June, as if to congratulate this decision from the ministerial meeting. In his message, Xi expressed satisfaction with China's relationship with Islamic countries based on friendship and mutual support. [50]

Iran's Denial of its Founding Philosophy:
Say No to the West and Surrender to China!

For decades, the leading countries of the Islamic world have complained about the oppression, occupation, and persecution of the Western world and have based their ontological positions on the opposition of America and Europe. Khomeini and his team, who declared the 'Islamic Revolution' in Iran in 1979, summarized their philosophy in international relations as "neither East nor West." In other words, they have not adopted the capitalism of the West nor the Marxist ideology of the East as a principle. But the founders of one of the most established civilizations in the Middle East ignored all their values, as did the OIC when it came to economic interests. For example, passengers on planes departing from anywhere in the world to Iran are reminded that they must cover their heads at their destination. Everyone, whether local or foreign, walks the streets of Tehran with their heads covered. Revolutionary guards warn those who break these rules and punish those who insist on breaking the rule. On the other side of the coin, today in China, those who cover their heads according to Islamic procedures are labeled as 'extremists' and sent to concentration camps. The administration in Iran, which sees women uncovering their heads as if they "surrender to the devil", has relied on the cruel sino-colony and does nothing for the Muslim women forced to uncover their heads. The mullahs, who preach about not selling the interests of the world, are about to turn into the incarnation of the words "He

is a dumb devil who does not speak out against injustice" regarding their administration's surrender to money from an irreligious regime. Religious leaders in
Iran, who gave Salman Rushdie a fatwa on death row because he wrote a book
called the Verses of Satan, continue to pretend that they have no idea about the
fact that the irreligious regime has banned the Qur'an. reacting to France's recent statements The Islamic Revolutionary Iranian regime, which almost tried
to declare war for caricatures insulting our Prophet, made an agreement with
the sino-colonial regime instead of supporting the Uyghurs, Kazakhs, and other
Muslims who were sent to prisons for teaching Islam to their children. Acting
from the perspective that this agreement would strengthen its economy, Tehran
will cooperate not ' in the commercial field but also in military security and energy issues, while opening the doors to China. The future answer to this deal is that
Beijing will reach out to Iran in the Middle East and change the balance of the
region. So, the collapse of the "Neither East nor West" argument gives the new
Colonist of the East the strategic keys. Because what is happening in Pakistan
today is a harbinger of what will happen to Iran in the future.

Proclamation of Sino-colonialism:
"The Future of Our Country Depends on China"

Neighboring the East Turkestan lands occupied by China, Pakistan is the
country where Beijing carries out the pilot practices of sino-colonialism in
the geography extending from Asia to Europe. As Prime Minister Imran Khan
stated Pakistan has become so attached to China now that it acts as if it was
unaware of the genocide activities against Muslims right next to it. [51] Displaying dramatic examples of the insensitive attitude adopted by the Organization
of Islamic Cooperation, Pakistan criticizes the organization when it comes to
Kashmir. However, when asked about the situation of Muslims in East Turkistan, it becomes a "door-wall" as comm' defined in the Uyghur language. Imran
Khan, while answering questions from journalists at the World Economic Forum held in Davos in February this year, said he did not "know much" about
the oppression of Muslim Uyghurs. [52] Today, the whole world public opinion
knows that; Pakistan is one of the countries that know the situation of Uyghur
Muslims best because it is a neighbor. If the rulers of a country express that
they do not know much about the persecution that their own people know and
oppose, it comes to mind here that the state officials who made this statement
are no longer the leaders of their own state, but the rulers of a country that
exploits them. Just like the silence of OIC, whose founding purpose although is
to protect Muslims living in non-Muslim countries, against China, also Imran
Khan claims to be the "Global Defender of Islam" on the one hand, but he does

not see the Sinification of Islam by Beijing, on the other hand. The Prime Minister of Pakistan, who talked about women's rights, freedom of headscarf, and Islamophobia in UN meetings, also complains about the marginalization of Muslims in Western countries. But when it comes to the Chinese Communist regime's forcing Uyghur and Kazakh Muslim women to uncover their heads, Pakistan's opposite attitude declares to the world that it is a victim of Sino-colonialism. Because, as he admits, his future is now in Xi's hands. [53]

Pakistan's Prime Minister Imran Khan also sees how desperate he is by looking at the developments in Bangladesh. Bangladesh, another Muslim country in remote Asia today, is one of the countries China is trying to exploit. Bangladesh's government, which was in the middle due to the tension between China and India, shook hands with the Beijing regime. They are caught between the colonial hawks of the Beijing government and condemned themselves to the investments they sent. The agreement, which was signed between China and Bangladesh in July last year and abolishes the customs duties, is described as a victory by the Beijing government. The neo-colonial mentality, which increases its influence on the economy of Bangladesh economically, is also happy to politically bind another country in Asia to himself. But experts warn that the developing state of Asia, Bangladesh, will fall into a debt trap with this agreement. [54] Another area in which Bangladesh is dependent on China is the military area. This young country, which declared its independence in 1976, is an important country for Beijing to maintain its political and military superiority in South Asia. Because the Beijing regime uses Dhaka as leverage in terms of balancing India's military power. The government of the country has based its perspective on international politics on the philosophy of "Make friends with everyone, do no harm to anyone." However, it was not easy for the young country to maintain this and the country's dependency on China is increased. [55] Even though their government made a deal with the Chinese communist regime, the people of Bangladesh stood up against the persecution of Muslim Uyghurs, Kazakhs, and other societies, and organized demonstrations for this purpose. [56]

Another issue in which the consequences of the Sino-colonial communist regime's crackdown on the Muslim world are seen is the massacre of Rohingya Muslims by Myanmar soldiers. Myanmar is one of the key gates to South Asia for the Belt and Road Initiative, Beijing's favorite colonial initiative. The part of the BRI that starts in Kunming in China and covers Myanmar is the China-Myanmar Economic Corridor (CMEC). This corridor passes through Mandalay and extends to the Kyuapkhyu port. Another project in the area close to this port is the Kaladan Multimodal project. This project covers the sea route between the port of Sittwe and Kolkata in Myanmar and extends from the land to Paletwa and Kaletwa in the north direction. [57] These regions are the borders of Myanmar with China in the North and Bangladesh in the North West. Both Kyuapkhu port and Sittwe port are located in the Rakhine region, where Rohingya Muslims were forced to leave. Rakhine is what the Islamic world describes as Arakan. [58] It is seen that the colonialist Beijing had an impact on the genocide of Muslims in Arakan, the point of CMEC opening to the Indian Sea. Because the date when the oppression experienced by Rohingya muslims turned into genocide is just before Beijing began accelerating the BRI. The Beijing government thinks that this region needs to be "cleaned" to realize its projects in Myanmar. For this reason, the Beijing government slapped the backs of those who perpetrated the massacre of Myanmar soldiers against Muslims, which the UN Human Rights Commission President Zeid Ra'ad al Hussein described as "ethnic cleansing". China's Ambassador to Myanmar, Hong Liang, tried to legitimize the attack of Myanmar soldiers on Rohingya Muslims by defining them as "internal affairs". The same ambassador later said China would continue to stand behind Myanmar. When the issue came to the agenda of the UN Security Council, the cruel regime did what was expected of it and vetoed the decision prepared against the Myanmar administration for the continuation of the colonial order. [59] The power of the Islamic Cooperation Organization, the umbrella organization of the Muslim states that laid the red carpet in Beijing's BRI project, was sufficient for Myanmar in the face of this genocide and decided to raise this issue to the International Court of Justice against Myanmar. [60] The organization could not say a word against the sino-colonialist China, who openly defended the massacre on Rohingya Muslims. The argument used by China in supporting the Myanmar government is similar to the one it uses to make the world buy the oppression and persecution of Muslims living within its borders. This argument is the term "fighting extremism". Although it is known that the key to the Rohingya Muslims' escape from this persecution is Beijing, no administration has taken a step in this regard. The Islamic world has been hypnotized by the economic promises of the sino-colonial country and denies the truths that stand out in front of everyone.

Malaysian Politics as Another Victim of Belt and Road Initiative

While one arm of the sino-colonial Beijing regime is gripping on Myanmar, its other arm extends from Malaysia to Indonesia in South Asia. Remarkable developments showing the extent to which the Beijing government's neo-colonial activities extend have been experienced in Malaysia. Malaysia's former prime minister Necip Rezak has been one of the most supportive of China's BRI project. One of the biggest projects of BRI in the Asia Pacific region is planned in Malaysia. The size of the railway project between Kuala Lumpur and Kota Bahru is approximately 14.5 billion dollars. Malaysia expects an investment of 98 billion dollars from BRI in the long term. [61] However, when things didn't go as expected, the opposition saw that the country was under a debt that it could not bear economically, and the country entered the election process. This situation would ruin the plans of the China, the Beijing government, which immediately took action in Malaysia and attempted to intervene in the democratic elections of the Malay people. In other words, Beijing responding "this is my internal affairs" to those who speak out against the atrocities it inflicts in its country, did the opposite in Malaysia. In a way that is rarely seen in world politics, the Embassy of China in Kuala Lumpur dared to tell the Malaysian people how they should vote to elect Najib Razak. However, this attempt was repulsed by the Malay people and Razak lost his job in the elections in July 2018 and a corruption investigation was initiated against Razak. The Beijing administration, on the other hand, acted with the logic of "The old king is dead, long live the new king" and sent Foreign Minister Wang Yi to Mahatir Muhammed, who became the Prime Minister after Razak. After the meeting, Wang explained that 'relations between the two countries are strong'. But developments have shown the opposite. Two weeks after the election, Mahathir visited Beijing and on his return from Beijing said that BRI projects could be suspended. Mahathir regarded BRI as a sign of China's neo-colonialism due to corruption in the projects, a huge debt undertaken by his country's economy, and its dubious contribution to the local economy. [62] Malaysian Government then held meetings to review the projects. The political turmoil in the country did not end and Mahatir Muhammed resigned earlier this year and Muhyiddin Yasin was appointed in his place. Muhyiddin's decision not to deport Muslim Uyghurs has also been recorded as a positive development. [63]

While the news that Uyghurs in Malaysia will not be deported has not yet been forgotten, the real surprising news came from Indonesia. The Indonesian government deported 4 Uyghurs to China with the allegation of "terrorist crime suspects". [64] Indonesia, one of the largest countries in the Islamic world in terms of population with its population of 267 million, is of great importance for the "Maritime Silk Road", one of the domination projects of the sino-colonial mentality. Indonesia is also the place where Chinese President Xi declared BRI in 2013. Indonesia is one of the important gateway points of global maritime trade with its islands, whose number is not exactly known, and its maritime borders in a wide area extending from Australia to the Philippines and New Zealand in the Pacific Ocean and to the Indian Sea. It is therefore a country that the sino-colonial regime wants to keep under control. President Joko Widodo, or Jokowi as he is known, wants to carry out his development in the maritime field by relying on China. The amount of investment Indonesia wants to receive under BRI is over 170 billion dollars. [65] With the effect of these huge projects worth billions of dollars, the administration of a large Islamic state like Indonesia does not see the pressures made against Muslims in China. The Indonesian people are aware of the genocide committed against Muslims by Beijing and are organizing protests for them. But these protests are not seen from Jakarta's government buildings. The "this issue is the internal affairs of China "approach of the Indonesian Government, whose hands are tied due to the aid and financial support from the Communist Chinese regime, is striking. Not ' the administration but also some Islamic scholars in Indonesia have also been victims of Beijing's manipulations. Delegations who were taken to East Turkistan by special invitation were shown pre-arranged places and told that the genocide claims were a fabrication of the West. Nahdlatul Ulema called for "Stop human rights violations against Uyghurs" after those who attended this pious visit returned to Indonesia. However, this call found a place in western newspapers just after the news that the Nahdlatul Ulama movement was manipulated. [66]

Africa

The situation of Muslim countries in Africa in the west of the Indian Ocean is weaker than in Indonesia in the east. As is mentioned early we will talk in detail about the effects of Sino-Colonialism in Africa, many countries in the African continent are among the weakest victims of China's debt and aid trap. For example, Sudan is one of the countries that receive the most aid from China among African countries. According to figures from 2018, the amount of aid sent amounts to 60 billion dollars. However, this aid has not been free of charge, companies under the guidance of Sino-colonial Beijing have gained the right to invest in energy in Sudanese soil. Sudan's total debt to the Communist Chinese regime is $ 6.8 billion as of 2018. 2.9 billion dollars of this debt is for energy and 2.5 billion dollars for transportation infrastructure. Sudan has a debt of over 800 million dollars regarding water resources. [67] Sudan, one of the countries sanctioned by the United States, is under the guidance of China in international relations. For this reason, Sudan is also among those who have signed a letter of support for China on human rights at the UN Human Rights Commission. Nigeria, one of the largest countries of the African continent in terms of the Muslim population, was also among 37 countries supporting China that ignored the Muslim genocide carried out by the Beijing government and beyond that, applauded it. [68] The Nigerian government has also borrowed $ 6.2 billion from the sino-colonial system. More than half of this debt, or 3.4 billion dollars, is for transportation investments. [69] Given the principle that "the borrower also takes orders", it is not possible for Muslim countries in the African continent to object to China's colonialism and its war against Islam. Another Islamic State in the north-west of the African continent, Algeria, is among those supporting Beijing at the UN. Algeria, one of the biggest victims of France's colonial activities, has become the fifth-largest trade partner of the sino-colonial regime in Africa. [70] In return for this commercial partnership, the effectiveness of the Chinese communist regime in North Africa has also increased. The Arab Spring protests that started in 2011 did not lead to a change in China's colonial plans in the region. Although the regimes had changed in the aforementioned countries, the fact that the new rulers need Beijing to survive in economic terms is also an indication that they are open to exploitation. This is a sign that none of the Muslim leaders in Africa will speak out against the war initiated by the Beijing against Islam. Because the genocide of Muslims or the demolition of mosques in China is ' an "internal matter" for them.

Turkey

Considering the weak economies and weak political power of African countries, it may seem reasonable that these countries do not break Beijing's promise in terms of the real politics of international relations. Turkey is granting shelter to tens of thousands of Muslim Uyghur today. Although, in 2019, 22 states made statements condemning China at the UN Human Rights Commission. But Turkey is not among those states. However, Turkey is the ' Muslim majority country which has spoken out against China's human rights abuses in East Turkistan. Furthermore, from time to time, Turkish ministers made statements in the Turkish parliament supporting the Uyghurs while saying "We're protecting you, we got your back." There are some traces of economic dependence on the sino-colonial system in this stance of Turkey. In 2018, China lent $ 3.6 billion to Turkey for transportation and infrastructure projects. The non-governmental organizations and the public, who immediately took to the streets when there was a situation against Islam anywhere in the world, could speak out after the news about East Turkistan became widespread in Turkey. Beijing is watching the reactions of Turkey and other countries while rubbing its hands.

It is out of the question for Turkey, to mobilize the countries against Sino-colonial China, even though Turkey holds much influence over other Muslim countries and Turkic countries in Central Asia. Nations such as Kazakhstan, Turkmenistan, and Tajikistan, which are sandwiched between Russia and China today, almost ignore all the cruelties of China whenever the human rights violations of the Beijing regime are raised in international organizations. In fact, it would seem that these states should be the first to defend the

Uyghurs, Kyrgyz, and Kazakhs because of shared religion and the sameTurkic origins as the other Muslim communities in China.

Central Asia

A painful example of being unable to defend both the religious brother and the blood brother is seen in Central Asia. These countries, which have become involved in the BRI project of Sino-colonial China, began to enter the hegemony of Beijing economically and politically. Kazakhstan, a bordering neighbor through East Turkistan, can barely save people carrying Kazakh passports from concentration camps. Tajikistan is one of the countries where Beijing has made its presence felt both economically and militarily. The first examples of the Sino-colonial 'debt-trap' practice have also been seen here. Tajikistan, which borrowed money from Beijing for the projects about its coal mines, became unable to pay its debts in 2011 and transferred an area of 1,158 square kilometers in the Pamir mountain to the Chinese Communist Regime. One of the places where Tajikistan is helpless against China is the Gorno-Badakhshan Autonomous Region on its eastern side. China wants to keep the region under control by deploying troops in this area at the foot of the Pamir mountains. [71] Afghanistan, located in the south of Tajikistan and neighboring Pakistan and Iran, is a country that the sovereign countries constantly want to control after the Russian war that started in 1979 and lasted for ten years. China, which has already turned Pakistan into a satellite state, wants to increase its effectiveness by taking advantage of anti-Americanism in Afghanistan. For this purpose while using the Covid-19 outbreak as a tool, on the one hand, China became involved in Afghanistan immediately after Trump stopped talks with the Taliban and hosted the Taliban administration in Beijing, on the other hand. This is an indication of how China's "good Muslim, bad Muslim" policy is hypocritical. The Sino-colonial regime continues to genocide Muslims within its borders while sitting at the table with the Taliban abroad. [72]

Saudi Arabia

Again, the situation of Saudi Arabia, which considers itself the leader of the Islamic world, is no different from Turkey. The Saud Kingdom, which says that they are the servants of the two most important holy places of Muslims, the Kaaba and Al-Masjid an-Nabawi (Prophet's Mosque), is also the center of the Organization of Islamic Cooperation and have more teeth than other countries in the organization. Although it has the honor of welcoming millions of Muslims every year on the occasion of the Hajj, Saudi Arabia has begun to fall under the guidance of the Beijing government just like the other Muslim states. Saudi Arabia is always first to defend China in the UN since Riyad has bad marks when it comes to human rights. It is a shame that a state, which is the guardian of the tomb of the Prophet, is on the same path alongside a "demonic regime" that insults the Prophet and the religion brought by him and wants to erase all traces of Islam in its own land. No one here opposes the development of economic relations between the two countries, but if this economic partnership develops in line with the wishes of one side, it means that a new colonial order is being established here in terms of international real politics. If this Neo-Colonial state describes the genocide it inflicted on Uyghur Muslims as a "war with extremism" The sad truth is that the oil-producing Islamic countries, which started an oil embargo in 1973 because the American army supported the Israeli Army, take the opposite attitude towards the new invasion attempt against Muslims. In a period when one country did not need to occupy another country militarily to invade or exploit it, and when it was able to enslave these countries with its economic systems, the oil-producing Islamic states with 'black gold power' in their hands who are carrying water to China's mill means voluntary surrender to the sino-colonial system.

Egypt

At this point, it is necessary to remind of how Europe's two major countries, France and Britain, brought the world to the brink of a new war over control of the Suez Canal. The Egyptian President of the time, Nasser, nationalized the Suez Canal Company, stating that the Suez Canal, located within the borders of Egypt, should be managed by their own company, not by the Channel company established and managed by two European countries. In 1956, France and Britain's attempt to recapture the canal during the period when the Cold War was at its most widespread failed despite the defeat of the Egyptian army with the joint reaction of America and Russia. After this date, the British colonialism of the Suez Canal, which had been continuing since 1881, ended and the canal was completely dominated by Egypt. Today, there are no other similar challenges against colonialism in the history of the Muslim and Arab world. Because Sisi, who came to power in Egypt in 2013, has sacrificed Suez, the key point of the Middle East, to his economic interests and paved the way for its colonization by China again. In doing so, he did not see Sino-colonial Beijing's pressure on the Muslim world.

There is a common saying in the Islamic literature that "the Qur'an was revealed in Mecca and Medina, and read in Egypt". This statement reveals the importance of Egypt in terms of the Qur'an and religious education. The history of Al-Azhar University, whose foundation dates back to the Fatimid period, is a witness to this truth. But there has not yet been a loud voice about the genocide committed by the Chinese Communist regime against Muslims from Egypt and Al-Azhar University. The Egyptian government's sacrifice of Muslim Uyghur students to the oppressive Beijing is one of the bitter examples of the last period. The Chinese government also deported these oppressed people to concentration camps and prisons and committed all kinds of cruelty to them. He also demands the rent of his tooth and nail" was staged in Egypt. But the appetite of the neo-colonial Chinese mentality is so ravenous that it started to eat the Islamic world by seizing the lands of East Turkistan first. Later, he passed through Pakistan's Gwadar port and Sri Lanka, slaughtered the Rohingya Muslims, from there reached the Strait of Hormuz, put Suez canals under his hand, set his eyes on North Africa, and sent the message "It's your turn" to the world. The repercussions of this message and the effects of the new colonialism program, which Beijing has marketed as a Belt and Road Initiative project, to the countries will be discussed in more detail in the following chapters.

Summary

In summary, the Organization of Islamic Cooperation and its member countries do not want to see the genocide and persecution of Muslim Uyghurs, Kazakhs, and other Islamic communities in China due to their economic and political interests. These countries can very easily hide behind the "separatist and dangerous" arguments of the Chinese Communist regime or say that it is Beijing's internal affairs. However, it is wondered how long an organization that the patron of the Muslim world and the leading Muslim states is will refuse to acknowledge this war against Islam. Today, there also remains a question mark regarding on what grounds the OIC and member countries, which bear the responsibility of protecting the religion they belong to, will ignore and blow-off the demolition of mosques, deletion of Islamic verses and hadiths from the mosque walls, instruction of the communist doctrines and the principles of Xi Jingping through the sermons and preaches given in the mosques.

In short, the evaluation of the actions of the PRC regime from the perspective of the Uyghurs clearly reveals that the great destruction and demolition, whose signs are clearly visible, are actually not seen by many who ought be first to recognize. The meaning of this statement is that the Organization of Islamic Cooperation and 57 member countries, and Muslim communities in other countries have begun to knuckle under the rule of the Chinese government, which built the sino-colonial regime. In the next chapter, the atrocities and genocide inflicted by China on the Islamic ummah in East Turkistan and how they constitute a warning for other countries will be examined.

4

The Occupation and Sinification of East Turkistan

"In this torture, the hands of the prisoner were mostly subjected to torture. But the prisoner's hands were tightly tied at first so that the whole body suffered from pain and the prisoner would not move. Then the prisoner's hands would be inserted into the hole of the spinning wheel and the spinning wheel's arm would begin to be rotated. As the arm was turned, the prisoner's hands would be clenched. On the one hand, the needle was inserted, and the blood of the prisoner was shed. Often the prisoner's fingers and wrist bones would be broken, leaving people crippled." (1)
Isa Yusuf Alptekin

THE PROPHET MUHAMMAD stated the following in Hadith-i Sharifs, which is known to many people: "Believers are like a body in loving each other, pitying each other and protecting each other. When one part of the body is sick, the other parts are also suffering from insomnia and febrile illness for this reason." Considering Mecca and Medina, The Holy Lands, as the heart of the Islamic world, then East Turkistan can be considered as the hands. Like the Queen of Spain, who saw Islam as a disease, the authoratian Chinese regime, which views Muslims as chickpea grains to be crushed, has unfortunately squeezed Muslim states into the 'spinning wheel' torture machine that İsa Yusuf Alptekin spoke of in his memoirs. China has put East Turkistan, the hand of the Islamic world in Asia, into such machinery and is crushing and destroying it. The difference is that China didn't just stick a needle to bleed one dry, it has also drugged the Muslim states with sino-colonial methods so that they wouldn't feel the pain of East Turkistan. When the communist dictatorship puts its hands on the spinning wheel machine, it completely takes control of other regions, weaving the Muslim countries into itself, and these countries will realize that they are trapped, however at that point it will be too late. As is often said by the people of Turkistan, if the Islamic and also the Western world do not want to 'give an inch and lose a yard' they must stop this neo-colonizer of the 21st century as soon as possible. They should also pay close attention to what the people of East Turkistan are going through, which will be explained in greater detail in this chapter.

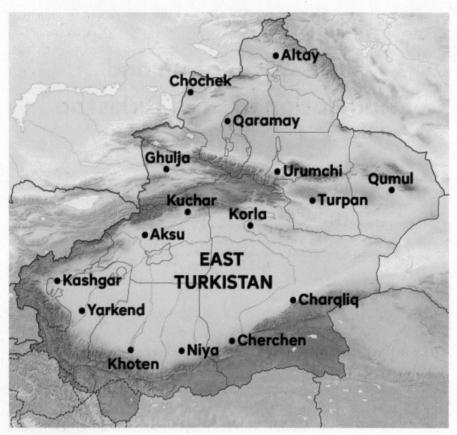

East Turkistan (Center for Uyghur Studies)

Geographical Location and Importance of East Turkistan

Located at the easternmost point of the Turkic and Islamic world and occupied by China, East Turkistan has borders which stretch about 1.82 million square kilometers. It borders Kazakhstan, Mongolia, Kyrgyzstan, Afghanistan, Tajikistan, and Pakistan. The population of East Turkistan, which is at the center of Central Asia's connection with East Asia, is about 25 million. The population distribution in the region has been deliberately changed over time and as a result, the Han population, which was 5 percent before the 1960s, currently makes up around 45-50 percent of the population of East Turkistan.

When the geographical structure of East Turkistan is examined, it is seen that one-third of its territory is desert. In the northern region are the Altai mountain ranges, and in the south there are the Himalaya, Karakorum, and Ural Mountains. The mountains of Tangri Tagh divide the lands of East Turkistan in half. The remaining part in the north is known as the İli Basin and the remaining part in the south is known as the Tarim Basin. The capital of the country, Urumqi, is located in the north, and Kashgar, one of the historical centers, is in the south. There are more than 300 rivers, called "derya" in the Uyghur language. The longest of these is the Tarim Derya with a length of 2,179 kilometers. The Turfan region is famous for its fertile soil, and fruits and vegetables are grown even in the winter season. In East Turkistan, there are very rich coal mines in the Ural and Altay Mountains and in the vicinity of Urumqi, Kashgar, Kuchar, Karashehir, and Turfan. As well, there are copper and gold reserves providing an abundance of underground wealth in the regions of Turfan, Aksu, and Ili. There are uranium mines in five regions, and tin, ammonia, mercury and lead mines, which are also important underground resources. The Taklamakan desert, which covers a large area in the country's territory, has oil reserves. It is stated that together with the Taklamakan, the total oil reserves in the Turfan and Çungarya Basins are 160 billion cubic meters. [2]

East Turkistan is Not a Part of China!

Today, the Chinese Communist regime considers the occupied territories of East Turkistan as part of its dominion. Using its power of influence via manipulation of international public opinion, China has managed to exert its dominance in areas which vary from diplomatic relations to media organizations. Even the Turkish press uses terms such as 'Xinjiang Autonomous Region' when reporting about Uyghurs. Is East Turkistan part of China or is it in the Central Asian region like other Turkic Republics? The answer to this question will give clues about the justification for the genocide committed by the sino-colonial regime against the Muslim Uyghurs, Kazakhs, and other Turkic communities.

The language, culture, clothing, food, customs, and traditions of the people living in that territory have no resemblance to China or Chinese culture. On the contrary, it is almost the same as that of the peoples of Kazakhstan, Kyrgyzstan, Tajikistan, and Uzbekistan. If you look at the map, those who visit East Turkistan, located right in the middle of Eurasia, will see a trace of the Turkic people rather than a Chinese land. [3] James A. Millward states that this place is a center of attraction, based on the phrase "Geographical Center of Central Asia Within a Driving Distance" seen on a signboard in Urumqi. In other words, from this point of view, Millward's determination that "East Turkistan is part of Central Asia" reflects historical facts, contrary to China's claims. [4] The root of this fundamental difference in discourse lies in the lack of any academic consensus on the borders and definition of Central Asia, and that nobody has objected to the Chinese claims that "there is no East Turkistan, it is Xinjiang Autonomous Region" (Xinjiang Uyghur Autonomous Region), neither in the field of social sciences or diplomacy. Another point is that Chinese historians, who look at the issue from the perspective of ' Beijing, describe the period from the 8th century until the 18th century when the Chinese did not have any claim to these lands as if these lands belonged to China and describe the peoples living there as if they were the Chinese people (minzu). [5] Trying to build its imperialist ideology through its historical resources, China used the term "xiyu" for the regions which made up East Turkistan during the Qing dynasty. The imperial administration of the period named these lands as Xinjiang, or Sinkiang, with a pragmatic approach after the occupation in 1884. Xinjiang means 'New Frontier'. The Republicans who destroyed the imperialist system and the Communist Party leaders who came to rule after the Republicans translated almost all of the names in Turkistan into Han Chinese following their assimilation policy. The Chinese Communist Party named the region it occupied in 1949 as the 'Xinjiang Uyghur Autonomous Region' in 1955. [6] Also, it should be stated that, as it has been started from the beginning, the real name of the homeland of Muslim Uyghurs is East Turkestan, and it will be referred to as this in this work.

Why is East Turkistan, the Heart of the Silk Road, Important?

Before examining the atrocities and genocide committed by the Chinese Communist regime following the invasion of East Turkistan, it is necessary to look for an answer to why the communist dictator Xi Jinping and the Beijing Regime do not want to give up that land. First, we can look to its geographical location, which should also be examined from a historical perspective. While the science of history cannot be based on counterfactuals, if East Turkistan were a fully independent state, it would be considered a key country in international relations in Central Asia. In other words, sino-colonialist plans would not be easily implemented, because China's neighbor to the west would be East Turkistan, along with Central Asian countries Kazakhstan, Tajikistan, Kyrgyzstan, and Uzbekistan. They together would contain the geopolitical power that could stop Afghanistan from becoming an economic and political colony of China. Thus, the sino-colonialist enslavement of the Turkic communities could be brought to a stop. China would not be able to put into practice its long-term plans to take over the world without destroying East Turkistan, which is seen as the eastern castle of the Turkic-Islamic World. For this reason, China continued to batter down the gates of this castle. When examining the Yalta Conference in February 1945, where the great powers divided the world amongst themselves, one can see the pragmatism behind the Soviet Union's "gifting" of East Turkistan to China. Russia, which has invaded other Central Asian countries, did not want the existence of a state that would trigger independence movements. Russia accepted many countries like its own backyard, but the politics of international relations are tied to the economy, and with the Soviet Bloc in shambles, Russia was forced to recognize the independence of those states. Russia, not wanting anyone else to garden in its backyard, supported leaders who would obey its orders in those countries of the former USSR. At this point, with the possibility of the existence of an independent state called East Turkistan, it can be predicted that these countries could come together and form an alternative geopolitical alliance. For this reason, occupied East Turkistan seems safer for Russia today in terms of controlling its backyard. Given that China has launched the sino-colonial plan it calls the 'Belt and Road Initiative', which also includes Central Asian countries, it is clear that China does not tolerate a Muslim presence and can never grant independence to East Turkistan.

The second part of the answer is that East Turkistan is vital to China's growing economy. For the PRC, which accelerated its economic growth after becoming a member of the World Trade Organization in the 2000s, the most important need is the supply of underground resources and energy. Information about the wealth of the Uyghur territory can also be found in the online announcements from the Communist Chinese Regime. According to the data obtained from Chinese sources, it has been proven that there are already 76 mineral reserves in East Turkistan, with a total of 134 types of mineral reserves being discovered in these lands. Five of them are larger than those found in the northern parts of China. Again, 8 mineral reserves make up one of the largest resource pools discovered in China to date. The possible size of oil reserves is 30 billion tons and natural gas reserves are 10 trillion cubic meters. This corresponds to a third of the country's oil and gas resources. The rate of natural resources per capita in Uyghur lands is twice the average of China. [7] That is why the sino-colonial Chinese regime will never want to relinquish its control over these lands. Oil and gas are essential for the sustainable economic growth of the Beijing regime. One of the purposes of the genocide of the Muslim Uyghurs, Kazakhs, Kyrgyz, and other communities, who are the main owners of East Turkistan, which has not become Chinese land either in the past or today, is to erase the Muslim Uyghur identity from history and not leave these fertile lands in the hands of a non-Han Chinese society. If the situation expressed above happened, that is, if East Turkistan were an independent state today, it would have an important place in the world economy with these large energy sources. In this case, the sino-colonial mentality that wants to destroy them will also have to knock on the door of the Uyghurs.

The third point is that the Uyghur people are the obstacle for the Beijing regime, which is driven by Han Chinese nationalism, to capture all the lands it claims to dominate. The Muslim Uyghurs never compromised their identity or religion despite the occupation of the Qing emperors, the pressure of the Kuomintang, or the persecution of Mao. China's authoritarian administrations, which saw that they could not destroy Uyghur identity through oppression and persecution, tried to change the population balance by forcing Han Chinese to migrate to the region. But the communist regime, which did not achieve the results it wants, wishes to crush the region with an iron fist, and erase the traces of Muslim Uyghurs from that land. This is especially apparent with Xi in office. China has also increased its genocidal activities in the name of wiping Uyghurs out of history, by accelerating the Belt and Road initiative that it has prepared for becoming the world's largest economy and increasing its international power as an alternative to the West. This is the main justification for the establishment of concentration camps. As long as Muslim Uyghurs exist, East Turkistan will never be Chinese territory. As a matter of fact, Mehmet Emin Buğra, one of the leading figures of East Turkistan, wrote that the Uyghur people will not give up this justified cause, as if he predicted today's situation.

"Is East Turkistan's fight for independence over? This may be the reason why, today, China does not allow any opportunity to demand social and political rights by poisoning the spirit of the people with hostile and false propaganda and bloody terror, to destroy the national talent. However, those who examine the psychology of the people of East Turkistan well and consider the nationalism feeling strengthened as a result of their struggle with the eye of history and politics will answer this question by saying "It is never over - it will never be over". [8] The atrocities mentioned in Mehmet Emin Buğra's statement have been systematically applied in every field for decades.

Brief Overview of The History of East Turkistan

The Huns were the first to establish their dominance in the geography of Central Asia, including East Turkistan. The Huns controlled East Turkistan in 300 BC. In the following centuries, Tabgac (386-534) and Göktürks (550-840) ruled these lands. Uyghurs settled in the region in the 9th century. In the following period, when the Kyrgyz captured the Uyghurs' capital, the Uyghurs migrated to the Kansu, Turfan, and Kashgar regions. The existence of the Uyghur state continued until the invasion of Genghis Khan. After the Kyrgyz period, Ngo-Nie Tegin, one of the prominent names of Uyghurs, revived the Uyghur state by choosing Mengli, the nephew of the Khagan who was killed during the invasion, as the new Kagan. The Uyghur state in this region continued to exist until it merged with the Karakhanids and took part in the establishment of the Karakhanid Khanate. [9] East Turkistan remained under Uyghur rule until the 18th century, after the Karakhanids, when both Russia and China began to encroach.

The invasion attempts of China, which started from the 18th century, can be evaluated by examining three periods in the history of East Turkistan. The first is the period between 1755 and 1865, the second period is between 1877 and 1944, and the last one is the Chinese Communist invasion in 1949. In 1863, Yaqup Beg succeeded in establishing a state with its center in Kashgar. This state, also known as Kashgaria in some sources, was supported by the Ottoman sultans. The period in which this independent state was established is also the period known as "The Great Game" in history. Britain, who wanted to be effective in Asia, seemed to support Yaqub Beg while also gathering information about the rulers in the region within the scope of traditional British espionage activities, and pursued their weaknesses. Although Britain initially saw East Turkistan as a buffer zone between Russia and China, it turned a blind eye to the Chinese occupation of East Turkistan and did not respond to Yaqup Beg's calls. After Yaqup Beg died in 1877, this state did not live long. Taking advantage of Yakup Bey's absence, China immediately attacked and occupied the lands of East Turkistan. The homeland of the Uyghurs was declared as the 19th province of China in 1884 by the order of the Qing Emperor, and the name of East Turkistan was changed to "Xinjiang", meaning "new border". However, this occupation did not prevent the Uyghurs from trying to achieve independence. With the establishment of the Republic of China in 1911 under the leadership of Sun Yat-Sen, and the collapse of the imperial system, the lands of East Turkistan suddenly faced a chaotic situation due to both the civil war and the desire of the Russians for this region. After a struggle for independence in the city of Kumul in 1931, a victory against the Chinese was won. The Islamic Republic of East Turkistan, which Mehmet Emin Buğra formed during the uprising he started in Hotan at that time, was established in Kashgar on 12 November 1933. Khoja Niyaz became president, and Sabit Damollam became prime minister. Mehmet Emin Buğra, the pioneer of the independent state and the preparer of all conditions, continued to support the Muslim Uyghurs with all his strength in this new step and worked to keep the Republic alive.

Kashgar, the capital of the Republic, fell in February 1934, subject to a heavy attack by the Soviet Union, who thought that the creation of an independent state in East Turkistan would harm their interests in the region, with the support of both the Chinese and the Dungan Muslims. This young republic collapsed with the fall of Hotan in June of the same year. [10] In the period between 1934 and 1944, East Turkistan was under the influence of Soviet Union. Stalin's regime has made those involved in the establishment of the Islamic Republic of East Turkistan 'harmless', one by one. Along with Khoja Niyaz, thousands were either imprisoned or killed. The Uyghur people's next attempt to establish a state was the establishment of the Sharqi Turkistan Republic (Second East Turkistan Republic) on November 12, 1944 in Ghulja. The fight, led by Kazakh Osman Batur, who showed great resistance in the Altai region, lasted until 1951. Unfortunately, the foundation of this republic coincided with an unfortunate period after World War II, when America, Soviet Union, and Britain planned to share the world among themselves. After the Second World War, the leaders of the Soviet Union, America, and Britain came together in Yalta to share the lands among themselves. In the meeting held in February 1945, decisions were made that would affect both the situation of Europe and the fate of today's Central Asian countries. At the meeting, it was decided that Soviet Union would fight against the Japanese in the Pacific. Subsequently, Chinese and Russian leaders met in Moscow in June of the same year and signed the China-Soviet agreement. As a result of the agreement, Soviet Union cut off its support for the Uyghurs fighting for independence in East Turkistan, a concession it made at the Yalta Conference, pushing the Uyghurs into the hands of China. Dark days had begun for the Uyghurs. As Lutpula Muttelip, who was executed by warlords during this period, once described it, "These vast lands became hell for me".

Three Effendis (Üch Äpändi) Period

One of the important periods of East Turkistan Muslims' resistance against Chinese occupation is the Three Effendis Period when Mehmet Emin Buğra, İsa Yusuf Alptekin, and Dr. Mesut Sabri Baykozi acted together. These three important figures, who came together in exile, made significant gains in the name of East Turkistan's independence in the years immediately before the Communist Party's invasion. Mehmet Emin Buğra, one of the Three Effendis, was born in Hotan in 1901.He completed his education there between 1922 and 1930, earning the respect of many with his knowledge and oratory, and added 'Excellency' to his name. He was one of the founding leaders of the Islamic Republic of East Turkistan in 1933. After the fall of this republic, he was forced to leave his homeland and moved to Afghanistan. [11] Isa Yusuf Alptekin was born in 1901 in Kashgar. He studied in both madrasas and Chinese-language schools. In 1932, he founded the East Turkistan Citizens Society in Beijing and published a magazine called "The Voice of Chinese Turkistan (Chini Turkistan Avazi)". He was elected to the National Assembly of China in 1936. [12]

Dr. Mesut Sabri Baykozi, born in Ghulja in 1887, came to Turkey in 1904 and completed his high school education. After returning to his homeland in 1914, he placed himself at the forefront of the national struggle. Mesut Sabri Baikozi especially focused on the issue of education and established many schools. In

1933, when the Russians invaded the province, he went to China via India, where he was elected as a member of the State Council. [13] These three leaders in three important centers of East Turkistan met in 1943 in Chongqing, China, and set out together for the national struggle. The Three Gentlemen made a series of attempts for East Turkistan when they met in Chongqing between 1943 and 1945. Among the numerous attempts of these names, the struggle they made for the adoption of articles related to East Turkistan to the commission established by the Chinese Government to prepare a new constitution in 1943 was remarkable. They made suggestions for the Chinese Constitution such as "Acceptance of people of Turkistan as a member of the Turkic nation" and "Change of the word of Xinjiang into Turkistan in the fourth article of the Constitution". After these proposals were heard in the Chinese public, Chinese nationalists reacted with great repercussions. While the debates about the constitution were continuing, the Three Effendis came to the conclusion that the Chinese were keeping the people of East Turkistan busy. When the East Turkistan Republic was established under the presidency of Ali Han Töre in İli on 12 November 1944, the Three Effendis found the opportunity to go to their homeland. [14]

The Communist Invasion of 1949 and the Declaration of Autonomy on Paper!
In 1949, Mao's People's Liberation Army (PLA) captured all of East Turkistan with the help of the Soviet Union. A delegation of East Turkistan officials, including Ahmetjan Kasimi, who led the Uyghur people at that time, were put on a plane to go to Beijing on August 24th, 1949. They disappeared, and the Soviet claimed as a plane crash caused by an accident. The Uyghur nation, which was then leaderless, entered a difficult period. [15] After the People's Liberation Army (PLA) gained dominance, the 'migration of Han Chinese' program was initiated in 1950. In 1955, the Mao regime declared East Turkistan autonomous and recognized it as the "Xinjiang Uyghur Autonomous Region". [16] The inspiration for this autonomous system came from the Soviets. The Mao regime, which was inspired by the Soviet Union while establishing the communist regime and then supported by the Soviets while developing its policies, followed the same perspective in its policies towards East Turkistan. [17]

At this point, it should be examined how the concept of autonomy is sinicized and used for the system of dictatorship. In short, the territory of East Turkistan is one of five regions that are legally considered 'autonomous' in China today. Although the autonomous system is defined as the independent movement of a region in its internal affairs in political science, the Chinese Communist regime has developed a system in accordance with its goals in this field, as in many other fields. For example, in Article 116 of the Chinese

Constitution, it is stated that autonomous regions can take decisions in order to enforce and protect their rights and to allow the nations living there to experience their political, economic, and cultural characteristics. Even Mao once said that "minorities' languages, clothes, habits, and religious beliefs will be respected." [18] However, the same article contains provisions that these decisions cannot go beyond the wishes of the Central Beijing government and the Chinese Communist Party. In other words, although it is autonomous in name, East Turkistan/Xinjiang is the place where the Chinese authoritarian regime has implemented all of its dictatorial methods. Since the occupation in 1949, the local government has no administrative power. According to the Constitution, all decisions are subject to the approval of the National People's Congress, which is under the control of the current Premier Xi Jinping. Definite expressions were never included in the articles regulating regional autonomy in the Chinese Constitution. In this system that allows the central authoritarian regime to act as it wishes, although autonomy has been granted "within the limits defined by the Constitution and the law", the concept of "autonomous region" has no real meaning since the CCP regime decides what the limits of supposed autonomy are.

East Turkistan After Occupation, First Examples of Assimilation 1949-2009
The Chinese Communist regime's genocide against Muslim Uyghurs has its roots in the invasion of 1949. The following totalitarian approach is put forward as the justification of the persecution since 1949 in the book titled 'Chinese Solutions to Ethnic Nationalism', which was prepared by taking into account the working philosophy of the Central Administration of the Communist Party of China by Shiyuan Hao, a member of the Chinese Academy of Social Sciences: "For the renewal of the Chinese nation and the resolution of ethnic nationalism, China must root out these historical legacies with its imperialist powers." [19] The policies developed by the Beijing government to remove the traces of Muslim Uyghurs from those lands are based on two foundations. The first is to ensure that Bingtuan (the Xinjiang Production and Construction Corps, or XPCC), which was established together with the People's Liberation Army and soldiers from the Guomindang, dominated the region economically. The second step is to change the demographic population structure of the region by moving Han Chinese to the region. Looking at the practices of both policies in the field, it will be seen that the gradual elimination of the people of East Turkistan by assimilation is aimed. These assimilation policies have been turned into genocide.

Since the Mao era, new discourses have been constantly developed towards Muslims in East Turkistan and they have been tried to be criminalized. The first argument, used in the early years of the communist occupation to suppress and oppress the people in the region, was defining the people as "counter-revolutionary and ultra-nationalist". Starting from the 1980s, throughout the 1990s and until the September 11 attacks, 'Pan-Turkism, Pan-Islamism' proponents or 'separatist' definitions were an excuse to apply pressure. After the September 11 attacks, the concept of "War on Terror" developed by the USA was replicated by China and applied to East Turkistan. Since then, the Beijing Communist regime has carried out its repression and genocide against Muslim Uyghurs, Kazakhs, and other minorities by developing three concepts: 'war against terrorism, separatism, and fundamentalism'. How these discourses are shaped will be seen in more detail in the following chapters.

Muslim Uyghurs Being Forced to Leave their Homeland

When the PLA of the Communist regime completely took over East Turkistan with an iron fist, the remaining prominent names of the Muslim Uyghurs and the soldiers of the past Guomindang period were faced with three options. Cooperate with the Communist regime, flee abroad, or be destroyed. [20] After the communist regime captured their homeland, the Muslim Uyghurs who had the opportunity took refuge in West Turkistan, the Soviet Union. About 70,000 of the purged soldiers of the Sharqi Turkistan Army crossed the Soviet border. Among the forced migrants, there were many names such as Ziya Samedi, Abduruf Mahsum, Gheni Batur as politicians, soldiers, and scientists.

Leading figures such as Isa Yusuf Alptekin and Mehmet Emin Buğra, who decided that it would be impossible to protect the rights of the Uyghur peoples by staying in East Turkistan, also crossed into India and Pakistan by road and took refuge from there in Turkey. The Uyghur Diaspora, of which they laid the foundations, made a great contribution to the cause of East Turkistan, which was becoming an important issue in international public opinion. However, hundreds of people lost their lives in this migration. The following notes in the memoirs of Isa Yusuf Alptekin will contribute a little to understand these difficulties: "Some of our friends who had to make their animals cross from this cold water several times a day had frozen feet and their flesh was rotten. When the horse my children had ridden slipped and was about to roll onto the abyss, four or five people held the horse and saved my children from death. Another person's child was caught under the knocked down horse. We immediately saved the boy by cutting the ropes that tied the items to the horse. The children who took this trip with us could not speak out of fear of danger. You would understand the horror from their blood drawn faces." [21]

Leading figures from those who remained in East Turkistan were also cap-

tured by Chinese soldiers. The number of Uyghurs imprisoned or killed exceeded 100,000 by 1953. Among those killed by China are names such as Abdulaziz
Chingizhan Damollam, who was educated in Egypt and raised Uyghur youth
after returning to his homeland. The number of people who took refuge from
the Ghulja region to today's Kazakhstan was also quite high. After the Soviet
Union decided to open the gates, people crossed the border in buses. However,
disagreement between Mao and the Soviet leaders made these passages difficult. In 1962, the Chinese Communist Regime announced that it would no
longer allow buses. At the time of the publication of this decision, panic broke
out among those who were at the border and many people died after being fired
upon by soldiers. After this incident, 67,000 Uyghurs crossed over to Kazakhstan within a few days. The Mao regime also decided to close the borders completely in 1963. This decision means that the Chinese Communist Regime, whose
connection with the outside world was Russia, closed its doors to the world.
Mao first initiated the "Great Leap Forward" program to move past this impasse
and then tried to consolidate his dictatorship with the Cultural Revolution.

Fighting Against Counter-revolution (!) and Pressures in the Political Scene
The Communist Party under Mao, whose relations with Khrushchev deteriorated after declaring the People's Republic of China (PRC), started various attempts to adopt its own ideology. One of them was the Hundreds of Flowers
Campaign. The announced purpose of this campaign was to allow people to
criticize party politics. The "flower campaign" that started in 1956, one year
after the declaration of Uyghur lands as "autonomous", suddenly turned into
artificial roses whose thorns would make others suffer. Those who made these
criticisms and voiced them loudly were targeted. The name of the campaign was
changed and became an Anti-Rightist Rectification Campaign. In other words,
"fight with the counter-revolution". In occupied East Turkistan, it was used as
a means of punishing the elders, students, and teachers of the Uyghur people.
As Sean R. Roberts, author of The War on the Uyghurs reported, 1,612 Muslim
Uyghurs were labeled as 'local nationalists' and sent to labor camps. [22] In other
words, the likes of today's concentration camps were built in those days. The
struggle against this so-called counter-revolution has also turned into a period
in which practices reminiscent of medieval inquisition courts were carried out.
According to Mehmet Emin Buğra, the people were gathered in the squares
for the politicians whom the Communist Party calls criminals. Communist mi-
litants placed among the people shouted insults at these people and shouted
slogans such as "we want the death penalty for these traitors." The so-called
judges of the cruel regime, after the continued uprising of the people, stood up

and listed the crimes of "espionage, disrespect for Mao" and similar crimes against political criminals and sentenced them to death. Later, these people were publicly executed, shot in front of a crowd. There is one purpose of playing these theaters, which remind of Ancient Rome's arenas: to send a message to the people that if you defy the party's will, your end will be the same.

The Disaster of the Cultural Revolution

While the so-called "Great Leap Forward Program" continued in the homeland of Muslim Uyghurs, on the other hand, prominent people of that region started to be oppressed with labels such as "nationalist" or "far-right". In this process defined as "style correction operation", everyone who opposed these policies of the central government in Muslim lands was targeted, especially people who wrote works in the field of culture and literature; their works were subject to censorship and destruction. From 1957 to 1959, approximately 9,000 intellectuals and former East Turkistan soldiers were sent to labor camps, and some were even killed. Members of the "Literature and Artists Association", which was an active institution at the time, and teachers and academics in higher education institutions were dealt a great blow with the instructions of Wang Enmao, the party secretary of the period. The poet and linguist Abdurehim Sarp, who was among those who were tortured, was arrested, tried, and persecuted in prison. All his works were prohibited. Former Culture Minister Ziya Samedi was also arrested at the time and tortured in prison. Thanks to the initiative of writers in the Soviet Union, he was able to survive. A literary and historical scholar was sent to a labor camp without trial and sentenced to 20 years. Qajigumar Shabdan, of Kazakh descent, was sentenced to 22 years in prison in 1958. These names are just a few of the intellectuals that the Chinese Communist regime wanted to destroy at that time. [(23)] But as a result of the failure of the great leap forward program and the starvation of millions of people, Mao backed down from this decision.

Mao's abandonment of the "Great Leap Forward" program is actually intended to quell criticism from within the party that China is dragging out the disaster of absence and hunger. However, Mao made his last move to build the dictatorial regime with the "Cultural Revolution" that began in 1966. This move served two purposes: first, the elimination of Mao's opponents, and second, the construction of the communist authoritarian regime throughout the country. For this reason, the greatest persecution was seen in lands inhabited by non-Chinese nations such as East Turkistan. The result of this step taken by Mao, who considered himself more revolutionary than Lenin, to spread his power to the whole country like an iron fist and to deify himself, was a massacre. As a matter of fact, the headline "Cultural Revolution: 50th Anniversary of Mass Murders" was used by Euro News on the 50th anniversary of this so-called Cultural Revolution and summarized everything very clearly. (24)

Those who defended this so-called Revolution based their ideas on two points. The first was to implement a "liquidation policy" just as Lenin did in order to protect the regime. The second was to allow criticism of the communist regime. The first of these two points was applied. In other words, purges and atrocities ranging from the confiscation of people's property to killing them were carried out. This revolution was a movement that Mao mobilized the youth and the army for to carry out a large-scale "purge". The nature of all authoritarian regimes in history is that they are closed to criticism. Fervent believers of Mao's Revolution were needed to carry out such a great revolution of cruelty. Mao's lead soldiers were teenagers and young adults between 14 to 30 years old. These young men were called the Red Guards. The most ardent leaders of the Cultural Revolution are the so-called "Gang of Four", including Mao's wife Jiang Qing. As the revolution spread, the power of these four persons within the party grew. The 'Little Red Book', featuring Mao's thoughts on the revolution, became a symbol of the revolution. The cost of the revolution was the killing of more than 10 million people, the deaths of 30 to 45 million people from starvation, and the torture and imprisonment of 20 million people who were labeled as "counter-revolutionary" by Chinese authorities. Persecution had become so widespread that even villagers had been slaughtered. Academics, teachers, artists had been subjected to mind-boggling tortures. (25)

The territory of East Turkistan was the scene of a power struggle between party leader Wang Enmao and the Red Guards who opposed him. This power struggle led to more oppression and persecution of the Uyghur people than any other place. A policy of assimilation unprecedented in history has been implemented, both with the acceleration of Han Chinese immigration and with violent policies. The young people, who took to the streets with Mao's fiery speeches, especially targeted old habits, old ideas, and old traditions. Han Chinese youth, who were displaced to East Turkistan, committed all kinds of deeds that pushed the boundaries of humanity in order to gain the favor of the party. (26) The culture and religious beliefs of the Uyghur people have turned into areas where these young people showed their strength. Muslim leaders, scholars, clerics were attacked in those days in which even the traditional Muslim hat, the "doppa" was banned. The beards of these people were forcibly cut off. Mosques, masjids, places of worship, shrines, tombs, and many places with historical values were destroyed. In some places, mosques were even used as pig stables for the purpose of insulting Islam. Uyghur women had their hair cut by force, and they were forced to wear Han Chinese clothing. Uyghur scientists, doctors, artists, academics, theatre players, and musicians were also sent to labor camps for "retraining". [27] Before the cultural revolution in East Turkistan, there were 5,500 mosques, 107 of which were in the historical city of Kashgar. When the so-called Cultural Revolution ended, ' 392 of these mosques remained in use, two of them in Kashgar. [28]

The so-called cultural revolution that lasted for 10 years had a major impact on the dictator Mao and his team's policy on the Uyghurs. As a result, the cultures, religions, and languages of the Muslim Uyghur people were damaged. In the same period, the population of Han Chinese in the region increased by six-fold, from 300,000 to 1.8 million.[29] The Cultural Revolution ended with Mao's death in 1976. The remains of this period, which are rare in world history, have been collected in a museum in Chengdu city. [30] The expression "Such madness will not happen again", said by the Chinese who visit the museum, is a sign that nobody wants to remember that period. [31] During the cultural revolution, the oppression and persecution of the Red Guards targeting Uyghur culture, life, and beliefs once again triggered the resistance against the Communist regime in East Turkistan. At that time, the East Turkistan People's Revolutionary Party (ETPRP) was established for the struggle for independence. Members of this movement resisted both the Red Guards and the People's Liberation Army (PLA). But with the arrest of 6,000 Uyghurs in 1970 by the Chinese regime, this movement did not last long. [32]

The First Reaction March Against the Communist Regime by Uyghur Students

Deng Xiaoping, who took power two years after Mao's death in 1976, decided to transition to a free-market economy in his first years. The people in autonomous regions had found the opportunity to feel relatively comfortable. However, the Beijing government did not make this so-called freedom policy towards the Uyghurs without provision. One year after Deng came to power in 1978, the Soviet Union occupied East Turkistan's border neighbor, Afghanistan, to expand its hinterland in mid-1979. This move, which will impact the balances of the region, suddenly led to an inevitable change in China's East Turkestan policies. Some of the Han Chinese who settled in East Turkistan fled from East Turkistan. ' the Chinese soldiers remained. Chinese soldiers even dug tunnels for shelter. Tunnel-shelters were built in the inner streets of the cities. Beijing introduced new freedom policies for the Uyghur people. Mosques were opened, they tolerated religious education, and allowed Uygur literature and Uygur cultural publications. Beijing government made cooperation with the US on those days, even picked up riding animals such as horses, mules and donkeys, from Uyghur villages, and loaded with weapons, and sent them to Afghanistan. Even at that time,

Han Chinese cadres were given administrative positions in East Turkistan, and local people in other positions. None of these promised steps were taken. While the occupation of Afghanistan by the Soviet Union continued, the 1980s was a period when Muslim Uyghur youth engaged in intensive activities to protect their religion and culture. China's outward expansion policy has created an environment of freedom in the territory of East Turkistan for a limited period of time in terms of education, culture, and economy. Muslim Uyghurs, Kazakh and Kyrgyz people also started numerous programs in these three areas in order to educate new generations and prepare them for the future by taking advantage of this environment of freedom. Scholars such as Abdurehim Öktür on culture and Turghun Almas on history issues, my father-in-law Abbas Borhan on scientific issues, Zordun Sabir, Zonun Qadir, Teyipjan Eyup, Abdukerim Ghoji, Qayyum Turdi, Turdi Samsaq, Abdullah Talip, and Haji Yakup published books and journals in all fields. Abbas Borhan magazine called "Wisdom is Power" (Bilim Kuchi), Abdurehim Öktür's book "Iz", Turghun Almas's book "Uyghurs" and Zordon Sabir's book "Ana Yurt" are among the first works that come to mind that guide the new generation. While the wisdom of the Uyghur generation increased with these publications, many Uyghur scholars provided religious and spiritual training for progress in a spiritual context to keep the Uyghur identity alive. Here, it is important to list some of these religious scholars to honor them, for each of them as they have educated hundreds and thousands of Uyghurs in the same way as informal religious institutions. They are: Abdulhakem Mahsumhajim, Abdulahadhan Mahsumhajim, Muhammedali Akhun Khelpitim, Muhammed Zakir Khelpitim, Abdullah Rozi Damollam, Muhammed Qurban Damollam, Muhammed Abdullah Mahsum, Shamseddin Ezizi Karihajim, Abdugheni Karahajim, Abdulkadir Damollam, Muhammded Abdullah Mehsum, Ebulhasen Karahajim, Abdullah Karim, Shahi Merdan Damollam, Abdulhamit Yusuf Damollam, Qabil Karim, Hamut Mahsum, Abdullah Karim Qarakash, Sulaymanahun Damollam, Abulhamithan Damollam, Ebuydullah Meruf Damollam, and Mehmut Damollam. Many of these scholars were persecuted by the communist regimes and spent years in prison. As soon as they were released, they took over the chair again in the name of the education of the Muslim people. Based on the importance of economic independence in public life, Uyghur entrepreneurs started many initiatives in business life. Uyghur businessmen established a large number of enterprises and contributed to the economic development of East Turkistan. These initiatives also contributed to the solution of the employment problem at the time, and increased the level of social welfare. Cultural activities such as theaters, poetry nights, and similar activities aimed at enlightening the public in East Turkistan were most intensely organized in the 1980s. The plays of Uyghur youth staged in theaters have attracted great attention. In these theaters, the works of East Turkistan writers were staged to enlighten the society and raise awareness of young people.

Young people, who grew up with this education, made their first march against the unfair, discriminatory and wrong policies of the Chinese communist regime in East Turkistan in 1985. This march was first done in the Eastern Bloc countries. The punishment for criticism of the system by the people living under the rule of communist regimes in the Iron Curtain countries during the Cold War, as in the case of East Turkistan, was being sent to labor camps. However, this punishment did not discourage Uyghur youth. Student leaders, including my wife Rushan Abbas, the Founder and Executive Director of the Campaign for Uyghurs today, and Mehmet Tohti, Executive Director of the Uyghur Rights Advocacy Project, based in Ottawa, Canada, organized a large demonstration on December 12, 1985, against the policies of the Chinese Communist Regime. Mijit Amet, who was the student president of Xinjiang University Students Association at the time, died a few days before the demonstrations. Demonstrations started by students gathered in the garden of Xinjiang University continued with a march to the Communist Party building in the city center. This demonstration, which was stated to be attended by more than 7,000 students in some sources, was recorded as one of the biggest demonstrations in the Eastern Bloc countries and the Chinese communist regime until then. East Turkistan students held one of the biggest student demonstrations before the Tiananmen massacre, one of the bloodiest events in China's recent history. Dolkun Isa, who heads the World Uyghur Congress, said that one of the largest peaceful demonstrations in China before Tiananmen took place in East Turkistan. These demonstrations, which Dolkun Isa narrated in detail in the "The Diplomat" magazine, also changed his life. Dolkun Isa, who was 20 years old during the demonstrations, and his friends rejected the fact that the people of East Turkistan were not allowed to make their own decisions, even though its official status was autonomous.

Dolkun Isa, who studied physics at Xinjiang University at this time, continued his activism through various platforms. The Students Science and Cultural Association was founded under the chairmanship of Dolkun Isa. Rushan Abbas served as vice president, Waris Abubekir as secretary-general, and Ekrem Hezim took charge of planning. It should be noted here that Waris Abubekir was martyred in the concentration camps established by China in East Turkistan in 2019. However, in need of taking a new step in the pursuit of this right, Isa organized a huge march on 15 June 1988 by gathering his fellow students. Thousands of students gathered on the university campus and held hours-long talks with Communist

Party education officials during the demonstrations, which they called "Meeting Against Ethnic Discrimination Policy", demanding that the policies of discrimination against Uyghurs be ended. The negotiations were inconclusive, and the Communist Party's police dispersed the students. Dolkun, who was the leader of the demonstration, was arrested and jailed on the same night. Isa, who was imprisoned for 4 months, was released but was not allowed to return to school. Seeing that the pressure of the Chinese government had become unbearable, Dolkun Isa was forced to leave his hometown and took refuge in Germany, just like Isa Yusuf Alptekin and Mehmet Emin Buğra. [33] In December 1985, 300 Uyghur students in Beijing protested the separatist content of the movies that were showing in theaters at the time. A year later, demonstrations were held in many cities against a book that insults Islam.

The events of Tiananmen Square, one of the major demonstrations in China, attracted the attention of international public opinion. One of the leaders of the demonstrations, which the world remembers with the picture of the "man standing in front of the tank", was Örkesh Dölet of Uyghur origin. Örkesh, known as Wu'erkaixi, was among the student leaders who expressed democratic demands against the Communist Party regime. With the withdrawal of the Soviets from Afghanistan a while ago, when it became clear that the lands of East Turkestan would not be under the influence of Moscow, Beijing resumed its oppression from where it left off. Despite the bloody suppression of the Tiananmen events by the communist regime and the subsequent environment, Muslim Uyghurs did not give up their struggle for independence and seeking their rights. Major events took place in the years following the Tiananmen events. These were in Barin, Hoten, and Gulca.

1990 Barin and 1995 Hotan Events

The 1980s were an intermediate period when the people of East Turkistan felt economically free after the communist occupation. But this period did not last very long. The independence of the Turkic republics in Central Asia with the collapse of the Soviet Bloc in the 1990s worried the Chinese Communist regime. Fearing that the independence movements in Central Asia would spread to East Turkistan, China started to increase its political pressure on the Uyghur homeland. These persecutions extended to the prohibition of the printing and publication of books and even the prohibition of song lyrics. The pressures of the Communist regime, which wanted to destroy the idea of independence before it sprouted, had also been an indication that the Uyghur people opposed the integration with China. The freedom of the Muslim people was restricted by propaganda of "Separatists" and "Pan-Turkism and Pan-Islamism" as excuses. Several mosques and Qur'an courses were closed after Tumur Dawamat, the government representative at the time, declared that "the biggest threat is separatism". Religious officials, teachers at the Qur'an courses, and Community leaders, whom the regime regarded as "repugnant" persons, were immediately dismissed. Some of those dismissed had been jailed. It was forbidden for civil servants to worship, whether they are members of the communist party or not. Those who did not comply with this ban were dismissed from the office.

The first movement against these pressures came in April 1990. There had been a number of incidents in Barin district, south of Kashgar. Unfortunately, no clarity has yet been provided as to how and why the events began. It is stated in various sources that the events started when a group of Uyghur youth came together to protest the Chinese Communist Regime's oppression against the Uyghurs. According to another source, in a mosque in Barin, people took to the streets with the call of a Kyrgyz group that opposed the Communist Party's discrimination against Muslims and nuclear weapons testing. It was also reported that government buildings were seized in incidents involving approximately 200 demonstrators. [34] However, the demonstrations ended with the armed intervention of the police. Foreign media reported that the loss of life was 60, while the Chinese government made a statement that one party member and 15 demonstrators died. The demonstrations, which began on April 5, lasted about 5 days. During the events, 10,000 soldiers were sent to the Barın. After that, this figure exceeded 20,000. After the soldiers took complete control in Barın, they detained almost everyone regardless of their age. 102 of these people were sent to labor camps. There is no clear information on how the judicial process was run there. [35]

The Beijing government, which had violently suppressed the demonstrations, immediately tried to force Uyghur leaders in the diaspora to bear the blame. In this context, Isa Yusuf Alptekin, who was in Istanbul, was targeted. The city of Barin was taken under blockade. After the incident, the oppression in Barin increased further. Now the individuals approved by the government would serve in mosques. Madrasas providing religious education were closed on the grounds that they supported the demonstrations, and the government sealed the doors of 50 places of worship in Aksu. Projects of 100 religious institutions planned to be built in the medium and long term were canceled. All media channels were censored and ' a limited number of journalists were allowed to enter the region. The government once again targeted teachers and intellectuals in order to ensure public order, and these people were sent to labor camps. This incident also caused the events in East Turkistan to be heard for the first time in the international public opinion. For the Muslim Uyghurs, it was one of the indicators that the period of temporary relief there had ended and that the Communist regime would continue to rule those lands with an iron fist. After this incident, between 1990 and 1995, 1,831 Uyghurs were arrested across East Turkistan for "alleged membership in separatist, counter-revolutionary organizations". The Chinese regime implemented further measures to control religious life, and forced clergymen to take an exam proving their loyalty to the Chinese Communist Party before serving in mosques. The Beijing regime decided to accelerate the so-called integration of the Uyghurs with "Document No. 7", which revealed the government's goals at that time and came to light many years later. [36] Document No. 7 proved that China's pressure on Uyghurs would increase.

These repressive policies of the Beijing government were not appreciated in the Muslim Uyghur community, and there was pushback. As a result of these reactions, demonstrations also occurred in Hotan in June 1995. Two imams were arrested for reciting verses from the Quran outside the framework drawn by the government in their sermons and conversations. This arrest led to a public outcry, and people began to protest. The demonstrators walked all the way to a government building and surrounded it, but police and military forces dispersed the public by force. The Chinese government said 66 policemen were injured during the events but made no mention of civilian casualties. The statement of the Beijing government was a repetition of the rote rhetoric of closed government systems: "A small group of counter-revolutionary criminals deceived believers by using religion and provoked people against the party, the government and the security forces..." The government's retaliatory operations continued after the demonstrations were suppressed. In the following days, hundreds of people were detained, including those who went to the mosque for Friday prayers. There were even people who were imprisoned for 3 months just for going to the mosque. 20 people alleged to have been involved in the incidents were given up to 16 years in prison.

Ghulja Events

"Document No. 7" dated March 28, 1997 was leaked, which shows the pressure applied in East Turkistan in the 1990s, and points out that the military and security units would work more strongly and actively on the Muslim people. The document also stated that constructions of mosques should be stopped because the Communist regime sees mosques as the place for separatist ideas. The document, which includes considerations for strict surveillance of religious activities, also laid the foundations for the practice, which is still being applied today, of creating files for each person. According to the document, the creation of files containing personal data about people engaged in religious activities or who have the idea of independence outside the official framework is one of the pieces of information contained in the document. But the strict and repressive implementation of this document led to the outbreak of new events in East Turkistan. Bad news this time came from Ghulja in February 1997. [37]

The prohibition of "Meshrep" meetings of Muslim Uyghurs is one of the main reasons that led to the start of the events in Ghulja. Meshrep meetings are meetings where young people meet with people who will guide them, and various issues are discussed both in a cultural and religious sense. These meetings, which were banned after the Communist occupation, were allowed again in 1994. The importance of Meshrep meetings is to raise awareness, especially to the next generation, of the pitfalls they can fall into, from alcohol to drug use. The communist regime took one more step and banned these meetings in Ramadan in 1996 within the context of increasing the pressure on Muslim Uyghurs after the events that started in Barin and continued in Hotan. This ban, which was introduced in the last week of the month of Ramadan, which is the holy month of Muslims, caused a great reaction among the people. Soldiers and police officers of the Chinese Communist dictatorship kept watch at the gates of mosques on the Night of Qadr, which is the most sacred night for Muslims, and did not allow young people and women to enter the mosques. This ban on those who want to perform Tarawih and Tahajjud prayers caused a great reaction. The detention of the young people who attended the Meshrep meetings was effective in the growth of the events. When it was heard that the detainees were tortured to death at the police station and their bodies were handed over to their families, the people became angry and took to the streets. Thousands of people marched towards the government building, including children and women. Explaining that their purpose was to voice their complaints and that they do not want to cause any outburst, the group placed women and children in the front row of the march. However, after the Chinese police and soldiers ignored the women and children and opened fire randomly, the youth began to clash with the police. All those who tried to stop the police and soldiers with sticks in their hands were shot.

Dozens of Uyghurs lost their lives as a result of the shooting at demonstrators in Ghulja. According to the official statement made by Wang Lexquan, General Secretary of the Communist Party, on 11 July 1997, 17,000 people were arrested and sent to labor camps. Abduhelil Abdulhebir, one of the comunity leaders of the Uyghurs who was trying to raise the awareness of the Muslim people by organizing Meshrep meetings, was among those exposed to persecution. In addition, independent sources noted that more than 300 young people arrested by the Chinese police were sprayed with cold water at -30 °C on a cold winter day and that these people froze to death. To date, no detailed information on the condition of those detained has been available. According to the findings of Amnesty International, an international human rights organization, more than 200 Uyghurs were sentenced to death after being tried in showpiece courts, and more than 90 Uyghurs were given life sentences. The number of soldiers sent to the region in order to prevent news leaking from the region and to keep the events confidential was 40,000. To this day, no independent organization has been allowed to investigate this incident. This is one of the blackout attempts made by China, which has been committing genocide in East Turkistan in recent years, to prevent any incidents that would condemn it in the future. However, an unidentified person brought the images he took during the events to Bishkek, the capital of Kyrgyzstan, and gave them to Ilgar Alptekin, a son of Isa Yusuf Alptekin. Ilgar Alptekin brought these images to Turkey and these images were published on one of the TV channel. This event attracted the attention of all international human rights organizations. In the following period, information was also heard in the public that the bodies of people arrested in the events in Ghulja and sent to prison were used for organ trade in China. A nurse working in the prison stated that blood samples were collected from political prisoners who were not sentenced to death for the use of their organs. This, in turn, revealed another dimension of the Chinese Communist regime's crackdown on dissidents. [38]

Exploitation of the September 11 Attacks

Three weeks after the demonstrations in Ghulja, 3 bomb attacks were carried out on public transportation vehicles in the capital Urumqi. The Chinese regime created phantom Uyghur organizations in East Turkistan to blame these attacks on to justify their new draconian policies against Uyghurs. The regime began to take steps to limit religious life for its own purposes. For example, people under the age of 18 had been banned from going to mosques. Wanting to break the Uyghurs' ties with Kazakhstan and Kyrgyzstan, the Chinese government managed to keep countries in the Shanghai Cooperation Organization, a newly established organization which includes the aforementioned nations, silent for the human rights violations against Uyghurs. [39] In 1999, the Chinese National People's Congress reassessed the crimes under the headings of "being counter-revolutionary" and "committing crimes against the state" and changed the stipulated penalties into the death penalty and aggravated life imprisonment.

The opportunity that the Chinese Communist regime sought to increase pressure on Muslim Uyghurs came with the September 11 attacks. The Chinese Communist regime, which had previously called Uyghurs "separatists" or "extremists", immediately clung to the American government's "War on Terror". The

Chinese government, which first responded to US President Bush's "call to fight international terrorism", also included the past events into this call. After a year, the same discourse continued and the events that occurred in Hotan, Ghulja and Barin in the 1990s were also included into this concept. The Beijing administration wanted to reframe these actions that were carried out against the Chinese regime's oppression, maltreatment, and ethnic discrimination, by painting them as separtist extremism.[40] A new phase started in the propaganda mechanism and the concept of "War on Terror" was adopted by China to shift world public opinion. As a matter of fact, the Beijing government, which has made various initiatives in this area, started to turn this into an advantage starting from 2001. The Beijing Communist regime carried out its propaganda through the Shanghai Cooperation Organization since the One Belt and Road project was not operational at that time. The agreement drafted by the Shanghai Cooperation Organization in 1999, which envisages joint action within the scope of combating terrorism, separatism and radicalism, was signed by China one year after the September 11 attacks. The curtain of the pressure and genocide applied by the Chinese regime against Muslims in East Turkistan has been the "war on terrorism" argument, which was developed by the USA after September 11. It is also noteworthy that the Chinese media used the "war on terror" argument of some western states against the Uyghurs at that time. As a result of the attempt to evaluate every event that has occurred since the 1990s under this argument, millions of Uyghurs living in East Turkistan were sacrificed.[41] In fact, the events between Han Chinese and Uyghurs in 2009 were also evaluated in this context. The Beijing government has begun to violate the rules of international law and all the conventions it has signed in order to utilize an event that happened on the other side of the world for its own benefit. Based on its own pragmatist doctrines, China has developed a new policy towards East Turkistan. Acting on the principle of "hard strike", it has increased systemic pressure, considering all Muslims as "dangerous creatures that must be crushed as soon as possible". For this reason, if a Muslim living in East Turkistan grows his beard by adopting the tradition of the Prophet Mohammad, this person is defined as dangerous by the Chinese regime and registered as a member of dangerous organizations. In the meantime, the Chinese administration has always specifically pointed to the East Turkistan Islamic Movement (ETIM) in every incident. However, the USA removed ETIM from the terrorist organization list in 2020. [42]

Economic Assimilation and the Misery of the Great Leap Forward
One of the first actions of the Chinese government after the invasion of East Turkistan was land reform, as briefly mentioned earlier. As Dillon briefly sum-

marized, the main goal here is to weaken Uyghur society in a cultural and religious sense and disrupt the structure based on traditions and beliefs. [43] The Waqif (Foundations) Structure, which is one of the institutions that sustain the spiritual unity of Muslim societies, has broken down under the name of this reform. Through this step, China immediately nationalized the lands belonging to mosques, shrines, and religious schools, taking the advice of the Soviets. The goal of nationalization is to break down the Waqif Structure, which dates back centuries and sustained Uyghur society in a material and spiritual sense. Isa Yusuf Alptekin, one of the leading figures in the East Turkistan cause, emphasized that land reform was being used mercilessly against the Muslim Turks. Alptekin stated that the lands confiscated by the communist regime were divided into three. First, the most fertile lands were given to Chinese soldiers. These lands are the places where the Bingtuan system, where more than 2.36 million people work today, was established. The second group of lands was allocated to Han Chinese who later migrated there. The remaining infertile and non-arable lands were distributed to the Muslim people. Although owning land, even if it was unfavorable, pleased the public for a while, a new page was opened in assimilation and persecution that started with Mao's Great Leap Forward project announced in 1958. All the small lands distributed to the public were re-nationalized under the name of the cooperative, and people became workers, not owners of their land. [44]

In 1953, a workers aid group of 117,000 people was formed for land reform in East Turkistan. In the process of cooperating, the "Decision for Cooperation in Agricultural Production" was declared in the region. All tools and agricultural equipment were confiscated along with the land from the local people. In the same year, Chinese soldiers were brought to key points of the economy, while Muslim Uyghur lands were confiscated again. 10,800 of the soldiers - 1,470 of them of senior rank - deployed in East Turkistan were employed in local government institutions, companies, and institutions. In 1954, the number of cooperatives established was 150, covering 44 percent of the Uyghur people. A large number of people from mainland China, especially young Han people, were sent to the homeland of Uyghurs. For example, in November 1955, 6,000 Han Chinese young people came to the land of the Uyghurs. By the end of 1955, there were 4,576 agricultural cooperatives, 2,890 animal husbandry cooperatives, and 86 handicraft cooperatives in these lands. 2,351 private institutions belonging to the Uyghur people were also included in these cooperatives. Starting in 1955, the Mao administration also changed the cooperative system there. China decided to transfer all cooperative enterprises to the newly created "communes". About 5,800 cooperatives were transferred to the newly formed "people's communities". The number of these communes was 542 at the time. As a result, the process of eliminating private property, which began with cooperatives, was accelerated. The Uyghur people, who are able to live in the cooperative system, have suffered a great deal with the transition to the communal system. With the seizure of the labor of farms and shepherds in 1959, hunger and misery began to be seen among Uyghurs. The materials needed for survival started to be limited as rationing was introduced. As a result of the humanitarian crisis caused by the unmet need for basic food, more than 300,000 people, including children and babies, died. [45]

While the assets of the Uyghurs were being seized, the regime also implemented a new level of cruelty. According to the statements of one of those who witnessed that period, the process of becoming a cooperative did not proceed as expected. [46] Tens of thousands of people were persecuted. Isa Yusuf Alptekin tells that people whose lands were taken away were turned into workers who were forced to work for next to nothing. Those who were given these lands were transformed into workers working for peanuts in cooperatives. Their homes, their vineyards, their home gardens had been plundered, and nothing was left. Shacks were built in each village for the construction of the so-called "commune life". Children were separated from their families and placed in other sheds, and the elderly were placed in other places. While the elderly were given the duties of cooking and cleaning, the rest were employed as workers without making any distinction between men and women. Mao's so-called Great Leap Forward now evolved into the "great labor camp system". The people were awakened by the soldiers' whistles in the mornings, and after eating a small bite, they were taken to the field or another working place on foot. People worked up to 18 hours a day, both during cold winter days and hot summer days. Because men and women worked in separate places, families are divided. The permission given to women who give birth is ' three days. Some of the women, who worked as slaves in the fields before the end of the puerperium, died due to hard conditions. They were just casualties of training, sacrificed for the Great Leap Forward. There is no need to mention that those who were sick were not treated. They were also among those who were ignored for the survival of the Communist regime. When someone tries to rise up, their reward is to be killed with machine guns. [47]

In the same period, the breakdown of relations between China and the Soviets and the withdrawal of Soviet support put Mao in a difficult position, and Mao stopped the Great Leap Forward Program in order not to give an opportunity to his opponents. The place where Mao's ambition to make China a superpower stopped was the so-called "Great Leap Forward" program. Contrary to its establishment philosophy, no one was satisfied with the results of the top-down approach of communism. During this period, a passport procedure was initiated, even within the borders of the country. The hatred that started in this period when people living in cities were forcibly sent to villages resulted in the cultural revolution turning into mass murder. [48]

Forced Demographic Change and Community Life

The most important issue for the sinicization of the territory of the Muslim Uyghurs by Mao and his followers was the migration of Han Chinese to these lands. Although the population of Han Chinese living in the region was very small at the time when Mao launched his "Great Leap Forward Program", this population increased exponentially. This migration policy was carried out by the XPCC, established in East Turkistan on the instructions of the central government and known as Bingtuan. This unit, which was composed of paramilitary persons, including former soldiers from the Kuomintang (Guomindang) era, built new farms and unique cities on the lands allocated by the government.

Bingtuan, or XPCC as it is used in the west, was established in 1954, one year before Mao declared East Turkistan an autonomous region. When establishing the People's Liberation Army (PLA) in 1949 and establishing Bingtuan 5 years after the occupation of the lands of the Muslim Uyghurs, China used dismissed veterans and commissioned these soldiers to "cultivate and protect the territory of the border regions." For this reason, the most fertile lands in the land reform were implemented immediately after the occupation was given to the XPCC. This organization, which was established with former soldiers, grew rapidly with the employment of Han Chinese brought to the region and had a large share in the economy of East Turkistan. Bingtuan, one of the paramilitary organizations that Mao established after the communist revolution, was distinguished from the others with its economic power. This organization has been touted as a success of China's economic revolution, both during Mao's period and in the later periods. As a result of the systematic settlement of Han Chinese and their employment in Bingtuan, the number of semi-soldiers in the XPCC has gradually decreased, and these semi-soldiers have been replaced by civilians. Since 1967, with the intended migration of Han youth to the region, the population of the city of Shihezi, where Bingtuan was founded, reached more than 2.3 million. After this, the number of Bingtuan in 1975, membership then fell to 1.77 million. In 1982, after Deng Xiaoping took over, Bingtuan was transformed back into a semi-official organization and was connected to the Party. Since then, this organization has been acting as a state within a state, and its economic size has surpassed many leading companies in the world. Today, the headquarters of XPCC is in Urumqi. It has 174 farms and 4,391 companies in 142 sub-regions, and the number of members has increased again and reached 2.3 million.[49] This institution, which is operated as a semi-official semi-private company today, is one of the economic tools of China in implementing the new era of colonialism policies. Bingtuan has taken control of every area in East Turkistan, from underground resources to production, which keep the economy afloat. [50] The economic hegemony functions of the organization will be discussed in the relevant chapter together with the One Belt and Road Initiative.

The Great Leap Forward Program, which started in 1958 and was implemented in the whole of China, was implemented with more severe and oppressive methods in the country of Muslim Uyghurs. As mentioned earlier, the goal is to damage the Muslim Uyghur family structure and destroy their religious and national identity. With the abolition of religious institutions after the communist occupation, restrictions on people's fulfillment of the requirements of their religious beliefs, that is, worshiping such as praying and fasting, began in this period. Communal life, in which Han Chinese culture is enforced, is also part of the assimilation process. The goal is to build a socialist system by destroying all religions, languages, and cultures. [51] But as mentioned in the second chapter, the great leap forward program has cost millions of lives.

Another practice carried out during the Mao era was to send university students to the lands that China occupied on the western borders for a so-called development program. The first team of 6,531 people from Border Supporting han Youth was sent to East Turkistan in 1954. Two years later, 55,000 young Han people were sent to the Henan region. The number of Han Chinese who migrated to East Turkistan between 1950 and 1978 alone is 3.7 million. The proportion of the Han Chinese population, which was 5 percent in 1949, increased to 40 percent in 1978. [52] New programs were also put into operation in order to maintain control over the territory of East Turkistan. The Partnership Assistance for Xinjiang (Duikou yuan Jiang or Duikou zhiyuan) program was first announced in 1996. The program to encourage Han Chinese to work on the territory of Muslim Uyghurs, especially in public institutions, was updated again in 2010 and announced for the second time. [53] On the other hand, there were also Han Chinese who emigrated spontaneously after the 1990s due to the incentives given by the central government to the employees.

While the number of Han Chinese living in Uyghur lands was around 300,000 in 1957, it is seen that this figure increased to almost 1.8 million in 1967, excluding those who were sent there under the Bingtuan program. In 1982, the Han Chinese population there reached 5,287,000. [54] The proportion of Han Chinese in the population rose from 6 percent in 1949 to around 40 percent in 2008. Recently, this ratio is around 50 percent. The systematic placement of Han Chinese in East Turkistan has not been accepted by the Uyghur community, because Muslim Uyghurs believe that this program is contrary to the 'system of autonomy'.

Community leaders and community leaders saw that behind the Han Chinese migration to the region was the desire to assimilate Uyghur culture and identity. Another system implemented by the Beijing government within the framework of assimilation policies in the employment of young Uyghurs as permanent staff. In this system, which was implemented in the early 1960s, the ratio of non-Han Chinese in management positions was initially over 55 percent. While this staffing was allowed, non-Han Chinese were not given key positions. As the assimilation policy in the territory of Muslim Uyghurs accelerated, the number of these cadres also decreased over time. During the cultural revolution in 1966, almost all of these cadres were liquidated. At the beginning of the policy of foreign expansion, people who were not Han Chinese were started to be recruited. However, as Han migration increased in East Turkistan, the number of Muslim Uyghurs in the administrative cadres gradually decreased. [55] In recent years, the administration has completely come under the control of the Han Chinese.

Although the Uyghurs were allowed to develop their own businesses in East Turkistan for a while with the foreign expansion and economic liberalization, a successful result could not be achieved at this point due to political pressures. Wanting to sinicize the Muslim lands, the Beijing government planned the assimilation of Uyghur people among the Han Chinese that had migrated to Uyghur lands and thereby completing the so-called integration. In some cities, although Uyghurs have partially adapted to the current system in economic terms, such a development has not been achieved, especially in rural areas. Although very few Uyghurs were economically well off, this was seen by the Uyghurs as another version of colonialism, as the Han Chinese were both constantly growing in population and being economically advantageous. While the so-called volunteer Han Chinese of the Mao period came to the region initially, now those who want to take advantage of the economic advantages of the region and get rich with border trade have started to come. The activation of the railway between Kashgar and Urumqi in 1999 increased the migration of Han Chinese from the south to the northern borders. The economically advantageous position of Han Chinese and the increasing population of Han Chinese in the region created the perception for the Beijing government that the Uyghur region is now "colonized". The Beijing government, which did not fulfill the rights promised to Uyghur Muslims continued to gradually restrict these rights, despite being an "autonomous region" in the 1990s. [56]

When examined in terms of the labor market, the income gap between Han Chinese and Uyghurs has grown as a result of the policies of the Beijing government. Members of the Han community who emigrated to East Turkistan found better jobs than the local people there. Uyghurs have hardly found jobs in high-income energy and technology fields. Local people have been able to work in low-income jobs or under the counter sectors. [57] There are two main sectors that make the East Turkistan economy strong: cotton and oil, also known as "one black and one white gold". As the energy sector is largely under Han Chinese control, the control of large modern farmland in cotton production is also in the hands of the Han Chinese. With the influence of the Bingtuan, Han Chinese were in a better position economically. [58] These emerging inequalities started to be felt more, especially after the 1990s. The reflection of the pressure on Muslim Uyghurs, who are increasingly oppressed both economically and in terms of social rights, are the events of 2009.

Systematically Keeping the Uyghurs Illiterate

One of the most critical areas in assimilation and genocide against Muslim Uyghurs, Kazakhs, and other communities is education. The Qing emperors who descended from Manchu did not change much in education in 1884 and beyond. The Chinese government has built Chinese education institutions in a few places for the children of the Chinese officials who migrated there. These schools were later closed during the period of the independence movements that began in 1863. After the First Republic, which did not survive after the death of Jacob Bey in 1877, the Chinese once again attempted to invade the region. During this occupation period, schools providing Chinese education and bearing Chinese architectural features were opened in many parts of East Turkistan. After the year 1884, when East Turkistan was named "Xinjiang", children of community opinion leaders and religious leaders who could revolt against the Chinese were forcibly enrolled in these Chinese schools. Although they explain to the public that their purpose is to introduce Chinese culture to the Uyghur people, as Isa Yusuf Alptekin said, their real intention was to sinicize the Uyghur people. The Chinese rulers aimed to break the resistance of Uyghur children against Chinese culture and also to hold them hostage. China wanted to forcibly place the children of influential people in the region in these schools to prevent national uprisings. The people of East Turkistan did not send their children to these schools, despite both propaganda and administrative pressure. Muslim Uyghurs did not want their children to be given Chinese names in these schools, to force their children to wear Chinese clothes, have their hair cut by force, and to prevent children from performing their religious practices in short, to raise Uyghur children like Chinese children. [59] However, this attempt was not successful.

In the same period, towards the end of the 19th century, new schools were opened in the Uyghur homeland, especially in the provinces of Kashgar, by taking the example from the west in order to eliminate the lack of education of the people. Especially, modern school systems called "Huseyniye Schools" initiated by Bahavudun Bay were established and spread throughout the country. [60] On the other hand, the emperors of the occupying Qing dynasty did not give up their efforts to change the education system in East Turkistan. For this, it established a separate unit for education in Urumqi in 1905 and appointed a Chinese chauvinist administrator as ruler. The following statement of this ruler is one of the clearest signs that the emperors aimed to assimilate the Uyghur lands: "The Chinese schools are closely related to the life and survival of the Chinese state in East Turkistan and constitute the vital point here. That is why we have to take this issue carefully and open a lot of schools." However, the statement of the same administrator while describing the system of schools as "The level of the schools opened will not be high" is a sign that the purpose is not education, but controlled ignorance of children. One of the examples of choosing children of people with leadership potential is the father of Isa Yusuf Alptekin. His grandfather hid Alptekin's father for a long time and then wanted to shave his hair in the style of the Manchu and show him as a skinhead, but when this was discovered, he was sentenced to 6 months in prison. Alptekin's father, who was forcibly sent to school, was even given a Chinese name. [61]

Two systems were implemented in the schools that were established in Kashgar, and whose education system was changed during the period of the Islamic Republic of East Turkistan. These two systems were established as government-opened schools and schools opened by private foundations. Demand for foundation schools has increased over time. The biggest problem at that time was the difficulty of finding teachers to work in schools. For this reason, in 1934, 300 students were educated at universities in Central Asia and became teachers. However, after 1942, during the Kuomintang period, pressure on the Uyghurs increased, and many intellectuals were arrested and imprisoned. [62] Madrasas, which are very important in the Muslim Uyghur society and are the institutions of an educational tradition that has been ongoing for centuries, have suffered greatly after the occupation of the Communist Party. The madrasas, which were closed during the Cultural Revolution, were secretly reopened in the 1980s. As in many other areas, this issue was reignited in the 1990s, and madrasas started to be closed one by one. Teachers in madrasas and religious officials who preach in mosques were sent instructions to comply with the Chinese Communist Party's program, and they were all disqualified from their positions by various exams. Teachers deemed to be out of line with the party were removed from their posts. In the face of these pressures, the people of East Turkistan found an intermediate formula and established unregistered religious education institutions. [63]

Frequent Change of Alphabet

After the people of East Turkistan became Muslims, they started using the Arabic alphabet instead of the old alphabet they used earlier. After the 14th century, the Chagatai language, which used Arabic letters, which became widespread in Central Asia, was adopted in the societies there and used in this way for centuries. During the reign of Sheng Shicai, one of the governors who served in the region after the Republican revolution in China, they tried to use the Latin alphabet in 1937 after being influenced by other countries of the Soviet Union. Although some Uyghur intellectuals supported the use of the Latin alphabet, Arabic letters continued to be used widely. [64] Because the Uyghur territory was on the border of the Soviet Union both during and before the Communist occupation, the influence of the Russians was also observed in the alphabet changes in East Turkistan. After Mao's decision that people living in autonomous regions should be educated in their own language, Uyghurs were allowed to continue using the Arabic alphabet for some time. By 1956, under the influence of the Soviets, the Cyrillic alphabet was used in some regions. This trial process took two years. In 1965, the Latin alphabet based on Pin-Yin, a Latinization of Chinese, was adopted instead of the Arabic alphabet in all of East Turkistan. This transition is one of the large-scale moves that affected society as a whole. The Chinese Communist regime made another decision towards Muslim Uyghurs who used the Latin alphabet until 1983 and allowed the use of Arabic letters again. Uyghur language based on Arabic letters have been used since then. [65] Changes in the alphabet used by a society repeatedly for almost three generations have been one of the biggest factors that will cause society to remain ignorant. It is clear that these practices are part of the Chinese Communist regime's programs to make the Uyghur community and other Muslim peoples forget their identities and their heritages.

One of the issues that should be emphasized about education is bilingual education. The bilingual education system was implemented in the autonomous regions both during the Republican revolution period and in the early periods of the Communist Party's occupation in East Turkistan. As time passed, the communist regime began to rewrite the laws and removed education autonomy in East Turkistan. Uyghur language education in the region has been abolished over time, starting from primary schools to universities. Education is one of the areas where the effects of the Cultural Revolution, which is a black mark in China's history, are most deeply felt. Universities where Muslim Uyghurs are educated, as in all of China, have remained closed for 10 years. Both teachers working in secondary education and academics from universities were sent to labor camps. [66] In the 1980s, although Uyghurs were given the freedom of education in Uyghur to protect their own culture, after the collapse of the Soviets and the events in Hotan, Ghulja and Barin, the pressure on education started to increase. One of the most important policies of the assimilation program implemented since the 2000s has been the changes in "bilingual" education. The Beijing government, which spent a great deal of money on teaching Chinese to everyone in the region, took the first step in monolingual education in 2002. At Xinjiang University, education in the Uyghur language is prohibited in all departments except the Uyghur Language Course. Two years after this event, all children from kindergarten were obliged to take Mandarin Chinese lessons. Apparently, this decision was made so that non-Han Chinese can receive bilingual education. But the main goal was the opposite. [67] In recent years, bilingual education has been completely abolished and 'Chinese education is provided in schools. This is the result of the assimilation and genocide policies applied there. [68]

Another step was taken to ensure that the languages of Muslim Uyghurs and other societies are forgotten and unusable is to steadily reduce the number of works published in languages other than Chinese. On the one hand, the number of Chinese broadcasts in all communication channels is gradually increasing and the programs broadcast in other languages are terminated one by one. Another practice is to forcibly send younger generations for education in the inner parts of China in groups in order to separate them from their native languages. The study named "Xinjiang Classes" started in 2000 as 12 institutes, and by 2006 this figure reached 10,000 students in 26 regions. In these schools, brainwashing activities were carried out in which Muslim Uyghurs were taught predominantly communist doctrines. The students participating in that program stated that the schools are no different from prisons. In these schools, programs have been developed to prevent religious activities, such as praying and fasting, which help students preserve their Muslim Uyghur identity. [69] How this educational system was reinvigorated as a genocide tool against Muslim Uyghurs will be seen in more detail in the following chapters. The Chinese regime argued that the Uyghurs were sent to the concentration camps for job benefits, and also claimed that the education system at that time helped Uyghur youth to find jobs. But their real intention was to erase the Muslim Uyghur identity. As a matter of fact, it has been seen that the students who attended these "Xinjiang classes" are unable to adapt or even are unable to speak their own language when they return to their communities after many years. Uyghurs continued to be excluded by the Han Chinese despite this so-called training. [70]

Censorship of Uyghur Language and Literature

Attempts to eliminate written works that help Uyghurs preserve their identity in East Turkistan, the homeland of the world-famous linguist Mahmud al-Kashgari, have been described in the previous chapters. The greatest destruction occurred during the Cultural Revolution. Pressure on Uyghur literary works was also partially reduced in the early days of Deng Xiaoping, who came to power after Mao. But this period of relief lasted 10 years. After the events in Barin, the old order was restored and heavy censorship began to be applied to the publications aimed at defending the independence and culture of Muslim Uyghurs. After 1991, a set of censorship rules were instructed to all journals, publishers, and bookstores. For example, Homeland (Anayurt), a book written by Zordun Sabir in Uyghur, was censored three times and later was completely banned. The Beijing government, which did not want to allow the idea of independence to flourish in East Turkistan with the collapse of the Soviet Bloc and the rising independent Central Asian nations still fresh, banned the works of writers such as Abdurrehim Öktür and Turghun Almas, who are among the advocates of Uyghur nation's heritage. China has banned the distribution of audiotapes containing poems that have gained much appreciation from Uyghurs. Deng's reform process was interrupted without making any progress, and during the Mao era, the prohibitions began to be applied again and more heavily. Meanwhile, the Beijing government declared the ideas of writers such as Öktür and Almas as "separatist" and "Pan-Turkist and Pan-Islamist". [71]

Events of July 5, 2009

One of the important breaking points in the recent history of East Turkistan, the homeland of Muslim Uyghurs, is the events of July 5, 2009. These events, which took place on the 60th anniversary of the Chinese Communist Party's occupation, are the result of the Beijing government's decades-long colonialist, assimilationist policies towards the region. These events are an indication that the "integration policies" initiated after the Communist Regime forcibly seized the lands on which it could not claim any rights, neither historically, socially, culturally, nor religiously, were not working. These events are a declaration that the irreligiousness vaccine was tried and failed to transform a Muslim society. They are a sign that "harmonization projects" attempted through the Han Chinese migrated to the region have never been accepted by the Uyghur people. The events, which were one of the important breaking points in the recent history of East Turkistan, and allowed the genocide policies towards the region to be implemented more rapidly and violently, should therefore be examined under a separate heading. Many points regarding the demonstrations that took place in Urumqi on July 5, 2009 are still not fully clarified.

Road to July 5

One of the assimilation policies of the Chinese Communist Regime against Muslim Uyghurs for years is that Uyghur youth are sent to work in factories in the interior regions. The aim here is to assimilate Uyghur youth under the guise of "integration" by placing them in factories where Han Chinese are in the majority. Not ' men, but also girls were sent to factories in Han Chinese majority regions. About 10,000 Uyghur girls between the ages of 18 and 20 from the provincial regions of East Turkistan were placed in industrial zones in the southern part of inner China between 2006 and 2007. Another goal here is to get them to marry Han Chinese and make them forget their Uyghur identity completely. Although the program is declared to be "voluntary", it is clear that when the Chinese communist dictatorship is the power behind it, those who object to this situation will be accused of being "separatist" and "extremist". Families stuck in this predicament unwillingly sent their children to these factories. [72] Young workers sent to these factories were employed at low wages and some of them could not even get any wages. For example, 213 young girls from Yarkent city of Kashgar province were allocated 75 dollars per month in the factory where they were assigned. However, the factory management constantly found an excuse and did not pay a salary and made Uyghur youth work for very little or no pay. [73] Despite their children being employed hundreds of kilometers away for nothing and being subjected to political pressure in these factories, a significant proportion of Muslim Uyghur families have continued to preserve their own culture and identity. The Beijing regime's assimilation program called "Foreign Expansion to the West" did not achieve the expected success. The problems that grew due to the treatment of Uyghurs as foreigners in their own lands and the "alienation" problem of some of the Uyghurs, rapidly advanced towards the social explosion point. [74]

China, which hosted the 2008 Olympics during a period of tension between the Uyghurs and Chinese regime, has also used this international organization to make unfair accusations against the Uyghur people and criminalize them. For example, an explosion in a mine operating illegally in the provincial areas of Kashgar in 2007 in which a security guard died, was reflected as if there was an armed training camp there. As the start date of the Olympics approached, the raids, arrests, and detentions of the Beijing government on the so-called armed cells increased and the people of East Turkistan were almost taken into the security circle. The Beijing government has taken unimaginable steps, banned Uyghurs from staying in hotels in Beijing, and around 5,000 East Turkistan residents were detained without any justification during the Olympic games. It was intended to prevent Uyghurs from making their voices heard in this international sport event. Before the Olympics began, there were two suspected attacks in both Kashgar and Kucha, the details of which were not clear, and the Beijing regime detained hundreds of people. [75]

The Chinese Communist regime's crackdown on Muslim Uyghurs during the 2008 Olympics deeply affected social life in East Turkistan. The Muslim Uyghur people were systematically portrayed as both "extremist" and "dangerous" through the propaganda of the Chinese Communist Party. This, in turn, increased tensions between the two communities. The situation in the region had come to a point where the slightest spark could cause a social explosion. In addition, insulting rhetoric against Uyghurs was repeated constantly. The unrest between the two peoples was thoroughly exposed in June 2009.

Police and guards intervened in the incident in the Shurand toy factory in Shaoguan city in Guangdong province after two Han Chinese girls alleged they were abused by two Uyghur youths. After the Uyghurs explained the situation to the security guards, the two young girls left with the guards. Around 1:45 after midnight, a large group of Han Chinese with axes and sticks and iron bars in their hands arrived at the dormitory where the Uyghurs were staying. Two Uyghur teenagers were beaten to death. After the killing of these two young people, the other Uyghurs immediately took action and confronted the Han Chinese. Security guards did nothing when the incidents started. A large number of security vehicles came to the area where the dormitories were located in the morning and there was a harsh intervention against the Uyghurs. About 20 Uyghur youths were killed during this incident. Wounded Uyghur youths were taken to the hospital under the direction of the officials led by Wang Ying, a member of the Chinese Communist Party Committee of Guangdong Province. The proceedings against the organizers of the attacks were deliberately slowed down and every precaution was taken to avoid the media coverage of the incident. [76] In the research conducted after the events that grew until 5 July and turned into a massacre, it was revealed that the allegations that Uyghurs abused Chinese girls were false. These groundless claims have led to one of the important breaking points in the history of East Turkistan.

Demonstrations Spread to Urumqi

Although the events in Shaoguan were hidden by the Chinese press, the Uyghurs in East Turkistan learned what was happening here via the Internet and social media posts. Demonstrations began in the capital Urumqi and other cities in response to the unjustified killing of Uyghurs. New details of the tragic incident in which dozens of Uyghur young people lost their lives were published on the websites, and people who lost their relatives started to seek justice. Some students at Xinjiang University and other schools started a hunger strike, calling for justice. At the end of June, a discussion panel on the subject was held at Xinjiang University. Here, it should be taken into consideration that in

131

accordance with Article 41 of the Chinese Constitution, citizens have the right to criticize any institution or ruler of the state. Based on this article, the leaders of the Uyghur people appealed to various authorities to investigate the issue. However, state authorities continued to ignore these applications. Realizing that they will not get any results from official channels, Uyghur youth started demonstrations. At the same time, the Chinese police increased their provocative behavior against the Uyghur people. Uyghurs took to the streets to organize peaceful and nonviolent demonstrations for justice about the events that took place in Shaoguan. The vast majority of Uyghurs did not protest. However, a small group of demonstrators were detained by Chinese police on July 4. After this incident, the tension reached its peak. [77]

The protesters, whose numbers are estimated to be around 200 in some sources and around 500 in some sources, marched towards the city square shouting slogans. However, unlike others, this demonstration was a march in which the leaders were the ones who participated in the integration program developed by the Chinese Communist Regime for the Uyghurs, and were seeking justice for the events in Guangdong, and who were members of the Communist Party and even who trust the party. For this reason, a significant part of the demonstrators consisted of university students. [78] The marching groups arrived at the square at around 4:00 pm and continued their protests peacefully. As the hours passed, the number of demonstrators increased even more. There were people coming from other cities to join the protest. The government sent thousands of police and soldiers there to quell the demonstrators. While Uyghur youth held a peaceful demonstration without showing any outburst or using violence, a small group of people acted violently by trying to direct and provoke the participants. It is unknown who this group of people emerged out of nowhere and where they came from. One of the memorable events of that day is the burning of buses. It is still not determined who burned these buses. While the attitude of the Chinese police in previous demonstrations is obvious, it is well known that the young people who carried out their demonstrations peacefully would not be involved in such a provocation. However, this wave of violence caused by the small group trying to provoke the demonstrators suddenly swept everywhere. Around 18:30, 2.5 hours after the protest began, soldiers began to disperse the demonstrators by using water and tear-gas. Approximately 80-90 demonstrators were injured at first due to the electric nightsticks and aggressive dogs used by the police. Armed guards then stepped in and surrounded the demonstrators. The group, which tried to defend itself in panic, was confronted by armed soldiers. With the instructions of the provocateurs who infiltrated among the demonstrators, the demonstrations suddenly turned into a battle and Chinese soldiers neutralized the protesters by using their weapons. [79] A city bus was burned during the incident and the Han Chinese suffered from the demonstrations. The next day, this time, the Han Chinese attacked the Uyghurs. To quell the events, the government sent tens of thousands of troops to the region. With the end of the events, raids were carried out on the homes of Uyghurs and people started to be detained. The bill of the Beijing government for this massacre was the death of hundreds of Uyghurs, the injury of 1,000 people, and the detention of approximately 4,000 people. The Chinese government, as usual, announced the figures according to its propaganda and said that ' 200 people died, and most of them were Han Chinese. The number of detainees was stated as 684,000. One of the Han Chinese who killed two Uyghurs in Shaoguan was sentenced to death and the other to life imprisonment. The Uyghurs, who were detained and arrested, were tried in show process by courts. To date, 35 Uyghurs have been sentenced to death. Those who "confessed their guilt" under torture were sentenced to life imprisonment. The Chinese Communist authoritarian regime carried out all kinds of cruelty to destroy the Muslim Uyghurs, and this was another tactic, just like the events in Barin, Hotan, and Ghulja. The Beijing government also claimed that the World Uyghur Congress was responsible for the demonstrations.

East Turkistan and a New Stage in Colonialism After July 5th

The Chinese government saw the demonstrations that started in Guangdong and spread to Urumqi and other East Turkistan cities to disrupt social integrity. The communist regime once again demonstrated that it would never tolerate the people of East Turkistan to be independent or to become a free people, as it was determined to keep the territories it occupied within its borders and to sinicize the people of this region. Article 4 of the PRC constitution states that it protects all nations' rights and interests regarded as minorities. However, this article also states that these nations will be given these equal rights as long as they are 100% Chinese. The real-life reflection of this article, which also prohibits the actions that cause divisions in society, is different. Although it is said that the constitution respects and protects differences, diversity is never allowed in reality. China's ' expectation from both its own people and the other people it occupied is that they stay within the framework drawn by the Communist regime. For this reason, the events in Urumqi were seen by the regime as a danger of division in the territories it occupied. As a result of this point of view, the Chinese regime started the genocide process by going one step further in its assimilation policy to prevent similar events from happening again.

With the events of July 5, the Chinese government has revealed that it does not want to kill two birds with one stone, but to kill a flock of birds. China blamed the World Uyghur Congress for the events. The second goal of the authoritarian Beijing government was to use the "war on terrorism" to reframe these events as separatist extremism. The Chinese Communist Regime manipulated the Urumqi events since it could not impose accusations of separatism and extremism against Muslim Uyghurs in the international arena until then. The regime administrators gathered in Urumqi on July 8, 2009 and issued a statement claiming that the demonstrations were carried out by "extremists," "separatists," and "terrorists." The Chinese regime has tried to portray the World Uyghur Congress and its leaders as if they had plotted all three crimes. The third goal was to destroy the Uyghurs. For this reason, thousands of people were detained overnight, regardless of whether they have a connection with the incident or not. Many of these people were never heard from again. Young people were targeted not ' in Urumqi but also in other cities, and these young people became victims of the regime police. Its fourth goal is to escalate tensions between Han Chinese and Uyghurs even further. Just like the westerners who went to exploit Africa in the 16th century considered the local people as "uneducated, backward and dangerous," today's neo-colonial Chinese government made the Han Chinese view the Muslim people as "uneducated, backward and dangerous." As a result, the "enlightened and developed" Han Chinese were re-assigned to this region to raise East Turkistan people. [80]

Another effect of July 5th was that bilingual education in Uyghur and Chinese in East Turkistan started to be restricted. The aggravation of security policies to put Muslim Uyghurs under complete pressure and transforming East Turkistan into an open prison by establishing advanced technology-based systems accelerated after these events. The number of security guards serving in Urumqi increased from 20,000 to 70,000. While this change was taking place, Uyghur-origin police and soldiers who did not follow the Chinese regime's instructions and did not torture their kin were immediately dismissed. [81] The authoritarian Chinese regime rapidly began to build systems to keep the people of East Turkistan under control and surveil them. A year after the demonstrations, 40,000 new security cameras were installed throughout East Turkistan. In Urumqi, barriers were placed between the regions inhabited by Han Chinese and Uyghurs. Restrictions were placed on public travel. The number of security points on the streets increased. Strict monitoring was applied especially against conservative people coming to Urumqi from rural areas. In the public sphere, Uyghurs are restricted from showing their traditional and religious beliefs in schools and public institutions. [82]

The severe implementation of the intervention in social life, of which we see more severe examples today, was experienced again after 2009. Like in George Orwell's novel 1984, the cadres were deployed to monitor and control all aspects of society to strengthen the dystopian authoritarian regime. In line to sinicize the whole world, practices aimed at interfering with the Muslims' religious life in the region and preventing Islam's practices were more widely implemented. While doing all this, the Communist Chinese authoritarian regime, which tells the world that it is "fighting against terrorism," restricted communication channels so that no one is aware of what is happening in the region. Access to social media channels such as Facebook, Twitter was blocked, and restrictions on international phone calls were imposed. News sites and all internet sites that provide information on the Uyghurs' culture, literature, and social life were closed. [83]

A final point to be emphasized regarding the July 5 incidents is that the Bingtuan's leaders keep the "security concern" constantly in mind to maintain their dominance in the region. Thomas Cliff, in his study of the July 5th process, emphasized the need for "instability" by Bingtuan executives to receive continuous funding from the Beijing government. Thus, the July 5 turned into an "instability card" that enabled both Bingtuan and the Han Chinese there to consolidate their social and economic order. The increase in police forces in the region and restriction of Muslim Uyghurs' freedom after each incident is supported by the Han Chinese and increases their dependence to the Beijing. [84]

Accelerated Development or the Rise of Neo-colonialism

Why East Turkistan is indispensable for the Chinese Communist Regime, and why China will not stop occupying the region was discussed at the beginning of this chapter. One of the Beijing government's policies to erase the traces of Muslim Uyghurs on this land is the migration of Han Chinese to the region. As a result of this policy, which started in the Mao era, the region's population structure is changing. But it is difficult to say that the Han Chinese community that migrated there was pleased to be living there. The Chinese occupation government needed to invest more and make the Han Chinese feel comfortable economically. While doing so, the regime began to propagate a new perception of the Uyghurs as "the other". According to the Chinese Communist Party's long-term perspective on the region, the first method to be followed for Muslim Uyghurs' assimilation is to attract Han Chinese to the region through economic investments. It was thought that Uyghurs will lose their own culture by becoming rich. This context aimed to include the Muslim Uyghurs and other minority community members into the economic system. The main intention behind this goal is that, as just mentioned, as people get richer, they become more dependent on the central Chinese government that brought this prosperity to them and forget their origins. This initiative has resulted in some development among groups and cities such as Urumqi in the North. Some Uyghurs Muslim have developed economically with the Special Economic Trading Areas (SETAs) prepared for the regions at Kazakhstan and Kyrgyzstan's borders. [85] Among the Uyghurs, there have been those who developed economically and became wealthy thanks to border trade. The Khorgus region, on the border with Kyrgyzstan, and Kashgar, on the border with Kazakhstan, were designated as the center of this project. Kashgar is the place where the effects of the project are most obvious.

In East Turkistan, Kashgar is an important center for Uyghurs due to their identity and historical characteristics. Since Kashgar's sinicization is also critical for Beijing, this city has been declared a joint city with Shenzhen, one of China's most important industrial regions within the scope of the "sister region" project applied for the integration of East Turkistan. [86] While an economic region was being built, Kashgar's appearance was changing. Some places in the historic city have been demolished, and their appearances were sinicized. Han Chinese companies' weight has become more visible, although some have benefited from economic programs to improve their businesses among the Uyghurs in the city. When Chinese companies gave priority to Han Chinese in employment, the desired interaction between the two communities did not turn out as expected. The low number of people who can speak Chinese among Uyghurs kept the Han Chinese perception that "Uyghurs are backward and dangerous people." [87] As a result, the tension between the two communities has never subsided, and the Beijing government's plan to advance economic prosperity in the region's exploitation and assimilation policy has failed. In this case, the Chinese Communist Party regime decided to put the second card in its hand on the table. With the addition of the concept of "war on terror" to the definitions of "extremist" and "separatist" used by the Chinese administration against minorities, the genocide against Muslim Uyghurs, Kazakhs, and other communities has accelerated to make East Turkistan a complete Chinese territory. The Communist dictate, who wanted to dominate the world economically, decided not to allow another society, culture, and religion to exist in these occupied lands opened to the West. The construction process of Nazi-style concentration camps, which the whole world speaks about today, started simultaneously with the One Belt and Road Initiative announcement, which is the implementation tool of China's neo-colonial plan. In other words, the communist dictatorship decided that if "money did not assimilate the region, then it should be destroyed."

5

Uyghur Genocide

"In the camp, the officers were women; the managers were men. Managers call a group of young girls every day 'for questioning,' but in reality, they raped and tortured them. Even difficult applications such as inserting electric sticks into their genitals became a daily routine. One day, a young girl from the class where Qelbinur lectured was called for 'interrogation,' and this girl returned after two hours, unable to walk. The officers took that girl away, and she never came back. Qelbinur, who could not bear the things she saw and heard, became sick and was taken to the hospital and then suspended from duty." [1]
Qelbinur Sedik

XI JINPING is the son of Xi Zhongxun, one of Mao's comrades, who invaded East Turkistan with Mao in 1949. Taking the first step towards the CCP in 1974, Xi quickly rose with his ambition and political moves. He became the Party Secretary General in 2012- he became the President of China. He sees himself, along with Mao and Deng, among the greatest leaders in China's history. [2] As a result of Xi seeing himself as the successor of both Mao and Stalin, a period began when many projects were developed for China to dominate the world, while ignoring the value of human life. [3] By making a constitutional amendment at the 2018 National People's Congress, Xi made the decision to keep himself in power as long as he wanted to just like every dictator and authoritarian ruler. In the voting held on March 11, the "democratic majority", with 2,958 votes against 2 rejections and 3 undecided votes, lifted the restriction of serving Presidency two terms of five years each, granting Xi the right to be the President for life. [4] Unlike his successors, Xi has started to implement policies that will allow China to dominate in the global sphere. In this context, the One Belt One Road Project was one of the first projects announced. The project was announced in 2013, one year after Xi took over China's rule. East Turkistan is the key point of this project.

When Xi Jinping announced the One Belt and Road Initiative, a remarkable incident occurred in the Forbidden City area in Beijing. A vehicle accidentally plunged into the crowd, killing 5 people. With this aggressive action allegedly carried out by the Uyghurs, an incident similar to the previous violent acts in East Turkistan has occurred for the first time in China's inner parts. However, suspicions were expressed that this attack was an international terrorist attack. Expressing this doubt, Roberts has suddenly become the target of the Chinese regime. [5] Although the attack's motivation has been discussed, this event has triggered the Beijing government's new policies towards East Turkistan. The Chinese communist regime, which has made it systematic propaganda to associate the Uyghurs with terrorism, has started a new war against the Uyghurs. Roberts notes that the term "self-fulfilling prophecy," which the American sociologist Robert Merton described, that false evaluations about social events turn into reality over time and cause social and political problems, are seen in the events in East Turkistan. [6] In other words, imputations such as "separatist" and " terrorist threat" used by the Chinese Communist regime against all Uyghurs began to be perceived as if these attributions were true, with the intervention of the Uyghurs in some events. In the 1990s Uyghurs struggled to protect their identity, religion, and culture, which were heavily suppressed by the Beijing government. The event in which the tension between Han Chinese and Uyghurs turned into a social explosion on July 5, 2009, with the violent and bloody crackdown of the Chinese police of the demonstrations of Uyghurs. The inclusion of the actions taken due to social ruptures and the motivation of social-cultural demands into the definition of the "global war on terrorism" and the increase in assimilation and colonial oppression against East Turkistan is an unmitigated "self-fulfilling prophecy", as Roberts said. The vehicle attack in Beijing in 2013 opened the doors for the Xi administration to implement its colonial and genocidal policies even more intensely. In the following period, violent incidents involving the names of Uyghurs continued to occur in East Turkistan. Xi made the expected statement after a group of assailants committed violence against civilians with knives in the city of Kunming on March 1, 2014, when many people died. And after the incident, he instructed: "to punish violent terrorists heavily under the law and do everything to maintain social stability." [7] However, it is not even clear whether the Uyghurs carried out this knife attack or not. The Beijing government has also exploited this unsolved incident for its own purposes. Many incidents took place in East Turkistan in 2014. Along with the stabbing of a pro-government cleric in Kashgar, Beijing has tightened its security policies in this city, and 27,000 people have been detained. [8]

Xi: "Absolutely, No Mercy!"

It has been noted that the timing of this attack coincided with Xi's visit to East

Turkistan after he became head of the CCP and the state. During his visits to the region, Xi often voiced this "Strike hard campaign" while warning that such attacks should be prevented while they are still in preparation. The sign that the Beijing government will resort to all kinds of violence in the genocide against East Turkistan has been the words of Xi to the Chinese authorities in the region as "there is no mercy." The public learned this statement with the documents leaked to the press later. [9] Simultaneously, according to the information in various sources, Xi saw the mosques' people during his Kashgar trip. He scolded the Chinese officials by saying, "What have you done so far? Are these people still here?" This event has shown that radical changes will be implemented in policies regarding the region. After this high-level study tour held between 27-30 April, a "work conference on Xinjiang" was organized in May with Xi's instructions. Xi himself gave a speech there, showing the importance he attaches to the region. [10] With its special strategic location, East Turkistan is geopolitically important for realizing the Great West Development Strategy and energy and transportation projects.

For China to achieve its long-term goals, the region must fully integrate with the mainland of China. For this integration to occur, the so-called "separatism, extremism, and war on terror" must be eliminated. [11] As long as the target of these three arguments, which China constantly brings to the agenda and attributes to every event, is the Muslim Turkish identity in the region, East Turkistan will never be sinicized. Uyghurs and other Muslim Turkic societies are expected to leave their languages, religions, and cultures aside and become Han Chinese.

Xi set several goals in implementing the "strike hard" policy for East Turkistan. The first is to take drastic steps to end so-called acts of violence. The second is radical changes in education. In other words, the aim is to educate Muslim Uyghurs and other society members, be completely free from feelings based on own identity and Islam, and place the values of socialism in society. In the third step, what needs to be done is Islam's sinicization, as described in the previous sections. The fourth step is the aggravation of border controls, and the other is the establishment of virtual security. In other words, the establishment of the system that turns East Turkistan into a virtual prison today. The last step is establishing an order that will allow the people living in the region to obey the Communist party and the Chinese government completely. [12] These policies of Xi Jinping towards the homeland of Muslim Uyghurs are partially different from his father, who knew the region well and was responsible for the region during Mao's period. When Father Xi took office in charge of regions such as East Turkistan, he initially waged a brutal war against those who resisted the occupation. [13] He killed more than 90,000 people. He liquidated all the soldiers who remained from the period of the Second East Turkistan Republic. When there was no one left to oppose him, he began to use the method of 'soft power'. Acting against human nature, Xi Jinping is trying to destroy the Muslim Uyghurs, Kazakhs, and other communities in East Turkistan through dictatorial methods and Nazi methods. For this purpose, one of his first actions was to build concentration camps there.

In 2015, 60 years after East Turkistan was declared an autonomous region, the Chinese Communist regime adopted another decision on Muslim Uyghurs. China's National People's Congress passed the Security Bill in July. With this law, wide powers are provided to follow and monitor every step of those who oppose the regime. A few months after this law, another document called 'testimony to ethnic equality, unity, and development in Xinjiang' was published in September 2015. This document further increased the pressure on Muslims under the name of the communist regime's fight against 'separatism, extremism and so-called terrorism.' For example, no public officials are now allowed to go to the mosque. From this point of view, if an officer goes to a mosque, it means that he is involved in "religious extremism". In December 2015, before Chen Quanguo, who was the Party Secretary-General in Tibet, was appointed to Xinjiang / East Turkistan, a new Anti-Terror law was passed. [14]

All Crimes in the UN Genocide Convention Committed

One of the most terrible genocides the world has ever seen before East Turkistan is undoubtedly the Nazis killing millions of Jews during World War II. The leader of the Nazi Party, the Führer, Adolf Hitler, was responsible for the genocide. Hitler had always considered himself a wise thinker. Hitler believed that race determined people's characteristics and abilities. According to the Nazi ideology he put forward, people's physical structures, ways of thinking, organizational abilities, intelligence, cultural pleasure, and other characteristics depend on race. Therefore, according to Hitler, societies that are not of the master race must be destroyed. According to Hitler, these were mainly Jews, Romani people, people with disabilities, Poles, and even African-origin Germans that are not part of the master race and thus should be viewed as enemies that should be destroyed. There is ' one master race: the Aryan race from which the German race is descended. [15] This irrational point of view of Hitler caused millions of people to be killed in World War II with a brutality that is hard to describe in words. The victorious states, who did not want those dark days of world history to occur again, prepared the United Nations 'Convention on the Prevention and Punishment of the Crime of Genocide' by saying "never again." The UN General Assembly meeting in Paris on December 2016, 1948, opened the genocide convention for signature and accession with its resolution 260 A (III). The convention came into force on 12 January 1951. [16] Not long after the signing of the UN Convention on Genocide, a new genocide began in East Turkistan in the People's Republic of China, the new Iron Curtain country of Asia. In Article 2 of the UN Genocide Convention, acts that can be considered as genocide are listed. The occurrence of any of the following acts constitutes the crime of genocide;

In the present Convention, genocide means any of the following acts committed with intent to destroy, in whole or in part, a national, ethnical, racial or religious group, as such:

· Killing members of the group;

· Causing serious bodily or mental harm to members of the group;

· Deliberately inflicting on the group conditions of life calculated to bring about its physical destruction in whole or in part;

· Imposing measures intended to prevent births within the group;

· Forcibly transferring children of the group to another group.

In the 3rd Article of the Convention, which actions will be punished, as follows;

a) commit genocide;

b) To cooperate in committing genocide;

c) To directly and publicly incite the commitment of genocide;

d) Attempting to commit genocide;

e) Participating in genocide;

The next article clearly stipulates that the perpetrator of any offenses in Articles 2 and 3 should be punished. [17] In 1949, when the contract was opened for signature by the member states, the convention was signed by Taiwan representing China, not the current regime for China. However, the Chinese government did not approve the agreement immediately, and the agreement did not immediately go into effect. In 1971, with Mao's attempts at the US, the Chinese administration replaced Taiwan in the UN, and the People's Republic of China (PRC) ratified and put into effect the convention, which it had signed in 1949, after 12 years in 1983. It is noteworthy that Mao, the PRC founder, did not immediately approve the convention signed by today's Taiwan, because the atrocities and repression carried out by Mao and his administration during the Cultural Revolution of 1966 in East Turkistan, Tibet, and other occupied territories fit under the definition of acts described in the UN Genocide Convention. For example, with the lable of land reform in East Turkistan, the living conditions of the people in the region were forcibly changed, births were prevented with child restriction, and those who opposed the regime were sent to labor camps and subjected to physical and mental torture. In this case, even sending thousands of people to labor camps ' in East Turkistan for opposing the regime can be considered part of the genocide. However, at that time, the Mao administration carried out its policies without considering this convention of the UN. The convention was ratified and entered into force during the Deng period, which came to power after Mao and pursued a moderate policy towards the autonomous regions' peoples within foreign expansion policy. Seeing himself as the greatest leader of the communist regimes after Stalin, who destroyed millions of people in Gulag labor camps, and Mao, who was responsible for the deaths of millions of people including his own people during the great leap forward program and cultural revolution, Xi and his regime started to commit the crimes of genocide described in the UN convention just like the Nazis. Like Hitler's point of view, Xi and his Comminist Party representatives in Xinjiang also consider the Han Chinese to be the most superior race. Therefore, it is a disease, a crime, for a person in the region to have a Muslim and Uyghur identity, and they must be destroyed. The reflection of this view has been the commitment of acts within the scope of genocide, such as establishing concentration camps, the forced sterilization of women, and the separation of Uyghur children from their families. These crimes will be discussed in the following chapters in detail. The world is facing a new black era, but economic interests have made them forget the promises of 'never again.'

Nazi Concentration Camps Rebuilt in East Turkistan

The days reminiscent of Nazi-era Germany were felt more intensely in the homeland of Muslim Uyghurs after 2016. The Chinese Communist dictate started to build concentration camps in East Turkistan in 2014. [18] In other words, the first camps were established one year after the announcement of the One Belt and Road Initiative. Even in the Muslim Uyghur community, there was a story about an incident told by word of mouth. According to this story, Uyghurs living there were also employed in the construction of these camps. When one of these workers asked the Chinese about the construction, he answered, "Don't worry, many of you will be work here soon." Of course, it isn't easy to verify whether this story actually happened. However, the events that took place later showed that what this Chinese person said came true. Since 2016, Muslim Uyghurs' connections living in the diaspora with their relatives in their homeland have gradually started to break off. For example, Gulruy Asqar, whose story was featured in a research published in the Financial Times, learned that his nephew Ekram Yarmuhemmed was taken away by the Chinese police a while after moving to America in 2016. What happened to Yarmuhemmed constitutes one of the most striking precedents of Xi's war against Islam in the eyes of Muslim Uyghurs. Gulyar Asqar thought that his nephew was taken away by the police because of the money he sent from America for him. According to Yarmuhemmed's friends, the Chinese police found some money with the Holy Quran's records in a search in the apartment where Yarmuhemmed lived. As a result of the show trial, he was sentenced to 10 years in prison. [19] The number of camps established by the communist dictator to erase Islam's traces in East Turkistan has started to increase since 2017. When these camps, which were inspired by the Nazis, were first heard by the international public, namely in April 2017, approximately 3 million Muslim Uyghurs, Kazakhs, and other communities were sent to these concentration camps. [20]

Xi and Chen's Perspectives Reminiscent of the Nazis

The first thing that comes to mind in world history when it comes to concentration camps is when the Nazis set up to destroy Jews. All countries, especially Europe, have promised 'never again' so that humanity will not face a black mark like the Holocaust. After 75 years since the Holocaust, the world has again faced genocide and the destruction of concentration camps. This time, the genocide atrocity occurs in East Turkistan, which China occupied, who wants to exploit the world. As explained in previous chapters, the excuse China told the world about the construction of these camps and the real goal it conceals are completely different. Chinese President Xi argued at a meeting after the Australian Strategic Policy Institute reported new camp constructions in East Turkistan. According to Xi, camps are necessary and should continue for a long time to educate the people of East Turkistan from the correct (!) perspective. On the other hand, this perspective is the sinicization of East Turkistan people, either by genocide or by assimilation. As a matter of fact, Xi expressed this situation as follows: "It is necessary to guide all ethnic groups in creating a correct perspective about the country, history, and nationality." [21] According to President Xi, Uyghurs can show "extremism in religion," which is detrimental to China's interests. This, as Roberts explains, is the perpetuation of non-existent facts about an incident constantly brought to the agenda, and these non-existent facts turn into "self-fulfilling prophecy" as a result of the evaluation of unrelated events in the same scope. The concept of "extremism in religion," brought to the agenda by Xi and other Chinese rulers are used to heathenize a Muslim society and to justify even genocide for this purpose. For example, according to a new regulation issued in March 2017, the so-called "anti-extremism law" prohibited Muslims from growing their beards. [22] The definitions of crimes such as "growing a beard" and "performing religious practices" in the concentration camp documents in Karakash published by the Uyghur Human Rights Project also show how the Communist dictator views the concept of extremism in religion. (23)

Documents revealing Xi's authoritarian approach to Muslim Uyghurs in East Turkistan were published in the New York Times, one of America's leading newspapers, in November last year. These documents also contain Xi's statement of "no mercy," recorded as a black mark left in history. The documents, which span about 400 pages, include a series of secret speeches Xi made to government officials. In these conversations, of course, there is no direct instruction on the establishment of concentration camps. According to John Bolton's Book Xi Jingping had explained to Trump why he was basically building concentration camps in Xinjiang. (24) However, Xi freed the administrators in the region to apply "dictatorship" methods to eliminate the so-called religious excesses in East Turkistan. According to Xi, who constantly uses the concept of "religious extremism," which is completely ambiguous and whose framework is drawn by the regime, religion is a virus, and this virus must be destroyed. The regime leader, the practitioner of new-era Nazi methods, has again revealed that the Beijing government's rhetoric against Muslim Uyghurs has changed. Although previous rhetoric has consistently stated that separatist ideas from the outside are effective, Xi has been looking at the matter from the inside. In other words, there is no danger from outside; it is the thoughts of the Uyghurs that are dangerous. (25)

Although Xi's predecessors thought that the unrest and Uyghur's struggle in East Turkistan would be resolved by economic development, the new era's dictatorial leader demands ideological treatment to reshape Muslims' thoughts. He expressed this at a conference as follows: "The weapons of the democratic dictatorship must be used without hesitation and hesitation." Xi pointed out that comprehensive surveillance and the intelligence-gathering campaign is needed for East Turkistan to make this region a Chinese land and to eliminate the resistance of the Uyghurs to protect their own culture, language, and religion, and emphasized the transformation of these lands into a prison surrounded by virtual walls and digital wall. Xi, who opened the door to all kinds of methods from face recognition systems to genetic tests and big data collection and surveillance systems in these conversations hidden from the public, also supported blacklisting citizens, as described in the novel 1984. Xi described this as "We communists must be like a people's war." In his speeches during the same period, Xi said that the brainwashing activities in prisons and these camps should continue after leaving the camps. (26) After Xi's instruction, the thing to do was set up camps and send people there.

Xi sent like-minded people, who have a similar style to Adolf Hitler's propaganda expert Joseph Geobbels, to the region to realize this inhuman plan. Chen Quanguo, who implemented heavy security policies in Tibet, was appointed as party secretary to Xinjiang. Like President Xi, Quanguo became a practitioner of Nazi methods and had his name written on the black pages of history with the words he used: "Round up everyone who should be rounded up" [27] Quanguo addressed this instruction to the police and other security guards, who lined up before the operations to be carried out in Urumqi in February 2017. He ordered the police and security forces to be crushing and to prepare for a devastating attack. [28]

Being a Muslim is Enough to be Sent to Concentration Camps

While the world has not yet forgotten the suffering of the Jewish Holocaust, everyone is wondering why the new method of establishing concentration camps is being faced. As explained at the beginning of this chapter, the main reason is that East Turkistan territory is an obstacle to the Asian Red Giant China's goals of ruling the world. Although it has been under occupation by the Chinese Communist dictators for more than 70 years, the Muslim Uyghurs, Kazakhs living there are exposed to this genocide because they never accepted sinicization. According to Xi, who is guaranteed to stay forever as the head of the Communist Party and China with the new law passed in 2018, the blue flag of East Turkistan should be painted with the colors of the red flag of China. Aiming to Sinicize all kinds of beliefs in East Turkistan and all the lands he occupied and gave so-called autonomy, Xi wants to change every religious belief within the framework of communist doctrine. Along with Islam, Buddhism, Catholicism, Daoism, and even Protestantism were put on the target. According to this perspective of the authoritarian Xi regime, if an Uyghur or Kazakh demonstrates any behavior or dress that indicates that they are Muslim, they have not accepted to be Chinese. The punishment for refusing to be Han Chinese is to be sent to concentration camps, be subjected to all kinds of torture and punishment, and undergo brainwashing operations. When looking at the crimes against those sent to the camps, both in the Qarakash documents and in the documents that the public later learned, ' the traces of a paranoid mentality will be seen.

In Qarakash documents, concentration camp victims are classified according to their crimes. According to the document, which tells a tiny part of the persecution in East Turkistan, the so-called crimes are listed as follows: "Failure to comply with the birth control program. Sharing unsafe posts on social media, growing a beard, wearing a veil, practicing religious duties, applying for a passport, traveling abroad, being a relative of a prisoner, traveling within China, watching an illegal media channel, having a relative abroad, not listening to the neighbourhood committee officials, talking to overseas countries by phone..." [29] Innocent people were sent to concentration camps for other reasons not listed here. If these articles listed in Qarakash documents are acted upon, everyone in the world should somehow be sent to these concentration camps. The criminalization of even the most natural behaviors of man appears in an authoritarian and dictatorial regime. According to this point of view of the Chinese administration, everyone in the world is guilty and must be punished. Who knows, with the One Belt and Road project, Xi's goal is to rule such a world.

PRC officials' statements have always been the same against the allegations that Muslim society was subjected to genocide by Nazi methods with false crimes that shocked humanity. These places are not concentration camps but "holiday education centers," according to them. What kind of an education center is this? The main elite of East Turkistan people were exiled there first. From poet, academic, lawyer, doctor, singer, fashioner to the businessman, anyone who keeps society afloat is currently in the camps. The Chinese regime also uses a method such as sending the relatives of prominent Uyghurs living abroad to these camps to get revenge. The most dramatic example of this is the abduction of the sister of my wife Rushan Abbas, the founder of the Campaign for Uyghurs. When we heard the news about the camps and the disappearance of my entire family, Rushan Abbas took the rostrum to speak about China's persecution. Rushan participated on a panel at a think-tank in Washington and was vocal about my family's disappearance. Six days later, her older sister, Dr. Gulshan Abbas, was abducted by the Chinese regime in Urumchi. For more than 2 years, no one has ever known what happened to Dr. Gulshan Abbas. Someone from the hospital where she used to work said that she was detained when Radio Free Asia reported contacted the hospital. In this case, the following right question arises: If these camps are "vocational training centers" [30], as Xinjiang Governor Shohrat Zakir said, then for what training does Dr. Gulshan Abbas, a retired medical doctor who speaks fluent Chinese language, need? She has not violated the Chinese state's laws, and has not committed a crime. Having spent her life helping the patients, the reason Dr. Abbas was sent to the concentration camp was a retaliatory action by the Chinese regime for Dr. Gulshan Abbas's sister, my wife Rushan Abbas' activism and advocacy work in the United States. The survivors of these camps are speaking about what has happened in these camps and stating that those aren't re-education or vocational training centers but concentration camps in the full sense.

Increase in the Number of Concentration Camps and Forced Labor Centers

German-born Adrian Zenz, who has conducted extensive research on human rights violations in East Turkistan, notes that the sending of people to concentration camps in East Turkistan began in late 2013. The first example of the Chinese regime's so-called retraining programs for Muslims was seen in the city of Turpan in August 2013. A program was initiated in this city because young men were transformed through education in four subjects, one of which was to grow a beard. Another example is the inclusion of 259 'problematic' people in a closed training program for 10 days in the Kashgar region. A similar practice was seen in the province of Ili in 2015, and a secret training program was implemented on 42 people. The first practice of the so-called retraining program in its present sense in East Turkistan was carried out in 2014. A three-stage training program was initiated in Kashgar's Konashahar district to "eliminate the excesses," and those deemed problematic by the regime aligned with the CCP's line. In this district, 3,515 people were forcibly included in the 203 sessions until the end of 2014. Muslims who participated in this program later returned to "secular life." In 2015, 3,000 Uyghurs were trained in training centers in Hotan and lost their so-called "religious extremism". The order established in the facilities here is partially similar to the military order. In the same year, 5,000 people in Ghulja and about 2,000 people in Lopnur participated in the CCP doctrine program. [31] Small groups were sent to the concentration camps until 2017, and after that date, everyone determined "problematic" by the government was taken to these camps. The recruitment of new people in CCP training centers and local governments in 2017 was the first sign of expanding the so-called training centers. For example, it was recorded that 110 retraining center officers and 248 police officers would be employed in Karamay. While the number of those sent to these camps in previous years was expressed in thousands, this number increased to hundreds of thousands and even exceeded millions in 2017. [32]

This brutal operation against Muslim Uyghur, Kazakh, Kyrgyz, and other communities does not comply with international law or norms. Zenz notes that certain quotas are set for Muslim-majority regions and that people are imprisoned without legal justification to fill these quotas. In his report dated 2018, the German researcher Adrian Zenz pointed out that with Chen's appointment to East Turkistan, there was a serious increase in the number of people sent to the camps. [33] On the other hand, the Communist regime transformed some old public buildings into concentration camps and used them. According to the CFR figures in 2017, the number of camps in East Turkistan is 1,200. [34] After the concentration camps came to the forefront in the world, public opinion and the human rights violations in the camps were loudly voiced. The Chinese government made one of its thousands of years of insidious maneuvers. It made an interesting statement to reduce reactions. Shohrat Zakir, the governor of Xinjiang, held a press conference in December 2019 and declared, "Those who stayed in retraining camps are now graduated." [35] In fact, it was soon understood that this explanation was a distraction. Because neither Dr. Gulshan Abbas nor millions of other oppressed people ever gained their freedom. What actually happened was that after the Chinese communist regime completed its brainwashing activities in the camps, a significant number of these people were sent to factories that were set up next to the camps to work as a slave. Trying to downplay these centers built by the systematic inspiration taken from the Nazis, the Beijing regime continued to build new camps within the borders; it did not let anyone in.

ASPI published the latest report on the continued construction of camps in East Turkistan. According to the ASPI report, while the party officials in East Turkistan made statements about the graduation of the people in the concentration camps, they also built new prisons on the other hand. According to the findings of the institute, more than 380 new facilities have been built recently. These new buildings were determined based on satellite photographs, descriptions of those staying in the camps, and data obtained from the region. The Chinese communist regime has built huge concentration camps in East Turkistan. According to the report, while violence and oppression against Muslim Uyghurs have been increasing since 2017, new camps have been built to send hundreds of thousands of East Turkistan residents behind locked gates. Existing detention centers were expanded both last year and this year, while new detention centers were built simultaneously. The Institute classified camps in East Turkistan from a low-security level to a high level of security. Of the 380 camps identified in the report, 108 were rated in the category of a low-security level. These facilities were formerly a school and hospital-like buildings. These buildings have been converted into detention centers with equipment such as wire fences and security cameras. Those held in these facilities are allowed to go home on weekends while working in factories on weekdays. These places are also facilities shown to delegations from abroad for propaganda purposes. [36]

The facilities found to be used as "retraining centers" is more than 380. These so-called training centers have been implemented since 2017. As of 2019, the security measures in these centers have been further increased. These buildings are equipped with higher security measures than the places mentioned in the previous paragraph. They have high walls, wire mesh, watchtowers. In these compounds, where there are classes for brainwashing activities and courses about the regime, there are also showcase gardens to make people feel completely imprisoned. These facilities are right next to the factories where Muslim Uyghurs, Kazakhs, and other work like slaves. In ASPI's study, 72 settlements are included in the third category. Large thick walls surround these facilities, security guards are stationed at the main entrance gates, and watchtowers and six layers of barbed wire are placed on the walls. The administration buildings are built in a completely separate location from the prisoners' wards, and entrance and exit to the facilities are provided through a single door. These 107 buildings described in the report are prisons where high-security measures are fully implemented. Those sentenced to long-term imprisonment are kept in these facilities, which were expanded after 2017. Some of these are next to buildings with lower security levels. [37]

Although the Chinese Communist Regime tells the world that there are no human rights violations in East Turkistan and claims that the people in these camps live "happily," it is a fact that the Regime ruled these places with an iron fist. Since it also does not allow neutral observers to enter the occupied territories, it is impossible to determine the extent of the persecution. However, with the research of ASPI on the camps, it was revealed that new camps were built in the region, and the existing concentration camps were continuously expanded. According to the institute's research results, the compounds of 61 remand and detention facilities were expanded between July of 2019 and July of 2020. Half of them have been converted into high-security prisons while previously being used as a retraining center. For example, a 100,000-square-meter detention camp, built on a 60-acre plot in the city of Kashgar, with 13 five-story residential buildings and surrounded by 14-meter-high walls and watchtowers, has been in use since January of this year. The concentration camp in Dabancheng, near Urumqi, the capital of East Turkistan, has been used as one of the largest detention centers. With the new buildings added in 2019, this detention center has reached enormous dimensions and is now 1 kilometer long. [38]

In time, the Beijing government accepted that the numbers in these concentration camps, which were the biggest black mark of the recent period after the Nazis, reached enormous numbers. But while accepting this, they portrayed this system of cruelty, which they started in the name of destroying a society, as a success in the sinicization of people. Documents released by the Beijing government in September of this year contained information about concentration camps. The document also shows the Chinese government's perspective on the Muslim people living there. According to the Chinese communist regime, this backwardness in some regions of East Turkistan that is not fully developed economically is due to the conservative nature of the region's people. It is stated in the document that people were sent to concentration camps to eliminate this so-called backwardness. Since 2017, as Chinese government says, 1.29 million people have been forcibly taken from their homes by the authoritarian communist regime each year and sent to camps. A third of these figures are in the southern part of East Turkistan, a rural part. Considering that almost 1.35 million people are sent to so-called education centers each year, it is thought that almost more than 4.5 million people have been taken to these camps to date. This figure also coincides with the numbers of organizations reporting human rights violations in East Turkistan. [39] The statements of Chinese President Xi that he is satisfied with the operations in the region and maintain these operations are evident from the fact that it is impossible to protect the Muslim and Uyghur identity in East Turkistan in the future.

Not a Re-education Center, but a Center of Persecution

Is this order in which Muslim Uyghurs are forcibly recruited really a system in which people are retrained, as the Chinese communist regime claims? For a long time, the Beijing government denied the new version of the Uyghur genocide launched in 2014 and has not allowed real information about the region to leak today. Certain people were invited to certain areas, and they were all deluded. For the communist regime to establish a new colonial order globally, Muslim Uyghurs, Kyrgyz and Kazakhs, and other nations must be destroyed.

If we evaluate the accounts of people who went to East Turkistan and saw the concentration camps, China did to the Uyghurs worse than what the Nazis did to the Jews. said Canadian academic Olsi Jazexhi of Albanian origin is one of China's names to East Turkistan for propaganda. Olsi Jazexhi saw the genocide committed by the Beijing government there and announced it publicly when he returned. "Forgive me, my Chinese friends, but there is no law in the world that will find what you do to those people fair," Jazexhi explained. Dr. Jazexhi later spoke at the conference organized by the Uyghur Academy and said: "I have seen that by imprisoning and scaring Muslim Uyghur, they are trying to pressure them to forget their identity. We have seen the assimilation policies organized in a very systematic way to decrease Uyghur's dominance." The Canadian academic said that he did not expect to see people still being filled in camps like slaves and imprisoned in the 21st century and said that he said "Peace be with you" (An Islamic style greeting Assalamueleykum) to a Muslim he met in the camp, but he replied "hello" in Chinese. Dr. Jazexhi said: "Muslims can't even say 'peace upon you' there. They treated people like monkeys there." [40] Emphasizing that the Chinese Communist Regime followed the paths of the Nazis, Dr. Jazexhi points out that the records of the Beijing government's crimes regarding the genocide in East Turkistan have been systematically destroyed so that in the future, they will wash their hands and act as if nothing had happened. Dr. Jazexhi also added, "Those who remain in those camps are neither terrorists nor extremist people. Their rime is being a Muslim. The Chinese were forcing them to abandon their culture, language, and Islamic faith. In the camps, there was pressure to eat non-halal food, drink alcohol and offer their allegiance to communist doctrine," he said of his observations. [41]

China's Persecution Centers Through the Eyes of Witnesses

The main goals of the Chinese Communist regime in carrying out genocide through concentration camps and other methods are obvious. As exemplified under various headings above, the Beijing government wants the lands it occupies to be completely sinicized. To fulfill this, it is making it so that the Muslim people who live there will give up the religion of Islam, the Uyghur peoples will be detached from their identity, the use of their mother tongue is banned so as to disconnect them from their past, the separation of children from their families and the forced sterilization of women and the economic collapse of the region to eradicate the lineage of Uyghurs, Kyrgyz, Kazakh, and other peoples. According to this goal, of the millions of East Turkistan Muslims subjected to genocide, very few people survived the Chinese Communist regime's persecution. Many of them were also able to leave China due to the interlocutor States' initiatives, as they carried the passports of other countries. As they left the concentration camps, they were pressured that they would certainly not speak against the Beijing government. The reason for this pressure is to hide the facts about how the PRC committed genocide in the homeland of Muslim Uyghurs. In response to all the authoritarian Chinese regime threats, brave Muslim Uyghur and Kazakh women have told the world public the details of the genocide in East Turkistan. The details of what kind of hell the victims have endured are given below.

Qelbinur Sedik, a Living Witness to Uyghur Genocide

World public opinion became aware of concentration camps when China began to realize its extermination policy against Uyghurs. However, the accounts of East Turkistan teacher Qelbinur Sedik show that systematic assimilation and genocide began much earlier. Sedik, who was forced to teach in concentration camps, gave an account that was disturbing and unsettling.

In her 28th year of teaching, Sedik first encountered China's eradication steps in 2004. According to an instruction notified to her school, "education will be given in two languages," that is, it will be given in Uyghur and Chinese. But the actual application of this order means that almost all courses are given in Chinese. After 10 years, she learned that a close colleague had been tried, also learned in 2016 that the mother, father, and brother of the same friend were arrested and taken away. Her friend quoted the police as saying to them, "If you pray, you will be in prison for 10 years; if you read the Quran, you will be in prison for 8 years." In November 2016, administrators at the school held an exam to select successful teachers. Qelbinur successfully passed this exam on both educational skills and political ideology. On February 28, 2017, it was reported to Qelbinur, who was called from the school's human resources center, that she was assigned to teach language to 'ignorant' illiterate people who do not speak Chinese. A confidentiality agreement was also signed with her for this duty. She was told to meet the police on the morning of March 1. Qelbinur, who met the police at the bus stop and was taken to concentration camps located at the mountains' foot, was put through a security search and taken to the control room. There she saw through security cameras the cell-type classes in which prisoners were kept. The head guard shouted, "training begins."

The prisoners' rooms have no beds, ' blankets, and the rooms receive very little light. Qelbinur counted 97 people, 7 of whom were women and 3 of whom were very old. Then the officers took her to her first class. 70 male inmates in the classroom have grown beards, just sitting on simple plastic chairs. She traditionally said, "Peace upon you," but no one had replied to her. Some were crying quietly. She immediately realized that her word was inconvenient and started the lesson by telling them, "I came to teach you Chinese." She showed them the letters one by one and asked them to repeat; she silently prayed to break free from this torment as soon as possible. When she helped distribute food at lunch, she found that they are given hot water instead of rice soup. The security guards even counted slices of bread. Qelbinur signed a six-month contract. During this time, she taught 97 prisoners, addressed by number. A prisoner named Osman, one of Urumchi's wealthy persons, once upon a time recognized her and begged her to see the sun for 5 more minutes every day. One day Osman disappeared, and later Qelbinur learned that he had died of a brain hemorrhage due to high blood pressure. Another teenager in her class fell ill, but the officers ignored him. This person was taken to hospital after his health deteriorated, but he still passed away. Because of the systemic pressure, malnutrition, and convictions in health conditions, the prisoners had lost their health over time, and some were unable to walk. The second group came on March 20, including teachers, people in business, religious elders, and even those who were arrested just for the crime of conversing on Facebook. Qelbinur taught communist anthems instead of teaching them Chinese, as these newcomers were more educated. One day, Qelbinur saw that her businessman neighbor had also been taken away. His crime is to make a phone call with his son living in Kyrgyzstan; the police said to them, "Calling abroad is a big crime." Of the 600 Uyghurs in his neighborhood, 190 have disappeared within a year. In their place, Han Chinese settlers began to appear.

New groups were constantly being brought to the concentration camp where Qelbinur was working. The number of detainees had exceeded 3,000. Guards would take 7-8 people to the torture chamber every day. Screams in the basement torture rooms can be heard everywhere. A police officer told Qelbinur that there were four types of electric shock devices. These are "chairs, gloves, helmets and an iron rod inserted into the genitals." Qelbinur, who underwent a so-called voluntary but actually compulsory forced sterilization operation in July 2017, experienced one of the most difficult moments of her life. When she went to the hospital, she saw Uyghurs; heaven knows why. The regime now regularly controls women every year and sterilizes them. German researcher Adrian Zenz's report, which will be mentioned in the future, contains more information.

In September 2017, Qelbinur was reassigned to another location as she waited to be released from concentration camp hell. The new place of duty is the camp where women are kept. Qelbinur Sedik found that about 10,000 women stayed there. 60 of them were over 60, and many of the rest are young girls in the spring of their lives. These young women were brought there because they were educated in Korea, Australia, Turkey, Egypt, America, and Europe. When they came to see their families, they were immediately arrested and sent to the camps. Qelbinur's daughter was also studying abroad. She decided to kill her if she ever comes back. And what Sedik says about the women's camp is appalling. There are no toilets in the dormitories, buckets that are changed once a day. In the morning, everyone is given 1 minute to wash their face. The right to have a bath once a month (!) is allowed to them. Women began to get sick one by one. All prisoners had to go to the infirmary every month. The prisoners were given an injection, a blood sample is taken from them, and a substance is given to them to swallow. A nurse told Qelbinur that prisoners were given a substance to help them sleep and calcium because they stayed in the dark for too long. But the truth is not so; prisoners were systematically sterilized. A young student died due to the drugs given. In the camp, the officers were women; the managers were men. Managers call a group of young girls every day 'for questioning,' but in reality, they raped and tortured them. Even difficult applications such as inserting electric sticks into their genitals became a daily routine. One day, a young girl from the class where Qelbinur lectured was called for 'interrogation,' and this girl returned after two hours, unable to walk. The officers took that girl away, and she never came back. Qelbinur, who could not bear the things she saw and heard, became sick and was taken to the hospital and then suspended from duty.

Life in East Turkistan has also become unbearable outside the camps. Qelbinur Sedik once saw 8-10 women standing by their children playing in the street. Police cars that came there suddenly gathered all the women, put sacks on their heads and handcuffed them, and took them away. The children were left in tears. After a while, Sedik saw that a group of young people released from the camp were walking in an injured condition. Forcibly retired in 2018, Qelbinur once again underwent a forced sterilization operation that year. This torture was repeated a year later. The order sent is that all women up to the age of 59 should be subjected to this persecution every year. Qelbinur, who applied for a passport on the occasion of her daughter's wedding when she saw that it would be impossible to live there anymore, was given a passport a year later after long interrogations. She knocked on the doors of 23 departments to get a passport. She finally reached Europe in October 2019 and met with her daughter. Qelbinur Sedik, who was unable to recover from the impact of what she had experienced for a long time, said: "I cried, felt humiliated, abused and psychologically attacked. But I worked in the camp, and I knew what would happen to me if I objected. I've seen young girls there, but I've never seen a Han Chinese. At first, I couldn't talk about anything due to fear about my family and my husband. But now I have decided to fight to raise my voice for my people." [42]

Zumrat Dawut, A Life Falling Apart

In East Turkistan, about 1.5 million Uyghurs have been taken from their homes every year since 2017. One of those millions of Muslim Uyghurs is Zumrat Dawut, who is married to Imran Muhammad from Pakistan. The Washington Post, an American-based news paper, published Zumrat Dawut's story. According to this report by Emily Rauhala and Anna Fifield, it all started in March 2018 with a phone call from a nearby police station when they were sitting at home. On her way to the police station, she told her family that it would not last long, that she would meet with the police and come back immediately. She was unaware of what was going to happen to her, so she just put on slippers and left. However, neither that day nor the next day was she able to return home, and she returned a week later. The Chinese police took her to one of the dark interrogation rooms at the police station, where her hands and feet were tied on a metal chair. During the 24-hour interrogation, she was questioned about everything from her phone calls to bank accounts. During the interrogation, the police threatened and intimidated her by telling her "Nobody can save you from here, nobody can answer you. "Even your God can not hear

what is done to you here." The next day, she was taken out of the police station with her hands tied, a black bag on her head, and taken in a police van to
the Medical Center first and then to the concentration camp. She was forced
to change her clothes in front of men in the concentration camp. After the
prison proceedings were completed, she was sent to a ward where hundreds
of women like her were staying. [43] Dawut saw hundreds of women piled up
like fish, because there was no room in the wards. People slept in turns, some
sleeping while others were standing. After being awakened every morning
by music that deafens the ears, she had to run to take advantage of the water
that was available for a very short time. Before breakfast, detainees pay their
respects to President Xi and the Communist Party. The guards then take them
to larger wards called classrooms. She had to sit on the floor for hours learning
Chinese and listening to party propaganda. Propagandist teachers constantly
tell them that "the Islam they believe comes from another country" and try to
make being a Muslim look like a disease. The wards are monitored 24 hours a
day. One day, she wanted to give a piece of her bread to an old woman who was
suffering from diabetes and was writhing because she couldn't take medica-
tion. The sick woman did not want to accept her offer, fearing that she would
be caught on cameras. But she gave it anyway. A short time later, the guard
arrived at the ward and beat up Dawut. Dawut couldn't get up for a while. From
time to time, she was allowed to make video calls with her family in Urumqi.
But before these calls, she was taken to a makeup room and was certainly told
not to look sad. Dawut refuted the lies of China, who lied to the world, claiming that these places are education centers, not concentration camps, in her
statements to NBC News: "It's a prison. If these places were a training center,
they would not have chained us, beat us, tortured, or pressured us there. If they
were training centers, we would go home every day after class, we would not
be torn from our families" [44]

Zumrat Dawut had the opportunity to get out of the concentration camp,
where she stayed for about 2 months, through the diplomatic initiatives of her
Pakistani husband. On her way out, she was made to sign a commitment that she
would never worship again and that she would not tell anyone what happened
there. She also paid a $2,500 fine for violating China's two-child limitation law.
The communist regime did not stop with this, but offered her a method of 'spa-
ying'. Dawut, who was worried about going back to the camps and being unable
to reunite with her family, was compelled to accept "this voluntary operation".
On October 22, 2018, she went to the hospital and was operated on in the company of government officials. As soon as she left the hospital, they convinced the
local security officials that they would visit her husband's sick father living in

Pakistan and left China. Dawut and her family lived in fearful days until they arrived at the airport in Urumqi and got on the plane. She thought that the Chinese nightmare would never end. Dawut, who came to Pakistan, received a phone call from her brother after a short while. Her brother texted her saying the police officers were looking for her. This was a sign that Pakistan is not safe for them either. Saying that "Pakistan is now a Mini-China", Imran Muhammed took his wife Zumrat Dawut and their children and came to America using the tourist visa he had previously obtained and applied for asylum there. Dawut does not receive any information about the condition of his relatives in Urumqi. Dawut sums up the reason for all the atrocities she has suffered in one sentence: "They want the annihilation of Uyghurs." [45]

Ömer Bekali, "There were Also Those Who were Brought to the Concentration Camp with the Whole Family."

Organ trafficking is one of the most inhumane crimes committed by the communist Chinese regime in East Turkistan, in addition to the crime of genocide. Uyghurs, Kazakhs, Kyrgyz, and other Muslims who were the targets of the genocide, as well as members of Falun Gong in China proper, are among the target groups for organ trafficking. Ömer Bekali, who was arrested in Urumqi in March 2017, is one of the victims of the concentration camps. Bekali, the son of a Uyghur mother and a Kazakh father, started to travel between East Turkistan and Kazakhstan for trade purposes after becoming a citizen of Kazakhstan in 2008. After completing his work in Urumqi, where he came for a tourism fair in March, he went to visit his family in Pichan. The day after he visited his family, on March 26, 2017, police came to his door and told him that they wanted to meet with him and threatened him saying "You don't know us, but we know you." This incident shows that China violated all international rules for genocide. When asked why he was arrested, he answered, "You are suspicious for organizing and supporting illegal activities". He was handcuffed and taken to the hospital. He underwent a very detailed examination at the hospital, where his blood samples and DNA samples were taken. The first thing that came to mind of Bekali, who heard the talks about him while he was waiting in the hospital, was that he would be operated on and one of his organs would be removed. After his procedures were completed, he was taken to the police station in Pichan. There, he was put in a cell next to 13 Uyghur youths bound in chains. The next day, he was interrogated by a three-person delegation, including a person from Karmay. This delegation made accusations against him such as "you helped people to get passports, you received money, you said you would help them with a visa". Then he was then taken to Karmay for further investigation. Bekali, who was handed over to the Jarenbulaq police station in Karmay on 3 April, was interrogated by a Han Chinese police chief the next day. The chief of police started his speech by swearing at Kazakhstan and said that Bekali's citizenship would not help him. Bekali's 43-year life was thoroughly investigated and an element of a crime was sought. Bekali was asked questions about events that never actually happened, such as helping some people travel to Turkey or Syria. When he denied all these baseless allegations, Bekali was taken from the police station and sent to prison in Karmay.

During his stay in prison, his feet were chained even while he was in the ward. These chains on their feet were removed ' when representatives of Kazakhstan's Embassy arrived for a visit. Bekali said, "Every time I tried to get up, I lost my balance due to the chains that were constantly attached. It was like hell. I had lost all my hope" about the prison conditions. On November 4, he was released from prison and taken to a concentration camp to stay for 20 days. This concentration camp was no different from a prison. There were guards and security cameras everywhere. During the transfer, he underwent a detailed examination for the second time. Bekali, who said he saw people of all ages in the camp, described the conditions as follows: "There were teachers, officers, people of different backgrounds. There were even whole families, parents, and children. Those who completed their prison sentences were brought here. Those who worked in the state sector were accused of being hypocritical. There were even people brought in just because their clock was adjusted to the Urumqi time zone." Before leaving the camp, Bekali heard an officer saying, "It's time to bring in those with official records." After that date, doctors, teachers, and lawyers began to be brought into concentration camps. Every morning and before every meal, prisoners were made to read aloud words praising the Communist Party. Bekali, who said that anyone who missed these rituals was punished, noted that he was trained in communist doctrine every day of the week. Those sent to the camps had no chance of completing the so-called training before two years. Those staying in the camp did not have the opportunity to defy the orders of the staff there. Anyone who objects was immediately punished with beatings or put into cells. Saying that the Chinese regime claims that these so-called training centers liberate people's thoughts, Bekali said, "actually, the thing asked from prisoners is to listen to the party's orders" and emphasized that the opposite methods are followed. Bekali, who was not allowed to contact his family during his stay in the camp, informed the officers that he wanted to apply to the court in Karmay. On the 19th day, an officer came and said, "If you speak Chinese, they will come to see you," and he shouted in Uyghur, "Shoot me or send me back to prison; I do not accept your teaching." Thereupon, Bekali was thrown into the cell, and his arms bled while trying to get rid of the handcuffs. When the handcuffs were removed,he was not given any food. The next day, the camp officials called him and told him that he could return to Kazakhstan. As he left the prison, he shocked the officers by saying, "I can speak four more languages, including your language. I do have a master's degree in your language, and I was not going to learn it from uncivilized, and uncultured people like you." Bekali, who told the police at the door that he would seek his rights all the way, said that one purpose of the camps was to cut the people from their own nation. [46]

Raping of Young Women in Front of Other Prisoners!

"China describes it as a political camp, but it's a prison set up in the mountains." Sayragul Sauytbay is one of the few people to get a chance to be freed from concentration camps, and she refuted the propaganda of the Beijing government with this sentence. Because Sauytbay stayed in these camps as both a mandatory teacher and a prisoner, she witnessed how genocidal crimes, like Nazi crimes were committed. She also published her testimony, a book called The Chief Witness.

The signs of how the communist Chinese regime will sinicize the people of East Turkistan had already been seen before the concentration camps for Sayragül Sauytbay, her family, and other Uyghurs were put into operation. Her son's mouth, who was studying in kindergarten in 2016, was taped because he spoke the Kazakh language. After this event, her husband went to Kazakhstan, taking their two children. She planned to join them later. However, the Beijing regime's evil methods immediately came into play, and her passport was confiscated. She would not be able to see her children for a long time. After a while, the Communist Chinese regime's 'Friendship Service' knocked on Muslim Uyghurs' doors. 'Staffed relatives' come and stay in the houses for 8 days every month. During their stay, Muslim and conservative Uyghurs are forced to drink alcohol and eat pork in an attempt to sinicize them. Muslim people were asked to share their beds with these staffed guests. In the most intimate part of the house, they were tortured by forcibly sharing the same bed with an unrelated person. Those who opposed were immediately notified to the relevant authorities and sent to the camps. Staffed officials also took photos of every crime they committed and passed them on to their Chinese superiors. After this move, the next step for bringing down the Muslim Uyghur family was "to take down anyone to be taken down" and send them to camps.

As of 2016, it is heard almost every day that an acquaintance or a relative has been picked up and taken away. Now women and men prepare small bags and wait ready at the door. The expected day came for Sauytbay, and she was taken to a concentration camp. Because of her medical education and her profession as a teacher in her past, the camp administrators forced her to become a Chinese teacher. She taught Chinese to the prisoners in the camp and made them sing the songs of Communist propaganda. 5 cameras were monitoring her cell. The other prisoners were deployed in a 16-square-foot space in groups of 20 people. All the women had their hair shaved off, held in inmate clothes and handcuffs. Chinese cosmetics companies used the prisoners' hair to make wigs. These wigs and false hair products were caught at American customs. Because of her medical background, Sauytbay was also assigned to the infirmary. During this assignment, she witnessed prisoners being given drugs, even though they had no disease. Sauytbay later learned that these drugs were sterilizing female prisoners. Sauytbay also witnessed guards raping a young girl in front of 200 prisoners and punished prisoners who were uncomfortable watching it. She personally experienced one of the most shameful scenes in human history. Sauytbay, who was sent from the camp after 5 months of imprisonment, managed to find a way to go to Kazakhstan, where her family lives. Sauytbay, who was taken to court for trespassing on the border with Kazakhstan, was sentenced to a detention period; fortunately, she was not extradited to China. Sauytbay and her family applied for asylum in Sweden, and after her request was approved, they settled there. "I have to tell the world what I have experienced," said Sauytbay, who wrote a book about the experiences she went through to announce the genocide suffered by Uyghurs. She is still subject to threats and blackmail by the 'long arms' of the Chinese government, but she calls on the world to take action for Uyghurs despite this. [47]

The ordeal of the East Turkistan people, which began with being sent to concentration camps, continued after completing the so-called training there. In the repression process, which begins with the police station and continues with the concentration camp, the Muslim people are shown two ways. Some of them are sent to jail for fabricated crimes that have been found by researching their lives before the concentration camp. While some of them are held in concentration camps, a significant portion of those staying in the camp are forced to work as slaves in factories where production is made for western companies.

First, Choose a Crime From the List, and Then Go to Court!

The Communist Chinese regime does not care about the rules of international law and universal human rights principles. Prisoners held in concentration camps for a certain period of time are tried in showpiece courts and sent to prison. According to a study by German media outlet Deutsche Welle (DW), which interviewed survivors of the camps, the Beijing government has taken another step to continue the pressure. The victims, who spoke to DW and escaped the camps, taking refuge in other countries, said that one day the officers came with a list in their hands and asked them to choose a crime that they did not commit from this list. Among the crimes on this list, there are articles that no one can define as a crime in normal life, such as wearing a headscarf, performing prayers, growing a beard, making phone calls, or traveling abroad. These lists are the same as the 'objectionable religious activities' document distributed by the Beijing regime in East Turkistan in 2014. One of the witnesses interviewed by the German broadcasting channel said that he had a list lit on his hand while he was being treated in a hospital for tuberculosis. Another was one employed as a teacher at the camp. While he was teaching, a staff member came and handed him the list and asked him to choose one. The officers threatened them by saying, "You have to choose a crime from the list. If you don't choose a crime, it means you don't confess your crime. That means you'll stay here forever." Prisoners forced to choose are caught between two emotions: the worry of not seeing their relatives for a long time after choosing a crime from the list and the comfort of learning how long they will stay between four walls. Prisoners who are taken to showpiece courts immediately after choosing their crimes did not even have a legal representative. The crimes they select from the list are read in the face of the detainees in these courts, and they are asked to promise that they will not commit that crime again. According to one of the witnesses, the expression expected from prisoners is as follows: "I regret my crime, I promise that I will not commit this crime again." The witness, who was sentenced to 2 years of imprisonment, was suddenly thinking about what he would do for two years, and on the other hand, he was grateful when he saw the others with 10 years of prison. The so-called Chinese Communist regime courts gave the heaviest punishment to those who committed objectionable crimes such as "regular worship." [48] The imposition of the heaviest punishments on the religious shows that the ' purpose of the Beijing regime is to remove Islam's traces. DW's applications to the relevant Chinese authorities for these explanations were not answered. In response, the links to the statements made by the official authorities were sent. [49] In these showpiece courts, prominent Muslim Uyghurs, Kazakhs, and Kyrgyz received the highest sentences. Filmmaker Hursan Hassan, award-winning academic Rahile Dawut, writer Yalqun Rozi, Abdulqadir Jalaleddin and thousands more are among those who were sent to concentration camps by the Beijing government and punished for fabricated crimes.

The German broadcasting channel also interviewed people in the diaspora whose relatives were in concentration camps. According to these interviews, many oppressed people commute between prisons and concentration camps. And some are punished twice in a row. After the so-called courts were finished, these people began to disappear. Some were chained to their hands and feet and transported to prisons. A significant number of those who were called by their names never returned. Most of the rest were sent to work in factories as slave laborers.

China Has Resurrected the Order of Slavery!
It has been centuries since European colonists used the people they kidnapped from Africa as slaves. Slavery in America was abolished in 1865. After a century and a half, world societies were once again faced with the reality of slavery. The Communist Chinese regime first brainwashed the people it had gathered in camps in East Turkistan. Those deemed potentially dangerous by the regime were sent to prison, and the rest were employed as slaves in factories. Many companies, including Western giant firms, exploit the labor of Muslim Uyghurs and other societies. The Australian Strategic Policy Institute published a report last March with the title of 'Uyghurs For Sale.' With this report, the Institute revealed that slavery had been resurrected in the 21st century, again. The report states that between 2017 and 2019, 80,000 Muslim Uyghurs were sent to work in factories outside East Turkistan. But according to the information received from the region, this figure is much higher. According to ASPI's findings, these workers are employed in factories during the day and then attend ideology vaccination classes prepared within the framework of communist doctrine in the evenings. The enslavement program, which the Communist Chinese regime maintained as a social engineering, also serves international supply chains' economic interests. The factories where these victims of forced labor worked make production for 82 well-known brands worldwide. The semi-military order established in the factories turns Uyghur slave workers' lives into hell by keeping them under constant surveillance. [50]

After the report was published, it could not be discussed in the international public as it deserves. The fight against the Covid-19 virus epidemic, which came again from China, was on the world agenda. However, details in the report indicate that a 'slave market' was established in East Turkistan. When the postings of the intermediary companies supplying Chinese workers are examined, the following statements can be seen: "Our company is ready to send a large number of workers from the Xinjiang region on state bail. Government-led, working units, high quality, safe, and reliable. Male and female ratio and age characteristics differ." Moreover, a caricatured Uyghur man and woman were placed in the ad. Another ad has this title: "1,000 ethnic minorities are waiting for online reservations." Details of the announcement are striking: "The Xinjiang administration organized 1000 people educated in Xinjiang and passed political and health qualifications. They are aged between 16 and 18 and are registered by the Xinjiang administration. Factories may apply to Xinjiang police stations. It starts with a one-year contract. A chef from Xinjiang can also be supplied for easy management. Employees will be at the factory within 15 days after signing. Anyone who needs an employee can apply immediately. Advantages of employees in Xinjiang: They are suitable for the semi-military management system, they can handle difficult jobs, there is no loss of personnel, they work during the contract. The minimum order limit is 100 workers". In this "slave market" system of the Beijing administration; there are also factors that encourage (!) local administrators and intermediary companies. If a company arranges slave labor in Xinjiang, it receives about $3 per person. If the worker is sent to another region, this price increases 15 times, and the company earns a bonus of $43.25. Factories that accept Muslim slave workers are given $145 if the contract is made for a year, and $720 if made for 3 years. [51]

Western companies listed in the ASPI report as having benefited from the forced labor system include: Abercrombie & Fitch, Acer, Adidas, Alstom, Amazon, Apple, ASUS, BAIC Motor, Bestway, BMW, Bombardier, Bosch, BYD, Calvin Klein, Candy, Carter's, Cerruti 1881, Changan Automobile, Cisco, CRRC, Dell, Electrolux, Fila, Founder Group, GAC Group (automobiles), Gap, Geely Auto, General Motors, Google, Goertek, H&M, Haier, Hart Schaffner Marx, Hisense, Hitachi, HP, HTC, Huawei, iFlyTek, Jack & Jones, Jaguar, Japan Display Inc., L.L. Bean, Lacoste, Land Rover, Lenovo, LG, Li-Ning, Mayor, Meizu, Mercedes-Benz, MG, Microsoft, Mitsubishi, Mitsumi, Nike, Nintendo, Nokia, Oculus, Oppo, Panasonic, Polo Ralph Lauren, Puma, SAIC Motor, Samsung, SGMW, Sharp, Siemens, Skechers, Sony, TDK, Tommy Hilfiger, Toshiba, Tsinghua Tongfang, Uniqlo, Victoria's Secret, Vivo, Volkswagen, Xiaomi, Zara, Zegna, and ZTE. [52] The bill that prohibits American companies from benefiting from this system, in which the Chinese Communist Regime used East Turkistan Muslims as slave workers, passed the American Congress. [53]. The discussions held in the Senate on this draft law at the time of this study could not be completed due to the election process. But it has also been reported that Apple, the global giant, is lobbying for changes to the law that would eliminate its own crimes. [54] In the first period when the virus was outbroken from Wuhan, China, while all countries stopped their production activities within the scope of anti-virus measures, the Beijing government continued to send the slave workers from East Turkistan to work in the inner regions. In February and March, tens of thousands of slave Muslim workers were sent to China's interior parts. [55] The public also revealed that the forced labored Uyghur also manufactured the masks sent by the Beijing government within the scope of lobbying and influence efforts in the countries affected by the virus and the masks produced for commercial purposes. According to the research published in the New York Times, while there are ' four businesses producing masks and similar materials in East Turkistan, this number has now increased to 51. It is clear that 17 of the companies that started to produce masks also benefited from the forced labor program. The masks produced in these factories have been delivered to many countries of the world, including America. [56] The reactions from many western countries, especially America, continue to rise to stop this inhuman system created by the PRC in line with its economic interests and goals of becoming a world leader. Most recently, Canadian parliamentarians defined the events in East Turkistan as genocide and asked the government to impose sanctions on China. Likewise, the Uyghur Human Rights Act, which was enacted with the support of almost all Congress and the Senate in the USA, was approved by President Trump. The decision to impose sanctions on the responsible Chinese authorities was published. Despite all these international pressures, the pressure of the Beijing regime on the people of East Turkistan continues. While women were separated from their husbands and children sent to work in factories, they were also forcibly spayed.

The Muslim Generation is in Danger of Annihilation

One of the crimes that the United Nations accepted as genocide is to take measures to prevent births in a society. The Chinese Communist Regime, which changed Muslim Uyghurs' living conditions to be considered part of genocide, also committed another crime by preventing Uyghur and Kazakh births. The forced sterilization of women, mentioned in the previous pages and described by those held in the concentration camps, is a systematic practice initiated against women in detention and all women by China. How the population rate of Muslim people in East Turkistan decreased with this sterilization program was stated in the report published this year by German researcher Adrian Zenz. The report with the title of "Sterilizations, IUDs, and Mandatory Birth Control: The CCP's Campaign to Suppress Uyghur Birthrates in Xinjiang."

Was published by the American-based Jamestown Foundation and announced by the AP News Agency. According to both the information told by the witnesses and the examinations made on official data, the Chinese government regularly checks whether minority women are pregnant in East Turkistan and forces hundreds of thousands of women to sterilize or even abort with intrauterine devices (IUD). As a result, IUD and sterilization methods declined throughout China, increasing rapidly in East Turkistan. As mentioned in the Qaraqash document, which contains a list of crimes attributed to those sent to concentration camps, the Beijing government considered it a major crime not to comply with birth control. Even in places like Hotan and Kashgar in East

Turkistan, the Uyghur community's population fell by 60 percent from 2015 to 2018. This rate is 4.2 percent in general in China. While the population growth rate in East Turkistan was 4.06 per thousand in 2018, this rate decreased to 2.58 per thousand among the Muslim population. While 200,000 IUDs were used in the region in 2014, this number increased by 60 percent in 2018 and exceeded 330,000. These devices are not used in other regions of China. [57]

Darren Byler, of Colorado University, said: "Here the goal is to reduce their presence, if not completely assimilate them. It's an easy method to assimilate them in China's crowded population." From the University of New Castle in the UK, Joanne Smith Finley said: "This is genocide, and it must be stopped. This is not a genocide with mass killings, but it is a slower, more painful, and chilling genocide. These mean genetically reducing the population of the Uyghur people." Representatives of the Chinese Regime claimed that this report and the news were unfounded and that everyone in East Turkistan had to obey the law. [58] However, what happened to Qelbinur Sedik, a teacher in the camps, and what she saw around her showed that the Beijing government's statements were intended to conceal its crimes. Since the People's Republic of China sees the Muslim presence in East Turkistan as an obstacle to its long-term neo-colonial plans, they think this obstacle should be eliminated by violating international values and human rights. If necessary, Muslim children are taken from their families and placed in dormitories to be raised as communists.

900 Thousand Missing Children?

One of the issues which are needs to pay attention is the kidnapping of the children of Muslim Uyghurs, Kazakhs, and other members of the society. According to the news published by the New York Times on December 28, 2019, approximately 500,000 non-Han Chinese children were placed in the communist regime's public schools as boarders. The Beijing Government, which sent parents to concentration camps, also sent their children to boarding schools to be raised under the communist doctrine. Based on the figures in the official sources of China, the studies revealed that the Beijing government placed half a million children in boarding schools in East Turkistan and also built new orphanages in every city. The goal of the Chinese government is to transform one in two schools into a boarding school in all cities, starting with towns with a population of more than 800. The order of the boarding school systems of the Chinese Communist regime is very similar to the military system. It is very difficult to get information about schools, they are constantly under security control. The main purpose here is to erase the Muslim identity, which President Xi sees as extremism, from children. [59] The Beijing regime wants to train generations that will serve as lead soldiers in the construction of the new colonial system. Starting from kindergarten, children are taught "to love the Party and China." As a result of this doctrinairism, children have become unable to recognize their families. Abdurrahman Tohti, who lives in Istanbul, is one of the living witnesses of this. Tohti, who found his child by seeing a photo posted on social media, discovered that his child no longer spoke the same language as him.

In the research published on the World Uyghur Congress website and reported by Radio Free Asia, it was confirmed that the children were sent to orphanages by contacting local authorities in Kashgar regions. Although the Beijing government has made statements that children are well cared for there, according to employees, the actual situation is the opposite: "There has been a significant increase in the number of Uyghur children brought in recently. Among them are 6-month-old breastfeeding babies, as well as 12-year-olds." When the inspector or outside guests arrive at these schools, the facts are hidden by preparing a child or two for show. An Uyghur who served there said: "Even their parents are not allowed to learn the fate of children. They stay in closed buildings that are almost beyond the reach of birds." He also stated that the children were being placed with Chinese families. In its report, which Human Rights Watch (HRW) draws attention to the issue, it is stated in the records that the Communist Party Secretariat of the Uyghur Region has ordered all orphans to be placed in state orphanages by 2020. While the rate of children placed in kindergartens was 24 percent in 2017, it is aimed by the Beijing administration to increase this figure to 100 percent by the end of this year. According to the BBC's research, the money spent by the communist regime for the construction of boarding kindergartens and orphanages is 1.2 billion dollars. Researcher Adrian Zenz briefly emphasized what happened as follows: "According to the evidence obtained, it should be called a cultural genocide." [60] In the research published by Adrian Zenz in October, it was stated that there had been an extraordinary increase in the number of East Turkistan children studying in boarding schools in the last two years. The number of students going outside the city, which was 500,000, increased by approximately 380,000 between 2017 and 2019, and this number reached almost 900,000. Throughout East Turkistan, there has been an increase of 76.9 percent in the number of children who have been educated in boarding schools since 2017. [61] Rushan Abbas, an activist who struggled to stop the genocide to which the Uyghur people were subjected, said: "Uyghur children whose parents are kept in concentration camps or forced to work as slaves in factories are brainwashed in the orphanages of the Chinese Communist Party. Many are being starved and beaten. Uyghur families today live under unbearable conditions. They are facing genocide." [62] The world public opinion did not give the deserved response to this call of Abbas. In the international order where the Chinese regime, which has committed so many crimes in the name of genocide, is elected a member of the UN Human Rights Commission, it is difficult to break from the chain of economic interests formed by the Beijing Government with its neo-colonial ambitions. For this reason, even Muslim countries do not raise their voices against the destruction of the traces of Islam in East Turkistan.

8,500 Mosques Destroyed by China:
Why Does the Islamic World Remain Silent?

Cultural genocide is another crime committed by the Chinese communist regime to destroy the Muslim people of East Turkistan, targeted for neo-colonialist ambitions. While the number of concentration camps and their area is increasing, historical mosques, cemeteries, and mausoleums are demolished. Details of how the historical and cultural heritage in the region has been destroyed are given in another report by ASPI, founder of the Xinjiang Data Project. This systematic destruction, reminiscent of the destruction during the Cultural Revolution, when the mosques in East Turkistan were turned into pig stables, aims to leave no trace of Islam. In the demolition project that started in 2017, 16,500 mosques have been damaged so far. 8,500 of them were destroyed. In the historical region of East Turkistan, 5,931 mosques in Kashgar, 2,900 in Hotan, 2,540 in Aksu, and 1085 mosques in Ili were either damaged or destroyed. Together with other cities, the total figure is 16,500. In Hotan, where all of the mosques were demolished, ' a showpiece building in the city center was left untouched, and a limited number of people prayed here for the Friday prayer. In Kashgar, all mosques are closed. [63]

A similar example of the red guards of the cultural revolution turning mosques into pig stables took place in Kashgar, and a mosque here was turned into a bar. The destruction was limited to mosques and targeted shrines that have an important place in Uyghurs' lives. For example, Imam Asim's mausoleum and outbuildings, where thousands of Uyghur Muslims come together every year with various events, have been severely damaged. What kind of destruction has been carried out is clearly evident when past satellite images are examined. In the newly captured satellite data, there are ' traces of trees there.

According to some images shared on social media, a previously closed mosque in East Turkistan was used as a restaurant with alcohol in Ramadan last year, and Han Chinese people drank and danced there. Many historical mosques were turned into restaurants or cafes after their features of being places of worship were eliminated. Pictures of Xi, communist doctrine slogans, and regime propaganda were hung on mosques' walls, and the historical writings there were dismantled. Nathan Ruser, one of the researchers, said that "Destruction is being carried out in a way that has not been seen since the Cultural Revolution." Rachel Harris, an expert on Uyghur music and culture at the University of London, reviewed the report and said: "What we see here is the deliberate destruction of places that are the heritage of the Uyghur people and the heritage of these lands." The following statement of Zang Xunmou, the Director CCP United Front Work, the unit of the Chinese government that monitors the work on these issues, also shows the aim of the regime: "The ultimate goal in religious studies is to complete the process of sinicization from inside and outside." While these demolitions were carried out in front of the eyes of the whole world, no statement has been made by the Organization of Islamic Cooperation, the roof organization of Islamic countries. The OIC continues to see no evil, hear no evil, speak no evil. On the other hand, the United Nations Educational, Scientific and Cultural Organization (UNESCO) and the International Council on Monuments and Sites (ICOMOS) also remained silent. ASPI has called on these two organizations to take action and stop this destruction that China has started. [64] The Australian research organization and organizations working in the region explained that the biggest problem they faced during the period when they prepared this report was that the Beijing regime restricted access to information and avoided providing information to people with the regime's advanced technology systems. The regime has turned East Turkistan into an open prison, not with the fence of concentration camps but also with virtual firewalls.

"1984" Come True: Digital Genocide!

In 2018, International Human Rights Watch (HRW) acquired one of the programs used by the Communist Chinese Regime in East Turkistan to monitor the Muslim population there. Thanks to the program developed by the Integrated Joint Operations Platform (IJOP) and established by the Beijing government in the region, the regime detects potentially dangerous people and immediately detains them and sends them to concentration camps. HRW's report investigating this practice's effects in 2019 revealed how this program was used as a weapon. IJOP Application is used for three main functions:

· Collecting personal information.

· Reporting activities and situations that may be considered suspicious.

· Marking people who may be considered threats with a red flag.

The IJOP application marks activities that cause people to be sent to concentration camps and are considered criminal activities as dangerous. The application can consider many natural behaviors such as praying, greeting a neighbor, entering the building through the back door as suspicious. According to the same system, if a person has made a new friend and this person has a connection with abroad, that person is also considered dangerous. [65]

Details of how the heavy surveillance systems established in the region surrounded the Muslim population were also conveyed in a documentary broadcast on Frontline, one of the American Broadcasting Channel PBS programs at the beginning of this year. According to the documentary prepared by Robin Barnwell and Gasbeen Mohammad, every moment of people's life in East Turkistan is observed 24 hours a day, 7 days a week. According to the new legal regulations valid in the region, all citizens must download a special application to their phones. Thanks to this application, security guards can connect to the citizens' phones, and a police officer who takes the phone can send all the data of that person to the IJOP center with the application on his phone. For this reason, all information such as SMS messages, photos, and searches made on the internet are collected at this surveillance center. After the September 11 attacks, China, which started a war on everything based on the US's argument, started to equip entire East Turkistan with security cameras. In East Turkistan, which has turned into a test laboratory for every new technology in security, programs have been used to interpret every data, from face-scanning systems to making sense of the person's walk. Therefore, when a person starts running on the street, he/she can be perceived as a potential threat and can be arrested at the first security point. Thanks to the QR code systems placed on the houses' doors, all information about who lives in the houses can be displayed. If a person in the house is not registered in that house, this means a suspicious situation. Given that the number of technology companies operating in East Turkistan is 200,000, it is understood that people are unable to breathe. Chinese President Xi's proposal to use the QR code for international travel is also a sign of how he will establish order if he dominates the world in the future. The Han Chinese who act as agents are added to the data obtained from digital sources in East Turkistan. Thus, the IJOP system analyzes using all these data and currently builds the world's largest data banks where personal data are collected. Among the project partners of these programs are American and other Western companies. As expected, the Chinese regime never complies with the universal rules of human rights when performing these practices. As a matter of fact, a technology company's response in the region to the Frontline team has gone down in history. The officer, by referring to the Uyghurs, said: "What human rights? They don't have any rights." [66] From the point of view of the Communist Chinese regime, as long as the people of East Turkistan do not accept sinicization, they can be the workers who will be employed as slaves in the factory, the patients who need to be treated because they believe in Islam, or an entity that will donate their organs when necessary. The daily lives of these entities and their genetic information are collected and stored for future use. That is why the Chinese regime collects everyone's DNA in all autonomous regions and inland China regions, starting with East Turkistan.

East Turkistan Catalogued, Time to Collect DNA of Other Peoples

It is now an undeniable fact that the People's Republic of China (PRC) collects people's DNA in areas such as East Turkistan and Tibet. This is proved both by official documents and by the accounts of those sent to concentration camps and those served there. To date, the Chinese government has made defenses against publications on DNA collection such as "for research purposes" and "to assist in tracking criminals." But the collection of millions of people's DNA suggests that data are being aggregated to be used in building new management systems in the future, not for research. According to the ASPI report, the number of people whose DNA samples are collected by the program, which was launched in other regions and occupied territories in the west, exceeded 70 million. In some sources, it is also stated that this number exceeds 150 million. In the genetic data collected by the Chinese regime, repetitive cataloging of DNA regions specific to the Y chromosome, known as short tandem repeats (STRs) in technical terms, is performed. The science of genetics has explained that Y-specific STRs are similar between males of the same male lineage. In this case, with the Y-STR sample taken from any man, it is possible to obtain information about that person's father and male relatives' identity. Thus, the Communist regime combines these Y-STR data with other data to reveal the pedigree of people. DNA samples are undoubtedly of great importance in catching criminals. However, while in many countries DNA data is destroyed after being collected and processed, the Chinese government's desire to keep these data indefinitely raises the question of what purposes it will be used for in the future. Also, the absence of any legal regulation on DNA collection allows China to act as it wishes without being accountable. This poses a risk to the future of societies. [67] The Beijing government uses its own public health units and private companies when collecting this data. They are a part of this system that attacks individuals' privacy and makes private companies also accomplices. For example, 140,000 DNA test kits were sold to Huangrui Scientific Instruments company, which sells medical, chemical, and scientific products in Hunan province, and the public security bureau by the American-based Thermo Fisher company. This company, which is among the 500 largest companies in America and criticized for developing practices against human rights in East Turkistan, has not made any statement to date. The kits Thermo Fisher sent can extract the DNA of a fifth of the men in that city. The Chinese Forensic Genomics International company also boasts its activities in this field. [68] Likewise, Chinese President Xi regards the concentration camps he established in East Turkistan, the surveillance systems based on advanced technology, and the results he achieved by crushing and destroying the people through steps such as Islam's sinicization success. However, rising Chinese nationalism constitutes the greatest motivation for Xi and the policies he developed. Nationalist movements that have become widespread in social media and internet channels in recent years tolerate all kinds of oppression against the Muslim people living in the region.

Hostility to the Muslim Populace Increased with Han Nationalism

After the Mao administration captured East Turkistan in 1949, the biggest and most important goal of both the Mao regime and subsequent administrations and today's Xi regime was the region's complete sinicization. The method used to rule millions of Muslims is the same as the methods described in George Orwell's novel 1984. In his book, Orwell asks, "How does man rule over a man?" and then answers the question: "By agonizing." The reflection of the ruling by agonizing is genocide camps. In implementing such a method, "an enemy" is needed to strengthen nationalist feelings among its supporters and support genocide policies. The enemy in East Turkistan's territory is Uyghurs, Kazakhs, and other communities who believe in Islam. In China, where the whole country was ruled with an iron fist starting from Mao until the Deng period, the regime began to banish criticisms of its own policies by promoting Han nationalism. Especially after the Tiananmen events in 1989, Han Chinese feelings of nationalism were raised to strengthen the Communist regime and the Chinese people. To keep these feelings alive, Islam has been targeted as the enemy. [69] An order in which Han nationalism has become stronger by every incident and the Muslim people in the region are no longer "seen as a human being" has been established in East Turkistan. The policies of the Chinese Communist regime towards Muslims were welcomed among Han Chinese, where nationalism was strong. Han Chinese applauded the sending of thousands of people to concentration camps one night. Chinese nationalism, "humiliated" by western states during the opium wars in the 1800s, is living its golden age in the Xi period. The fascistic thought that the Chinese will rule the world and that Chinese culture will prevail everywhere has shown that the practices depicted in the novel 1984 can also be implemented in real life. The nationalism that nurtured the communist regime and was raised through the Han Chinese is similar to the approach of dividing people into two groups of "good" and "evil," which is described by Orwell in his book "Prophecies of Fascism." [70] Because, according to Chinese nationalism, Han Chinese always represent "good" and Muslims represent "evil." The Han Chinese, who regard themselves as superior and their desire to have endless power, which is the constant aim of every nationalism, have always been in favor of "one of us", with fascistic feelings rather than in favor of the people, despite all the apparent shreds of evidence of the communist regime's genocide in East Turkistan.

Chinese, who tolerate the destruction of people in concentration camps, describes the Muslim Uyghurs as "ignorant, inferior and backward" since they are not "one of them". He treats Muslims there as lepers and does not allow them to live in their own apartments. Han nationalists treat the people of East Turkistan, whom the regime is trying to hold back in economic and social terms, as foreigners in their homeland. In other words, Chinese fascists, who migrated to the region, want to drive out the true owners of the Uyghur territory. The Han Chinese, who occupied cities such as Kashgar and Hotan, which were once the educational and cultural centers of the world, ignore the civilization that existed there before and constantly humiliate other societies. This racist nationalism found among many Han Chinese, who hate Muslim Uyghurs through the provocation of regime-backed propaganda, is equally exclusionary against other nations. Attacks and exclusion targeting African descent in China have increased at a time when all people stand up against racism after the murder of a young black by the police in America. People of African descent were kicked out of their apartments, fired from their jobs, evacuated from hotels, and beaten in the streets. The words of an African university student who taught English to a Muslim Uyghur youth is one of the most striking examples of Han Chinese fascism: "It is really difficult to live in a country where you constantly have to hide when you go out. I don't really know what the purpose of the Chinese is in both accepting foreign students and making their lives difficult at the same time. Living as a foreigner in China is like living in hell." [71]

As stated at the beginning of this chapter, Han nationalism, the PRC's supporter and its policies, has one goal. To become the world's new superpower. It acts by destroying every obstacle that stands in its way to becoming a superpower. All kinds of genocide crimes are committed there, as the Muslim people living in East Turkistan are also seen as an obstacle to the Beijing government to be destroyed. Very few of the atrocities and tortures carried out behind both real walls, and the world has noticed virtual walls. The stories of the survivors of the concentration camps are ' the tip of the iceberg.

In terms of the Communist Chinese Regime, the destruction or extermination of the people in the region does not prevent economic projections. The Bingtuan, or XPCC, as described in the previous chapters, continues its activities with approximately 2.39 million employees and thousands of companies. There are very few people from Uyghurs, Kazakhs, and other communities in this organization, based on Han Chinese nationalism. This economic model created by the XPCC is also wanted to be exported to the world by the Chinese regime through the One Belt and Road Initiative. In the next chapter, XPCC and BRI will be examined from this perspective.

6

The Bingtuan – Xinjiang Production Construction Corps (XPCC): The Chinese Version of Exploitation

"Bingtuan is a weird mixture of 'party, army, government and private sector'. All of the above, but still none of the above... for the Uyghur community, Bingtuan is a symbol of ethnic hostility" [1]
Prof. Dr. Ilham Tohti

THIS IS HOW UYGHUR scientist Prof. Ilham Tohti, who was sentenced to life imprisonment after being arrested in January 2014, describes the Bingtuan, the biggest colonial system of the Chinese Communist Regime. The Xinjiang Production and Construction Corps (XPCC), or as it is known, Bingtuan, is one of the world's largest paramilitary, semi-public, and semi-private sector organizations. This giant organization is reminiscent of the East Indian Company, founded by the British royal court with the approval of Queen Elizabeth I of England for colonial activities of the British Empire in Asia. The East Indian Company, which continued its activities until 1874, had its own army, its own region, thousands of sub-companies, and it had a larger organization than the world's giant companies today. The company even collected the taxes itself through agreements with the administrations of the countries they exploited. [2] The most striking factors that turned the East India Company into one of the world's largest organizations and even made it superior to the Chinese emperors in the Opium Wars are that it both had royal power behind it and controlled Asia's trade channels. The Chinese, who were "humiliated" by the British, want to take the world under their control with Bingtuan, which they established in East Turkistan and are planning with the Belt and Road Initiative (BRI) they developed. British colonists enslaved the people of Asia and Africa, and the Communist Chinese regime uses Uyghurs as slaves today. While tea was the most important commercial commodity for the British, cotton and oil ranked first as the most important commodity for Bingtuan today. The world has slowly started to be exposed to the truth about the colonial corps Bingtuan, mostly after the US wanted to impose sanctions. America has blacklisted Bingtuan for its human rights violations.

Bingtuan, the colonial corps of the Chinese Communist regime directly and indirectly manages 862,600 companies. It operates in 147 countries, including America and the UK. It has 2,114companies in the US alone and has partnerships with 71 American companies. Founded in 1954, Bingtuan now operates as a state within East Turkistan and works directly under the Beijing government. The communist Chinese regime exploits East Turkistan lands with this colonial army and develops new policies to destroy the Muslim people to have all the wealth there. In this chapter, the emergence and growth of this economic monster created by Mao will be discussed.

What is Bingtuan?

The Bingtuan model was first established based on military units in various parts of China before East Turkistan. Military units engaged in agriculture were established throughout China, not ' during the Mao era but also during the Imperial era. Those in these units also had to engage in agriculture to fight, to earn a living, and to care for their families as a state duty. Depending on the situation, some have been active in military matters, others in agriculture and production. However, the military units established in the northwestern regions, including East Turkistan, have served China's colonial ambitions since the imperial period. [3] Except for the homeland of Muslim Uyghurs, 12 Bingtuan organizations were established in 18 regions until the 1970s. All but the one in East Turkistan were short-lived and liquidated after a while. Although the purpose of the Mao regime for establishing Bingtuan in the Muslim people region is explained as the development of the "new frontier" (Xinjiang) under occupation, the main and real purpose is the sinicization of East Turkistan. The official establishment of Bingtuan is based on the decision of "104,000 PLA soldiers to be assigned for civil affairs" taken at the National Congress of the Chinese Communist Party on October 7, 1954. [4] Approximately 100,000 soldiers of Guamindong, also known as soldiers of the Nationalist Chinese government, were included in the PLA troops. [5] Bingtuan, which was a part of the "grand plan for the borders" of Lui Shaoqi, one of the most powerful figures of the Mao period, actually played a critical role in the continuation of the colonization of East Turkistan for both controlling the western regions and sinicization, as Seymour said. [6]

Bingtuan's most important mission in terms of border protection emerged in the war between India and China in 1962 and the Ili region near the Kazakhstan border. [7] The official responsible for the northwestern regions of the authoritarian Mao regime during this period was Xi Zhongxun, the father of today's Chinese President Xi Jinping. In some sources, there is information that Xi Zhongxun sent members of the remain of "National Army" (Milli Armiye) of Muslim Uyghurs, Kazakhs, and other societies from the independent East Turkistan Republic to the war with India in 1962 to eliminate them as "war casualties." Apart from the Sino-Indian War and the events in Ili, Bingtuan's main mission is to own and therefore protect the claim that East Turkistan occupied by the Mao administration is Chinese territory. For this purpose, Bingtuan, rather than using military methods, kept non-Han Chinese societies under economic pressure and seized the region's most fertile lands. In the so-called land reform carried out by the Mao government, Bingtuan was given the most fertile lands in East Turkistan. The 20,865 prisoners, most of whom were political detainees, were sent by the regime in 1951 to work in Uyghurs' vast lands and later joined the Bingtuan team. With the Soviet style method of sending criminals to labor camps applied by the communist regime, the number of prisoners in Bingtuan exceeded 160,000 for a period. 100,000 Han Chinese who had "volunteered to develop the west" were migrated from various regions to East Turkistan. [8] Mao's administration also sent 40,000 women from China's Hunan and Shandong regions to reinforce these soldiers. These women, who were told to be soldiers, were forced into marriage with the soldiers there, and the number of Han Chinese families was wanted to be increased in this way. These women were also employed in the fields under Bingtuan. [9] One year after the cultural revolution started, the number of members exceeded 2 million, with hundreds of thousands of people who went to East Turkistan and joined Bingtuan with the guidance of the authoritarian communist regime that started a new campaign especially for young people. [10] But Bingtuan was also affected by the chaos of the cultural revolution. Dozens of people died in the period known as the "January 21 incident" in early 1967, and the regime completely transformed this colonial organization into a military unit. The liquidation decision taken in 1972 for similar semi-military organizations in other China regions was also applied for the XPCC. The number of Bingtuan members, which was 2.3 million before the cultural revolution, declined to 1.7 million in the period 1974-74.

When Bingtuan was first established, it was planned as 12 regions and 10 regiments under these regions according to their activity area. However, this method could not be implemented. In 1969, each region was instructed to establish its structure. The Bingtuan Support Service Department, which was established and other units, started to operate in transportation and mining. In December of the same year, it was decided that all Bingtuans should be gathered under the military unit in East Turkistan. Soldiers are assigned to manage all units. In 1975,

3,257 PLA soldiers were appointed as directors of Bingtuan units. [11] Bingtuan, which could not achieve economic success for many years in the first period of its establishment and was partially closed during the Cultural Revolution, was revived after Deng Xiaoping came to power. In addition to 137 farms cultivating 808,000 hectares of land from its establishment until 1972, Bingtuan established 58 new agricultural zones. Bingtuan expanded its activities towards the Tarim Basin between 1958 and 1966. Bingtuan, which played a role in establishing the Karakoram highway extending from Gansu to Pakistan in East Turkistan, has been structured according to a division to control the Muslim lands, especially in the northeastern, northwestern, and southwestern regions in East Turkistan. [12]

Reactivated in 1980, Bingtuan is divided into two main branches. These are the East Turkistan Agricultural Industry (Xinjiang Agriculture) and Trade Group. The effects of the outward expansion policy in the economy initiated during the Deng period were also felt, and Bingtuan has entered into joint ventures with countries such as the United States, Japan, Germany, Turkey, Singapore, Italy, Denmark, and Thailand, as well as the World Bank. On the other hand, it made a significant trade with the Soviet Union over the barter system. [13] By the 1990s, Bingtuan regained the human resources it lost during the cultural revolution, and the number of members increased to 2.4 million. [14] The most important change in Bingtuan's history was made towards this millennium, before China's membership in the World Trade Organization. This amendment was the dismissal of the PLA and the People's Armed Police Force (PAP) in commercial matters in July 1998, the designation of Bingtuan as a "company" in August, and the approval of its special courts and prosecution offices in December. [15] In other words, the legal ground for Bingtuan's "state within the state" position known by the public has been provided. Bingtuan, which expanded its structure apart from the administration in East Turkistan occupied by the Chinese Communist Regime, has continued to grow in the strategic points of the Muslim people's lands since its establishment. In particular, Bingtuan, which established a colonial order in the waterways, became a quasi-government institution, exploiting the region's resources and having no responsibility. Bingtuan's structure, defined as a mixture of 'party-state-military' when established, has taken the form of 'Party-Government-Military-Enterprise' over time. [16]

The Transition from Communist Bingtuan to Capitalist XPCC

One of the organizations that gained the greatest advantage of the period, when the People's Republic of China came to the fore with cheap labor and rapidly expanded its economy, is undoubtedly Bingtuan, or XPCC, which has taken a corporate appearance by leaving behind its military appearance. Bingtuan's name was heard worldwide after the US decided to sanction human rights violations in East Turkistan. Bingtuan, which attracted the international community's attention, continued to exist as a failed business for a long time after the 1950s. But this crucial regime, that the PRC has put forward since the 1980s, has the communist idea in terms of politics but has a more capitalist view than western states in terms of economy, also saved Bingtuan from financial failure. Bingtuan has now become one of the most ruthless players of savage capitalism. The size of the lands that Bingtuan seized forcibly, demonstrating the prototype of the PRC's management logic, in the period when it was first established is approximately 55,300 hectares. [17] In time, Bingtuan started to seize the fertile lands of East Turkistan piece by piece. In 1995, the size of the lands administered by Bingtuan increased to 6.8 million hectares. [18] Bingtuan, which carries out its establishment in East Turkistan divided into 14 regions, owns 174 agricultural enterprises under these regions. [19] Looking at China's publicly disclosed data, the number of companies 100 percent owned by Bingtuan, together with direct partnerships or indirect partnerships, is 861,600, as stated in this chapter's introduction. Bingtuan, which includes 12 percent of the working population in East Turkistan, has 17 percent of the region's gross national product. [20] Bingtuan has a great share in the "one black and one white - oil and cotton" sectors that form the basis of East Turkistan's economy. Bingtuan alone is the largest producer of cotton in East Turkistan. It controls 37 percent of cotton production there. This, in turn, is of great importance for China, which is the second in the world in cotton production. [21]

Another element that underlies Bingtuan, the Neo-colonial Chinese Communist regime's capitalist system, effectiveness in East Turkistan's economy is that it controls a significant part of the water resources. Nearly all of the XPCC's agricultural holdings were seized from the Muslim Uyghur people and were established along East Turkistan's rivers. Bingtuan, which allows the Han Chinese who migrated to the region to settle in a way that they do not need local governments in East Turkistan, gains an advantage in controlling water resources and dams and, consequently, industrialization and urbanization. Especially with the urbanization in the Tarim Basin regions in the south and taking steps to facilitate the lives of the Han chinese who came here, a social structure dominated not in the north of East Turkistan but also in the south. [22] Bingtuan is more than just a company that produces and sells what it produces; it is also a typical example of state capitalism. While expanding its factories, on the one hand, it also has a say in the management of some existing cities in East Turkistan. It also builds new cities with their own factories, schools, homes, police force, courts, and prisons. Bingtuan's administrative and political authority is as strong as that of the Communist Party Secretary in Xinjiang / East Turkistan. It runs its own system directly under the Beijing government, or rather under President Xi. Urbanization continued to grow rapidly after the city of Shihezi, which was established as Bingtuan's center. In 2004, Bingtuan established 38 new small settlements in various key regions in a short time. [23] Apart from these small settlements, four more new cities were built until 2007. This figure had already increased to nine in 2016. It is estimated that the number of these cities will soon increase to 12. It is stated in another source that 18 more new Bingtuan cities will be established by 2030, seven of which will be completed in the short term and 11 in the long term. [24]

A Typical Example of 21st-century Colonialism

A group of companies' activities, such as establishing new factories, building roads, and establishing hospitals, are seen as a step to support social development and increase welfare. But when it comes to China and Bingtuan, the output of its colonial mentality is very similar to the East Indian Company. Bingtuan is a conglomeration of companies that exploit the lands occupied by a colonial state. The Communist Party regime has tried all kinds of methods since the invasion in 1949 to transform the Muslim people of East Turkistan, who do not share the same race, language, religion, and culture with China, into a group of brainwashed, atheist, communists loyal to the party and the state, against all historical and social evidence. As stated before, while trying to keep the administration of the region on the one hand, it also works to increase the population of Han Chinese in the region and to assimilate the Muslim people. Founded in 1954, Bingtuan was seen as an ideal tool for the Communist Chinese Regime to connect the region economically and socially to Beijing. As Cliff states it, the Communist Party administration concluded that the continuation of the control of the political and economic structure of East Turkistan was critical as well as the expansion of this structure and saw Bingtuan as an excellent tool for this. Because it has accepted that controlling the region economically and militarily will become more important in the future. Instead of providing non-profit social services during the Mao era, Bingtuan was transformed into a civilian-looking structure with no social and military responsibilities. [25]

It is undeniable that Bingtuan, which looks like a civil and economic structurefrom the outside, took the opposite steps when looking at Muslim Uyghurs' practices in their homeland. The first thing to be determined is that Bingtuan's economic wealth ' benefits the Han Chinese population's social and economic development. Today, approximately 90 percent of Bingtuan's members, which has a population of 3 million and interacts with 5 million people, are Han

Chinese. The rest are Uyghurs, Kazakhs, Mongols, and other nationalities. This figure shows that the authoritarian Beijing government has never had a goal of economically and socially developing the people of East Turkistan. Most of the organization members, which is the economic dynamo of the region, are former soldiers and Han Chinese, a sign that it exploits the natural and local resources of East Turkistan. One of the Chinese Communist regime's goals with the Belt and Road Initiative is to establish new Bingtuans in the countries involved in this project. If you look at Chinese investments in Pakistan today, you can see that Chinese people are working in factories established by Chinese banks, built by Chinese companies, Chinese companies, and these people are investing their money in Chinese banks rather than the business and economic advantage of the Pakistani people. In other words, as in Bingtuan's case, economic prosperity is developed in such a way that it is beneficial to the capitalist system of the Communist Chinese regime. At this point, it is necessary to pay attention to the following statement made by a writer on the Uyghurbiz website, which was established based on the work of the famous economics professor Ilham Tohti, who was sentenced to life imprisonment by the Chinese authoritarian government: "For decades, Uyghurs have been kept away from Bingtuan cities. Bingtuan is built on a single ethnicity, and Uyghurs are marginalized. The construction of Bingtuan increased the discrimination between the two societies in Xinjinag". [26] Countries that open their doors to China today should pay attention to this experience in East Turkistan.

The Bingtuan Labor Camps

One of the simplest facts of economics is that the most important expense for economic enterprises is personnel costs; as personnel costs decrease, the companies' profit increases. While it has become such a profitable and large enterprise in recent years, the number of Bingtuan members has not decreased; on the contrary, it has increased. But as the number of members increased, the rate of profit also increased. Is this an economic success story? The answer to that question is absolutely no. Because this organization, which has been operating as the economic apparatus of a communist authoritarian state since its first establishment, employs a significant number of prisoners. The method of sending detainees to labor camps, also known as "Gulag brutality," which became popular with the Soviet leader Stalin in world history, is still practiced by Bingtuan. Even in the first year of its establishment, more than 20,000 prisoners were sent to East Turkistan to work in Bingtuan. A significant number of these prisoners are political detainees. In 1955, this figure increased to 160,000. In the following years, there was a partial decline in the number of prisoners sent. By the 1990s,

100,000 prisoners were working in Bingtuan. Most of those usually sentenced to 5 years in prison in China are sent to work in Bingtuan. [27]

Bingtuan has its own prison, court, police and Public Security Bureau and Justice Department. In 1997, the number of Prisons in Bingtuan was 24. [28] Today, there are 36 agricultural enterprises where prisoners work. 22 of them are in Shihezi, in the 8th region of Bingtuan. In recent years, it has been noted that the Bingtuan prisons are located very close to factories. [29] The number of Han Chinese employed in Bingtuan factories, and agricultural enterprises has declined in recent years. But this reduction is not because the XPCC administration has begun to consider human rights, but because they found alternatives for Han Chinese detainees, that is, putting slave laborers in place. This labor source is the establishment concentration camps starting from 2014, to conduct genocide against the Uyghur Muslims in East Turkistan. Bingtuan's use of military elements against the Uyghurs emerged when the people protested the discrimination and oppression against them. Bingtuan soldiers were used in the events in Barin in April 1990 and in the Ghulja demonstration on February 5, 1997. During this demonstration, those detained were taken to the local government's police stations and prisons in East Turkistan and Bingtuan's prisons. One of the biggest incidents in which military elements were used to suppress Uyghurs' demonstrations was July 5, 2009. This information is confirmed in the documents published by China as follows: "The XPCC sent its soldiers and took security measures to suppress the demonstrations on July 5, 2009 immediately." [30] In the following years, the Bingtuan system continued to suppress the Uyghurs in East Turkistan.

On the other hand, the main reason why the United States imposed sanctions on Bingtuan is because of the inhumane system of governance it established in East Turkistan. People from rural parts of Southern East Turkistan were sent forcefully to work in cotton enterprises, one of Bingtuan's most important activity areas. Because China rules the region with a system closed to outside worlds, it is impossible to obtain true data. However, as it is stated in Lehr's study, it is estimated that a large proportion of Uyghurs sent to work from the southern part of East Turkistan were part of the forced labor system. [31] The method in which young people are forced to work in the cotton collection business since Bingtuan's establishment has continued until recent years. Even the issue of young people working in the fields was raised in China's parliament. The Congressional-Executive Commission on China (CECC) found that middle and high school students were forced to pick cotton in 2006, 2008, and 2011. [32] As mentioned above, the priority in the system established by Bingtuan has always been the Han Chinese. Therefore, it is impossible to see people from other societies than Han Chinese regarding recruitment or influential positions. As a result, a model that is completely closed to the outside and which exploits the land it occupied, forces the people to work as slaves, has been created. For this reason, organizations that do business with Bingtuan need to carefully examine what structure they are facing because this parallel state structure is not an enterprise conducting economic activities as it appears from the outside.

An expert from East Turkistan who travels abroad on business occasions knows the Bingtuan model very well and does not want to mention his name. He drew attention to the latest actions of XPCC at a meeting he attended in Europe in November of this year. According to this expert, the United States sanctioned the XPCC was seen by the Chinese regime as an attack against its own models. As a result, Bingtuan's demands have been met without question in East Turkistan, dominated by Bingtuan. Neighborhood officials are used as unpaid workers, especially in Bingtuan enterprises, in the name of reducing costs. Even ordinary public members were taken to work in Bingtuan enterprises by these 'sheku' officials. Bingtuan also markets Muslims held in concentration camps to the factories in other parts of China. When a factory needs staff, it immediately contacts Bingtuan. The Bingtuan administration also acts as a slave market owner, sending Muslim Uyghurs who are in concentration camps or prisons to temporary work in these factories. The Bingtuan mentality, the slave Lord of Modern times, continues to earn money through the bloody labor of the Muslim people, colonialism. Because of America's sanctions, Bingtuan's managers think, "If America wants to punish us because of you, then we will punish you." And these managers continue their actions and attitudes that will cause them to be punished for genocide if the International Court of Justice tries them. This cruel attitude of Bingtuan's slave lords has spread to the guards of the prisons they run. Another witness who gave a speech at the same meeting and did not give his name for his family's safety said that some guards had set up a system that could be regarded as human trafficking, in which they sent personnel to Chinese factories in return for money. As a result, today, the Chinese Communist regime and those who rule the Bingtuan model have helped establish and operate detention facilities that will be considered part of the Muslim population's oppression in Turkistan and crimes of genocide. Bingtuan also took part in establishing advanced technology systems that turn the lives of the people of East Turkistan into hell. These systems include many systems such as face scanning, phone applications, cameras on the streets, code reading systems placed on the doors of the houses. It is, therefore, necessary to pay attention to Lehr's these statements: "These activities mean that it is a key factor of what the U.S. Holocaust Museum calls crimes against humanity. However, identifying XPCC-connected businesses can be difficult due to hidden ownership structures." [33]

It is necessary to remind once again that Bingtuan, which the Chinese Communist regime has used as a Trojan horse for the world's economic domination, operates in more than 140 countries. Especially after Xi Jinping took over and declared himself president of China permanently, the Beijing government seems to have taken tougher steps towards becoming the world's dominator. The Belt and Road Initiative (BRI), which is presented to the international public as if it will promote each country's social and economic well-being equally', is the cute face of China's neo-colonialism system. Given the examples of Pakistan, Egypt, and Sri Lanka, it is a fact that in the Bingtuan model, companies similar to Trojan horses will establish their economic order in the countries covered by the BRI in the future and will exploit these countries. This organization, which operates in many fields such as cotton, advanced technologies, and banking today, will not need local people in business or bankers in the countries where it carries its establishment. In other words, in this ostensible economic game whose rules are determined by China, the house will always win.

7

The BRI: The Chinese Version of Colonialism

President of China Xi Jinping first announced the Belt and Road Initiative (BRI) during a speech given on September 7th, 2013 at Nazarbayev University in Kazakhstan. His speech was titled "Promote People-to-People Friendship and Create a Better Future". (1)

BEFORE ADDRESSING THE BRI, it should be noted anecdotally that the choice of Kazakhstan as the place where the BRI was first announced, the new plan for the construction of world rule of the PRC, is not an ordinary step for Xi and Beijing government. Kazakhstan is the place where, according to Chinese thought, the method of state intervention in the economy dating back hundreds of years, in other words, the state capitalism, was applied for the first time and the ambition of China to take control of trade routes was first implemented. Silk, which was produced in China in the 2nd century BC, is transported to Rome by crossing through Asia. And then it is sold at very high prices. Realizing this price difference or high-profit rate, the Han emperor Wu-Ti immediately nationalized all silk production in his lands. The second step, mentioned by President Xi in his speech, is that Zhang Qian was sent to explore the territory of today's Kazakhstan or Turkestan at that time. (2) After this discovery, Emperor Wu-Ti ordered the creation of the Silk Road. As it is stated in the article of Prof. Dr. Alimcan İnayet, the Han Emperor first built outposts along the way. However, because of the high cost of building outposts, the difficulty of controlling the outposts, and the increase in the cost of silk, this time he planned to invade those lands. (3) One of the reasons for the Battle of Talas, in which the Chinese and Muslims confronted for the first time, was resistance to this occupation. Huns, Göktürks, Karakhanids and many other Turkic khanates established on that land stood as obstacles to the invasion attempts of China. But the historically, economically, and geographically im-

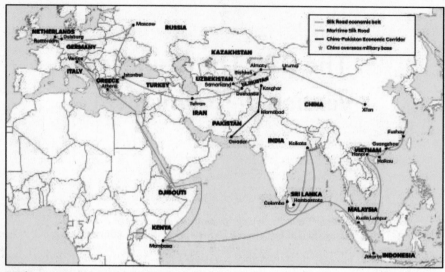

BRI (Geographical Intelligence Service–GIS)

portant territory of Central Asia has come under Chinese control after centuries of resistance. It is necessary to remember that history will not repeat itself from the perspective of seeking answers to many of the world's current questions in the past experiences of history. China, which wanted to conquer the whole of Asia for its own economic interests 2,000 years ago, desires to become the world's biggest colonial power again today. While Han emperors nationalized silk production at that time, today the authoritarian Xi regime expropriates economic activities in East Turkistan and other occupied lands with Han Chinese nationalism. Centuries ago, silk was important to China, and Turkestan lands had to be occupied for this silk. Today, white gold, in other words, cotton, is important, and keeping East Turkistan under occupation is the priority of the China. Emperor Wu-Ti wanted to take control of historical trade routes. On the other hand, President Xi is keen to seize not ' the trade routes that are the projection of the historical Silk Road but also the sea routes. In short, China, which adopted colonialism as its motto in the years before Christ, has appeared before the international public opinion as a neo-colonialist. As the Albanian Canadian Scholar, Olsi Jazexhi said, Beijing is determined not to make past mistakes, while the rest of the world is watching history repeat itself once again.

What is the BRI?

Chinese President Xi Jinping announced the 21st Century Maritime Silk Road in Indonesia in October, just one month after he declared the Silk Road Economic Belt in Kazakhstan in September 2013. The PRC covers the geography starting from China and expanding to the Central Asian countries, Russia and Europe, the Indian Ocean, the Persian Gulf, and the Mediterranean basin thanks to the Silk Road Economic Belt. The Maritime Silk Road, on the other hand, includes a sea route starting from Chinese ports and extending to Europe through the South China Sea and South Pacific, and a second sea route starting from South China and extending to the South Pacific. These two projects to be carried out together were first named as One Belt One Road (OBOR), and eventually evolved into the Belt and Road Initiative (BRI). One month after these speeches, it was decided at the 18th Central Committee Meeting of the Chinese Communist Party to start studies for the BRI as soon as possible. In order to cooperate with Russia, another superpower in Asia, Xi, and Russian President Putin came together in February 2014 and reached a consensus on many BRI projects. In his speech in Indonesia, President Xi also announced the establishment of the Asian Infrastructure Investment Bank (AIIB). A year after the BRI was announced, 21 Asian countries signed a memorandum to establish the AIIB. [4] The first major meeting of the BRI member countries was held in Beijing in May of 2017.

There are also unique bodies within the Chinese government that have significant influence on foreign policy. These bodies, called Leading Small Groups (LSGs), act as coordination centers for both the Chinese Communist Party (CCP) and state interests. These bodies, which had a more active role in Xi's period, were also created for the BRI. This body, named BRI LSG, has been active since 2015 to oversee, coordinate, and implement the initiative. Although the main mission of the LSGs is about foreign policy, Yang Jiechi, a member of the State Council in the body established for the BRI, is directly related to foreign policy. The other four members follow the China-related aspects of BRI. The chairman of the BRI LSG is Vice Chairman Han Zheng. BRI LSG's office is also in the National Development and Reform Commission (NDRC). [5] Within the scope of BRI, in addition to the two main initiatives titled land and sea, a "Digital Silk Road" initiative has been established. The Beijing government says that the importance of this digital structure will increase gradually. For this, it announced the Belt and Road Digital Economy International Cooperation Initiative. This initiative was supported by Egypt, Laos, Saudi Arabia, Serbia, Thailand, Turkey, and the United Arab Emirates. Another important step is China's 'action and connection' agreement for the BRI. 85 standardization organizations from 49 countries participated in this agreement. Steps were taken to ensure cooperation in tax matters with the participation of 111 countries and to establish common interests with 49 countries on intellectual property rights. [6] According to the figures for 2019, the number of countries included in this neo-colonial initiative of China is

136. Besides, 30 international organizations have also been part of the BRI and 195 agreements have been signed so far.

New Colonial Economic Corridors

Within the scope of BRI, which Beijing attaches great importance to in having a say in the future of the world, structures called "Economic Corridors" have been created in order to create various attraction areas in the region that will extend from Far Asia to Europe. Looking closely at these economic corridors, which will be detailed below, it will be seen that these corridors will serve China's plans to gain access to the warm water ports and to have a say in the strategic transportation and logistics areas of the world and for neo-colonialism. The social, economic, and political changes at the places where these economic corridors pass will be discussed in detail in the following sections.

The New Eurasian Land Bridge Economic Corridor (NELBEC) is one of the corridors connecting BRI to Europe. In this economic area, which is the projection of the China - Europe Connection Platform, it is desired to connect West China to Western Europe. The first dig in this section was done in Serbia. Construction began on the Belgrade-Stara Pazova section as part of the Hungary-Serbia railway project. In the geography stretching from China to Europe, Russia and Kazakhstan are among the countries connected.

China-Mongolia-Russia Economic Corridor (CMREC) is an economic region that includes the trio of China, Russia, and Mongolia. In this leg of BRI, the Chinese side of the Tongjiang-Nizhneleninskoye railway bridge was completed in October 2018. Construction of the Heihe-Blagoveshchensk Road Bridge is underway. The preliminary design of the Moscow-Kazan High-Speed Railway is finished.

China-Central Asia-West Asia Economic Corridor (CCAWEC). In this corridor, the development of energy and mutual trade as well as infrastructure investments are covered. China, Kazakhstan, Uzbekistan, and Turkey have signed international land transport. Likewise, China-Pakistan-Kazakhstan-Kyrgyzstan and China-Kazakhstan-Russia, and China-Kyrgyzstan-Uzbekistan land transportation projects were prepared. The $28 billion deal was put on the agenda with the Saudi dynasty within the scope of the China-Saudi Arabia Investment Cooperation Fund. Partnerships established with Iran in the economic, military, and security fields are also considered within the scope of this corridor.

China-Indochina Peninsula Economic Corridor (CIPEC) is one of two economic corridors that will extend China's economic influence to the south of Asia. The Kunming-Bangkok Accelerated Road was completed for the construction of this corridor. Construction of the China-Laos and China-Thailand railways are underway. It is aimed to increase cooperation between China and Cambodia,

Laos, Myanmar, Vietnam, and Thailand.

China-Pakistan Economic Corridor (CPEC) is one of the key points of the BRI. The number of projects to be carried out at CPEC is about 45. 8 of the 10 special free economic zones to be established within the scope of the Belt and Road initiative will be established in Pakistan. CPEC is also given importance because it is the first gateway of China to East Turkistan, that is, China to the West. A special Joint Operations Committee was established for this purpose. Gwadar Port, Peshawar-Karachi Highway, Karakoram Highway, Lahore Metro, and many similar infrastructure works are on the agenda.

Bangladesh-China-India-Myanmar Economic Corridor (BCIMEC) is the second economic corridor covering South Asia. It is the economic structure that China attaches the most importance to after CPEC. For this purpose, a separate structure has been made, especially in Myanmar. For this, a special committee was formed just like in Pakistan and this committee has separately implemented the China-Myanmar Economic Corridor (CMEC). [7]

Declared Goals and the Hidden Agenda of the 'Belt and Road Initiative'

The main objectives of the BRI, Xi's new colonial initiative, are listed as follows: "Developing common economic policies by improving communication between states and increasing regional cooperation. Ensuring connections by completing infrastructure work in a coordinated manner. Ensuring trade agreements, regulations, and financial integration. Strengthening relations between people through student, cultural and tourism activities".

For other countries, the most attractive aspect of the BRI is infrastructure investments. While countries have the opportunity to make their own infrastructure investments, China aims to use considerable economic tools to finance these huge projects. According to the data of the Asian Development Bank, developing economies in the region need the support of 26 trillion dollars in order to sustain their infrastructure investments and growth. Here, China has targeted developing countries with its colonial cunning. Taking advantage of the needs of countries with weak economies, which are in the lowest rank according to the Human Development Index of the United Nations, will provide significant political gains to China. Myanmar and Pakistan, ranked 148th and 150th in this index, are mostly targeted by China. Another tactic that China has engaged economically here is that it subsidizes Chinese companies with its own financial instruments and does not give foreign companies breathing space. The Communist Party has injected huge amounts of cash into state-owned banks. These banks also finance Chinese companies with long-term debt at low-interest rates, with a system that is seen as a state guarantee in a sense.

As a result, Chinese companies with access to cheaper financing are disabling their foreign competitors in tenders. For example, in 2015, a Japanese company lost the tender to a Chinese company for a high-speed train project in Indonesia. But on the other hand, the project has not been started since it was announced. Because the project has been constantly reviewed due to problems, its start has been delayed many times. [8]

On the other hand, thanks to the advantages that countries on the other side of the projects provide to China, progress in some projects continues. The steps that were taken under the China-Pakistan Economic Corridor (CPEC) between Pakistan and China can be given as an example of this. Pakistani leaders also attach great importance to the CPEC. Prime Minister Imran Khan has exempted the China Overseas Port Holding, which works for CPEC and will build the Gwadar port, from the tax. The Gwadar port area, which forms the key point of BRI's both Silk Economic Road and Maritime Silk Road project, has been leased to China until 2059. [9]

"China was Positioned as a Benign Master, Receiving Tribute from Its Neighbours"

The Belt and Road Initiative needs to be evaluated in two ways for China, both in terms of domestic politics and international relations. The lands of East Turkestan occupied by China, are important in terms of being at the center of China's route to the Indian Ocean and the Middle East through the ports in Pakistan. For this reason, the sinicization of the region is one of Xi's priorities. Therefore, the acceleration of the genocide against the Muslim population in 2017, when the BRI's official meeting at the level of heads of state was held, is a sign of this priority. In terms of internal dynamics, it is important to note the words of Suisheng Zao from Nottingham University Asian Research Institute: "The BRI reminds the Chinese people of the glorious days of China's empire". President Xi uses the BRI to market his story to his people that the PRC is the world leader. Pictures of the world leaders shaking Xi's hand and showing their honor for the 2017 meeting of the Belt and Road Initiative and its other organization are shared on all broadcast channels. Giving the message to his own people that "I am the leader of the world," Xi also feeds the vein of nationalism among Han Chinese. But what Xi actually did, as Zao puts it, is portray the image of a "China was positioned as a benign master, receiving tribute from its neighbours." [10] Executives affiliated with this position is observed to behave like neighborhood bullies and ignore reactions from the international public, disregarding facts and the opinions of others. For example, China's Foreign Minister Spokesperson recently shared a fake picture showing an Australian soldier holding a knife to the throat of an Afghan child, on his official Twitter account. The Neo-Colonial Chinese regime declared that it would not apologize for the social media post, although the editor of the photo said the image was not real and Australian Prime Minister Scott Morrison denied this post as "a disgusting insult". In other words, position of these neo-colonialists which wet its neighbor's beak and his staff "bullied" the Australian government, which opposed China's interests in the Asia Pacific, by breaking down the rules of international diplomacy.

Baogang He says that together with BRI, Xi Jinping provides a great opportunity to increase and legitimize his power in the country. He also points out that Xi used this opportunity to overcome the term limits in the Chinese Communist Party. Using the long-term execution of the "Chinese Dream" project with the BRI as a lever, Xi guaranteed his chair for a lifetime with the changes made in 2018. [11] Thus, Xi will be able to maintain his reign forever by changing the traditions of his own party like Mao and Deng, who ruled China until their death. Today, when we look at the countries with the highest social and economic welfare, it will be seen that the functioning of democracy is as healthy as the functioning of the economy in those states. So, Xi proposes equal development for all while introducing BRI to the world. However, healthy economic development is not an easy process if there is no democracy. The strong leader image that he gained outside his country, Xi, who rules his own people with an iron fist, is fostered with BRI in China, where there is a hierarchical system from start to finish and no democratic order.

The Foreign Policy Agenda that Xi Hid Behind with the BRI

Chinese Foreign Minister Wang Yi needed to make a public statement shortly after the announcement of the BRI and emphasized that this initiative was different from the Marshall Plan, which was aimed at sending aid to various countries and gaining allies. Wang Yi said that BRI is a collaboration between member countries and certainly not a cold war-like tool to be used for geopolitical purposes. [12] Indeed, even this statement itself is problematic. In international relations, the impacts of BRI-like projects where many countries come together are not seen with explanations but with the reflections of that project on the field. Looking at the BRI from a foreign policy perspective, it will be seen that the BRI has turned into a very useful lever for Chinese President Xi to become the new leader of the world and to build "a colonialism on which the sun never sets". As stated by Suisheng Zao, while the support of the participating countries is received with investments and infrastructure projects, countries that oppose BRI are punished directly and indirectly. Thus, those states were faced with a choice. One of the most dramatic examples of states faced with making a choice has been seen in Taiwan's relations with African countries. As discussed in the previous sections, it is the African people who pay the bill for the "debt trap" heavily. Almost all of the African leaders, who inevitably chose the colonialist Xi regime when they were presented with either China or the West, broke diplomatic relations with Taiwan. [13] Today, there is one country in Africa that recognizes Taiwan as a state: Swaziland, now known as Eswatini. [14] A similar situation arises in China's election as a member of the United Nations Human Rights Commission. Today, all willing and unwilling victims of China's neo-colonial policies support the Beijing regime in every vote.

Reminding that the "low profile" policy in foreign policy has been changed despite the foreign expansion policy that started with Deng Xiaoping in the 1980s, Christopher K. Johnson noted that the Xi administration is on the way to rebuild the past period in terms of politics, economy, and culture in Asia. [15] Xi, who sees the BRI as important in terms of enabling China to communicate more intensely with the world, aims to put his signature under China's position in the international order while strengthening its power in domestic politics with this initiative. [16]

China Needs the BRI for Economic Growth

The Belt and Road Initiative has expanded China's power in the Asia and Pacific region to developing countries in regions extending from Africa to Europe. With the impact of the rapid growth in its economy, China has focused especially on the countries under the scope of BRI, not the regions where it competes with the western countries in the field of foreign trade. In the trade war initiated by US President Trump, Xi led China to the developing countries with the advantage of the BRI. As Zhao noted, these steps also benefited Xi's great power diplomacy. [17] The Belt and Road Initiative has enabled the establishment of a new economic network centered on China with producers and consumers in East Asia, Central Asia, and South Asia. The biggest factor in why Xi and the Communist regime attach such great importance to the Belt and Road Initiative is the export-led growth of China's economy. China, which has grown its role in the production economy since 2000, has attracted factories from all over the world to its own country while progressing towards becoming the factory of the world. The greatest opportunity that China offers to both its own manufacturers and western companies is cheap labor. Recently, the use of Muslim Uyghurs as slaves gives China an advantage in cheap labor. On the other hand, the need for raw materials has increased gradually in order to maintain the wheel of the economy to make their own production cheaper and at the same time to provide raw materials to producers.

As Kleven points out, the number of African countries participating in the BRI draws attention as a significant part of the underground wealth needed by the industry of neo-colonial China is found in Africa. 39 countries from Africa are on the BRI, which makes China the continent's largest trading partner. [18] In the report, in which the first six years since the start of the BRI are evaluated and published on the official website, it is stated that China has invested 90 billion dollars in BRI countries. [19] States in Africa immediately accept these investment and credit offers from neo-colonial China, with the thought that they will support their economy. However, this situation results in those countries falling into a debt spiral after a while. [20] Today, the total debt of African countries to China is 148 billion dollars. [21] The neo-colonial logic of the Xi regime is about "giving one, taking two." For example, China, which wants to maintain its aluminum industry, has loaned 2 billion dollars to Guinea, which has the world's largest bauxite reserves, to access the bauxite mines in this country. [22] On the other hand, the government of Guinea has given a concession to the Chinese aluminum company Zibo Rundi for a 25-year reserve of 1 billion tons. [23] Considering that the Gross Domestic Product (GDP) of Guinea was approximately 11.4 billion dollars in 2019 [24], it will be seen that the debt given by neo-colonialist China is not payable. What happened in the case of Zambia, on the other hand, shows that the "equal development for all" motto, which is often repeated for the BRI, of the neo-colonial Communist Chinese Regime does not make sense. As stated in Kleven's article, Chinese companies that obtain the right to operate copper mines employ workers brought from China instead of the Zambian people in this country. The unemployment rate has increased in Zambia, where mining has an important role in working life. The disregard for the occupational safety of the few local people working in the mines reveals that the neo-colonial Beijing mentality values the Chinese. [25] Zambia's GDP is 21.06 billion dollars in 2019. (26) The amount of loan given by China to this African country is almost half of the country's gross national product, which is $ 9.8 billion. [27]

As seen in the case of Guinea and Zambia, China's foreign policy developing on the axis of BRI, in Kleven's words, "exhibits a model of exploitation and unilateralism similar to the old colonialism of Western powers." [28] According to Xi, the important thing is to realize the "Chinese Dream". China needs to transport raw materials and energy at low costs from other countries, especially from African and Middle Eastern countries, for the growth of the Chinese economy based on the neo-colonial system. And in turn, the cheap products manufactured in China should be sent to other countries through the most possible shortest routes. In this respect, when we look at the BRI's announced routes, it will be seen that the strategically important ports and trade routes are covered by the BRI. So, in Zhao's words, "The BRI will create an infrastructure network to expand China's economic access to Eurasia, Africa and beyond." [29] From a historical perspective, one of the main motivations in the colonial activities of European navigators extending from Africa to the American continent is the discovery of new routes in maritime trade and control of newly occupied points through ports. The striking examples of this are the Portuguese sailors' seizure of Ceuta, which is just across Gibraltar, and the British control of Chinese ports for a long time. Neo-colonialist efforts under Xi have been pursued through gaining partnership status and operating rights by investing in ports on sea routes from Asia to Europe through BRI. Critical points in which China has a say directly or indirectly in its management include the following: Three ports in Malaysia, Indonesia's largest port Tanjung Priok, Sri Lanka's port of Hambantota, and Pakistan's port of Gwadar in the Asia Pacific region and Abu Dhabi ports and Haifa Port of Israel in the Middle East. [30] The special economic zone built right next to the Suez Canal in Egypt and the port owned in Greece are also indicators of China's economic power extending from Asia to Europe through BRI channels. Just as Portuguese and Spanish sailors found alternatives to the Mediterranean under the control of the Genoese and Venetians, these sea routes mean the same for the neo-colonial Chinese administration. Because instead of the Malacca Strait under the control of the American navy, which is on the important sea routes in the Asia Pacific, China has its own ports to manage. [31]

China's Intention to Increase the Value of its Currency and AIIB

It is necessary to mention here two important points which can be found by reading between the lines on the official website for the BRI, [32] where the developments in BRI are explained. The first one is the special payment system that China has established to make its own currency valid like the dollar in the international market. A system has been established for each country that is a member of the initiative to use the official currency of China, the Yuan when making payments and money transfers. This system, the Cross-border Interbank Payment System (CIPS) has been used by 60 countries. The Chinese government has signed a mutual currency exchange agreement with 21 BRI member countries, while it has also cooperated with the financial regulatory agencies of 35 states. As it is stated at the beginning, all projects in all stages of BRI are insured by Chinese insurance companies to make sure "the house wins". The amount of the policies signed by the Chinese Export & Credit Insurance company is 770.4 billion dollars. [33] In other words, the countries in the BRI project ' open the way for the Chinese neo-colonial army to tender the projects and regulate local laws. As in the case of Sri Lanka, after the tender is granted, it is again China that wins, builds the project, finances the construction, works in the construction, insures and operates the project, and finally receives all the facilities when the debts go unpaid.

Under Xi, Asian Infrastructure Investment Bank (AIIB) has been established, which will provide financing for new projects that they promised to develop while announcing BRI. The real purposes of the establishment of this bank, as Jianmin Jin listed, are: "To challenge international financial powers, to secure its geopolitical power, economic advantage, and to establish a new facility for moderation between countries with or without capital." [34] In other words, a system that protects and improves itself is proposed by Xi management, not a system that is equally distributed for the benefit of the BRI member countries. Referring to the research of Erica Downs of the Brooking Institute, Jin pointed out that China could use AIIB as a curtain, instead of being directly in the process while trying to increase its influence on other countries. In the international system, China has developed its own model instead of models that it considers to be a stumbling block to its neo-colonial aspirations and wants to influence globalization by "using soft power". [35] The Chinese regime, which makes propaganda that organizations such as the International Monetary Fund (IMF) make loans to other countries, establishes a new economic order with AIIB in its own version. AIIB is a tool for the security strategy prepared from the perspective of Asian countries to establish their own security, as Xi stated in his speech one year after the BRI was announced. In the economic leg of the new security strategy, AIIB has been designed as an alternative to the World Bank, which is dominated by America and Japan. [36]

Digital Surveillance System Surrounds the World

While the world is struggling with the Covid-19 virus from his own country, neo-imperialist Xi Jinping has tried to turn this disease into an advantage in order to spread the authoritarian order to the world more. On the one hand, while increasing its diplomatic influence under the name of "health assistance", on the other hand, it brought up the travel proposal with "QR Code". If it is remembered that East Turkestan has turned into a digital prison, it is highly likely that the information collected with this code will be transferred to the Integrated Joint Operations Platform (IJOP) of sino-colonialist China. This proposal should be considered as part of BRI's Digital Silk Road - DSR system. It has been stated that 16 countries have officially been members of the DSR announced in 2015. However, since the details of most of the agreements made with 134 countries in the BRI are not known, the number of those connected to the DSR system is higher. Many developed countries in the Middle East and Africa have been included in the DSR program, especially due to the need for communication infrastructure. Membership in the DSR, which means the Chinese Communist regime's export of the methods used to control and suppress the opponents and the societies in the occupied territories to other countries, also means the expansion of authoritarian management mentality. Because leaders who accept this system are given opportunities to follow their opponents, to control them and to destroy the concept of private life. Because the countries participating in DRS have been given training on how to monitor and censor the internet. Since the center of the service provider systems is also in China, all data will flow there. As a result, the sino-colonialist China will be able to use its data to bring the country it wants to its knees and to take control. The next step is to include every country exploited by China, which has established a private internet system in its own country, into this system and the global internet network is fragmented. [37]

Military Bases of Neo-colonial Chinese Soldiers Abroad!

As mentioned at the beginning of this chapter, the Emperor of China, who started the construction of the new historical Silk Road in order to control the wealth obtained from silk production in the 2nd century BC, first built outposts on important routes and then occupied them. Xi's neo-colonial plans are also traces of what Emperor Wu-Ti did. He told the international public that the historical Silk Road would be revived first. But like the outposts that Emperor Wu-Ti built elsewhere and later occupied, Xi has begun to establish bases in other countries for the People's Liberation Army (PLA). The first example is the establishment of a PLA base in Djibouti, known as the Horn of Africa, at the crossing point of the sea trade routes from the Indian Ocean to the Red Sea. There is no clear information on how many Chinese troops have been sent to Djibouti to date. Some sources indicate that there are about 2,000 PLA members. This base includes personnel not from sailors but also from other military units. It has been noted on this base, which also has a helipad, that there are cyber and electronic warfare equipment and operations such as strategic naval communications, anti-terrorism, and intelligence gathering are carried out. At first, this base was claimed to belong to the Peacekeeping Force within the UN. However, this base serves China's neo-colonial goals and has the purpose of helping China in its competition against India in the Indian Ocean and at the same time protecting Beijing's economic interests. It is predicted that China will establish a similar base in Pakistan's Gwadar port in the future. [38] On the one hand, the aim of the Chinese administration, which proposes economic development and meeting in a "common destiny" to the world, to carry its military operations beyond its borders and to ensure that the world is governed by a new power with itself at the center.

China Expands Its Borders Step by Step

The Chinese Communist Regime, which has recently expanded its territorial waters with the artificial islets it has built in the South Asian Sea, is also expanding its land borders step by step. One of the most striking examples of this happened on its border with India. As stated in the report submitted to the Congress of America, China has violated the Indian border in a planned way. Dozens of soldiers lost their lives in the military conflicts that took place there. China intends to capture as many pieces of land as it can. [39]

The Chinese Communist regime is also growing its borders, piece by piece, by making moves for both economic and military purposes. The communist Chinese regime, which transformed Pakistan into its satellite country within the scope of the BRI, is building a second military base abroad, after Djibouti, through the Gwadar port project, which is one of the key points of the BRI project. The Communist regime, which saw India as its rival, took steps to increase military tension in the Himalayas and went beyond the border. Dozens of soldiers were killed in the conflict. China occupied a piece of land in Bhutan, which is located between Tibet and India, and built a village there, albeit a small area. The location of the place where this temple was built is disputed due to its borders, however, the Beijing regime has been expanding its borders inch by inch for a long time. According to Steven Lee Meyers in his analysis published in the New York Times, the Chinese regime, which has occupied and expanded its regional influence by expanding its land borders, is also making the same moves in the South Asian Sea. China, which accepts the artificial islands it has created here and expands its continental shelf, is also arming these islands despite the objections of the states in the region. [40] A similar incident is happening in Tajikistan. The activities that started as joint military exercises in Tajikistan have now morphed into the establishment of military bases there. The moves made by China within the scope of the BRI in Central Asia are actually the visible representation of the Chinese regime's long-term expansionist goals in the region. For this reason, Xi, who announced the BRI for the first time in Kazakhstan, is establishing operational associations that will bring countries in the region together under the concept of 'war on terror'. For this reason, the US Department of Defense's annual report submitted to the US Congress points out that China may establish military bases in Myanmar,

Thailand, Singapore, Indonesia, Pakistan, Sri Lanka, the United Arab Emirates, Kenya, Seychelles, Tanzania, and Angola. [41] These countries are also included in the list of countries participating in BRI. When the situations of the countries are examined in the following chapters, it will be clearly seen that Xi wants to increase his military presence in the world where he also wants to dominate economically in his way to be a superpower. The Belt and Road Initiative is just the initiative of Xi's Chinese Dream.

China Practicing What it Learned from Western Companies
Known for his research on China, James A. Millward pointed to an important historical fact in his article in which he questioned whether China was a colonial power. Referring to "Claudius Bombarnac", one of Julies Verne's lesser-known novels, Millward explained that in that novel, a train, departing from Europe passes through the Caspian Sea and goes to Beijing, was depicted. The novel mentions a nonstop train line from China to Europe. At that time, there was no such train line anywhere in the world. However, in the far corner of the world, in China, the giant empire of Asia, railways were built with Western companies and their loans. However, with the effect of these huge infrastructure projects, the empire treasury was emptied and an era in China came to an end. One of the main reasons for the collapse of the imperial system in 1911 was that the country fell into debt. [42] A century after this event, a train departed from the Chinese city of Shian on 1 November 2019, passed the Khorgas border gate of East Turkestan, passed through Kazakhstan and the Caspian Sea, and entered into Turkey from the Kars border gate on November 3, 2019. It came to Ankara on November 6, arrived in Istanbul on November 7, finally reaching Prague after 18 days of travel. [43] It is not possible to know if Jules Verne thought his depiction would come true one day. The speed of the developments in technology is increasing day by day. It is also possible to see that the dreams in Verne's novels can come true. There is another fact that stands in the eyes of the international public: An exploitation much more dangerous than colonialism that began in the 16th and 17th centuries in the world is being built under the name of BRI. The terrible reality faced by countries that are members of the BRI will be explained in the next chapter. In particular, the BRI, the most effective weapon of Xi Jinping's ambition to become a world leader, who came to power in 2012, has been used as a multi-functional weapon. While Xi makes many countries from Asia to Europe economically dependent on him, he also spreads the authoritarian order he implements in his own country to the whole world by strategically manipulating foreign policy. The proposition of Xi to use the QR code to the

world while turning the lives of Muslims in East Turkistan into hell with QR codes, phone applications, and advanced technologies shows what a future he dreams of. Not forgetting that the Qing dynasties "humiliated" the Chinese people by borrowing from abroad, Xi is now taking those countries under his command by lending to them.

8

Chinese Siege in the Asia-Pacific Region

"Most of us are Muslims and we follow the teachings of the Prophet Muhammad. We are all brothers in Islam in terms of rights, dignity, and self-respect. As a result, we have a special and very deep sense of unity." ***Muhammad Ali Jinnah (Founder of Pakistan)***

THESE STATEMENTS BY one of the leaders of Pakistan's independence movement and its first president, Muhammad Ali Jinnah, point to the importance of the unity and solidarity of Muslim societies. But today, the Islamic world has unfortunately lost this 'special and very deep sense of unity' that was mentioned by Jinnah. In particular, the atheist Chinese Communist regime does not respect the rights and dignity of Muslim societies in the territories it occupied in East Turkistan. It has gradually exported its inhumane genocidal practices established in these lands to other countries. By using its economic power in the Asia and Pacific region, it ensured that the leaders of the Islamic countries remained silent regarding the genocide of the Muslim people of East Turkistan. The western-centered colonial order that started in the 17th century and continued until the 1900s has now been replaced by the neo-colonial system of the Chinese Communist Party. Islamic countries, such as the developing Pakistan, are gradually turning into satellite states of Beijing as they open their doors to the economic pioneers of the China. Indeed, Pakistan's Prime Minister Imran Khan's statement that "the future of our economy depends on China" is a recognition of this weakness and desperation. China's border neighbor, Pakistan, is the first country in which the Belt and Road Initiative (BRI) has been implemented with all severe economic conditions. In this chapter, neo-colonialism activities in the Asia Pacific region will be discussed, starting from Pakistan.

Pakistan on Its Way to Becoming A Second East Turkistan!

The China-Pakistan Economic Corridor (CPEC) is one of the key foundations of the BRI. The number of projects to be carried out for CPEC is about 45. Eight out of the ten special free economic zones to be established within the scope of the Belt and Road Initiative will be established in Pakistan. [1]

The foundations of diplomatic relations between Pakistan and the People's Republic of China were laid in 1951, and Beijing has kept its relations with Islamabad warm since then. Pakistan was one of the first countries to recognize the Communist Party-state established after Mao's revolution. Moreover, this recognition continued by keeping the relations close in the period between 1960 and 1970 when China was isolated from the world. China has been Pakistan's military, technical and economic supplier for many years, as well as the supplier of nuclear technology and equipment. According to the common opinion of some experts, Pakistan has tried to keep its relations with China warm, in the same way that its arch-rival India has improved its relations with America. On the other hand, some experts think that China maintains its careful relationship while operating with the assumption that there are some anti chinese groups centered in Pakistan. In fact, Pakistan is an important leverage point in the rivalry between China and India. Husain Haqqani, former Ambassador of Pakistan to the United States, pointed out that for this reason, the Islamabad administration also regards China as supporting India. The Beijing government's military aid to Pakistan has therefore been seen as a troubling factor for India. From a broader perspective, there is a conviction that China is using Pakistan to prevent India's geopolitical power in South Asia. The origins of China's arms exchange with Pakistan date back to the 1960s. Since then, the Beijing government has supplied equipment to establish arms factories, as well as given direct arms sales to Pakistan. In particular, the arms embargo initiated by America in 1990 made Beijing more effective over Pakistan in this area. Looking at the balance of power between the two countries, there is no doubt that the weight is in favor of China. Pakistan is more dependent on the Beijing government. Likewise, after the 1960s, cooperation between the two countries increased in the areas of military relations and economic cooperation. In particular, mutual trade and energy agreements have come to the fore. Over the years, many mutual visits have been made and agreements have been signed as a result of these visits. The first official agreement was signed in 1963, and the free trade agreement was signed in 2008. [2]

The first step towards CPEC, was taken during Chinese Prime Minister Li Keqiang's visit to Pakistan in May 2013. During this visit, a Joint Statement on Deepening Comprehensive Strategic Cooperation was signed between the two countries. This signature has formed the basis for the CPEC agreement. [3] The Memorandum of Understanding on Cooperation for the Long-term Plan on China-Pakistan Economic Corridor was signed in July of the same year. This signature declared the establishment of the CPEC. The Gwadar Port project, which is the most important part of CPEC, was also signed in the same year. Subsequently, Pakistani Prime Minister Nawaz Sharif visited China and signaled that a new era had begun in the development of cooperation between the two countries. Chinese President Xi Jinping's return visit in 2015 was one of the turning points for the CPEC. During this visit, the two leaders signed more than 50 agreements in the fields of energy, infrastructure, and industry and thus set forth the framework of the CPEC. [4] CPEC covers investments of $46 billion over a period of 15 years. This figure was later revised to $62 billion. [5] Pakistan's Gross National Product in 2015 was approximately $270 billion. [6] In this case, CPEC constitutes one-fifth of the Pakistani economy. In his research published in The Brookings Institution, Madiha Afzal drew attention to the fact that important issues about CPEC such as the total cost, investment amount, and borrowing amount are not shared with the public. One of the opposition arguments used by Imran Khan, who was elected Prime Minister of Pakistan in the 2018 elections, against his predecessor Nawaz Sharif, is related to CPEC. Khan Pledged to review the terms of the CPEC when he came to power. However, Abdul Razzak Dawood, the Minister of Economy of the cabinet from which Khan took over, blamed his predecessor Sharif's government for the debt spiral of the country. Concerning CPEC, Dawood also said that the Pakistani side did not negotiate well with China. Upon receiving the negative reaction to this statement, Dawood immediately backed down and said his words had been misinterpreted. Dawood's statement was described as 'irresponsible' by dissidents, given the Pakistani economy's commitment to China. A more interesting development, according to Afzal, is that Pakistan's Chief of Staff, General Qamar Jawed Bajwa, was called to Beijing by the Chinese President 'by special invitation' to determine damage control. Xi's statement on this visit is even more remarkable. "BRI and CPEC are destined to succeed as flagships. Regardless, the Pakistan Army will provide security at all costs," Xi said. [7]

Xi Treats Pakistan's Chief of Staff as a Colonial Governor!

This statement by Xi and his calling the Chief of the Pakistani General Staff into his presence to make this statement shows the Beijing Government's point of view towards CPEC and BRI. Xi, the new colonist of the new century, treated Pakistan's top rulers as colonial governors. What is interesting is that both Chief of Staff Bajwa and the Pakistani opposition did not speak out against this rebuke and declared those who spoke against CPEC as enemies. Moreover, the Chinese administration had to postpone Imran Khan's visit to Beijing for 6 weeks due to ambivalence over the situation regarding CPEC. [8] The Neo-Colonial regime accepted Imran Khan's visit to China after downplaying its importance. In other words, what happened to Imran Khan in Pakistan showed that the increase in the economic welfare of BRI members is of no importance to the Beijing Regime. The ' important thing for China is ensuring that China's economic interests remain unharmed. The situation of those who oppose this is obvious. Pakistani Prime Minister Imran Khan had to take new steps to establish a middle ground between the Pakistani army and the Chinese regime.

In order to improve cooperation with China and make CPEC more effective, Pakistani Army took over the administration of CPEC from the Prime Ministry and raised its position to a supra-governmental one, thus the China-Pakistan Economic Corridor Authority (CPECA) was created. Retired General Asim Saleem Bajwa has been appointed as the president of what effectively functions as Pakistan's Bingtuan XPCC, which has a similar structure to the Chinese Bingtuan and now holds a stronger position than that of the government. The opposition parties reacted harshly to this, recognizing that this could mean the handover of Pakistan to China. Special powers granted to CPECA and the fact that CPECA will be controlled by the soldiers will make it intangible like Bingtuan. Just as the Chief of the Pakistani General Staff rushed like an equerry when the Beijing administration called him, the Pakistani army was now indirectly completely under China's control. The army has now started to work in the interests of Beijing concerning intelligence matters. The appointment of a military person to the head of a project that is said to be economically-indexed is important for China in terms of guaranteeing projects in countries such as Pakistan where political governments do not have longevity. Chinese military control of a very important project for Islamabad creates a weakness for a Pakistani governments a of any political persuasion. [9]

Secondary Base Abroad for the Colonial Chinese Military

Another point worth focusing on regarding CPEC is the Gwadar port project, which is the key point of the economic corridor. The project is critical for the neo-colonial Chinese administration to provide a path to the Indian Ocean and from there a reach to other strategic regions. The company that will take over the operation of this important port is China Overseas Ports Holding. According to a report by the American think tank C4ADS, China will take 91 percent of the profit from this project for the next 40 years. Another aspect of the importance of Gwadar for China is that after the first military base was established in Djibouti in Africa, China's second military base abroad will be established in Gwadar. The C4ADS report states that China has built a base in Jiwani near Gwadar. Gwadar is being transformed into a base of the Navy of China's People's Liberation Army Naval (PLAN). The Beijing government aims to increase the number of overseas troops coming into the country from 20,000 to 100,000, making Gwadar safe for itself. [10] The Pakistani rulers, who believe that CPEC is sufficiently mutually beneficial to Pakistan economically as well as militarily, supports the Chinese Regime's occupation of places such as East Turkistan and Tibet and in building artificial islands in the South China Sea, thus expanding its territorial waters. As a matter of fact, during the visit of China's Defense Minister Wei Fenghe to Pakistan, these issues were confirmed in the meetings with both President Arif Alvi and Prime Minister Imran Khan. [11]

New projects have been developed at CPEC this year as Khan came more in line with the Beijing government. In this context, another $11 billion deal was accelerated in September. The agreement also includes two hydroelectric power plants to be built in the Kashmir region, which will cost $3.9 billion. $7.2 billion was allocated for the renovation of colonial-era railways in the South Asian region. This project is the most expensive one that China has yet undertaken in Pakistan. This new economic zone to be established in the Punjab region in Faisalabad is an important indicator that CPEC itself is being accelerated. [12] These recent developments show how Pakistan's current prime minister, Imran Khan, is economically dependent on CPEC just like his predecessor Nawaz Sharif. The fact that Imran Khan initially opposed this project from during the Sharif era, but then accelerated the project, can be considered a sign that his hands are tied. Thus, Islamabad will become dependent on Beijing for the long term.

Sino-colonial Bingtuan System Established

So, is the CPEC really designed with Pakistan's economic interests in mind? It is not possible to answer this question with a clear "yes". Details of the CPEC plan published by Pakistan's English-language newspaper Dawn in May 2017 reveal that this young Asian country is progressing rapidly towards becoming a second East Turkistan (Xinjiang). Khurram Husain, the author of Dawn, who evaluated this plan, which was concealed by the Pakistani officials who signed the CPEC for a long time, stated that: "This plan envisions a deep and broad-based penetration of Chinese businesses and culture into society as well as in many sectors of the Pakistani economy". So in short, Pakistan will become part of China. According to the information in Dawn's publication, although issues such as energy, transportation, and logistics are on the public's radar, when the details of the project are examined, it is seen that the agricultural sector is at the center. [13] Data from the Pakistan Ministry of Finance reveal that agriculture plays a key role in the country's economy. The contribution of agriculture alone to Pakistan's economy is 18.9 percent and it constitutes 42.3 percent of total employment. [14] The abundance of agricultural projects in CPEC means that this vital sector is also being handed over to neo-colonial China. CPEC encourages Pakistani agricultural businesses to borrow loans from Chinese banks. Another remarkable point is that the Bingtuan model, which was mentioned in the previous chapters, has been transferred to Pakistan and Bingtuan has a significant share in CPEC. Bingtuan, also known as Xinjiang Production and Construction Corps (XPC), requires the introduction of agricultural equipment, new technologies, and precise irrigation techniques to Pakistan. Within the scope of CPEC, these policies are aimed at developing similar agricultural activities as those of Bingtuan in Chinese-occupied East Turkistan. Bingtuan's launch of products produced in East Turkistan's Kashgar region to Pakistan's domestic market is yet another issue. Cotton and textile production, which is one of the main fields of activity of the neo-colonial system Bingtuan, also appears in CPEC and the focus is especially on yarn and coarse fabric. Looking at the areas of the economic corridor such as agriculture, textile, and food production, the picture that emerges shows that neo-colonial China will again profit greatly through these ventures. In short, "Chinese businesses will play a leading role in every field." [15] Athar Hussain, Director of the London School of Economics Asia Research Center, emphasized: "CPEC is designed to provide China with more profit than other parties". [16]

The High Tech Surveillance System in Pakistan

In a Frontline Documentary program put out by the American Public Broadcasting Service (PBS), it was stated that the advanced technology-based surveillance systems established by the Chinese Communist Regime in East Turkistan have been exported to 60 countries so far. [17] The Neo-Colonial Communist Chinese regime included the implementation of its own advanced technology-based surveillance systems in its economic corridor agreements with BRI member countries. In a report published by Pakistani news outlet Dawn, it was revealed that a virtual corridor will be created through this economic corridor, and surveillance systems will also be established. Laying fiber optic cables from China to Pakistan has been an important agenda item since the beginning of the CPEC negotiations. The underlying element of the Beijing government's insistence on fiber optics is the use of Pakistan as a transit point which will establish the ability to deliver its own internet system to Europe and Africa with the transfer points built in Pakistan. This system, which will create an infrastructure for China's telecom services, creates security risks for Pakistan. The extension of fiber optic cables from Khunjerab to Islamabad and cooperation between the Chinese and Pakistani media are also included in the content of CPEC, but there is no information on the details of how this cooperation should be established. Thus, seemingly the goal is to distribute China's propaganda. The Neo-Colonial CPEC plan also includes the establishment of a 24-hour surveillance system in the area of Khunjerab. With this system, security cameras and scanners will be installed throughout the area. A similar model of this "Smart City" in Khunjerab aims to be established in Peshawar. [18] Representatives of other political parties in Pakistan reacted to the CPEC, which paved the way for China to settle in Pakistan in every field from agriculture to industry and military fields. Party representatives stated that CPEC, with this plan, reminded them of the British East India Company and gave this warning: "If we have to carry all the burden, it will be very harmful to us. Will this project be a national development or a national disaster? Loans from China would have to be paid by Pakistan's poor people." [19]

Concerns have also been raised about the sharing of intelligence between Pakistan and Chinese authorities. Some foreign citizens and journalists who have traveled to the region have reported being interrogated by Pakistani Intelligence regarding their connections to Uyghur activists or interest in this topic.

Pakistan Surrendered to CPEC Does Not See Genocide in East Turkistan

In the report where long-term plans were announced via the website where the Pakistani Government announced the developments regarding CPEC, there is a statement: " Xinjiang (East Turkistan) has made great economic and social progress since the implementation of the Western development strategy. Kashgar, one of the important cities of Xinjiang (East Turkistan), has opened up to the world, the rapid economic developments in the city have attracted attention and the city will develop further". [20] These expressions are the declaration that the oppression of East Turkistani people by the Neo-Colonialist Chinese regime was accepted by the Pakistani authorities and that the life of the Muslim people in the region is of no value to Pakistan. The fact that Imran Khan, who criticized the injustices against Muslims at every opportunity, ignored the injustices in East Turkistan, shows that he is bound hand and foot against neo-colonial China. Answering the persistent questioning of a journalist at the Davos meetings this year, Khan said, "China helped us. They came and helped us when we had fallen on the floor. This is why we are very grateful to the Chinese government." [21] Imran Khan, who was asked about East Turkistan before, said that he did not know much about the issue and ' brought up the situation of Muslims in Kashmir. The Pakistani government refuses to acknolwedge the genocide suffered by Muslims in East Turkistan and ignores the human trafficking problem faced by its own citizens. Referring to her report published by Associated Press, Madina Aflaz said that about 600 Pakistani women were abducted and forced to marry Chinese men, a very disturbing situation. Aflaz also stated that the Pakistani government is trying to put pressure on members of the press so that this issue is not covered. [22]

These recent developments have demonstrated how Pakistan's prime minister, Imran Khan, like his predecessor Nawaz Sharif, is economically dependent on CPEC. CPEC not transformed relations between China and Pakistan but also drastically affected Islamabad's relations with its neighbors. This effect will continue to be felt more, especially in its relations with Iran. Although there is a level of distrust between Pakistan and Iran, and there are border disputes between the two countries, China's pressure to implement CPEC and a massive $400 billion deal with Iran - this deal is expected to be signed soon - put Pakistan in a difficult situation. If the agreement between Iran and China is larger and more extensive than CPEC, one might wonder how China's relationship with Pakistan will be. On the other hand, China is likely to take both countries under its wing.

Testing Bangladesh, the Young Country of Asia, with the BRI

Another economic corridor developed by the Communist Chinese regime (in order to avoid putting all their eggs in one basket) and to ensure its dominance of all Asian lands in the name of the BRI covers the geography in which Bangladesh is located. The Bangladesh-China-India-Myanmar Economic Corridor (BCIM EC) starts from the Yunnan region and extends to the Indian port of Calcutta. Asia's two largest countries, India and China, agreed to create an economic corridor between the two countries in 2013, and then Bangladesh and Myanmar also joined this initiative. [23] However, due to the rivalry between the two major countries, no full progress has been made in this economic corridor to date. BCIM EC is expected to have a budget of $22 billion when implemented. The final figure has not yet been established, as work has not been completed to date. The Neo-Colonial Chinese regime expects to create a trade potential of 132 billion dollars with this project. As in other economic corridors of BRI, it is expected that major transportation projects, energy, and communication line projects will be developed in this economic corridor. [24]

Although BCIM EC has not started yet, the neo-communist Chinese regime has taken steps to implement new projects with Bangladesh under the BRI.

Bangladesh, which is located between India and Myanmar, has had to walk a precarious path. For the Bangladesh government, doing business with the sino-colonial regime means support for infrastructure projects. From the point of view of the Beijing government, attracting Bangladesh to its side has the advantage of having it as collateral to be used against India. To date, the amount of investments to be realized in Bangladesh under the BRI amount to about $10 billion. A significant amount of this figure is for the 6.5 km long bridge to be built over the Padma River. Establishing an industrial zone in Chittagong and opening a tunnel that will provide a connection to Paya Port. The Bangladesh government, trying to manage a balanced policy between India and China, intends not to take excess loans from the Beijing government as much as possible. Meanwhile, Chinese State-sponsored companies are involved in important projects such as the liquefied gas terminal and oil refinery at Payra Port in Bangladesh. [25] Pointing out that the Beijing government is using BRI for its neo-colonial activities, experts warn Bangladesh not to fall into China's debt trap. [26]

Bhutan, another small state located just north of Bangladesh, is yet another example of where the Chinese Communist regime attempts to expand its borders inch by inch in the South China Sea. This small country located just south of Tibet, occupied by China, is also a Buddhist kingdom in the Himalayas. China has built a new village in Bhutan, neighboring Tibet, using methods similar to creating artificial islands in the south china sea. Chinese regime stated that they established this new settlement according to the coordinates they determined. However, this village, which neo-colonialist China built according to the coordinates it claims as its own, is actually located within the borders of Bhutan. [27] It is also necessary to examine the conflicts in the Galwan Valley, the border region between India and China, which occured in June of this year, from the perspective of Bhutan. As a matter of fact, in the report submitted to the United States Congress, it was pointed out that China systematically increased tension. The report stated that the sino-colonial Beijing regime had planned the military conflicts in Galwan in advance. One of the signs of this is that Chinese Defense Minister Wei announced a few weeks ago that "China must fight to maintain order." Two weeks before the clashes, Global Times, one of China's neo-nationalist state-own propaganda machines, issued threats that India would "suffer a devastating blow" if it became involved in a Sino-American rivalry. In the report, it is stated that a thousand PLA soldiers were detected in the Galwan Valley in the satellite images obtained before the clashes started. [28] Both the debt trap incidents in Sri Lanka and the conflicts in Bhutan and Galwan Valley are events that can be considered as warning signs for Bangladesh. The first encounter Bangladesh had with the problems created by the sino-colonial system is the gathering of tens of thousands of Rohingya Muslims fleeing Myanmar soldiers on their border.

Traces of Rohingya Genocide Perpetrator Hidden in CMEC!

China held its first major event on the Belt and Road Initiative in Beijing in May 2017. This period is also the year thirty heads of state attended the two-day meeting. 2017 is also the year when pressure on the two Muslim societies in Asia increased and this pressure transformed into genocide. It is noteworthy that the deportation of millions of people to the concentration camps established in East Turkistan in 2014 and the genocide of Rohingya Muslims coincided with this "acceleration period". Ethnic cleansing is being carried out against two Muslim societies, which China sees as an obstacle to reaching Asia and Europe from the land and from the sea to the Indian Ocean and the Pacific. Since the events in East Turkistan are described in the previous chapter, there is no need to repeat them here, but there is a connection between the genocide suffered by Rohingya Muslims and the China – Myanmar Economic Corridor (CMEC).

The period when economic relations between China and Myanmar began to improve was after Deng Xiaoping's foreign expansion policy. With the population reaching 60 million in the 1990s, Myanmar became an especially important market for China. With its sailing point through the Yunnan region and the Bay of Bengal, China's access to new sea routes through Myanmar means that it will use a shorter route in the Pacific region instead of the Malacca Strait. This allows it to overtake the United States in terms of influence in the region. For this reason, sino-colonial China sees Myanmar as one of the countries it must dominate by the BRI for its own economic interests. Even before the BRI, it signed 75 economic agreements with Myanmar between 2000 and 2010 alone. Attempts to build the Myanmar economic corridor, therefore, date back to before the BRI. The development of CMEC has not been at the pace that neo-colonialist China wanted due to the political and economic difficulties that Myanmar was going through. In May 2017, shortly after the first major meeting on the BRI, Myanmar faced a new political crisis. As always, it was the neo-colonial Chinese regime that came to help Myanmar, which was condemned and isolated in international circles due to the genocide of Rohingya Muslims. The Myanmar government signed the CMEC agreement, another critical step for the development of the BRI in the region. [29] Looking at the details of CMEC, it is clear that everything proceeded in the way neo-colonialist China wanted. Because CMEC will connect the oil trade in the Indian Ocean to the Chinese state of Yunnan, it will also strengthen Beijing's hand in oil competition with India. [30] Another important aspect of CMEC for China is that it is one of the keys towards spreading its military power to every corner of the world. The Beijing government, which cooperated with the soldiers in Myanmar when they were in power, also cooperated with the new government in this context. This cooperation aims to provide a great advantage for the People's Liberation Army Navy, which desires to gain "blue water navy status" in the long term, with a base on both the Indian Ocean and the Pacific Ocean. [31]

There are 6 key projects in Myanmar under the umbrella of the BRI. Three of these are within the CMEC. The Kyaukphyu Deep Sea Port and the New Yangon Development Project are located in the border economic zones to be established in the Kachin and Shan states. CMEC, which encompasses 24 projects, starts from the Yunnan region of China and extends to the Bay of Bengal by covering the large and developed cities in Myanmar. These cities include Mandalay, Yangon, and Kyaukphyu Special Economic Zones (SEZ) located in Rakhine state. [32] Yangon is the final destination of the economic corridor starting from the Yunnan Region. The place most of note here is Kyaukphyu due to its location in the Rakhine state. This state is the region where Rohingya Muslims live. At the final point that will grant Sino-colonialist China access to the Bay of Bengal, the Rohingya Muslims, which China sees as an obstacle to its capitalist ambitions, live. This is a situation just like the Muslims of East Turkistan who are living at the geographical point of connection to Central Asia. While China destroys the Uyghurs, Kazakhs, Kyrgyz, and other societies in East Turkistan, which it occupies with its genocidal policies, sino-colonialist China also provides the greatest threat for the Rohingya in Myanmar or the Arakan Muslims as they are known by the Islamic world, to be subjected to genocide by the soldiers there. The Beijing government, which defends its own genocide as its "internal affairs", accepts the massacres in Myanmar, which are regarded as absolute crimes of genocide within the scope of the UN Genocide Convention, as "this is their internal affairs". The words of Chen, General Secretary of the Communist Party in Xinjiang/East Turkistan, bear reflection here. He said "round up everyone who should be rounded up," and the order "shoot everything you see and hear" given to Myanmar soldiers, as they confessed at the International Criminal Court. [33] The destruction of every obstacle that China will encounter not ' in the lands it occupied but also in the Asia Pacific region cannot be separated from the sino-colonialist mentality. Just as the streets of East Turkistan have been cleared of Muslim Uyghurs, Rohingya Muslims have also been victims of ethnic cleansing. During the "cleaning operation" in August 2017, 730,000 Rohingya had to leave their homes. The sad truth is that there is no voice from the Islamic world speaking out for East Turkistan nor against the real perpetrator of crimes against Rohingya Muslims. After Chi-

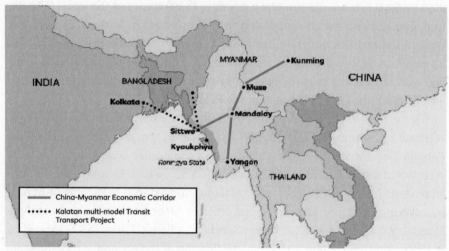

CMEC (The United Service Institution of India)

nese Party Chairman Xi Jinping visited Myanmar, 51 agreements were signed between the two countries and the total size of these agreements amounted to 46 billion dollars. [34] The Beijing regime has reached the Gulf of Bengal with the CPEC it signed with Pakistan, moving towards the east in the Indian Ocean, and with the CMECagreement signed with Myanmar, it gained direct access to the sea routes there and increased its international power.

Debt-Trap Risk in the Asia-Pacific

The Belt and Road Initiative will drastically affect the economic and political future of other countries in the Asia Pacific Region. Countries such as Cambodia, Laos, and Vietnam are also within the scope of BRI. The most important risk for countries such as Laos, Cambodia, and Seychelles is that they are weak against 'debt trap' diplomacy. The largest loaner country in the Asia Pacific region is China. A large part of this debt is for infrastructure investments, especially in Papua New Guinea. In the study of Lovy Institute, which includes detailed analysis on the subject, the critical threshold for the debt diplomacy trap was defined as 50 percent and above of GDP- debt at this level or above is categorized as risky. So this means that half of a country's per capita income goes to neo-colonial China. From this point of view, small island countries in the Pacific region, including Fiji, are at this risk. Likewise, Papua New Guinea, neighboring Indonesia, is also on the brink of risk. To date, there has been no China-based debt trap problem in that region. However, when the economic data of these countries are examined, the risks are clearly seen. [35]

China's Investment is Helping China again, not the locals

Neighboring Myanmar, Thailand is one of the countries under the influence of neo-colonial China. It also has geopolitical importance as it has a coast on the South China Sea. Since the military government in Thailand sees neo-colonialist China as the ' resource to keep its country afloat to ensure its legitimacy, it has come to a position to surrender its country's economy to Beijing. [36] Thailand's neighboring country, Cambodia, sees neo-colonialist China as one of its biggest allies. However, looking at the projects carried out within the scope of BRI, we encounter a similar situation to Pakistan and Myanmar. In other words, these countries fall into the position of being China's gateway to the Indian Ocean and the Pacific Ocean. We see that the same move was made in Cambodia to seize ports and establish free economy zones wherever BRI reaches. Here, the special economic zone is the Sihanoukville Special Economic Zone (SSEZ). Cambodia also means cheap labor for Chinese firms based in SSEZ. The Chinese state-owned company China Communications Construction Company (CCCC) is also undertaking a 1.9 billion dollar high-speed rail project. [37] Although BRI seems profitable for Cambodia, it still has some risks. Cambodia's debt to China is $4.2 billion. It is defined by the Global Development Center (CGDEV) as being at risk of debt shortages. CGDEV's research reveals that the debt problem carries great risks not for Cambodia but also for other countries. Another noteworthy point in this country is that most of the Chinese investments coming to Cambodia have gone to Chinese society there. In other words, it is the Chinese who both invest and benefit from this investment. This, in turn, harms Cambodia's local economy. [38]

China's New Islands also Threaten Vietnam

It is seen that the neo-colonialist Chinese regime, which sees the Asia Pacific region as its own backyard, has changed the security policy it has been pursuing in the region since the 1990s in a way that will benefit it through economic and political means. Deciding to turn the South China Sea into an inland sea, Beijing planned to reduce the effectiveness of the USA in the region at the Conference on Interaction and Confidence Building Measures in Asia (CICA) in 2014 with the ambitious actions of Xi. Xi wants to transform this concept into a new security policy called "Asia for Asians". [39] The main reason for this policy is that the magnitude of the trade passing through the South China Sea is 3.37 trillion dollars, according to 2016 figures alone. This sea, which is the crossroads of the world's largest maritime trade routes, is also the place where 40 percent of LNG liquefied natural gas transfers are made. This is why the sino-colonial Chinese government has built new artificial islands since 2013. These islands mostly violate Vietnam's territorial waters. [40] On the other hand, Vietnam, where western companies have moved their production bases in recent years, sees BRI as an opportunity for the infrastructure investments it needs. By 2040, Vietnam needs to complete its infrastructure projects. For this reason, the sino-colonial Chinese administration intends to make the biggest projects of Vietnam, which it confronts in the South China Sea, under the roof of BRI. [41]

"Laos will one day Become Part of Southern China"

Another country, where Sino-Colonial China wants to open BRI to the world through the Yunnan region, is Laos, a small country in Southeast Asia. The Beijing regime aimed to build a railway between the two countries and make this country a part of its own hinterland. The 5.95 billion dollar railway project will connect Laos' capital Vientiane and Yunnan's city of Kunming. The Mohan-Boten Economic Cooperation Zone, the special economic zone to be established on the border of Laos and China, will be one of BRI's doors to the world. The reflection of these investments in the public is also a sign of China's ambitions towards the region. Although the public describes these investments as the integration of the capital circulation of sino-colonial China, they wittily joke that "Sooner or later Laos will become a part of Southern China." But just as every joke contains a truth, underlying this wit lies the concern of turning into one of the satellite states of China. [42]

Indonesia, Key Country for the Maritime Silk Road

Neo-Colonial Chinese leader Xi Jinping announced the 21st Century Maritime Silk Road, the second main branch of the Belt and Road Initiative, in his speech at the Indonesian Assembly in Jakarta on 3 October 2013. [43] Indonesia is one of the biggest countries that China aims to increase its economic relations in the Pacific. The past issues that were particularly problematic during the seventies have been left behind as relations between the two countries begin to improve. Diplomatic relations were suspended from 1967 to 1990 during the reign of Suharto, the ex-president of Indonesia. In recent years, there has been an increase in trade with Indonesia, an important market for neo-colonial China. Until last year, the number of China's projects in Indonesia has reached 2,130, the total volume has increased to 4.7 billion dollars, and China's investments in the country have reached approximately 20 percent of the total foreign investment in the country. [44] The size of the trade volume between the two countries is 79.4 billion dollars. However, China is the second most invested country in Indonesia. [45] Indonesia's importance to neo-colonial China is more of this country's key geographic location on the sea foot of the BRI, rather than increasing bilateral trade and investment. As stated in some sources, Indonesia, which has 17,508 islands and is the largest Muslim country in the world in terms of population, dominates an area of 5 million squ-are meters together with the inland seas. It is located between the Indian Ocean and the Pacific Ocean, in the middle of sea routes. Because of this location, it has been considered important by western colonists in history. Following the Mataram Empire, the United India Company of the Dutch exploited Indonesia. The struggle for independence that started in the 1900s was successful after the Second World War, and full independence was declared in 1945. [46] The founda-tion of Indonesia's relations with China was laid five years after independence was declared.

The relations between the two countries have not developed as expected by China until recent years, and have been interrupted as in the Suharto pe-riod. In the neo-colonial period when Xi came to power, the Chinese Com-munist regime made special efforts to develop its relations with Indonesia for its imperialist ambitions. The purpose of Xi declaring BRI's sea projects is to keep the Asia Pacific country with its vast geography by its side. The Indone-sian government also sees the neo-colonial BRI as important for its economy. The amount of investment Indonesia expects under BRI is approximately $91 billion for 30 projects. Indonesian President Joko Widodo (known as Jokowi) even asked for special support from Chinese President Xi to finance BRI pro-jects. The largest of these projects is the high-speed train project, which will cost about $6 billion and will be built between the textile center of Bandung and the capital. [47] However, these projects are not progressing at the pace the Beijing government wants. Local legal regulations are an obstacle to projects.

The Indonesian Government, which sets its hopes on the BRI project of the Neo-Colonial Chinese Administration, in return remains silent, just like Pakistan, against the genocide of Muslim Uyghurs in East Turkistan. Despite the protests of the Indonesian people against China, the Indonesian government takes the rote rhetoric of the Beijing government into account. In fact, the Xi administrati-on went one step further, took the leading clergy of Indonesia to East Turkistan, and showed them religious activities organized there for show. Nahdlatul Ulama, the leader of the Muhammadiyah Movement in Indonesia, said during the visit that the news about East Turkistan was a "western fabrication" and they need more evidence. The Indonesian government, like Pakistani Prime Minister Imran Khan, considered it "an internal matter of China". [48]

The important point to note here is the developments in the South China Sea. Indonesian President Jokowi, who wants to benefit from neo-colonial Chi-na's BRI program, is also aware that the Beijing government wants to reduce Indonesia's dominance in the South China Sea. For example, in December 2019,

Chinese military ships accompanied Chinese fishermen to the proximity of Natuna Island, Indonesia's special economic zone. Indonesia responded to this move, which goes against the convention of international diplomacy, by calling the Chinese Ambassador to the Ministry of Foreign Affairs. President Jokowi went to the island of Natuna personally and followed the developments on the spot. In fact, it is not a new development for China to move warships around the region under the guise of accompanying the fishermen. China has faced Malaysia and Thailand in the same way before. However, for Indonesia, it is not about fishing, but about a critical issue-- like energy. The 46 billion cubic meters of gas in the Natuna Island area is of vital importance. Neo-Colonial China continues to build new artificial islets in the South China Sea with the pretext of establishing bases for its navy while expanding its navy. As stated by Felix K. Chang, one of the experts of the Foreign Policy Research Institute, China uses "Salami Tactics". In other words, China carries out gradual and designed actions against those who oppose its imperialist ambitions and thinks that "what I take is profit". China's goal is to break Indonesia's opposition by sending fishing boats more frequently to the Natuna Island region and forcing it to adapt to the presence of neo-colonial China, like Malaysia. [49]

Malaysia, the Country that China Ventures to Take Sides Even in Elections for the Sake of BRI

Malaysia, another Muslim country in the Asia Pacific region, is also one of the target countries of neo-colonial China. Malaysia is also one of the states with a large Chinese population in that geography. The origins of the relations between the Chinese Communist Regime and the Malaysian administration date back to the 1970s. In the period of "ping-pong diplomacy" initiated by Mao with the United States in 1971, the first steps were taken with the visit of Malaysian Prime Minister Tun Abdul Razak to China. Afterward, relations between the two countries continued with ups and downs. Since the 2000s, the trade balance has grown against Malaysia due to the export-led growth of neo-colonial China. With a population of over 31 million, Malaysia is an important market for China. Beijing has attached great importance to the inclusion of Malaysia in the BRI due to its coastline on the South China Sea and its location on sea routes. The two countries signed major projects under the BRI, with Malaysia's former prime minister Necip Razak taking a stance in favor of neo-colonial China. In the period when BRI was first announced, the amount expected by Malaysia for projects was approximately 98 billion dollars. The biggest share here belongs to the 14.3 billion dollar railway project between Kuala-Lumpur and Kota Bharu. This project is also one of BRI's biggest projects in the South Pacific. [50] When the BRI was announced in 2013, the Barisan Nasional (BN) coalition, which was in power in Malaysia at that time, attached great importance to this huge railway network, which is also known as the East Coast Rail Link (ECRL). However, the opposition opposed this project as it would transform Malaysia into one of China's colonies. The result of these objections was that the BN coalition lost the election in 2018. Here it is necessary to mention another issue. It is not acceptable for a country to take a side in the elections of another country through its foreign representatives, in international diplomacy. Taking sides in this way is considered as an "intervention in internal affairs". But for neo-colonial China, the argument of "internal intervention" is one used to fend off those who oppose the genocide in East Turkistan. This argument is left aside when it comes to neo-colonial policies and the party leaders who support them. The 2018 election period in Malaysia also coincided with the Chinese New Year celebrations. And in this period, Chinese Ambassador to Malaysia Bai Tian has consistently participated in the activities of the BN Coalition, which supports BRI projects, and showed that they support the coalition. This attitude of the ambassador has been seen and criticized by policy experts in Malaysia. However, these attempts of Beijing failed, and the Pakan Harapan Coalition, led by former Prime Minister Mahathir Muhammad won the election. The new coalition has examined many aspects of BRI's favorite rail project, including finance, under-planning, and the possibility of corruption. [51] Mahathir Muhammad criticized China's neo-colonial approach during his visit to Beijing after stopping two major projects under BRI. Mohammad, who met with Prime Minister Li Keqiang in Beijing in August 2018, answered a question about the free trade agreement at the press conference: "Free trade should also be fair trade". Mahathir warned against the sino-colonial system because of China's debt-trap diplomacy: "We must admit that the development levels of the countries are not equal. We do not want to experience a situation like the poor countries facing a new version of colonialism." [52] One year after Mahatir Mohammad became prime minister, after negotiations with China, he revised the ECRL project and decided to continue it by reducing its cost from $14.3 billion to $10 billion. [53] An investigation was initiated against Nacip Razak, who defended China's colonial project BRI because he gained benefits through these projects. Mahathir Muhammad, who resisted Neo-colonial Chinese rule, resigned from his post after a while. Given Mahathir's criticism of the BRI, the traces of the process that led him to resign can again be seen in Beijing.

'Salami tactic' for Malaysia

Malaysia, where the Beijing Government wants to be effective in its economy with huge economic projects and investments, is systematically violated by Xi's navy in its territorial waters. Malaysia, an island country like Indonesia, is also one of the transit points between the Indian Ocean and the Pacific Ocean. The neo-colonial Chinese administration's long-standing attempts to transform the South China Sea into its inland sea has been closely followed by international circles. Having declared himself the permanent president of China at the 13th National People's Congress in 2018, Xi also confessed what kind of hegemony he established by breaking the international diplomacy rules. Xi described his project to expand its territorial waters by building an island in the South China Sea as a major project. Malaysia is one of the countries most affected by the attempts of the Beijing government to dominate the seas by building artificial islets 1,800 miles away from the coasts of China. [54] However, the Malaysian government could not stand up against the neo-colonial giant Chinese regime. For this reason, Mahatir Mohammad, who became prime minister in 2018, could not raise a strong objection to the genocide of the Muslim population in East Turkistan and could not put any pressure on Beijing's encroachments in the South China Sea. His predecessor, Najib Razak, did not speak for two years when one of the Chinese coast guard ships anchored in Malaysia's territorial waters. Despite this attempt of Najib, who was able to meet with the Sino-Colonialist Xi about this issue ' two years later, the ship in question left its location and another ship anchored in its place. [55]

Sri Lanka, a Victim of China's Debt-Trap Diplomacy

Located in the Indian Ocean, just southeast of India, Sri Lanka is one of the most striking victims of neo-colonial China's debt-trap diplomacy. Sri Lanka's city of Hambonta is one of the important crossroads on maritime trade routes due to its location. This small country, which is located at the crossing point of thousands of ships every day, is one of the places that China has been trying to influence with colonialism for many years. In 2002, the Sri Lanka government decided to build a new port in this city. The Chinese government has proposed a $1.1 billion loan for the construction of the port. With its neo-colonial tactics, China demanded that construction be done by Chinese companies in addition to lending. After the government of Sri Lanka accepted both conditions, the construction of the port started and the port was opened in 2010, 8 years later. Hambantota port, after opening, started to lose money. When the Sri Lankan government was unable to pay even interest on the debt, the Chinese government immediately seized the port, a move that China has employed in the past. In return for Sri Lanka's debts, the operational rights of the port were granted to China for 99 years with the agreement made in 2017. The neo-colonial government of Beijing controls not ' the port but also the 15,000 hectares of the port area and even wants more. It forces the people in the region to sell their land, as it cannot legally claim it. [56] China's debt pressure on Sri Lanka is not limited to Hambarto port. The major share of the country's $66 billion debt belongs to the neo-colonialist China. The debt trap diplomacy experienced by Sri Lanka is one side of the coin. Colombo, one of Sri Lanka's major landmarks and once home to military bases, was sold to a Hong Kong-based company in 2011. There is an increasing number of Chinese companies on the streets of Sri Lanka. Lotus Tower, which is planned to be built in the city center to serve telecommunication companies, is also one of the incomplete projects. The president of Sri Lanka during this time, Maithripala Sirisena, stated that this giant project was also left unfinished by Chinese companies and that these companies took the project funds of $11 million and left. [57] Gotabaya Rajapaksa, who was elected President in 2019, stated that they will review the agreement to reclaim Hambarto Port, both during and after the election period. However, the neo-colonial Chinese administration, as if it had never heard of this call, continues to accelerate the renovation of the port. China's debt-trap diplomacy, which we can see here in the Hamborto Port and in African countries,, which we will discuss in the following chapters, serve Beijing's interests. The difficulties faced by other countries have no meaning for the Beijing regime.

Will the Maldives Become a Second Sri Lanka?

The Maldives, located west of Sri Lanka and one of the most important tourism centers of the world, is a country that is at risk of being caught in China's debt trap, just like its neighbors. The Sinamale Bridge, which connects the islands in the Maldives, has been a solution to the public's transportation problems, but has also created governmental concern of falling into debt. The current debt owed by this country is 3.1 billion dollars. This bridge was built during the reign of Abdullah Yameen, who supported the sino-colonial Chinese rule. The Yameen government, which imprisoned opponents just as the totalitarian rulers in China have, lost the 2018 elections in a surprise event. The fact that the so-called China-Maldivian Friendship bridge actually pulled the country into a debt trap was revealed. Mohammed Nasheed, who is parliamentary speaker, said the costs of the bridge were inflated. The old government and the Chinese parties claimed that Nasheed's calculations were wrong and stated that the real figure was 1.1 billion dollars. However, considering that the GNP of this small archipelago country is 4.9 billion dollars, even this figure shows that the Maldives has already fallen into a debt trap, just like Sri Lanka. [58]

9

Chinese Invasion
of the Middle East

"It is tough to stay away from hypocritical and self-seeking people. They show their fictitious love and hide their evil inside. As long as you keep them content, they love you, and as long as you give them, they become happy."

THIS EXPRESSION OF Ali ibn Abi Talib, the fourth caliphate of Islam, advises regarding relationships. It also points to an important danger for state administrators in relations between countries. The danger is that colonial governments, who consider their interests, seem to be friends of those states as long as they benefit from the countries they exploit. From the perspective of international relations, each country protects its interests and acts accordingly, revealing the lessons to be taken from this expression. This lesson is to watch out for the actions of self-seeking people. While choosing their allies to protect their interests, the governments of Muslim countries are expected to stand against both the exploitation of their people by another government and the neo-colonialist systems that commit genocide against other Muslim societies. Because it is the responsibility of the rulers of Islamic countries to make the best of one of the most well-known hadiths of Prophet Mohammad: "A Muslim is the brother of a Muslim". [1] However, when looking at the relationship between the Islamic world's ancient state of the Middle East, Iran, and its leading country, Saudi Arabia, with the neo-colonialist Chinese regime, it seems that Caliphate Ali's warning against "self-seeking people" and the Prophet's hadith on "brotherhood" meant nothing to them. The cost of ignoring these two principles will be paid again by the Muslim peoples.

Islamic scholars who revived the ancient Greek philosophy sources and enabled them to be re-learned in Europe grew up in the Middle East, the center of science and civilization of the period in the 11th, 12th, and 13th centuries. The Islamic world's scientific and scholarly progress declined due to the invasion of Baghdad and Basra by the Mongols in the 1200s, and the destruction of all scientific resources by burning them or throwing them into the Euphrates and Tigris rivers. The Islamic world still pays the painful cost of this destruction by falling behind Western civilization. Muslim societies face a new threat of destruction after a 7-century hiatus. The endless ambitions and self-interests of the neo-colonialist Chinese rule is gradually invading the Islamic world. Just as Ali ibn Abi Talib Ali put it, Sino-Colonialist Xi has an evil mentality that sees Islam as a "disease to be eradicated" behind his smiling face. It is important both for their people and for other Muslim societies that Iran, a country that once supported the view of "neither the West nor the East," and Saudi Arabia, the Servant of the Land of the Two Holy Mosques or the Custodian of the Two Holy Mosques are vigilant against this mentality. If China's genocide against Muslim Uyghurs, Kyrgyz, Kazakhs, and other societies in East Turkistan, and China's dominance in the Middle East through steps such as the colonial Belt and Road Initiative (BRI) are ignored, the Islamic world will experience the situation of "lock the stable door after the horse is stolen" again. This economic, political, and cultural threat to the Islamic world comes from the east, not from the west, this time.

Iran, the Country that Opened the Doors
of the Middle East to Sino-Colonialist China

Iran is undoubtedly one of the countries with the most primeval civilization in the Middle East. Iran, which can reach the Indian Ocean through the Strait of Hormuz, has a geographical position extending to the Middle East and Europe through Asia and Anatolia. Due to its advantageous geographical location and oil wealth, Iran is in an effective position in international politics. Iran, which was subjected to gradual isolation after the revolution in 1979, the hostage crisis in the American Consulate, and other events, still makes its power felt on the Shiite axis extending from Iraq to Yemen. While Western countries have sanctioned and embargoed Irano due to both its management style and nuclear ambitions, Iran has turned its direction to China. This change is a sign that the current Iranian regime ignores the founding philosophy of the Iranian revolution. Khomeini and his team, who came to power with the revolution in 1979, adopted the philosophy of "neither the West nor the East" to show that they would be a strong independent state. Khomeini's government defined the United States as the "big devil," which it sees as the vanguard of the capitalist system, and the Soviet Union, the representative of Socialism, as "the little devil." [2]

The Iranian government, struggling with an economic crisis for many years due to embargoes imposed by America and other western countries, has opened its doors to China. The Chinese government wants to use this indigence of Iran to reach the Middle East from both land and sea, along with Pakistan, and to carry out sino-colonialist activities in the Middle East.

Seeing the Iran Nuclear Deal signed in 2016 as an opportunity, China took action after the agreement was signed. President Xi made a historic visit to Iran, where he met with the supreme leader Ali Khamenei. President Rouhani signed the legal arrangement to pave the way for cooperation between the two countries shortly after the visit. The agreement between China and Iran covers 25 years. This agreement covers cooperation in the economic, political, and military fields. [3] Relations between the two countries are based entirely on mutual benefits and economic benefits. It has no ideological basis. Iran sees that China wants to dominate the world economically. However, Iran, which is subject to heavy sanctions by the USA, thinks that the ' economic power to oppose America is China. Iran is important for China-it will provide an advantage in the region to the BRI, expanding Xi's and the Chinese Communist Party's influence globally. China wants to take advantage of Iran's influence in the Middle East. [4] Relations between Iran and China, namely the Sino-Iranian agreement, also has a broad political base. The agreement between Iran and China is important for Tehran in terms of relations with China and America. Seeing that the tension between the two powers will increase even more in the future, Iran naturally uses its choice in favor of China instead of America. At the same time, China sees itself as a balancer between Russia and Western capitals. China takes advantage of Iran's position to increase its power in the Middle East. [5]

The point that should be emphasized about the agreement between Iran and China is that Tehran thinks that America's influence in the Middle East will decrease with this agreement. However, another point will be the reflections of this agreement on Tehran's foreign policies, because this agreement means that the Tehran regime will give up the ideals adopted during the Iranian Revolution, and must contend with the new issues caused by giving up these ideals. Iran, which adopted the philosophy of "neither the West nor the East" during the Iranian Revolution will have to compromise its independent foreign policy stance with this agreement. It is unclear how long the partnership between Iran and China will last. However, the priority given by Iran to implement an independent policy will be replaced by taking the priorities of the "new boss" into consideration. In other words, in the process following the agreement signed with the Beijing government, Iran will not speak in the international arena alone. The most striking example of this was seen during the epidemic of Covid-19.

The Iranian spokesperson and the Chinese ambassador warned the Ministry of Health after blaming China for the epidemic. The statement was retracted, with spokesperson Kianoush Jahahpour saying, "we all decided that we should respect the principles of diplomacy." [6] What happened after this statement, which angered China, showed that the Beijing government expects complete obedience from its partners in the international arena. Mutual respect comes ' after submission. On the other hand, Iran's regional enemies see this situation as an advantage, because China's desire to improve its relations with Israel and Saudi Arabia will limit Iran's regional movements.

$400 Billion Deal

It is stated that the historic agreement, which was announced to the public in July 2020 but whose preparations are not yet completed, includes 400 billion dollars. The agreement, first proposed during Xi's visit to Iran in 2016, was approved in President Hassan Rouhani's cabinet in June of this 2020. However, it has not been brought into the Iranian parliament. After President Donald Trump abandoned the Iranian nuclear agreement fostered by former President Barack Obama, which lifted sanctions and embargoes on Iran in return for strict monitoring of nuclear activity, the Iranian regime accelerated the negotiations with China, and the agreement was brought to the final stage. The New York Times, published a review of the 18-page first draft of the agreement. According to the analysis, the Beijing government will buy Iranian oil cheaply for 25 years in return for Iran's investments in banking, telecommunications, ports, railways, and many similar fields. The agreement, which was evaluated within the BRI scope announced by Xi to realize the Chinese Dream, will contribute to Beijing's extension of its economic and political power from Asia to Europe. It is expected that more Chinese signs will be seen on Iranian streets with the realization of high-speed trains, subways, and similar works within the scope of the agreement. With this agreement, China will establish a special free economic zone in Maku in the northwest of Iran, where the Shatt al-Arab river, formed by the confluence of the Tigris and Euphrates rivers, flows into the Persian Gulf. [7] As we have seen in other countries, these special free economic zones mean that the Chinese government will bring its own bank, its own security, its own employees, and its own insurance to these regions and establish its own system. This economic region to be established in the Persian Gulf could strategically turn into one of China's bases in the Middle East. This region is also critical in terms of oil transportation and will provide China with great strategic power.

It is a traditional sino-colonialist Chinese tactic to accelerate this agreement, which Iran hopes to provide economic relief, at a time when the US and other European countries are pulling out of the nuclear deal and experiencing difficult times due to the Covid-19 virus outbreak. The analysis of Ariel Cohen of Forbes Magazine summarizes everything: "Beijing exploits Tehran's growing desperation" [8]. The Beijing government's exploiting the desperation of the Middle East's ancient civilization to cheaply meet the endless need for oil. In addition, China has an opportunity to create future partnerships with Iran in the military and technology industries.

The Chinese Firewall System in Iran

Another point that draws attention in the draft agreement, which includes 5G investments in the field of telecommunications, is that the global positioning system Baidu, which will expand China's hegemony in cyber technology, will also be established in Iran. [9] Building this system means that China will have a central role in Iran's cyber field. On the other hand, this system offers the Iranian government more control over the internet. [10] This means firewalls and a surveillance system similar to the ones built by sino-colonialist China in East Turkistan to be installed in Iran. This part of the draft agreement, which covers 5G and internet investments, is also a response to America's sanctions against China's Huawei company, which carries out 5G investments in China.

With this agreement, China is making another move to increase its colonial power. Iran, in return, will exit the American and western financing systems and support China's new digital currency, e-Yuan. Also, Iran will have the opportunity to rid itself of concern over American sanctions and sell its oil. [11] On the other hand, this agreement can also be seen as an advantage when considered in terms of Iran's regional enemies because China's desire to improve its relations with Israel and Saudi Arabia will limit Iran's regional movements. Although Iranian officials think that they will increase their influence in the region with Beijing's support, the cooperation between China and Iran is completely contrary to the concept of "neither the West nor the East," which Iran independently implements. China, which wants to take advantage of Iran's regional power by doing a great cunning, does not want to be a party to the regional disputes contrary to what America does. [12]

The Common Hypocrisy

The Chinese regime wants to find a resource to be exploited and take advantage of finding an ally in the Middle East. However, another important point to be emphasized here is that Iran does not comply with the word of Islam, even if it is in its official name an Islamic Republic, and violates the principles of Islam for the sake of its economic interests. When an insulting step is taken against

Islam and the Prophet Muhammad, especially in Western countries, like other Muslim countries, Iran immediately reacts and even goes further by imposing the death penalty against those who commit these insults. For example, Iran issued a death fatwa on Salman Rushdie and attempted to suspend diplomatic relations with Denmark, which allowed cartoons insulting the Prophet Muhammad. But whenever the issue is about the genocide against East Turkistan and the Muslims living there, the word "Islam" in Iran's official name is forgotten, and the word "hypocrisy" comes in its place. Iran and China, which have agreed on economic, political, and military issues, are similar to each other in terms of "hypocrisy." Whenever asked, Chinese diplomats and foreign ministry spokespersons say that China's people have no problem with their religious freedom. However, they are engaging in hypocrisy by hiding the demolition of mosques in East Turkistan. [13] The parts of the houses of Muslims, where the Quran and other religious books were placed, were demolished, the Qur'an was collected from the houses, and the prayer rugs were removed. The fact that the Mullah regime, which does not allow women to walk on the streets with their heads uncovered in Iran, did not see the Muslim Uyghur women forced to remove their headscarves in East Turkistan is another example of hypocrisy. Iran's arguments to defend Islam are completely ineffective against the sino-colonialist Xi. The verses of the Qur'an, the hadiths of the Prophet Muhammad, and the names of the four great Islamic Caliphs were removed from the walls of the mosques in East Turkistan, and were replaced with communist propaganda doctrines and Xi's words. Did Ayatollah Ali Khamenei, who considers himself the supreme leader of the Islamic world, bring up any of these attacks against the Muslim Uyghurs when he met Xi in 2016? No news has been published so far that Khamenei issued a warning. Moreover, there was no objection from Khamenei or his assistants to the Beijing regime for changing Islam's principles and redefining these principles according to the Communist and socialist doctrine. The more painful situation for the Islamic world is that Pope Francis, the leader of the Catholic World, reacted to this genocide against Muslims in East Turkistan, not Khamenei, who regarded himself as the leader of the Islamic world. Pope Francis, who did not want to repeat the mistake of the Vatican, which supported the German Nazis during World War II, wrote the following statements in his newly published book: "I often think of people who are persecuted. The Rohingyas, the poor Uyghurs, the Yezidi people - what ISIS did to them was cruel - or the Christians who were killed by bombs while praying in the church in Egypt and Pakistan" [14]

Iranian opponents also criticize the Iranian government's agreement with the Neo-colonialist Chinese regime within the country. Ali Motahari, a former official of the Iranian Foreign Ministry, who criticized the Iranian government's silence on the East Turkistan issue, summarized the situation by saying, "Iran does not see China's pressure on the Muslims due to its economic interests." Motahari noted that it is a major failure for the Islamic Republic that the US, which Iran defines as the devil, condemns the oppression and torture imposed on Uyghur Muslims and imposed sanctions on China where Iran has not. [15]

Neo-colonialist China and Iran, whose words and deeds go against the grain, are determined to continue this cooperation for their benefit. However, on the chessboard in the Middle East, where the world's toughest moves are played, Iran faces the possibility of not establishing the alliance it wants with China. Because China has relations and agreements with countries that are both friendly and hostile to Iran, from Bahrain to the United Arab Emirates and Saudi Arabia. Neo-colonialist China makes deals not ' with Iran but also with other Gulf countries and Saudi Arabia.

Neo-colonialist Chinese Influence in Gulf Countries

The Sino-colonialist Xi Government takes steps within the scope of BRI not ' with Iran but also with the Gulf countries at the point of transition from the Indian Ocean to the Gulf of Oman and the Persian Gulf. The United Arab Emirates, Qatar, Bahrain, and Oman are also among the BRI countries. The projects in these countries are mostly about infrastructure and energy fields. UAE was one of the stopping points of Chinese President Xi Jinping, who visited BRI countries. While developing its relations with Saudi Arabia and Iran, China also attaches importance to the UAE in terms of maintaining the balance of power in the region and being effective, because the UAE has an important position in China's route from Eurasia to Europe. For this reason, relations between the UAE and China were accelerated when Xi came to power even before the BRI was announced. The mutual trade volume between the two countries, which was 287 million dollars in the 1990s, reached 42 billion dollars by 2012. [16] In 2019, this figure was 34.7 billion dollars, and the balance in trade favors China. The UAE's sales to China are $11.2 billion, in contrast to China's $23.5 billion exports. The UAE, which is primarily known as a financial center, is one of the places where Chinese companies are mostly located. As of 2019, there are 6,000Chinese companies, mostly in Dubai, and around 200,000 Chinese live in the UAE. [17]

After the BRI announcement, a new stage was started in the relations between the UAE and China. The relations that China has established with other countries within the scope of BRI includes political issues and transportation, energy, and finance fields to contribute to the growth of neo-colonialist China's economy. The Xi government wants to grow in the fields of energy, construction, nuclear energy, and logistics by making partnerships with other Arab countries in the Gulf and the Middle East at different levels to be more effective in the Middle East. Established within BRI's framework, the China-U-AE Joint Investment Fund has a size of 10 billion dollars. A bilateral trade agreement and a reciprocal transfer agreement, to increase the effectiveness of the Chinese currency, the Yuan, in the international market, were signed between the two countries. The neo-colonialist Chinese government took the step to seize and operate the ports on the BRI route to improve maritime transport in the UAE, just as it did the same in Iran and Pakistan. The container port in Khalifa Industrial Zone Abu Dhabi (KIZAD) has been given to the Chinese company COSCO for 35 years. China National Petroleum Corporation (CNPC) has become an 8 percent partner, with $1.77 billion, of the Abu Dhabi Company of Onshore Petroleum Operations (ADCO), one of the Emirates' largest oil companies. The Chinese regime considers Dubai, a financial center, as a center of attraction for Muslim countries' financial investments in the BRI. Two trillion dollars of global Islamic Capital whets China's appetite. For this, Dubai is critical. Chinese financial institutions and universities in Dubai organize annual joint meetings in this context. The huge size of construction projects in the United Arab Emirates is also considered an important opportunity for Chinese construction companies. [18] The second region in which China has invested the most is Jebel Ali Free Zone in Dubai. Since the Gulf countries are one of the world's largest re-export centers and a base to trade with western Asia, Europe, and Africa, UAE is a stepping stone for China.

The UAE, where China has invested billions of dollars, is a gateway for the Beijing government to the Middle East and North Africa (MENA). The rulers of the UAE, who are willing to be the guardians of this gateway, also intend to keep their economies alive with China's investments. Having signed many deals with China, the UAE does not see the region being gradually taken over by Chinese companies. Currently, the economic occupation of the UAE territories by China is not accepted as a problem by the Emirates. The UAE also opens its doors to Beijing for future generations to be educated with the neo-colonialist Chinese culture. Starting in the 2019-2020 academic year, the number of classes that teach Chinese in the UAE will be increased. The effects of Chinese education were experienced on the 70th anniversary of China's founding. To appeal to the Beijing government, Muslim children in Dubai have memorized the anthem of communist China, and videos were published about it. Sheikh Mohamed bin Zayed Al Nahyan Institute teaches Chinese with 200 teachers in 200 schools. [19]

One of the reasons why Chinese President Xi and the Emirates rulers get along well with each other because there is neither a democratic government nor a criticism mechanism in either country. China thanked the Emirates for supporting genocide policies in East Turkistan by equating not violating human rights to not interfering with others' right to sovereignty. The Emirates, who have no problem enriching themselves with China's blood money, defend their silence with the justification of "let's not interfere with China's internal affairs." [20] China also does not interfere with the internal affairs of the Emirates, but the Confucius Institutes, Beijing's soft power academic programs, propagate neo-colonialist China at two universities in the UAE.

China's Interest in Qatar's Natural Gas

For the neo-colonialist Chinese government, easy access to energy resources is essential. For this reason, China establishes systems that will exploit the energy resources by establishing separate alliances with hostile countries in the Middle East. One of the most striking examples of this is Qatar. Neighboring Saudi Arabia and strategically located in the Strait of Hormuz, Qatar has the world's largest outstanding liquefied natural gas (LNG) resources. China's ambassador to Qatar, Zhou Jian, speaking on the 71st anniversary of the establishment of the Chinese Communist Regime, also recalled the partnership agreements with Qatar to construct specialized ships for LNG, as China's perspective on the region is energy-oriented. Another importance of Qatar for China is the Chinese construction companies involved in infrastructure projects in Qatar. China Railway Construction company is building the Lusail Stadium in Qatar, which will host the 2022 FIFA World Cup. [21] China is the third-largest trading partner for Qatar, and the trade volume between the two countries is $11.5 billion as of 2018. The number of companies with a Qatar-China partnership is 181, and Chinese companies make investments in shipbuilding, petrochemical, technology, and tourism. The total amount of investment is 3.8 billion dollars. Neo-Colonialist China also has another strategic port investment in Qatar. One of the region's largest ports will be built to replace the existing Doha port at $7.4 billion. This port will be built by Chinese companies, just like other places. Huawei, which is the technological trojan horse of Sino-Colonialist Xi, also appears in Qatar. Huawei conducts communication infrastructure works in Qatar. [22] Strategic Cooperation between Qatar and China has been ongoing since 2014. The Qatar government wanted the support of the Asian giant, especially when they faced the Gulf crisis, and Qatar Emir Tamim bin Hamad Al Thani visited China in 2019. Although China makes 28 percent of its LNG imports from Qatar, it has silently supported the Gulf Quartet formed by the United Arab Emirates, Saudi Arabia, Egypt, and Bahrain, which excludes Qatar. [23]

In 2013, Emir Tamim bin Hamad Al Thani visited China. This visit during the BRI expansion period was welcomed by China, and Qatar was declared a "strategic partner." LNG is at the center of this strategic relationship between the two countries. In 2019, they decided to maintain this relationship. Qatar considers its relations with neo-colonialist China important for Qatar National Vision 2030 (QNV2030). America's support for the Gulf Quartet pushes Qatar into China's lap, just like Iran's example. The Qatar government cooperates with China in the military fields with the search for allies' motivation. In return, Beijing sees Qatar as a balance of power in the Gulf. The transfer of security and military technologies to Qatar within the scope of BRI and the increase in cooperation with Qatar are important for the long-term goals of sino-colonialist Beijing. This is why both the Gulf states and Qatar are vital to China as they are at the center of the trade corridor that will help keep this Asian giant at the center of the global economy. [24]

Strategically Located Country for Neo-colonialist China: Bahrain

Bahrain, which is a neighbor to Saudi Arabia and Qatar, in the Persian Gulf, is important for Beijing with its strategic location. Located on the transit point of the oil supplied from the Middle East, Bahrain is also an important location on the sea routes opening to the west. While developing the BRI strategy, the Beijing Government strives to keep its relations with Bahrain alive due to its strategic importance. The difference of Bahrain, which is the second transit point after the Emirate of China, which exports 2 trillion dollars to Asia, Europe, and Africa, from other countries, is that this country is the "pearl of the Gulf," that is, one of the important ports of the historical Silk Road. Bahrain is seen as Dubai for Chinese companies with its liberal economy, lifestyle, and dynamic management system among Middle Eastern countries. Bahrain stands out as it serves as a transit point for Xi's neo-colonialist rule, which wants to invest in both the Middle East and Africa. This is true for export and import as well as for money markets. [25] As of 2019, 134 Chinese companies have an investment of 835 million dollars in Bahrain. The project amount undertaken by construction companies in Bahrain is around 1.4 billion dollars. The trade volume between the two countries is around $1.6 billion in 2019. Chinese technology company Huawei is one of Bahrain's largest contractors in communications. It is seen once again that when sino-colonialist China enters a country, it lays its hands on every field from construction to communication. This is not limited to the economy, and the communist Chinese government's propaganda is deployed through the Confucius Institutes. The Confucius Institute, which China used as a soft power for its imperialist purposes, and was criticized by

Western countries, was also established in Bahrain. This institute operates in the University of Bahrain.

Important Junction on China's Maritime Silk Road, Oman

The first is the region in the South China Sea where Indonesia and Malaysia are located, and the second is the Arabian Sea part of the Indian Ocean. The geographical gateway of this second part is Oman. The fact that Oman, which stretches slightly from the Arabian peninsula to the Indian Ocean forms a junction on sea routes, makes it indispensable for sino-colonialist China to realize MSRI. Located in the middle of major shipping routes of both oil and cargo ships, another advantage of Oman is that it exports oil. Oman meets 6.9 percent of the oil needs of the Asian giant. Oman ranks sixth with $16.4 billion in crude oil supplies. [26]

Diplomatic relations between Oman and China began in 1978 when Deng Xiaoping came to power and launched a foreign expansion policy. Oman was the first Arab country to export oil to China in 1983. Oman's second export item has been natural gas, since 1997. Oman's position also became important in the period when Sino-colonialist China increased its domestic production and began to strengthen diplomatic relations with the Middle East and Gulf countries. The Beijing regime, which wants to take advantage of both oil supply and maritime transport together with MSRI, has invited Oman to take part in the sino-colonialist plan. The Oman government accepted the MSRI invitation with the idea to attract investment to its country. On the other hand, Oman is one of the countries that China has lent money to. Oman requested $3.6 billion from China in 2017. The Beijing government intends to invest in a special commercial zone and port in Oman under the BRI. A consortium of 6 Chinese companies has been formed for these investments to be used as both production and import and export centers. China also wants to establish an industrial city in Bahrain with a budget of 10.7 billion dollars. Considering that the Indian Ocean, where half of the world's container traffic and 70 percent of oil transportation are carried out has become the new junction of global trade, Oman with its two seaports is indispensable for sino-colonialist plans. The China's defense white paper of 2015, which summarizes China's regional imperialist goals, focused on expanding hegemony in the maritime field. Therefore, Chinese firms' investment of $10.7 billion in Duqm Port will offer sino-colonialist China the opportunity to establish alternative bases in economic terms and military terms. This port will turn into a connection point for a wide area from East Africa to the Pakistani coast. [27]

The fact that Oman cannot receive the investments expected from China in non-oil products weakens the position of the Sultanate in bilateral relations Because there are alternatives for the Beijing regime. Another challenge is that the importance of Oman's investments will decrease due to new industrial zones in Iran. Wanting to increase cooperation with Beijing on industrial zones and non-oil products, the government of Oman sold 49 percent of its electricity enterprises to the Chinese State Grid Company. In communication and technology, it is also expected that the companies of sino-colonialist China will come into play in the future. [28]

China's Expectation of "Let the War End, I will Earn Money" in Yemen

Although it does not take place in public opinion as much as Syria, Yemen is experiencing a great human tragedy due to the long-standing civil war. Cities have suffered greatly from this war. The reconstruction process, which will begin after the war, is the aim of sino-colonialist China. Yemen, the neighbor of Oman and located in the south of Saudi Arabia like Oman, attracts China's attention in BRI projects with its strategic location at the Red Sea entrance. Today, the Gulf of Aden is another important junction of sea routes from Asia to Europe. Although the Chinese regime does not directly express their desires in Yemen, it makes underhanded initiatives just like in Syria. Yemen, one of the first states to recognize the People's Republic of China in 1956, increased its economic relations with China after Xi came to power. An agreement was made for the power plant in 2012. In 2013, it was decided to expand the two container ports of Yemen. The Sino-colonialist Beijing government also supports Yemen's oil extraction activities, although it has fewer reserves than other countries in the region because China is ensuring the security of the line extending from Pakistan to Europe on the BRI's route. As stated before, China expects the war in Yemen to end and to profit from this country. [29] China, which does not directly intervene in the civil war in Yemen to confront Saudi Arabia, wants to bring the parties together and end this disaster. In turn, Saudi Arabia turns a blind eye to the pressures of the Beijing government in both Taiwan and East Turkistan and supports Beijing in this regard. [30]

Saudi Arabia, a Key Country for Neo-colonialist China's Oil Needs

The Chinese Communist regime has become one of the two most important actors in global trade with its export-oriented economy since the 1980s after switching to a state capitalist style of government. Considering that there are 60,000 factories in the Guangdong region, which realizes 'one-third of the total production of Communist Chinese regime, it will be understood why Saudi Arabia is important for the sino-colonialist capitalist system. The oil import amount of China, which alone realizes approximately 28 percent of the world's total production, is 238.7 billion dollars. 40.1 billion dollars of this figure is provided from Saudi Arabia. Forty-three countries supplied crude petroleum oil to China in 2019. Roughly half (44.8%) of Chinese imported crude oil originates from nine Middle Eastern nations ranging from $386 million from Egypt up to $40.1 billion for Saudi Arabia. [31] That is why the economic relationship between China, the worst enemy of Islam, and Saudi Arabia, where Islam's holiest cities and places are located, continues to grow.

Among the countries with which the Neo-Colonialist Chinese regime cooperates within the BRI, there are countries with which it cooperates in a few areas, as well as countries with extensive cooperation in every field. Although there has been trading between Saudi Arabia and China since the 1980s, the BRI has converted this into a comprehensive strategic cooperation with not ' Saudi Arabia, but many more nations. Undoubtedly, the hegemonic ambitions of Chinese President Xi have an impact on this development. Due to its oil and its political role in the Middle East, Saudi Arabia is one of the states that the Beijing government attaches importance to, such as Iran, Egypt, and UAE. Considering that the United States has extensive partnerships with the aforementioned countries, except Iran, it is certain that Xi, who wants to become the world's new superpower, will further develop its relations with states such as Saudi Arabia. Crown Prince Mohammed Bin Salman has been followed with keen interest by the Chinese government since he emerged as the most powerful name in the royal family of Saudi Arabia. Mohammed Bin Salman (or comm' known as MBS) who visited Beijing, in 2016, is a key figure in the development of relations between the two countries. Chinese President Xi visited Saudi Arabia in January 2016 and met with both the Saudi King and Crown Prince Mohammed Bin Salman. As a result of these negotiations, the size of the relations between the two countries based on oil was changed, and the relations were transformed into a comprehensive strategic relationship. Xi specifically requested that Arabia be included in the BRI. The Saudis have also shown interest in the China-Pakistan Economic Corridor (CPEC). [32] Taking part in CPEC will provide an important advantage in terms of Beijing's energy supply for both Arabia and China. The sino-colonialist Xi regime, which is about to turn Gwadar Port into a base of its own within the CPEC plan's scope, wants to make this point a new energy transfer center between Saudi Arabia and China. The Beijing government also takes steps to use its own currency in trade between the two countries. [33]

China Built the Mecca-Medina Railway

Relations between Saudi Arabia and China began 30 years ago. Relations, which began in 1990, have started to develop since Xi took over in China. In Saudi Arabia, the Mohammed Bin Salman factor is important. In response to China's

BRI steps, Saudi Arabia also wants the 2030 Vision Program to benefit from bilateral relations. As stated in the introduction to this chapter, the biggest reason why Saudi Arabia is important for sino-colonialist China is oil. In addition to oil, Xi sees Saudi Arabia as an important partner in its ambitions in the Middle East. Saudi Arabia is valuable for China because of its geographical location and because the two most important Islamic cities, Mecca and Medina, are in Saudi Arabia. However, the long-standing relationship between Saudi Arabia and the United States forces China to act carefully. [34] The trade volume between the two countries increased from 417 million dollars in 1990 to 73 billion dollars as of 2019. [35] The biggest factor in this increase is oil, and Saudi Arabia is one of the few countries that China's export numbers are higher than its production numbers in the import-export balance. Neo-colonialist Xi wants to take advantage of Saudi Arabia to ensure the success of the BRI in the MENA region. This is because Saudi Arabia, which has the Gulf of Aden to the south and the Red Sea to the west, is located in the European zone of the 21st Century Maritime Silk Road of Xi, and has influence in North Africa. Wanting to use the Red Sea as a step to MENA to develop its exports, the Beijing government has undertaken major infrastructure projects in Saudi Arabia. The most striking of these projects is the high-speed train line built by the China Railway Construction Corporation between Mecca and Medina. This line was completed and is operational. With the construction of this high-speed rail railway line, which is expected to be used during the period of Hajj, the most important gathering of the Islamic world, the neo-colonialist Chinese regime both opened a field of propaganda to itself and inflated the 2030 vision of Arabia. [36]

Establishment of UAV Factory in Saudi Arabia by China

One of the critical issues in military and security cooperation between Saudi Arabia and China is unmanned aerial vehicles (UAVs). In addition to the 20 UAVs purchased in 2014, 50 more UAVs were ordered in 2017. These UAVs are used in the War against Yemen. With an agreement signed with the China Aerospace Science company of neo-colonialist China, it was decided to establish a factory in Saudi Arabia to manufacture and produce UAVs. The UAVs to be produced here will be used both in Wars such as Yemen and will be sold to other countries in the Middle East. [37] Arms exchange between the two countries is expected to increase.

One of the critical issues between the two countries is that China guides Saudi Arabia, which it sees as the Islamic world leader, on genocide against Muslims in East Turkistan. Saudi Arabia has so far protected China's discourses and supported China in both "non-interference in domestic affairs" and "the fight against extremism." The statement made by Prince Mohammed Bin Salman during his visit to China shows how Muslim leaders have adopted China's discourse. The Crown Prince of Saudi Arabia, one of the countries that knows the extent of the humanitarian crisis in East Turkistan and the situation of the Muslims, said on the Chinese state channel CCTV that "China has the right to fight against terrorism and extremism." However, as Jonathan Fulton has stated, Saudi Arabia, unlike neo-colonialist China does not have the opportunity to censor all internet connections and technology in its country. Therefore, he will have to face the reaction of the Saudi people. [38] It is a matter of curiosity how much a government that says "I am the leader of the Muslims" will remain silent against the genocide of Muslims. The fact that MBS was keen on the issue of teaching Chinese to children in Saudi Arabia schools shows that Saudi Arabia cannot easily escape China's sino-colonialist trajectory.

Israel, the Country that Opened its Strategic Port to China

Israel has undoubtedly created one of the most surprising legs of Xi's flagship BRI. Relations between the two countries date back more than is known in public. During the "Ping-pong diplomacy" that Mao initiated with America in 1972 to both save China from isolation and take part in the UN Security Council, the foundation of the first relations between the Beijing government and Israel were laid. It is stated that former US Secretary of State Henry Kissinger, one of the most important defenders of the authoritarian Chinese regime in the world, also impacted the establishment of these first relations. The Beijing government, which saw the Jewish Lobby and Israel as the key to China's legitimacy and power in the international arena during the periods of Mao and his successor Deng, has always kept Israel alive behind closed doors. The Beijing government, which has to acquire the oil it needs for production mostly from the Muslim countries in the Middle East, has continued its relations with Israel in a low profile to avoid these countries' reactions. BRI initiated the process in which these relationships started to be seen.

BRI's sea route runs through the Red Sea and the Suez Canal to the Mediterranean and Europe. The cooperation of Sino-colonialist Xi with Israel while cooperating with the Gulf countries and Iran has attracted the attention of Western countries. That is the domination of the world by China. For this reason, China, which is not interested in the fight between the countries in the regions it wants to dominate, is calculating how to connect these regions to itself economically. China has already taken a step in this context, taking over the part of Israel's Haifa Port open to civilian ships. Haifa Port is of critical importance for the transport of natural gas resources in the Mediterranean to Beijing. The trade volume between Israel and China has increased in recent years. This trade volume, which was 10.9 billion dollars in 2014, increased to 14 billion dollars in 2018. [39] The railway line, which is planned to be built within BRI's scope and will connect the Red Sea and the Mediterranean, will ensure Israeli natural gas delivery to China. Israeli Prime Minister Benjamin Netanyahu, who visited Beijing in 2017, noted that there are a large number of investments in technology and infrastructure sectors within the relations between the two countries. In an interview with a newspaper, Netanyahu said China made one-third of high technology investments in Israel. Chinese companies undertook the Carmel Tunnel in Haifa and the rail system projects in Tel Aviv. [40]

China, which has 10 cities with more population than Israel's total population,expects to benefit from technological and scientific developments in Israel. For the Beijing government, which predicts that more sophisticated and more efficient studies will gain importance in every field from food to health, agriculture to water and biotechnology, it is important to establish a relationship with Israel. During Netanyahu's visit in 2017, 12 agreements worth $25 billion were signed between the two countries. Beijing's investment in technology companies in Israel has increased 10 times compared to the previous year as of 2016 and reached 16.5 billion dollars. [41] Expansion of Haifa Port and Ashdod Port, construction of Tel Aviv light rail systems, and the construction of Carmel Tunnel are among the most important infrastructure projects. The total investment amount of these projects is around 4 billion dollars. [42]

Paying attention to the balances in international relations, China does not want to oppose America, Israel's ancient ally, and tries not to offend the Muslim countries from which it has purchased oil. However, the point that should be expressed here is that Israel's exclusion by the USA during the Obama period opened a space for China in Israel. As the world's second economic power, the Beijing government sided with Israel when it needed it most. [43]

The Country Where China Wants to Act as an Ally Instead of America: Jordan

Jordan located just east of Israel and north of Saudi Arabia is one of the countries that sino-colonialist China wants to see as its ally in the Middle East. China was one of the partners of the Amman International Motor Fair held in Jordan when Xi Jinping announced the BRI. With Iraq on one side, Syria and Israel on the other side, Jordan is one of America's allies in the region. Jordan has also been one of the countries that the Chinese regime has knocked on its door within the scope of sino-colonialist steps in recent years. Jordan opened its doors to China for economic reasons and because China is an alternative power to America in the Middle East. The first royal visit from Jordan to China after 1999 took place in 2013, and China found another gateway to the Middle East in Jordan. [44]

When the history of the relations between China and Jordan is examined, it will be seen that Jordan always acted according to America in the past. During Jordan's Black September in 1970, the Communist Party of China (CCP) supported the Palestinian fedayeen in their attempts at overthrowing the monarchy. However, in the years following U.S. President Nixon's pivot to China, the Jordanian government would follow suit. In the 1980s, Jordan began to seek further relations with China. Deng's foreign expansion policy is one of the processes that bring Jordan closer to China. Sino-colonialist China has become Jordan's largest supplier over time. The result of this has been the "imbalance" in foreign trade, which reached 2.6 billion dollars in 2020. Since Jordan imports everything from shoes to air conditioners and vaccines from China, the import volume has increased to 2.7 billion dollars, and its exports remained at 164 million dollars. Jordan, which is also a member of the BRI, signed a 2.5 billion dollar project with China regarding oil production and agreed with China on the construction of a railway of 2.8 billion dollars. The free trade zone system, which is indispensable for the neo-colonialist system, also appears in Jordan. The system established by China is more attractive for Jordan, which failed to complete its economic program with the International Monetary Fund (IMF). Jordan has been hit hard by the Covid-19 pandemic. Tourismis of critical importance in its economy and as a result, Jordan needs China. Therefore, Jordan has been added to the list of sino-colonialist China allies in the Middle East. [45]

Lebanon, which Looks to China to Come out of the Economic Crisis

Lebanon is another country in which China shows interest in the Mediterranean basin. Lebanon, which has been in political and economic instability for a long time, is searching for an ally for support. Indirectly affected by the tension between America and China, Lebanon had to choose between the West's alliance and the economic power of the east. Lebanon, which has suffered from conflicts between Iran and Saudi Arabia for many years, is in an economic crisis where its currency has lost 80 percent of its value. The "benevolent" China, which took the stage under the pretext of supporting countries in need, has also shown itself in Lebanon. The following statement of an official from the government, who is supported by the Hezbollah group that Iran helped behind the scenes, clearly shows the position of Lebanon: "Our move toward China is dire. But we are not turning our back to the West." [46] The rescue package prepared by the IMF for Lebanon did not come into effect because the legal arrangements expected from Lebanon were not implemented. Hezbollah, which currently stands against the West, like Iran, prefers the Communist Chinese Regime instead of the IMF.

Hezbollah Leader Sides with China Seeking to Destroy Islam

Speaking of which, it is necessary to mention another matter. Some cartoons insulting the Prophet Muhammad have been published in France in recent weeks. Since such an insult against the Prophet Muhammad could never be accepted, all Muslims reacted to these cartoons. The Hezbollah leader in Lebanon, Hasan Nasrallah, one of those who reacted, considered the cartoons as "declaring a sort of war" [47]. Like his mentors in Iran, Hasan Nasrallah sees himself as one of the protectors and religious leaders of the Islamic world. Heaven knows why these so-called religious leaders have not reacted to Xi Jinping's removal of the Qur'anic verses from the mosques' walls in East Turkistan, nor to Xi putting his own words in their place. To date, Hezbollah leaders have not made a single statement regarding the anti-Islamic practices of China in East Turkistan. Whatever the Sino-colonialist Chinese regime did to destroy Islam, neither Ali Khamenei nor Hasan Nasrallah reacted to China. Although China is committing genocide against a Muslim population, it has a free hand in Muslim countries thanks to this unresponsiveness. China's plans for the Middle East also include Syria and Iraq.

Sino-colonialist China, the Secret Ally of Dictator Assad

According to the estimates of the United Nations, 400,000 people lost their lives in the civil war in Syria. 5.6 million Syrians have left their country since 2011. 6 million Syrians have been displaced, forced to leave their homes and move to another city. The bloodiest civil war in the Middle East's recent history is about to complete its 10th year. [48] The Beijing government watches the civil war in Syria from a distance according to its long-term colonial plans and supports the dictator Assad regime behind closed doors. [49] The sino-colonialist Chinese government, knowing that Syria will knock on its door in the future, is waiting for the time to take an active role in the country's reconstruction process after the civil war. As in Iran and Lebanon, the Xi regime, which is waiting with debt securities in its hand to help the dictator Assad regime, also appears in Syria. From Beijing's perspective, which uses the "internal problems" argument while defending the atrocities it uses to suppress opponents in its own country, the problems in Syria should also be resolved by the Syrians. China is opposed to the operation launched by Turkey. The Chinese government also acts together with Russia in voting about Syria in the UN. [50] The Sino-colonialist Chinese regime wants to increase cooperation with Assad in security matters by claiming that

East Turkistani people are among the groups that participated in the civil war in Syria. China wants to improve its economic relations with Syria due to its plans to become the new superpower with BRI. For the Chinese regime, which has never put all of their eggs in a single basket, Syria and Lebanon represent a route to the Mediterranean that is an alternative to the Suez Canal. [51] As the dictator Assad regime sees his country's economic future in the investments of China, he wants Beijing's support. In return for this support, neo-colonialist China built a $2 billion industrial park. Huawei company also aspired to establish Syria's communication system. [52] The Beijing government, never wanting to risk itself, will continue to wait to implement its colonial policies in Syria.

Iraq, the Third Country Where China Purchases the Most Oil

The Iraqi lands, where oil was found for the first time in 1827, became one of the places Western imperialist states wanted to seize after the Ottoman Empire entered the period of collapse. Iraq, one of the world's leading oil producers, is also the center of power conflicts and regional wars. Iraq has been at the center of power struggles after the war with Iran and the wars in 1991 and 2003. The communist Chinese regime's aspirations over the Middle East and Iraq date back to the Mao period. In the 1960s, China supported the state administrators in the region to prevent America and Russia from being effective in the region. The Chinese regime of the period, which applauded the collapse of the kingdom in Iraq and the proclamation of the Republic of Iraq by Abd Al Kasım, wished this to be an example for other countries. The first diplomatic relations between China and Iraq were established in 1958. However, members of the Communist Party established in Iraq were found dangerous by Al Qassim, and China was accused of supplying weapons to these groups. Relations between the two countries have deteriorated in this process. [53] The era of Saddam Hussein is the period when western countries imposed sanctions on Iraq and invaded Iraq twice. This key country of the Middle East has gone through difficult political and economic processes for years. Despite this, one of the rare countries that continued to benefit from Iraq was sino-colonialist China. [54] Iraq is China's third-largest oil supplier after Saudi Arabia and Russia. Iraq, which has a 9.9 percent share in China's oil imports, exported 23.7 billion dollars worth of oil to China in 2019. Iraq is one of the countries where China has a foreign trade deficit thanks to its oil advantage. [55] In 2018, the trade volume between China and Iraq exceeded 30 billion dollars. In contrast to Iraq's oil export of 20 billion dollars to China, China's export to Iraq is 7.9 billion dollars. Iraq, where official relations with China date back to the 1960s, is the first Arab country to participate in China's BRI project. The Sino-colonialist Chinese regime intends to develop its relations with Iraq further because it has significant oil reserves and is located on the historical Silk Road route. [56]

Iran's influence on Iraq is one of the controversial and troubling issues for both America and Western countries. The influence of Iran-backed groups in Iraq, which has not been fully stabilized since the invasion in 2003, is an undeniable fact. However, another power that the USA and western countries should pay attention to here is the sino-colonialist Chinese regime. Iraq, which signed the BRI last year, is essential for China due to its location as a transition point to the Eurasia corridor and oil. Iraq was among the 50 countries that did not see the genocide committed by China in East Turkistan and insteadpraised the Beijing Government. As Daniel Samet states, China wishes "to exploit the economic dependence of Iraq and other BRI clients as a means to advance its political aims." [57] One way China increased its colonial activities in Iraq, which had difficulty fighting the Covid-19 virus, was "mask diplomacy." Since the outbreak of Covid-19, Beijing has sent aid to many countries in the form of medical diplomacy. Iraq has been a focal point for China's efforts in the Middle East, and Iraqi health officials have had nothing but praise for Chinese efforts. [58] Upon arriving in Beijing on September 19, Iraq Prime Minister Adel Abdul-Mahdi described his visit to China as heralding a "quantum leap" in bilateral relations. [59] While Chinese companies are currently operating in many Iraq projects, it is expected that this will accelerate with BRI. Because China's modus operandi in its colonial plans around the globe is firstly to extend assistance to the specific area that a country needs help with most, and then to leverage that to work outwards into all other areas of use to its BRI project. [60] Today, a similar situation is happening in Iraq.

10

Chinese Colonization of Africa

"If you remain silent against the grabbing of a right, remember
that one day you'll also face this injustice and persecution"
Abd al-Latif al-Baghdadi

ONE OF THE MOST established and oldest educational institutions in the Islamic world is undoubtedly the Al-Azhar University in Egypt. For more than a thousand years, hundreds of thousands of students have been educated in Al-Azhar. Again, tens of thousands of students stayed in the dormitories of this ancient university. Al-Azhar University, which welcomed the scholars who were able to flee from the Mongols and the scientists from Andalusia, also has a distinguished position among the Muslim people of East Turkistan. Like Abdulaziz Chingizhan Damollam, one of the prominent scholars of our people, we left our country to study science, took refuge in Al-Azhar, thousands of kilometers away, and aimed to study there. Qutluk Shawqi and Abdulaziz Chingizhan Damollam were among those who went to Al-Azhar even before the Chinese Communist Party invaded East Turkistan in the 1920s, and were known as fighters for their cause. Abdulaziz Chingizhan Damollam, who first studied in India for 3 years in 1926 and then came to Azhar as both a student and a professor, is also an important role model for Muslim Uighur youth. Abdulaziz Chingzhan Damollam, who returned to his homeland in 1947 for the scientific development and for freedom of East Turkistan, continued his struggle during the Communist Party invasion in 1949, was arrested by this irreligious regime and put into prison, and was martyred by the atheist regime on February 2, 1951. But the path of knowledge and science that he and Qutluq Shawqi opened has never been interrupted. Some of the young Muslims from East Turkistan also found a way and were educated in Al-Azhar. "The magazine entitled: Voice of Turkistan", prepared by Ibrahim Wasil, who founded the Turkistan Charity Society in Egypt, was published until 1958. "Azad Turkistan" magazine, prepared by Muhammed Emin Islami, one of the pioneers of Uyghur intellectuals, is one of the traces left by the students of East Turkistan in Al-Azhar. During the Cultural Revolution, when the Chinese Communist regime closely followed the Muslims in East Turkistan, when all the doors were closed, the number of those studying at Al- Azhar was slightly cut. In the 1980s, some migrated to this unique educational institution in Cairo with the relaxation of some regime policies caused by the re-opening of the school. In order not to waste this opportunity given to us to leave the country at a young age and learn science, we had the opportunity to study in Al-Azhar, with the support of our family. 34 years ago, we arrived in Cairo on the 9th of September and joined a few Uyghur students like Abdulcelil Turan. While studying here, we met with the Deputy of Al-Azhar Dr. Ahmed Shalaby to share our issues and the problems of those who came before us, and for the development of religious education activities in East Turkistan. It was revealed during these meetings that Dr. Ahmed Shalaby had traveled to East Turkistan for years, contacted the science and wisdom circles of East Turkistan, and took steps in the direction of bringing some Uyghur students to Egypt. During these visits of Dr. Ahmed Shalaby decided to give scholarships to 10 Uyghur girls and 10 Uyghur boys every year, and 100 East Turkistan students to study in Azhar for 5 years in total. However, the Communist Chinese regime, which increased its pressure and surveillance in East Turkistan, also tried to close this door of education. It never allowed students from East Turkistan to take advantage of this opportunity. Especially after Xi Jinping became the president of China, the Egyptian authorities came under the influence of the Beijing government and the East Turkistan students who came to Al-Azhar for education were forcibly deported to China by the police. While the Egyptian government expelled hundreds of students in order to appease the sino-colonial Beijing regime, the administration of Al-Azhar University, which even gave scholarships to Muslim Uyghurs for a period, remained silent in the face of this injustice. The Sheikh of Al-Azhar and their deputies, who were visited twice a week by the officials of the atheist Chinese regime, have long forgotten the words of their Master, Abdullatif Baghdadi, who we quoted in the introduction to this article. This educational institution, which tells its students the importance of speaking out against injustice towards Muslims using the lessons taught in the Hadith, is in the assumption that the persecution of East Turkistan will not touch them one day in the future. If they do not take a stand against the sino-colonial Chinese government, these Al-Azhar Teachers will be guilty like they teach the principles of Xi and Communist doctrine, instead of the Qur'an and Hadith-i Sharifs in their lessons. To see how close this danger is, it is necessary to analyze the situation of the countries which were technologically and economically exploited by China, as we explored in previous chapters.

Egypt: Rulers Change, But not the Relations with China

Relations between China and Egypt have a long history. Egypt is the first African and Arab country to establish relations with China formally. The Egyptian government officially recognized the government of the Chinese Communist Party in 1956. Egypt later supported China's bid to become a permanent member of the UN Security Council. In return, China condemned the pressures of Britain, France, and America in the Suez Canal conflict. As of today, sino-colonialist China has been one of Egypt's critically important allies in military and technical matters. At the same time, China is one of the largest export markets for Egypt. In particular, crude oil and marble are the main export materials. Egypt's importance to neo-colonialist China became more vital after the Arab Spring. In recent years, Egypt's bad economic conditions combined with the Arab Spring has led to the emergence of Xi as Egypt's "savior". Even the Muslim Brotherhood Leader, President Mohammed Morsi, had one of his first high-level official meetings with his Chinese counterpart, Hu Jintao, immediately after taking office as head of state, and visited Beijing. During this visit, China lent 200 million dollars to Egypt and gave 300 police cars as a gift. Negotiations were held on both economic and political issues. Support from neo-colonialist China was important for the newly elected Morsi government. [1] After he was removed from power, Abdul Fatttah el- Sisi, who succeeded Morsi, also paid special attention to improving relations with sino-colonial Xi. He has therefore maintained support for the One Belt and Road Initiative (BRI), which was announced in 2013. At the heart of Egypt's worth to China is the Suez Canal. The Suez Canal, one of the key crossing points on the BRI sea leg, is the gateway to China's Mediterranean Sea. In a sense, it is the key to the Communist Party's ambitions to reach Europe. Although some European countries opposed this situation, the Egyptian government has supported China fully. During the negotiations held during Sisi's first visit in 2014, a consensus was reached on the development of cooperation between the two countries in economic fields, including mutual trade, infrastructure investments, aviation, and alternative energy sources, especially nuclear energy. [2] Egyptian President Sisi met with Chinese President Xi seven times and signed 25 agreements. These agreements are mainly related to energy and transport. Sisi also fully supports China's favorite project, BRI. Sisi, who wants to show how eager he is to cooperate with Beijing, participated in the 75th-anniversary events of the 2nd World War in Beijing in September 2015. President Xi returned this favor by visiting Sisi in Cairo 4 months later. This visit is the highest-level visit to Egypt since 2004. In 2016, at international meetings, Sisi went to China twice and met with Xi. In 2018, Sisi again visited China, where he attended the China-Africa Cooperation Meeting and praised the Beijing Government. Sisi's last visit to China was last April as part of the BRI. [3]

At this meeting, it was decided to cooperate not ' on economic matters but also on political issues. In particular, Sisi intends to apply the political practices of the sino-colonialist Xi and the Communist Beijing government in his own country. China wants to use Egypt as leverage against the Arab and African countries in the path of their new imperialist plans to exploit the world. The fact that Sisi has the same desire to have a say in Africa and the Middle East ' increased the Beijing government's influence on Egypt. China's apparent willingness to cooperate with Egypt on the military, law enforcement, security, terrorism, and transnational crimes is actually this desire. Even though the One Belt and Road Initiative seems to be at the center of the relations, it is noteworthy that the two states' relations have shifted from economy to political and military cooperation. In a sense, this means that China is establishing its both capitalist and repressive state model in Egypt. [4]

Sino-Colonialist China will Now Dominate the Suez Canal

Investments in Egypt constitute one of the most important parts of the Belt and Road Initiative (BRI) of the communist Beijing regime. To benefit more from the Suez Canal, China has decided to build a large special economic zone here. For this reason, the Suez Canal Economic Zone (SCZone) was announced in 2008. The sino-colonial Chinese government, aiming to produce and export from Egypt to Europe, Africa, and the Middle East, has been one of the biggest inves-tors of SCZone. However, the Arab Spring and the events after that delayed the realization of this goal. Sino-Colonial Xi's declaration of BRI in 2013 accelerated this project. SCZone is being established in Sokhna District, 120 km from Cairo. The reason for choosing this location is because it is close to China's Tianjin Technological Development Area (TEDA), which was previously built by China. TEDA is one of China's largest production and logistics centers built in Egypt. As soon as SCZone was announced, TEDA immediately took the stage as the first and biggest investor. Since TEDA is also the largest partner of SCZone, the two economic regions have started to be evaluated together, and its name has been changed to TEDA SCZone. [5] SCZone, which is being established on 461 square kilometers, consists of four main sections and 6 ports connected to the Suez Canal. After completing the first part of the project, 68 companies, including Chinese giant companies, showed interest here. Construction of the second part has started in 2016. The Egyptian government has given tax advantages to companies operating here. SCZone, which the Sino-Colonialist Beijing regime attaches great importance to opening up to African countries, offers Chinese companies the opportunity to export their products to 26 countries on the continent with zero customs, provided they label their products as "Made in Egypt." [6] The Beijing government has decided to increase the number of its investments in Egypt, together with BRI. The Chinese ambassador announced that the investment of 7 billion dollars would be increased to 15 billion dollars. [7] As part of another project, the Egyptian government has agreed with the Chinese company Hutchison Ports to construct a new container port in the Abu Qir region. Hutchison is one of the largest port management companies in the world. It operates in 27 countries, including Egypt. It also operates two of Egypt's largest ports: the port of Alexandria and the port of Abu Qir, whose projects were recently signed by parties. The company's goal here is to operate with an annual capacity of one million containers. [8]

Construction of New Capitol Delivered to China

Another project that the Sisi government has delivered to sino-colonialist China and its construction companies outside of SCZone is the new administrative capital project. Built between the Nile River and the Suez Canal on Cairo's east side, this city is 700 square kilometers in size. By comparison, it will be equal to Singapore's surface area. The city, which 6.5 million people can live in upon its completion, is being built by Beijing's state-owned company, the China State Construction Engineering Corporation (CSCEC). The center of this new city will be the tallest tower in Africa with a length of 385 meters. The project, which started in 2018, is aimed to be completed in 2023. [9] The cost of this new city is expected to be between 45 billion dollars and 58 billion dollars. Sisi, whom Sino-colonialist Xi sees as the guardian of Africa, aims to have his name written in history as the leader who built the new capital. [10] However, the most striking example of China's inability to contribute to the economic development of countries is seen in Egypt, contrary to what Xi claimed when announcing the BRI. Because the new capital of Egypt, where neo-colonialist China has established special economic zones to strengthen its economic hegemony, is also built by Chinese construction companies. In this case, no contribution is made to Egypt's local economy. On the contrary, experts point out that the people in Egypt are getting poorer. Timothy Kaldas, an expert at Cairo-based think tanks, criticized, "The government that spent billions of dollars tells the public that they have to tighten the belts." Another political expert, Hassan Nafaa, comments: "Sisi may want to put his stamp on history, but Egyptians do not see an improvement in their quality of life. Sisi will be remembered as the one who destroyed the middle class ". [11] On the other hand, it is stated that the new capital will be equipped with state-of-art technologies. This means that China, which will build the internet and security infrastructure of all public buildings in Egypt, up to the ministries' rooms, will have access to all kinds of information and documents. Another criticism is that this new city will not solve the problems of the historical city of Cairo, such as population crowding, water and electricity, and conditions of living. Because ' a certain number of very high-income people will live in this new city, this city will become a place where public officials ply between home and work. In Cairo, where the weekly earnings are 70 dollars, no civil servant can live in the new capital. [12] In other words, the Sisi government, together with its Chinese friends, is building luxury government ghettos where everything from A to Z will be in Chinese hands.

The Sino-colonial Chinese government agreed with Egypt in 2016 and burdened Egypt with 12.5 billion dollars of debt. Apart from that, nearly 20 billion dollars were injected into the Egyptian economy by China through financing, construction, and development projects. While the communist Xi regime sees Egypt as a stepping stone to both Africa and Europe, it also increases the country's debt burden. Although there has been no recent example similar to that of Sri Lanka, the share of foreign debt in Egypt's GDP is high. The debt ratio, which corresponds to 30 percent of the GDP in 2014, has increased at rocket speed since 2017 and reached 102 percent. It dropped to 93 percent in 2018. This percentage is well above the 77 percent that the World Bank has determined as the point of economic collapse. [13] The Egyptian government's debt to sino-colonialist China is $4.3 billion. A significant part of this figure belongs to the country budget, the banking sector, and the business world. [14] Undoubtedly, China's expectations for the BRI project are very high for the Egyptian government to be under such high debt. However, considering the country's economic structure and creating an economic region in the Suez Canal, building a giant new city that will cost billions of dollars and making similar investments means a debt-based economy in which the people will become poorer rather than generating economic development. China already dominates the system in SCZone rather than Egypt. If the Egyptian government cannot pay those debts one day, the world's most important commercial transit point will be taken over by the sino-colonial Xi regime.

Military Companies also Do Business with the Chinese
The Egyptian Military Organization is actively involved in these megaprojects

with Sino-colonialist China. Benha Electronics, a subsidiary of the National Authority for Military Production, and Kaha, a company in the chemical industry are among the companies that partner with Chinese companies. The Arab Organization for Industrialization (AOI), which oversees both the military and civilian sectors, has partnered with Shanghai Wanxiang in the development of the smart electric transportation system and with China North Industries Corporation on the localization of technology. [15] The fact that the soldiers play such an effective role in Egypt's relations with sino-colonialist China evokes Pakistan's example. In Pakistan, Prime Minister Imran Khan appointed a retired general to head the special unit he had set up for CPEC and placed him in a supra governmental position. On the other hand, in Egypt, Sisi himself is already a former soldier, and Sisi is appointing soldier-led companies at critical points. This is another area where Neo-colonialist Xi provided an example for Sisi. Because while Xi works with Bingtuan, a semi-military semi-civil organization in East Turkistan occupied by China, Sisi acts in the same way.

Uyghur Students were Deported to Please China

There is a dispute between Egypt and Ethiopia over claims on the Nile River. On the one hand, China conducts its relations with Egypt, and on the other hand, it does business with Ethiopia. China, which financially supports Addis Ababa, provides technical support for the construction of the Gilgel Gibe III Dam on the Omo River, just like the Tekeze dam. The Egyptian government considers dams and hydropower projects of Ethiopia on the Blue Nile as a security threat. Egypt, concerned that it will lose control of its water resources, is taking every step to win China's support. The detention and deportation of students from East Turkistan under the "suspicion of terrorism" is one such step that Egypt has taken. [16]

Especially since 2017, the Egyptian police have been raiding Muslim East Turkistan residents' houses and arresting them, and handing them over to the sino-colonial Chinese regime. The number of Uyghur students arrested by the police in July of that year alone is 90. According to two color codes, these students are divided into two groups at the police station as "green and yellow." Those in the yellow group were deported after being detained for a while. Others were released after 60 days of arrest, with their passports confiscated. Among the released Uyghurs, those who had the opportunity left Egypt immediately. It is known that 6,000 East Turkistan Muslims lived together with students in Egypt until before the raids. [17] However, in Egypt, not students from East Turkistan, but students from China have started to worry because the Communist regime waging war on Islam threatens other Muslim communities as well. This perspective has become even more apparent in recent years.

This is true not for Uyghurs but also for Hui Muslims. After a video of a Hui Muslim student reading the Holy Quran was published on the internet, this student suffered many insults. [18] To recall the question at the beginning of the article, it does not seem possible for the Egyptian Government to leave the trajectory of sino-colonialist China for economic and political relations. But why do the administrators of Al-Azhar University, once a place where students from all over the world come to study safely, wait to act? These administrators do not hear Muslim students' voices because of the doors they closed one after another, and the walls surrounding them do not mean that these painful truths did not occur. Until when will the rulers and scholars of Al-Azhar, the authority to which even the Egyptian people complain about the Egyptian government, ignore the war initiated by the sino-colonial Chinese government against Islam? Will the teachers, who explained that "the Qur'an can never be changed" in their lectures, close their eyes to Xi's attempt to rewrite this holy book? While a Muslim society is subjected to genocide in East Turkistan, the Egyptian scholars, who are a living example of the verse of Qur'an that says "Why are you saying things you didn't do?" continues to describe the hadith of "Muslims are like members of a body" as if nothing happened. It is necessary to remind the following slogan of those who do not speak against the persecution in East Turkistan: "Don't be silent! As you keep silent, it will be your turn!"

Neo-colonialist China who Turned Western Sanctions on Sudan into Opportunities

Sudan, located in the south of Egypt, is one of the countries in East Africa where western states have opened up space for sino-colonialist China for many years, like Iran. With the division of Sudan into North and South, Beijing again became "the house that always wins" in international disputes.

The origins of the relations between Sudan and the Communist Chinese regime date back to the Mao period. The Sudanese government of the period is another African state that first recognized the People's Republic of China in 1959. The relations of the two countries had progressed at low intensity until the 1990s, and after the revolution in Sudan in 1989, China started to be more active. In the face of conflicts in the country and international pressures against it, the Sudanese Government saw sino-colonialist China as a supporter of itself. During the Darfur Crisis, the Chinese regime underhandedly supported the Sudanese government to protect its interests in the region and avoid confrontation with America. [19] The Beijing government bestowed the helping hand Sudan needed against the American embargo that started in 1995. Sino-colonialist China immediately made a trade agreement wherever there was a problem and in this way increased its diplomatic power. In this way, China has shown itself in the capital city of Sudan, Khartoum. Greater Nile Petroleum Operating Company was established in 1997 with the support of China National Petroleum Corporation (CNPC) to operate in the petroleum fields in Sudan. In Sudan, where 133,000 barrels of oil per day are produced, sino-colonialist China controls 75 percent of this sector. Sudanese Foreign Minister Ibrahim Ghandour said that the Beijing government is investing in the oil sector and other fields and is interested in mining and construction. [20] Most of the investments are made in textile, cotton, gold mining, and animal husbandry. The biggest investment is in the oil field. CNPC has invested $10 billion in this sector.

On the other hand, protest demonstrations started in the country in 2018 as a reaction to the government due to the economic crisis and long-standing pressures in Sudan. In this process, the sino-colonial Chinese government did not intervene in any way and continued to resume its work after the crisis. At the end of these demonstrations, Omar Al Bashir, who ruled Sudan for nearly 30 years, was overthrown due to the coup in 2019. The Provisional Military Administration handed over the government of the country to the newly established Independence Council in August 2019 and Abdullah Hamdok was elected as the new prime minister. During the coup, Chinese diplomats immediately contacted the temporary military administration behind the scenes. Sudanese Oil Minister Awad al-Jaz, with whom Sino-Colonialist China has been doing business for many years, had been arrested. Awad Al-Jaz was also Bashir's deputy. Acting with the idea of "the king is dead, long live the king," the Beijing Ambassador immediately congratulated the military administration.

The Sino-colonial Xi regime wanted to reinforce its relations with the new Sudanese government by blocking the UN Resolution about 120 people who lost their lives during Khartoum's demonstrations. During the UN meetings in 2019, Chinese Foreign Minister Wang Yi met with the new Sudanese Prime Minister Hamdok and explained that the two countries' relations would be maintained. [21] Within the scope of BRI, the flagship of the Chinese Communist Regime, the Port Sudan Railway project in Sudan and the railway line project that will connect Chad, Cameroon, and Sudan are among the projects on the agenda. [22] However, no official joint memorandum was signed yet. This railway project is important for the Chinese government, which has always regarded the "win-win" logic as a priority. The new government, which intends to continue constructing the railway, which was initiated during the reign of the overthrown leader Bashir, wants to take part in BRI. The new Sudan government has also requested support from the Beijing regime, which has invested nearly $ 20 billion in Sudan for infrastructure projects. [23] On the other hand, Sudan owes 6.8 billion dollars to sino-colonialist China for energy and transportation issues. The Beijing regime gave loans to Sudan for a total of 68 different issues. [24]

Ethiopia Struggling to Pay Its Debts to China

Ethiopia, one of the most populous countries in Africa after Nigeria, is also one of the important administrative and political centers of the continent. The headquarters of international organizations such as the African Union, the UN Economic Commission for Africa, and the Intergovernmental Authority for Development (IGAD) are located in Addis Ababa, the capital of Ethiopia. The ability to reach the headquarters of international organizations and representatives of countries provides an advantage to Sino-Colonialist China. Ethiopia, where China has established diplomatic relations since 1970, is also in a position of importance to the European Union, America, and other western states. Another aspect that makes Ethiopia important is its relations with its western neighbor, the Republic of South Sudan. Ensuring political stability in South Sudan is the common wish of both Ethiopia and China. Because the oil in South Sudan is expected to support the energy needs of sino-colonialist China. This country is strategically important for the Xi and BRI plans in terms of controlling the Blue Nile. Because the dams to be built on this river are critical in terms of both Egypt and Djibouti's water resources and energy production. [25]

However, the high borrowing and non-payment risk, similar to what we see in other countries, is also in question for Ethiopia in the economic relations established between sino-colonialist China and Ethiopia. These words of Ethiopian President Abiy Ahmed about the Djibouti Railway, which was initiated by borrowing from sino-colonialist China but was interrupted because it was inefficient, is important: "What hurts Ethiopia is borrowing from some other companies or countries. For example, Ethiopia took a loan to build a railway, but Ethiopia was asked to repay the debt before the project was completed." [26] While China's investments in Ethiopia have grown by 52 percent, Ethiopia's debt to the sino-colonial Xi government has risen to $12.1 billion since 2000. This debt corresponds to 59 percent of the country's total debt. Ethiopia and China sat at the bargaining table as the Ethiopian-Djibouti Railway project, which Prime Minister Abiy complained about, further increased this debt amount. However, Abiy, who wants to take advantage of the BRI, has met with Chinese President Xi for new investments. [27] Within the scope of the memorandum signed in 2019, the 12 kilometre Addis Ababa beach project was decided within the scope of a five-year economic and technological partnership. Sino-colonialist China again carried out 70 percent of the road and construction projects within the scope of infrastructure investments.

248

Djibouti, the Place Where Sino-Colony Established its First Base Overseas

One of the smallest but strategically most important countries in Africa is undoubtedly Djibouti, located in Africa's Horn. Located between Somalia and Eritrea, Djibouti is in the Gulf of Aden's center at the connection point to the Red Sea. Its unique geographical location has made Djibouti one of the important gates of maritime transport. This is why the Xi government, which wanted to establish the colonial system of the 21st century in the new world order, established its first military base in overseas countries here. [28]

Sino-colonialist Xi has high expectations from this small country of Africa. Djibouti immediately joined the neo-colonialist initiative BRI, which was announced in 2013. The "strategic cooperation" between Djibouti and the Asian giant had been declared, and the People's Liberation Army Navy (PLAN) has its first foreign base in Djibouti. It has been stated that the Chinese soldiers sent to this base will act as part of the UN peacekeeping force. It is stated that the capacity of this base, which is rented from the Djibouti government for 20 million dollars annually, can be increased up to 10,000 soldiers. According to the determinations of the US Department of Defense, there are 8 hangars, underground facilities, unmanned aerial vehicles, and helicopters on the base. This base is a mile from the American base in the region. In a sense, this is the first place where the two countries' soldiers meet in another country. Although it was alleged that Chinese soldiers acted in harassment by shooting laser lights towards the American base, Beijing denied these allegations. [29]

Billion-dollar Investment for the Strategic Position, not Energy

This small country of Africa has no underground resources that can benefit the sino-colonial Chinese regime compared to neighboring countries in the region. However, Djibouti attracts large investments due to its strategic location. Since 2000, 1.5 billion dollars has been transferred for the projects carried out by China in the country. A significant portion of this money was used for the special economic zone built by sino-colonialist China. It is stated that the total amount of this project is 3.5 billion dollars. When the economic zone is completed, it is expected to reach an employment capacity of 200,000 and allow 7 billion dollars of trade. Chinese companies also have shares in the economic zone here. On the other hand, Djibouti is rapidly moving towards the debt trap of Sino-Colonialist China. While Djibouti's total debt was 50 percent of its GDP in 2016, this figure reached 104 percent in 2018. This percentage is well above the World Bank's risk standards. It is stated that Djibouti's debt to China was 1.8 billion by 2018. While this rapid borrowing raises concerns within Djibouti, the lack of transparency on debt borrowed from sino-colonialist China further increases this uneasiness. [30]

Suppose the government becomes unable to pay these debts in the long run. Djibouti would lose its feature of being an important country in terms of the strategic position for Africa, the Middle East, and Europe. It will face the risk of becoming a satellite state of China.

The Struggle of Nigeria, the Most Populous
Country in Africa, with Sino-Colonialist China

Nigeria is the largest Muslim country on the continent. Located in the Atlantic Ocean on the west coast of Africa, Nigeria's population is expected to surpass America within 30 years. For this reason, Sam Hill from Newsweek Magazine defined Nigeria as the future superpower of Africa. With a population of 200 million, Nigeria is one of the leading oil producers in Africa. 100 million dollars worth of oil per day is extracted in the country. But this is not a sufficient income for the large population, but oil accounts for 97 percent of Nigeria's exports. Similar to China, Nigeria has the potential to become one of the strongest economies of the continent with its large population, precious underground wealth such as oil, and its dynamic economy. [31] Seeing this potential, the Beijing government wants to make this Islamic country, like Egypt, one of its allies in Africa.

This most populous country in Africa is an important market for both state-sponsored companies and private companies of sino-colonialist China. The investment amount of 150 Chinese companies in Nigeria is over 20 billion dollars as of May 2019. China is the country's largest importer as of 2017. The import figure for China is about $9.6 billion, which is more than three times the share of Belgium, which ranks second. Although the Beijing authority says that economic relations are profitable for both states, the increasing number of products labeled "Made in China" on the streets of Nigeria undermine local production. What happened in the countries where Sino-colonial Chinese goods were sold are also happening here; that is, the local producers have to close their workshops. 300,000 people lost their jobs in the textile and garment industry in Nigeria. [32] This situation is the result of neo-colonialist China's business logic and its policy of enriching its own country and its people. Free private economic zones established by China in other countries are also found in Nigeria. Dozens of Chinese companies produce here and export their products with zero customs duty. As in other countries in Africa, a significant part of Nigeria's infrastructure investments are carried out by Chinese companies. It is estimated that the investment amount of train lines built by Chinese companies across the country will reach 20 billion dollars. [33] Nigeria's debt, the most populous country of Africa, to sino-colonialist China, is 6.2 billion dollars. Most of this debt belongs to the transportation infrastructure with $3.5 billion. The amount of debt in the energy sector is $1.2 billion. [34] As the Nigerian government borrows money from China; it remains silent against the Chinese Communist Regime's genocide and human rights violations against Muslims in East Turkistan. It also supports China's role in the UN. Moreover, Nigeria is one of the 'sensitive' countries. Visiting this country is considered a crime for the Muslim Uyghurs. The visit of Muslim Uyghurs to Nigeria is used by China as an excuse for being sent to concentration camps. [35]

Sino-colonialist China's New Moves in North Africa and the Moroccan Example

Chinese President Xi pointed to the Mediterranean region as a target when he announced the Belt and Road Initiative in 2013. While one branch of this colonial plan stretches from Asia to Europe following the traces of the Silk Road, another branch is the 21st century Maritime Silk Road (MSRI), which starts in the South China Sea and reaches the Mediterranean. These plans, covering almost more than half of the world, are the colonial moves that will enable the China to dominate the world in the future. North African countries with a coast to the Mediterranean are naturally the economic and diplomatic targets of the sino-colonialist regime. Even Morocco, which has deep-rooted relations with America in North Africa, is on China's radar.

The tourism country Morocco is a strategic partner. [36] However, Morocco's deep relations with America brought the two superpowers against each other in this country. While Morocco has made a $2.7 billion arms deal with the US in the last 20 years, China has infrastructure investments in Morocco. [37] China, which invested $1.25 billion in Morocco from 2014 to 2019, built one of Africa's longest bridges, the bridge between Rabat and Sale. France had originally been the largest foreign investor in Morocco- they have now been overtaken by China. The Atlantic Free Zone, Casablanca Finance City, and Tanger Med Port Complex in Kenitra are some of China's investments. Additionally, the King of Morocco also announced the Mohammed VI Tangier Tech City project, which bears his name. Chinese automotive manufacturers took part in this project, one of the largest technology regions in North Africa, to establish factories. The Chinese Cultural Center, which is the soft power used by China in international diplomacy, operates in Rabat. [38] The Kingdom of Morocco, which wanted to accept China's money while trying to protect its alliance with America, borrowed 1.2 billion dollars from Beijing in return for this investment. [39]

Sino-colonialist China is Now the Largest Supplier in Algeria

Algeria, which France has been colonizing for many years and regarded as its gateway to Africa, is at the center of the Belt and Road Initiative of sino-colonialist China. As a result of China's importance to Algeria, China's third-highest direct investment in Africa, was reserved for this country with 2.5 billion dollars. [40] Algeria is the third country where Sino-colonialist China sells the most weapons. Algeria, which adopts Marxist-left principles, as its administrative system, feels close to Beijing in this respect. This proximity also led to an increase in arms sales. [41] Xi's technological trojans ZTE and Huawei are effective in Algeria in the field of telecommunications. In 2018, the Algerian government agreed with the Xi regime to establish 5 new industrial zones. These special industrial zones will serve Chinese companies operating in the vehicle, electronics, and mining industries. These projects, which also include mining and port management, are among the largest investments that neo-colonialist China has made in the Mediterranean basin after Egypt. [42] China ranks first in Algeria's foreign trade, which is one of Beijing's oldest allies in North Africa.

While the Sino-colonial Chinese government made exports to Algeria worth 7.58 billion dollars in 2018, Algeria's exports were a sixtieth of this figure. As a result, there is a large trade deficit in Algeria. Algeria's highway in the East-West direction and the Algeria Opera House are among the leading investments of China in this country. One of the most striking examples of Sino-Colonialist China's method of bringing everything from the mainland, from banks to construction workers, while investing in one place, was once seen in Algeria. 50,000 Chinese who came to work on projects in the country constitute the largest Chinese community in Africa. [43] While the Xi's sino-colonial rule takes Algeria into a circle economically, on the one hand, it also takes steps to please the Muslim people there. The Chinese Communist regime, which demolished 8,500 mosques in the territories of East Turkistan, saying, "believing in Islam's religion is a disease," is building one of the biggest mosques in Africa for 1 billion dollars in Algeria.

Why is Sino-colonialist China Investing Less in Tunisia?

Although it seems stuck between Algeria and Libya, Tunisia is one of the North African countries that should not be neglected by the Beijing Government. Tunisia is better than other countries in North Africa, both in terms of the investment environment and legal regulations. After the Arab Spring events that started in 2011, Tunisia, completed its transition to the democratic system peacefully. Despite this, Tunisia attracted less investment compared to its neighbors. During the period when Algeria attracted 12 billion dollars investment between 2009 and 2014, Tunisia could obtain 110 million dollars from Beijing. Moreover, Tunisia gives visas to foreign investors and workers more easily compared to many countries. (44) While neighboring countries receive billions of dollars of investment from China, the reason why the amount of investment is so low in Tunisia is that the general rules of the sino-colonial system do not work in this country. Looking at the historical process, Tunisian leaders have been slower and more passive in relations with China. This has led the Beijing government to do the same.

Another issue is that Tunisia's investment costs are higher compared to its neighbors. The Tunisian government did not reduce these costs with taxes or similar incentives and did not provide a price advantage to sino-colonialist China and its companies. A critical point is that the laws for protecting the local economy and the environment are stricter compared to other countries. Foreign companies are obliged to employ the Tunisian people. Foreign companies can employ a maximum of 4 foreigners. (45) While there are 10 Chinese companies and $10 million Chinese investment in Tunisia, there are 4,000 companies of European origin and $12 billion of European-based investments. This is because the legal regulations in the country are similar to western standards. (46) Despite this, the trade volume with China has been increasing in recent years. The trade volume was 1.87 billion dollars in 2017. (47) After the BRI was announced, the Tunisian government, wishing to benefit from this initiative, became a member of the Asian Infrastructure Investment Bank (AIIB). After the Forum on China-Africa Cooperation (FOCAC) meeting held in 2018, the Tunisian delegation signed agreements with the Chinese side in various fields from automotive production to commercial centers and transportation infrastructure. Another business item was solar energy investments. (48)

Sino-colonialist China Awaits the End of Civil War in Libya

Libya, which has not been able to maintain its political stability after the Arab Spring process that started in 2011, is one of the countries where the Beijing government has not cut trade relations. Due to the civil war, many countries, including China, withdrew their citizens in this country for life-threatening risks and suspended investments.

The sino-colonial Chinese regime, whose energy needs are constantly increasing, continued to buy oil from Libya despite its turmoil. Libya's oil exports have increased by more than twofold between 2011 and 2017. China, which has never been a party in the conflict zones and preferred to watch the conflicts from afar, continues its "policy of not interfering with internal affairs," awaiting the end of the war in Libya and the construction projects it hopes to take after the war. For Beijing, it doesn't matter who wins or who loses. China hopes to see the winner as soon as possible and settle in the country with its banks and construction companies. On the other hand, the current Libyan government has made attempts to join the BRI. [49]

African Countries on the Edge of China's Debt Trap

Undoubtedly, African countries are at the top of the regions to which neo-colonialist China lends the most through BRI and other projects. The projects intended to be implemented within the scope of great goals lead to the second exploitation of the African continent in time. As of today, Africa's total debt to sino-colonialist China is 148 billion dollars. Almost one-third of this debt, approximately 44.2 billion dollars, is spent on infrastructure investments. The second-largest share belongs to the energy sector with 37 billion dollars. The mining sector comes in third place with 18.8 billion dollars. The amount of debt in communication technology is 9.3 billion dollars. Sub-Saharan countries are more vulnerable to the debt trap of the BRI, mainly because of their underdeveloped economies. [50]

Every Angolan Owes China $ 754

Located on the East Coast of Africa, Angalo's debt to sino-colonialist China is $43.2 billion. 17.6 billion dollars of this debt belongs to the mining sector, 7.4 billion dollars to the energy sector, and 7.1 billion dollars to the transportation sector. [51] Africa's second-largest oil producer, Angola, sells almost all of its production to sino-colonialist China. Angola, which constitutes another example of "debt trap" diplomacy like Sri Lanka, has borrowed from China since 1983. The amount of debts Angola has received to date is 60 billion dollars. Angola is trying to pay its due debt of approximately 25 billion dollars by giving all the oil it produces to Beijing. Needing infrastructure investments like other underdeveloped countries, Angola opened its doors to China in this regard, but eventually, it could not pay its debt to the sino-colonialist government. Finally, Angola had to give all of its income from oil, which is its greatest natural wealth, to China. As a result, the per capita debt of Angolan people to China is $754. [52]

Kenya's Rail Investment Made by Borrowing from China

Located in the south of Ethiopia and bordering the Indian Ocean, Kenya is one of the countries to which sino-colonialist China owes a large amount of money. 5.8 billion dollars of Kenya's 9 billion dollars debt belongs to the transportation sector. The country also owes 1.7 billion dollars in electricity generation. [53] After the Standard Gauge Railway project was completed and started to operate, it could not earn the expected profit in economic terms. This train line, which generates $9.2 million in revenue every month, cannot pay the debt arising from its investment because the periodic debt to be paid for the project is 350 million dollars. When this debt was no longer payable, Kimani Icnhung, Chairman of the Budget Committee of the Parliament of Kenya said, "our country's economy has suffered, and we can no longer pay this debt." [54] The first stage of SGR was made between Nairobi and Naivasha in the east direction. In the second stage of the project, the railway extends to the port city of Mombasa in the west direction and the Uganda border in the opposite direction. The part of the train line up to Mombasa has been completed. This line, which costs 3.2 billion dollars, cannot generate the expected profit due to insufficient freight transportation. [55] This railway project's inability to bring the expected profit and the debt burden it causes is an example of how the investments made under the BRI will harm the economies of the involved countries.

Zambia's debt to Sino-Colonialist China is $9.7 billion. Of this total debt, 2.9 billion dollars were provided for the transportation sector, 2.6 billion dollars for the energy sector, and 1.8 billion dollars for government programs. [56] In Zambia, whose total external debt reaches 12 billion dollars when the debts to other countries are added, the economy management is in great despair. Zambia, whose economy was heavily damaged due to the virus epidemic that emerged from China and spread to the world, could not fulfill its debt payment of $40 million in November and faced the risk of default. The Chinese government has delayed Zambia's debt payments for 6 months. However, it is doubtful how the country will pay this debt in the future. [57] The debt of the Republic of Congo to Beijing is 5.1 billion dollars, of which 2.8 billion dollars are from the transportation sector. Likewise, Cameroon's debt is $5.9 billion. Another country with high debt is Ghana, with a total of 3.7 billion dollars owed. [58]

The economic weakness of African countries against neo-colonial China has been on the world's agenda for a long time. Since it is not possible to include all the details of the BRI, ' sample cases are examined. However, researches and reports of independent organizations show that Africa is currently in a great debt trap. According to the findings of the Overseas Development Institute, 40 percent of Sub-Saharan African countries are on the verge of a major debt crisis. According to the data of the World Bank, the debt of 18 countries in Africa is more than 50 percent of the GDP of these countries. The total foreign debt of the African continent is 417 billion dollars. 148 billion dollars of this debt has been taken from China. The biggest problem here is that China turns the need for infrastructure investments in Africa into opportunities. The high cost of projects undertaken by Sino-colonialist Beijing in Africa is heavily criticized. On the other hand, the main reason why African countries want to borrow money from China is that they can borrow more quickly and easily compared to western institutions such as the IMF or the World Bank. [59] The statements of China that they support the development of Africa are empty promises. While the trade volume between Africa and China was 10 billion dollars in 2000, this figure increased to 190 billion dollars in 2017. The balance in this trade volume is undoubtedly in favor of sino-colonialist China. Half of the international contracted construction projects in Africa belong to the Beijing government and affiliated Chinese companies. While China exploits the continent's resources, it also endangers the health of its societies and the environment.[60] The increasing presence of neo-imperialist Chinese rule everywhere in Africa, from the economy to the environment and business life, indicates the re-colonization of the continent.

11

Chinese Influence on Turkey and It's Expansion of Central Asia

"Uyghur, Kazakh, Kyrgyz, Tajik,
Uzbek, Tatar are a great union.
because of the unity, we stay a life
We stay together like a family"
By Mehmet Emin Buğra

THE FOUR VERSES above are the last lines of the poem "Atamizning Oz Ogli Biz" by Mehmet Emin Buğra, one of the pioneers of the cause of East Turkistan. After the occupation of East Turkistan by the Chinese Communist Regime 71 years ago, Mehmet Emin Buğra Hazretim was forced to leave the county and go to exile. After staying in India for three years, he emigrated to Turkey in 1952 with his colleague İsa Yusuf Alptekin. As a leading country of both the Islamic and Turkic world, Turkey has become a safe place for upholding the rightful cause of East Turkistan and for those who had to leave their homeland. We did not have the opportunity to meet with Mehmet Emin Buğra, who died in Ankara in 1965. However, I had the opportunity to meet his daughter Fatima Buğra and prayed at the front of his graveyard in Ankara Turkey in 1986, also we met with Isa Yusuf Alptekin in Turkey and listened to him and took some lessons. İsa Yusuf Alptekin and Mehmet Emin Buğra both agreed that Turkey was very important for the fight against the sino-colonialist Beijing government. These expressions of İsa Yusuf Alptekin, clearly shows that Turkey's place in the eyes of the oppressed Muslims in East Turkestan is always different: "I cried. I was crying every time I saw Turkey's perfection and greatness. I was proud. I was saying to myself that there is at least one strong state of us, of Turks." As Hazretim wrote in his poem, the Turkic world, as nations of the same lineage that believe in the same religion, will be able to stop this colonial mentality. In this part of the study, in the light of the remarks by

Alptekin and Buğra, sino-colonialist China's economic, military, and political occupation attempts from Turkey to Mongolia will be discussed.

The Expectation of East Turkistani Muslims from Turkey

Yakup Beg, the leader of the first independent Kashgariye State established in the 19th century, wrote a letter demanding the support of the Ottoman Sultans. Both Sultan Abdulaziz and Sultan Abdulhamid the Second stated that they would support East Turkistani people . People of East Turkistan have always considered Anatolia as their second homeland, even in the crisis period when the Ottoman Empire fell, and the Republic of Turkey was established instead. Uyghur Muslims, during the struggle for independence in the aftermath of the Yakup Beg period and after the Chinese invasion in 1949, have come to Turkey through Central Asian countries, Afghanistan or India. Following the invasion of East Turkistan by the People's Republic of China (PRC), Uyghur leaders such as İsa Yusuf Alptekin and Mehmet Emin Buğra went to India and then reached Turkey. Both leaders continued this struggle on Anatolian soil until the end of their lives. Today, the fruits of the seeds planted by these two people can be seenin the activities of the Muslim Uyghurs in diaspora.

Aware of Turkey's influence in the eyes of both Central Asian countries and the Muslim people of East Turkistan, the sino-colonial Chinese government has always made a special effort to improve its relations with Turkey. On the Turkish Ministry of Foreign Affairs website, it is stated that diplomatic relations with the PRC were established in 1971. This date also coincides with the beginning of Mao's 'ping-pong diplomacy' with America. Relations between the two countries have been improved with Deng Xiaoping's launch of the foreign opening policies and increased to the level of 'Strategic Cooperation' in 2010. Both President Abdullah Gul and President Recep Tayyip Erdogan visited China. Turkey has been involved in establishing the Belt and Road Initiative (BRI), the sino-colonialist new world order of the Chinese communist regime. President Erdogan attended the first BRI summit in May 2017. Erdogan's next visit was in June 2019 on the occasion of the G20 meetings. Erdogan and the Chinese President met 5 times, including G-20 meetings. [1] Looking at the course of economic relations between the two countries, sino-colonialist China has also gained an advantage similar to those in many other countries. As of 2019, the amount of exports from Turkey to China is 2.58 billion dollars. On the other hand, the amount of imports is 6 times the export figure and is 18.49 billion dollars. The Turkish business sector exports mostly mineral products such as marble, chrome, copper, lead, iron, zinc to China. It imports especially electronic goods and mainly communication technologies from China. Cargo and cruise ship exports are among the important items. The size of the neo-colonialist China's investment in Turkey is $2 billion. Most of them are in energy, infrastructure logistics, finance, mining and telecommunications, and animal husbandry. Referring to the distribution of these fields, a situation similar to exports of sino-colonialist China to other countries is observed in Turkey. [2]

Turkey, an Important Transit Point for BRI

Situated at the crossroads of Asia and Europe, Turkey is one of the countries that the Xi regime maintained strategic cooperation to realize 'the Chinese Dream' and to dominate the world. For this reason, China has been attentive to membership of Turkey into the Belt and Road Initiative since its announcement. Using this key position, the Turkish government has been supporting the "Silk Road Economic Belt" and "21st Century Maritime Silk Road" projects. As a result of this support, Turkish President Erdogan attended the first BRI meeting three years ago. Turkey aims to implement the 'Trans-Caspian-Middle Corridor' project of the railway line from China to Europe. Turkey and China signed an agreement to include the Middle Corridor to BRI when it was first announced. [3] The plans of the Beijing Government for a railway starting from China to reach Europe have been realized. In this context, the first freight train between Xi'an - Ankara - Prague passed through Ankara on November 6, 2019, and reached Prague in 18 days. A ceremony, attended by the Turkish Ministers of Transport and Trade was also held in Ankara for this 42-car freight train belonging to China Railway Express. [4]

For the Sino-colonialist mentality, Turkey's ports, which are surrounded by seas on three sides, are as important as the railway routes. There have been 16 lines that are connected for Ro-Ro ships carrying containers between Turkish ports in the Black Sea and the Mediterranean Sea, and the Silk Road. For the development of these lines, the construction of a container port of 3.8 billion dollars in Mersin port on the Eastern Mediterranean coast, 870 million dollars in Filyos in the Western Black Sea, and 1.24 billion dollars in Izmir Çandarlı in the Aegean Sea have been carried out. [5] These three ports mean that the transit points of all maritime traffic around Turkey will begin to be operated by China. Currently, COSCO, China Merchants Holdings International, and China Investment Corporation have invested $920 million to acquire 65 percent of the Kumport port in Marmara, Turkey's inland sea. [6] The biggest advantage of this port from China's point of view is the shipment of products for the Turkish market. But it is also important since it is located at a point of transition to Europe. Two other important areas in which Sino-colonialist China has been investing are finance and energy. Various agreements have been made between Turkish banks and Chinese banks.

The most important signature in which energy and finance are intertwined is the $3.6 billion agreement with the Industrial and Commercial Bank of China (ICBC). In 2018, the agreement provided financing to increase the capacity of Natural Gas Storage facilities in Silivri and Lake Tuz. 20 percent of Turkey's natural gas consumption is provided from these two regions. [7] Another step that Turkey has taken with the Chinese side under BRI is the signing of a $5 billion agreement between the Turkish Wealth Fund and the Chinese Export and Credit Insurance Company (Sinosure). It is stated that the loan funds to be created by this agreement will be aimed at energy, petrochemical, and mining areas. [8]

It is seen that many large projects planned by Turkey in recent years are also planned as part of BRI. Eurasian Tunnel, the world's first submarine railway Marmaray, Yavuz Sultan Selim Bridge, and Çanakkale 1915 Bridge are among these projects. The Ankara-Istanbul high-speed railway, financed by China with a $750 million loan completed in 2014, was also built by a Chinese company. The next big step of this high-speed train, which is part of the fast railway project planned by the Sino-colonialist Chinese government from Beijing to London, is the fast railway line between Edirne and Kars. Which is an investment of about $30 billion. [9] Here, the point to focus on is that some critical projects are sold to sino-colonists at a low price, due to the difficulties of payment experienced in Turkey since the amount of long-term debt exceeds 300 billion dollars. The aforementioned Yavuz Sultan Bridge is one of them. China is also financing this project, one of the highest bridges globally, with $2.7 billion of loans. The bridge was sold to investors of sino-colonialist China for $688 million after the contractors who carried out the project failed to pay. The acquisition covers not the bridge but also 51 percent of the Northern Marmara Highway. [10]

Chinese Signs in Istanbul, in Which Many Uyghurs Live

Both the sino-colonialist China and Turkey see tourism as an important tool in addition to transport, finance, and energy to increase economic relations in all areas. Chinese tourists mostly visit Istanbul and many other popular tourist attractions in Turkey. In 2012 and 2013, there was an increase in the number of tourists from China with the mutually declared "country of the year" themes. As a result of the "Year of Tourism in Turkey." declared in China, 394,000 Chinese tourists came to Turkey in 2018, with a 60 percent increase compared to the previous year. [11] There is no doubt that Turkey, where tourism has a large share in the economy, is a big win for the Chinese people to be interested in. Istanbul Metropolitan Municipality has also hung Chinese signs at some public transport stations, perhaps out of the idea of making Chinese tourists feel at home. In a globalizing world, one can ask, "what's wrong with these signs?"

But Turkey's position, where a large number of Uyghurs have taken refuge, is different from other countries. While genocide committed in East Turkistan for sino-colonialist ambitions is obvious, local rulers are expected to be more sensitive to looking after the people of the same lineage and the same religion and language. For this, it is necessary to make the necessary arrangements for the Muslim Uyghurs, the majority of whom have taken refuge in Istanbul, to solve all kinds of legalizations problems as soon as possible. In addition to the steps taken to stop the genocide in East Turkistan, a stronger voice is expected from Turkey for Muslim Uyghur, Kazakh, Kyrgyz and other societies in the international area.

For the Chinese Communist regime, Turkey has maintained its position as an important country in the past, and today it is in a position where relations should be maintained well at every turn. For this reason, Chinese students have been researching institutes in their own countries and in Turkey for many years. The most famous universities in Beijing and Shanghai have Turkish Research Centers. On the other hand, whether the number of academic researches in Turkey is sufficient or not is a controversial issue. But as Ferhat Kurban Tanrıdağlı said, the sino-colonialist Chinese regime knows Turkey so well that it keeps Turkey as a 'strategic partner' while committing genocide in East Turkistan at the same time. The Confucius Institutes, which the Neo-colonialist Beijing government uses as a soft power to spread its hegemonic plans to the world, also operates in Turkey. There are Confucius Institutes in the Middle East Technical, Boğaziçi, Okan, and Yeditepe universities in Turkey. As a result of recent years, China's increasing economic and cultural pressures, even the establishment of "China-towns" in Istanbul, has been on the front burner. Another critical element is that the Turkish government has recently launched an economic initiative to attract foreign capital and stimulate the housing sector with a real estate investment of 250,000 dollars. And to no surprise, this initiative mostly attracted the Chinese. The TV channels of Sino-colonialist China have been abidingly describing how it is "easy" to acquire a Turkish house. [12]

Effects of Sino-colonialist China on the Press

To China, Turkey is seen as a strategic partner, making its presence felt through media outlets while receiving the support of Turkish politicians with huge investments and BRI to be effective in the Anatolian territory. In 2012, Turkuaz media agreed and decided to publish the Turkish version of China Today newspaper, which still operates in 150 countries. This agreement is one of the visible steps of the sino-colonialist Xi regime in the media. On the other side of the coin is the advertising factor. The effect of the advertising factor on the media is observed mostly on the genocide in East Turkistan. As in many countries of the world, Turkish press outlets mostly use the discourse of the sino-colonialist regime, "Xinjiang Uyghur Autonomous Region," when mentioning East Turkistan. Considering that the struggle against repressive and dictatorial regimes first began by denying their discourse, the Turkish media has a great responsibility. Because humanity needs to stand awake against China, the master of "smiling to faces while carrying a dagger on bosom," as stated by Tanrıdağlı. [13] Advertising is the biggest source of income for newspapers, and the Sino-colonialist Chinese regime uses this source very well. China transfers billions of dollars directly and indirectly to media outlets in Turkey and around the world. In return for these dollars, many members of the press apply "auto-censorship," sometimes spontaneously, sometimes at the request of the government. When a Turkish journalist starts to write a story about East Turkistan, they find themselves writing a sentence with the word "Xinjiang." Another critical issue is that companies, which are also an extension of the Sino-colonialist system, allow their partner companies to advertise to broadcasters to support their propaganda. Thus, they keep those broadcasters alive. They feed the shooters of bullets fired against the people of East Turkistan.

Because of the contacts of some political parties in Turkey with the Chinese Communist regime, every step taken on behalf of the people of East Turkistan is being smeared. These groups try to legitimize the oppression of the people of East Turkistan by the Chinese regime at every opportunity they find. First of all, it is necessary to accept the following fact from the beginning: the East Turkistan case is a cross-party case and a struggle for the existence of the Muslim people, which the sino-colonialist system wants to commit genocide against. Therefore, whether my wife Rushan Abbas as Executive Director of the Campaign for Uyghurs or myself as the Chief Inspector of the World Uyghur Congressa and co-founder of the Campaign for Uyghurs, our meetings with the party leaders in Turkey are our natural right to stop the sino-colonialist Xi's genocide on Uyghurs. Just because we live in another country never means that we serve that country's ambitions. We have ' one goal, to be the voice of the Muslim Uyghur people, to warn the world about the ambitions of the Sino-colonialist mentality, and to stop the genocide in East Turkistan. It is important to listen to Muslim Uyghurs who took refuge in the streets of Istanbul or another country for understanding the persecution of Uyghur people rather than paying attention to fake news produced by armchair outrunners of the sino-colonialist regime. On this occasion, we would like to express some of the issues contained in the statement at the meeting held on the occasion of the visit to Turkey in November and the celebration of the East Turkistan Republic Day:

- East Turkistan is a Turkic territory occupied by China. Even if you look ' at Chinese names, these facts are as obvious as the day.

- The East Turkistan cause is the struggle for national rights - law and freedom. It is the Chinese state that knows this fact and the dimensions it can reach best. Announced in September 2013, the "One Belt and Road Initiative" is just a reinterpretation of the historic Silk Road; its ultimate goal is described as "building the community of the common destiny of humanity." So "the Chinese Dream" is China's goal to dominate the world. "One Belt and Road Initiative" is the tool that will serve to achieve this goal.

While defending the East Turkistan cause, we warn as required by our sense of responsibility for the common interest of the Turkish Nation, just as our late leader İsa Yusuf Alptekin said: "Look at us, draw a lesson, get to know China, understand its black ambitions, and protect yourself."

Traces of Sino-colonialist China in the Balkan Countries

Chinese President Xi's neo-imperialist ambitions extend from Asia to Europe. BRI acts as a Trojan horse to make his presence felt in Europe, both by land and by sea. Economic wealth will flow to Beijing through port and infrastructure projects in Eastern European countries and the Balkans in the Mediterranean basin. The fact that the economies of the Balkan countries, which are Europe's backyard, did not fully develop, the need for foreign investment creates an environment for the Beijing regime to establish its hegemonic system there. In these countries, the positions of political administrations open to influence are another element that facilitates imperialist China's works. For the development of Sino-colonialist Xi's goals for Eastern Europe and the Balkans, the "16+1", that is, Central and Eastern Europe (CEE) platform was created, in which 16 countries participated. Finally, with the inclusion of Greece, it became the "17+1" platform. The fact that Asia's imperialist power in the very center of Europe led to such an initiative naturally triggered the reaction of the European Union (EU). EU countries have expressed that sino-colonialist China is creating Trojan horse initiatives that will undermine the continent's integration process. [14] China's neo-imperialist President Xi has staged the "divide and rule" tactic from Asia to Europe through the CEE countries.

His biggest project in the Balkans is the Port of Piraeus in Greece. This port is the gateway used by sino-colonialist Chinese companies to enter the European market since 2008. In the same year, China Ocean Shipping Company (COSCO), one of Beijing's companies, obtained the right to operate this port's second loading area for 35 years. COSCO, which later acquired the third loading area, finally bought 67 percent of the first loading area. During the acquisition process carried out by the Greek privatization administration, the PRC took control of an important gateway to Europe. Transport lines to Macedonia and Serbia will be created through this port. [15] Sino-colonialist China also has investments outside Greece, in Albania, Bosnia and Herzegovina, Montenegro, Northern Macedonia, and Serbia. While Western companies stay away from these countries due to uncertainties in the business environments, Chinese companies enjoy a huge advantage with state-owned banks. Since the European Union's essential environmental protection regulations are also flexed here, their risks are reduced. As of 2018, 2.2 billion dollars of bilateral trade volume, which was approximately 4.5 billion dollars, is with Serbia. So, China is profitable. Neo-imperialist China's exports are $3.4 billion. Serbia is also ahead on investments. In the period between 2015-2019, 10.3 billion dollars of the 14.6 billion dollar project was invested in this country. Most of the investments are for infrastructure and transportation. On the other hand, the debt trap problem in African countries and some Asian countries is also an issue for the Balkans. As of 2018, Montenegro owes almost 40 percent of its debt to China, followed by North Macedonia with 20 percent, Bosnia and Herzegovina with 14 percent, and Serbia with 12 percent. [16] The Balkan countries' debt to sino-colonialist China for their infrastructure projects is approximately 6.7 billion dollars. The billion-dollar borrowing of countries with relatively small economies is causing concern in Europe. Because, together with the unsustainable debt problem of projects in other countries, the exclusion of non-Chinese companies in the construction of these projects leads to an increase in costs and the problem of corruption. [17]

Among the Balkan countries, Serbia especially wants to keep its relations with China warm. In this context, a $3 billion trade agreement was concluded, including military products. China has a dream to make the capital Belgrade the crossroads point in Europe of the sino-colonialist BRI. Besides, the Serbian government has voluntarily opened its doors to high-tech surveillance systems that have been spread from East Turkistan to Kazakhstan, Kyrgyzstan, and Iran, and 1000 security cameras have been taken from Huawei to make Belgrade a "safe city." 85 percent of the $1 billion budget of the highway, which will extend from the ports that will connect China to Europe, to Montenegro's city of Bar, and then to Belgrade, is financed by China's Eximbank. Albania and Northern Macedonia also have partnerships with sino-colonialist China in key infrastructure projects. [18] One of the regions where Sino-colonialist China is most comfortable in the name of public diplomacy is undoubtedly the 17+1 countries. With political leaders' guidance, sino-colonialist China is seen as the miracle hand that solves their country's infrastructure problems. Thousands of kilometers away, ignorance of China's repressive steps both in its borders and in other countries favors the Beijing regime. [19] With the growing number of Confucian Institutes in capitals and important cities, the "Seven Dwarfs Awakening Snow White" tales about the new cruel actor of the imperialist order are being told to society.

Azerbaijan Should Also Support Muslim Uyghurs

Azerbaijan, which left the Soviet Union and gained independence in 1991, established its official relations with the PRC on April 2, 1992. Former President Heydar Aliyev's visit in 1994 was the first official high-level visit. Current President Ilham Aliyev has also visited China twice. During the second visit in 2015, a joint memorandum for BRI was signed. Baku-Tbilisi-Kars railway and Baku International Maritime Trade Port constitute the Trans-Caspian East-West Transport Corridor, the means for sino-colonialist China to reach Europe. Looking at the trade between the two countries; Azerbaijan's energy exports are strong, while China's exports, which cover all kinds of sectors, are in Beijing's favor. As of 2018, 752 million exports and 1.4 billion dollars of imports were realized. The investment of Azerbaijanis in Chinese companies is 1.7 billion dollars, compared to the investment of 120 Chinese companies in Azerbaijan of 800 million dollars. Another important sector in relations between the two countries is energy. Sino-colonialist China's state oil company, China National Petroleum Corporation (CNPC) and Azerbaijan's energy company signed a cooperation agreement in 2016. At the second BRI summit in 2019, agreements covering various areas amounting to $821 million were signed between the two countries. [20]

The main project of interest to Azerbaijan in the Sino-colonialist BRI initiative is the Trans-Caspian International Transport Route, a road network extending from China and Southeast Asia to Europe. The Beijing government, which wants to weaken the Azerbaijani government's strict restrictions on foreign capital inflows, wants to use this country's membership negotiations with the World Trade Organization as a lever. However, the Azeri government's sluggishness to some legal regulations could not ensure economic relations at the level expected by sino-colonialist China. [21] On the other hand, in 2005, when the Azerbaijani and Chinese sides met on the matters about East Turkistan, Taiwan, and Tibet as areas of conflict, Azerbaijan rejected Taiwan's claim to independence to gain China's support in the UN. After 10 years of high-level talks in 2015, the Chinese side asked for Azerbaijan's support of East Turkistan even asked Azerbaijan to reject Muslim Uyghurs' asylum requests and send them back to China. Although Azerbaijan does not have a high number of Uyghurs living its borders, the Azerbaijani government did not sign the declaration of "war with separatists," which the sino-colonialist Xi regime sought support in the UN. Here, the historical and cultural ties between Muslim Uyghurs and Azerbaijanis have an impact and should be an example. [22] Striving to maintain good relations with both states, the Beijing government unsurprisingly has maintained a "neutral position" on the relations between Armenia and Azerbaijan. One thing to note about Azerbaijan is that the number of Confucius Institutes, the soft power key of neo-colonialist China in Azerbaijan, is also increasing.

Sino-colonialist China Needs Turkmenistan's Natural gas

Another country in Central Asia with a coast on the Caspian Sea is Turkmenistan. Neighboring Uzbekistan, Iran, and Afghanistan, Turkmenistan is the world's 4th largest natural gas supplier. Turkmenistan, which was a part of the Soviet Union from 1925 until the 1990s, gained its independence on 21 October 1991. Turkmenistan has two similarities with Azerbaijan in terms of Sino-colonialist Chinese government. The first is that it is on the Silk Road project route, which extends to Europe. The second is undoubtedly natural gas production. After the Central Asia–China natural gas line was opened in 2009, Turkmenistan sent natural gas to China along with Kazakhstan and Uzbekistan.

Turkmenistan has not followed the neutrality policy in international relations and has not been involved in any international organization in that geography. Instead of selling natural gas to a single country, it acts by marketing it to many countries. [23] But due to the height of sino-colonialist demand, it sends a significant part of the natural gas it produces to China. In 2019, Turkmenistan shipped 30 billion cubic meters, while Uzbekistan and Kazakhstan exported 10 billion cubic meters. The decline in production worldwide due to Covid-19 this year has naturally affected both countries, especially Turkmenistan. [24] The dependence of a large part of its greatest economic asset on China puts the principles of neutrality of Turkmenistan in international relations into a challenge. Despite this, Turkmen rulers intend to strengthen energy exchange with sino-colonialist China, bringing it closer to the target of 60 billion cubic meters by the end of this year. China's national energy company CPNC has invested 4 billion dollars for the Bagtyyarlyk natural gas project in this context. Although the government of Turkmenistan does not want to dwell on this issue, it does not have a strong hand against sino-colonialist China. Almost all of Turkmenistan's gas goes to China, and this energy supply corresponds to a 4 percent share of the Beijing regime's total supply. As a reflection of the colonial and imperialist policies, the Chinese government causes competition between Russia and Turkmenistan on price, making the cost of energy reduced. China, which supplies natural gas from Turkmenistan at a low cost and makes Turkmenistan dependent, wants to increase cooperation in the fields of military and security. [25]

China Collaboration with Taliban

"China would be welcomed as an arbitrator in negotiations for peace in Afghanistan and should not leave matters of such great importance solely to the US." So said Maulana Samiul Haq, the so-called "Father of the Taliban," in 2018. An open invitation has been made to fill the vacuum already created by the American side in the initiatives launched to bring the Afghan people, tired of the 40-year power struggle, to an environment of peace and tranquility as soon as possible. [26] The Sino-colonialist Chinese regime watched this crisis right next to it from afar for a long time and did not intervene. All the Beijing Government has done is taking advantage of the September 11 attacks and blaming Muslim Uyghurs and trying to destroy the people of East Turkistan based on the US "War on Terror" argument.

Afghanistan, surrounded by Iran on the west, Turkmenistan and Uzbekistan on the east, Tajikistan on the north and China on the northwest is one of the geographies with the most deep-rooted Asia history. There is information that traces of the first settled life date back 9,000 years ago in some sources. Since it is also an important transit point from East to West, Afghanistan has been a place of power strife between major states in history. It was occupied by the Soviet Union, which wanted to increase its power in the region against China. In 1979, it was occupied by order of the then Soviet leader Brezhnev. More than 1 million civilians lost their lives in the war that lasted for 9 years, and 3 million people were injured and disabled. This war is an important breaking point in the history of Afghanistan. According to retired General Abdul Nasir Ziyai, who served during the invasion of the Soviet Union, the war in the country has never ended since that invasion. [27] Afghanistan has once again been hit hard by America's military intervention after the September 11 attacks. The American government has tried to destroy the Taliban because the Taliban has provided al Qaeda with Afghanistan opportunities. The United States mostly guided security-related issues. At the same time, the USA also focused on democracy, human rights, the fight against drugs, and development. This, in turn, is aimed at covering up the unsuccessful military operations. Another importance of Afghanistan for America is that it is a point of balance in the tension between Pakistan and India. For this reason, the beginning of negotiations with the Taliban has been on the agenda since the Obama era. [28] These negotiations continued during the Trump era but came to nothing.

The situation in Afghanistan is the same for the sino-colonialist Chinese regime, which constantly monitors the regions from afar and waits for the events to end, wherever there is a crisis or a troubled region in the world. China quietly followed the US and the coalition's end of security operations in the country, and then their talks with the Taliban administration. After 2013, with the introduction of the sino-colonialist BRI, low-density negotiation traffic between China and Afghanistan was initiated. Following the moves of America, China started talks with Afghan leaders in front of the press and Taliban representatives behind closed doors. The first visit of Afghanistan President Ashraf Ghani to China was in 2014. As a result of the security priority, it was announced that 15 Uyghurs had been extradited to China during Ghani's visit. In 2015, a secret meeting was also held with Taliban representatives and members of the Afghanistan Peace Council. During this meeting, Uyghurs, who are alleged to be separatists, were raised. [29] After American President Trump cancels talks with the Taliban in 2019, the sino-colonialist Chinese regime publicly announced its talks with the Taliban. Taliban leader Mullah Abdul Ghani Baradar and his accompanying delegation were hosted in Beijing. [30]

The long-term plan of the Neo-colonialist Beijing Government for Afghanistan is to establish economic dominance through the BRI. For this reason, it expects the conflict environment there to end first. [31] Afghanistan's rulers, unable to provide economic and social development due to decades of war, have also been knocking on the door of sino-colonialist China for a long time. Expectations for investments have been expressed since the previous president, Hamid Karzai. The critical point here is the tension between Afghanistan and Pakistan. Trade between the PRC and Afghanistan is quite small compared to other countries and is naturally in favor of China. The Afghans expect that their country's underground resources will be brought into the economy. Unfortunately, the alternative for this purpose is the Sino-colonialist Beijing Government. In this context, a $3.4 billion deal was signed for copper mines. The copper ore at the mine site, which was leased to China for 30 years, was found to be one of the largest reserves in the world. But from this agreement, the Afghan government did not get what was expected because the promised railway line to transport the mine was not built. The Sino-colonialist Chinese government is constantly making agreements to keep Afghanistan in its hands but does not follow up. The officials of the neo-colonist Beijing stated behind closed doors that they acted as if they were "investing" to prevent other states from accessing these resources. Besides the corruption problem in the country, the Afghan people still cannot benefit from the treasure on which they sit. For this reason, the American government criticizes Beijing for setting "bribe-fed debt traps." [32] The statements used by American State Department official Alice Wells, in her testimony in Congress, once again revealed the true face of Sino-colonialist Beijing, "China has made no economic contribution in Afghanistan. BRI is just a slogan. China has not taken steps to help Afghanistan's economic stability." [33]

Sino-colonialist Chinese Soldiers in the Territory of Tajikistan

Afghanistan's northern neighbor, Tajikistan, another Central Asian country, is a country where the neo-Colonist Beijing Government is slowly beginning to invade its territory. The Sino-colonialist Beijing regime, which is expanding its territorial waters by building artificial islands in the South China Sea, is deploying the People's Liberation Army (PLA) Units in Tajikistan under the name of patrol soldiers.

Tajikistan, one of three countries in Central Asia around the Fergana Valley, shares a 477 km border with China. One of the countries where Tajikistan established its first diplomatic relations in 1992 when it gained independence from the Soviet Union is the PRC. With the end of the civil war in 1997 in Tajikistan, the great states' interest in Tajikistan gradually increased. Undoubtedly, Tajikistan's strategic position in Central Asia played a critical role in this interest. Since the 2000s, the presence of the sino-colonialist Chinese regime in Tajik land has become increasingly noticeable. Tajikistan, which needs development and investment in all areas, from construction to agriculture to energy, is also a unique opportunity for sino-colonialist Chinese rule. The fact that a single-man regime is vulnerable to corruption in the country makes things even easier for sino-colonialist China. [34] Tajikistan, the economically weakest country of the former Soviet Bloc, has relied on Sino-colonialist China at the point of completion of the Rogun dam, especially to meet its energy needs. But since Russia is the executor of the project, the PRC did not look warmly at this proposal; instead, it tried to supply energy production from other sources. [35] Tajikistan is important for the Chinese government since one of the important projects of Beijing's colonial lever BRI, the Karakum Highway, which runs from occupied East Turkistan to Pakistan, passes through an area close to the border with Tajikistan, and Tajikistan also has a border with Muslim Uyghur territory. For this reason, the Beijing regime, which does not want its imperialist plans to be undermined, has increased its military presence as well as its economic presence in Tajikistan in recent years. In September 2016, China proposed setting up 11 checkpoints on the border and deploying troops towards the Afghan border. In October of the same year, even a military drill was conducted with 10,000 soldiers. [36] The increasing military presence of the Sino-colonialist Chinese regime in the region has also attracted the attention of the American government, and this situation was noted in the Department of Defense report submitted to US Congress. [37] Gerry Shih from the Washington Post newspaper personally examined the region and saw with his own eyes the deployment of PAP troops in Tajikistan's border with Pakistan and Afghanistan and confirmed that Chinese soldiers had been there for 3 years. However, both governments are not in favor of this military presence being known to the public. The presence of Chinese soldiers in Tajikistan, which dominates the Wakhan Corridor, is to give a message to Moscow by the Beijing regime. "They want to show the Russians where the red line is," an expert told the Post. The Sino-colonialist Chinese regime wants to play the "big game once again" that the British played in the region 150 years ago. On the other hand, they officially deny that there is a military presence there. But images published by The Washington Post reveal that sino-colonialist China de facto controls part of Tajikistan's territory. [38]

From the perspective of BRI, which is the outcome of the Beijing government's new era imperialist policy, Tajikistan is viewed from a more security perspective. Because the advantage of this small country is its geographical location, the Sino-colonialist government does not have an investment that attracts attention. As of 2017, the amount of Chinese investment in Tajikistan is ' $97 million. The trade volume between the two countries is 1.5 billion dollars as of 2018. [39] Tajikistan, which has no connection to the sea from anywhere, expects transportation infrastructure projects to take place within the scope of BRI. [40] In this context, the reconstruction of the Dushanbe Kulma Highway is carried out by Chinese companies with a 375 million dollar budget. [41] Beijing's expectation from Tajik leader Emomali Rahmon is that it will support its security-indexed policies connected to its repression policies developed against East Turkistan's Muslim Uyghurs. Tajikistan, which has already given some of its territories to Chinese control, is a country where the sino-colonialist Xi regime has implemented a plan to expand its territory step by step. Since Tajikistan's economy has become increasingly dependent on sino-colonialist China and borrowed from the Beijing government, it cannot go beyond Beijing's international political agenda.

Kyrgyzstan, the Country in Central Asia that Does not Have a BRI Project

Kyrgyzstan, one of the weak countries in Central Asia both geographically and economically, has been going through a turbulent period politically in recent years. Kyrgyzstan, with the lowest national income per capita in Central Asia, is a country where both Russia and China want to increase their influence. Russian Leader Vladimir Putin looks at Kyrgyzstan from a perspective of building Great Russia, while the sino-colonialist Beijing government looks from an economic perspective. Although Kyrgyzstan has no economic and strategic resources, it is part of the Fergana Valley, a Central Asia transit point, and has a geographically central position. There are five factors effective in the Sino-colonialist Chinese regime's view of Kyrgyzstan and other Central Asian countries. These are political and economic expansion, energy, the transit point to Europe, the economic interests to be achieved with the BRI, and making its neighbors more aligned with itself. According to this last article, the sino-colonialist Xi regime sees countries such as Kyrgyzstan as complementary to its domestic policy and agenda in the territories it occupies, such as East Turkistan. The communist Chinese regime practices such as the soft power Confucius Institutes and "debt-trap diplomacy" as reflections of their national security policies are also seen in Kyrgyzstan. [42]

The amount of investment of the authoritarian Chinese regime in Kyrgyzstan is about $3 billion. These are mostly in the fields of oil, energy, and transportation. However, due to political upheaval in the country this year, the Naryn Free Economic Zone project, which will cost $275 million under BRI, has been canceled. In Kyrgyzstan, unlike other countries, local people react against the projects of the sino-colonialist Chinese regime and the Chinese working there because they have lost their jobs. Last year, a large demonstration was held in Bishkek, the capital. Similarly, tensions broke out between villagers and Chinese employees at a gold mine operated by a Chinese company, and 20 people were injured. In Kyrgyzstan, where a striking example of the Sino-colonialist economic occupation program is taking place, the Naryn Free Economic Zone is the focus of discussion. The establishment of a logistics center the size of 300 football fields in this historical and cultural center caused protest among the Kyrgyz people. Among the reasons for this reaction, there are issues such as the damage to the ecological fabric, the failure of investors who promised to develop housing for the local people, and the introduction of cheap labor from China, causing an increase in local unemployment. [43] The second important point is that the Kyrgyz people react to the Beijing regime due to the oppression and genocide suffered by the Muslim Uyghur, Kazakh, and their lineage in East Turkistan.

This reaction of the Kyrgyz people and the growing political upheaval creates alternative opportunities for the sino-colonialist Chinese regime. In particular, the Chinese regime, which has placed private security companies in Central Asia in recent years, is spreading a similar practice in Kyrgyzstan under the pretext of increasing the security of both BRI and other projects. For this, lobbying is carried out in the Kyrgyz Parliament to make legal arrangements for security guards of Chinese private security companies who will serve as armed guards. Currently, the Chinese private security firm Zhongjun Junhong Anbao Jituan actively operates in China, Kyrgyzstan, and Uzbekistan via railway line. The more critical issue is that the sino-colonialist Xi regime attempts to establish a surveillance system, similar to the one in East Turkistan, in Kyrgyzstan, to monitor every citizen with security cameras. In this context, China National Electronics Import & Export Corporation, one of China's state-owned companies, signed an agreement with the Kyrgyz government. The Chinese government used the follow-up of anti-Chinese demonstrations as the reason for the establishment of this surveillance system. [44] However, as seen in the case of East Turkistan, once the Beijing regime's entered from the door, this is enough to make the whole system suitable for itself.

Sino-colonialist Influence in Uzbekistan, the Historical Center of Central Asia
Samarkand and Bukhara are two important historical cities of the Turkish-Islamic world. Uzbekistan, which contains these two cities, is also one of Central Asia's historical and cultural crossroads. After gaining independence in 1991, it was ruled by Islam Kerimov until 2016. Its resemblance to the Chinese Communist regime is that Shavkat Mirziyoyev, who became the president in 2016, decided to move to a free-market economy. This decision was undoubtedly welcomed by the Chinese regime. Because Tashkent, one of the important centers of the historical Silk Road, is also important for the new colonial plan BRI. Both the high-speed train between Samarkand and Tashkent and the private industrial center of 1.7 billion dollars are being established in this context. [45]

The size of foreign trade between Sino-colonialist China and Uzbekistan is 7.6 billion dollars as of 2019. Meanwhile, the balance is in China's favor. As of this year, the number of Chinese companies in the country is 652,000. Of these, 531 were established last year. It operates in all areas from petroleum to textile, communication to agriculture. Natural gas resources have an important place in the relations between the two countries, as in Turkmenistan and Kazakhstan. In addition to natural gas, 50 percent of raw materials such as copper and uranium are made in China. [46] That is, Uzbekistan is one of the energy sources that feed the production monster of neo-colonialist China. To increase energy transmission capacity, two countries agreed to build another new pipeline during Chinese President Xi's visit in 2013. The same special economic zones that the sino-colonialist mentality spread to the world under the BRI are also established here. Construction of the Dzhizak Free Industrial Zone has begun in Syrdarya. Xi Jinping's Trojans Huawei and ZTE also realize 157 million dollars worth of projects for communication and technology infrastructure. [47] The Uzbek government, which attended the first meeting of the BRI in 2017, signed an agreement of 23 billion dollars that will cover various fields. Currently, the Kyrgyzstan-Uzbekistan-China Railway line under BRI is the main project. [48] Despite all these figures, Oleg Limanov said that China's growing political influence in the region poses one of the most serious challenges for Uzbekistan and other Central Asian countries. [49] One of the moments when this challenge arises is undoubtedly the refusal of Uzbekistan and Kazakhstan to to oppose China on human rights and genocide in East Turkistan. Because the Sino-colonialist Chinese regime, which distributes debt to countries within the BRI scope, asks these countries to support its political ambitions in the international arena in return for every penny it gives.

The Country Xi Wants to Conquer: Kazakhstan

Sino-colonialist Xi Jinping made the first announcement of the Belt and Road Initiative (BRI), which will establish the new world order through his rule, in the Kazakh capital of Astana in 2013.

Kazakhstan is an important touchstone for the neo-imperialist ambitions of the Beijing government. The fact that these lands, which have an area of about 2.725 million square kilometers from east to west, become a part of sino-colonialist China means that Beijing's communist regime reaches the European gates with a line starting from the easternmost part of Asia. The neo-imperialist Xi government, who is pursuing this dream, has made clear this fact on sohu.com, one of the largest search engines in China. The website, which carried out an interesting psychological operation, published an article titled "Why Kazakhstan is eager to return to China" in April of this year. The article retells, in brief, the history of Kazakhstan, noting that leaders of many Kazakh tribes had pledged allegiance to the Chinese emperor. It also states that Kazakhstan had historically been part of China's territory and Kazakhs "do not have too many complaints" about being repeatedly invaded by China. [50] It is possible to see the traces of an imperialist and colonial spirit in every letter of this article, which reflects a mentality that could not prove with scientific data that even East Turkistan, which it occupied in 1949, belonged to itself in the past. In China, where the Internet is tightly controlled, the publication of this article is tolerated. Kazakhstan's foreign ministry summoned the Chinese ambassador to protest over this article, which insulted its independence. As expected, the sino-colonialist Chinese regime, which tested the limits of its hegemonic ambitions with this article, said that the article would not harm relations between the two countries. The Kazakh government is under China's influence due to the genocide suffered by its race in East Turkistan right next door. And although it fails to show the international arena's expected reaction regarding the problem in East Turkistan, it also tries to free its citizens in the region. [51]

The development of relations between Kazakhstan and the PRC began with its separation from the Soviet Union and its independence. The first high-level visit to Kazakhstan, China's second-largest neighbor with 533 kilometers, was by Prime Minister Li Peng in 1994. The border agreement between the two countries was signed at that time. Kazakhstan, which is also part of the Shanghai Cooperation Organization, led by Sino-colonialist China, is one of the countries that Beijing cannot give up because of its geographic location and rich underground resources. Kazakhstan has 2.2 billion tons of oil reserves in its territory and 12 billion tons in the Caspian Sea. Since 1996, oil has been exported from Kazakhstan to China. Beijing needs Kazakhstan to meet its 210 million tons of oil needs as of this year. [52] In 2012, zero customs trade was initiated for oil exports. Kazakhstan imports petrochemical products in return for crude oil exports. DUee to the decline in oil prices, Kazakhstan turned to find alternative markets, and the Beijing government started an industrial transfer to hold Kazakhstan. A $2 billion deal was agreed for this transfer in 2013. In 2014, the Chinese regime committed an additional $18 billion. Of the 79 projects prepared in this context, 56 of them were approved in partnership with Chinese companies. Although the agreements contribute to Kazakhstan's industrialization relatively, what the sino-colonialist China wants to do is transfer environmentally harmful industrial enterprises, which have been criticized by the international public, to Kazakhstan. [53] The biggest trade of Sino-colonialist China among the Central Asian countries is with Kazakhstan. The trade volume is $28.9 billion. Simultaneously, the Beijing regime's biggest investment is also in Kazakhstan, with an investment of $19 billion. [54]

After the announcement of BRI in 2013, the importance given to Kazakhstan by the sino-colonialist Beijing government increased further. The Chinese Communist regime considers Kazakhstan as the greatest partner of the New Silk Road. As a result, relations between the two countries have been transformed into "comprehensive strategic cooperation." During the visit of Kazakhstan's President Kassym-Jomart Tokayev in 2019, several agreements were made with the Chinese. These agreements, especially in energy, technology, and 5G infrastructure, are remarkable. [55] An investment of $5 billion in the road and rail sector by 2022 is also a part of BRI. Many major infrastructure projects to be realized within the country's 'Kazakhstan 2050' National Development Strategy are integrated with Sino-colonialist China's BRI plan. Kazakhstan, whose economy is more effective than neighboring countries, is indispensable for the continuation of sino-colonialist BRI plans, as it is the geography that connects China to Europe. [56] Various activities will be carried out in Kazakhstan with the soft power that the Beijing government calls "people to people" management. These issues were discussed during the visit in 2019. [57]

But it is also a question mark that projects covered by BRI are successfully executed. For example, the Khorgos Gateway Project, which forms the border between Kazakhstan and China, has launched with the slogan "We are building a new Dubai". It is the starting point of the 8 thousand km railway that will extend from China to Europe through Kazakhstan. However, it is controversial how efficient and profitable such a long road is for cargo transportation. A significant number of containers bound for Europe are returning empty. Incentives for the transport of containers have created a system where containers are sent, and money is earned, even if they are empty. Moreover, the fact that these projects do not contribute to the local economy indicates that BRI's discourse on equal development for all is not true for real life. [58]

Kazakhstan, the country with the largest borders in Central Asia is the place where China's hegemonic activities are most felt. An indicator of this is the public's common saying: "If you want to go abroad, learn English. If you want to stay in Kazakhstan and succeed, then learn Chinese" [59]. The fact that the young generation wants to learn Chinese to find a job shows that the criticism of Kazakhstan's people that their country has entered the hegemonic orbit of Beijing is justified. The Kazakh people also organized various demonstrations in Kazakhstan to oppose China's influence on their country under the name of investment. These demonstrations highlighted how much the country owes to China and sufficient information about the agreements with China is not provided to the public. According to the figures announced by the government a while after these demonstrations, the amount of debt received from sino-colonialist China for 55 projects under the BRI is $27.6 billion. [60] Another criticism of Kazakh people against sino-colonialist China is the issues of unemployment and equal wages. Various demonstrations were held in 2019 due to wage inequality between Kazakh society and Chinese workers. The demonstrations' result was that sino-colonialist China wanted to export the security systems it uses in East Turkistan to Kazakhstan under the pretext of protecting its own companies. Some of China's paramilitary state organizations, such as Bingtuan, are reorienting their services towards serving the BRI needs. In Kazakhstan, local sources have also speculated about the potential deployment of Chinese private security companies in the country, such as the Hong Kong-based Frontier Services Group. [61] Kazakhstan's indebtedness to neo-imperialist China in oil and natural gas issues is also a notable issue. Kazakhstan, whose relations with China started in the field of economy, is about to enter Beijing's political orbit. Naturally, it has not shown a clear stance on the genocide of its cognates on the other side of the border. Kazakhstan was able to take steps for the release of people with Kazakh passports in East Turkistan. Gulzira Auelkhan, who spent 15 months in the concentration camps of Sino-colonialist China and had a chance to flee to Kazakhstan, also warned the Kazakh rulers: "I do not believe that Kazakhstan and China are friends. The BRI project is part of China's expansion. They're trying to take over our country." The article with the title of "Why Kazakhstan is eager to return to China" that we mentioned earlier, once again confirms Beijing's imperialist goals.

Sino-colonialist Chinese Influence in Mongolia

One of the places occupied by Sino-colonialist China, such as East Turkistan, is the region known today as Inner Mongolia. With the end of the imperial period in China in 1912, independence was declared with the Russians' help, and the Mongolian Republic was established. However, the communist guerrillas of sino-colonialist China, taking advantage of the Chinese-Japanese war, established underground Mongolia organizations. These guerrillas formed neighborhood units during the Japanese occupation between 1935 and 1937. The communist organization increased its activities in Mongolia with the Japanese withdrawal from the region.After the end of World War II in 1945, Inner Mongolia was forced to join the initiatives of these PRC organizations. Northern Mongolia became a satellite state of the Soviet Union. The impact of power strife in Central Asia continues from that day to the present.

The Sino-colonialist regime, which established all kinds of pressure in Inner Mongolia, which it occupied, also wants to establish dominance over the Mongolian state. Xi Jinping, who has wanted to realize his imperialist ambitions since he took over China, also visited Mongolia in 2014. Neo-imperialist China wants to use Mongolia's underground resources and opportunities in the field of animal husbandry. While the trade volume between the two countries was $6 billion in 2013, the figure is expected to rise to $10 billion this year. The Xi regime, which wants Mongolia to be included in the scope of BRI, aspires to both infrastructure and superstructure projects. At the heart of the Beijing Government's interest in Mongolia is the trouble-free execution of its rule in Inner Mongolia. For this reason, one of the topics discussed during the visit in 2014 was 'security'. [62] However, the Mongolian people see their neighbors China's activities against their country as an outcome of the colonial mentality. This public reaction has paved the way for the presidency of Battulga Khaltmaa, who recently said that he would pursue an anti-China policy because China plays a major role in mining and foreign trade, which form the basis of the country's economy. But China has a 90 percent share in Mongolia's exports. Mongolia's coal and copper mines are also important to the economy of Sino-colonialist China. [63]

The Sino-colonialist Beijing regime indirectly wants Mongolia to enter its orbit in foreign policy. In 2016, after the Dalai Lama, the Religious and Political Leader of Tibet, visited Mongolia, China suspended its trade relations with Mongolia and asked for assurance that such a visit would not take place in the future. One step further from this happened when Mongolian President Khalmaagin Battulga announced a strategic partnership during his visit to America. At the end of the visit, the Chinese media published articles stating that Mongolia will inevitably come under Chinese domination. Some

Mongolian politicians also reacted to this incident, which resembles the article crisis in Kazakhstan. This is a sign that Beijing has found "funded supporters" who support China in the field of diplomacy. [64] Another step in which the neo-imperialist Xi regime completely sinicized the lands it occupied in line with its sino-colonialist aims was seen in Inner Mongolia in September of this year. Teaching the Chinese language in the schools, starting from this educational period, caused great protests. About 5,000 people were detained during the demonstrations. The people of Mongolia, who see that their cognates are under pressure from the Beijing government, also react to this. Chinese The public also protested foreign Minister Wang Yi's visit during the same period. In the statement made by Wang Yi after the visit, attention was drawn to each country's commitment not to interfere in each other's internal affairs. [65] The meaning of this statement, from the Chinese perspective, is that: "I apply the policy I want in these lands I occupied, even if you come from the same lineage, you cannot interfere with it." Being economically dependent on sino-colonialist China makes Mongolia's hands tied.

Russia and India's View of Sino-colonialist China's BRI Plan

The Aksai Chin region in the Karakash River Basin in East Turkistan, occupied by the Sino-colonialist Beijing Regime, is one of the major conflict issues between China and India. Tensions in the region, where the two states fought over claims in 1962, have risen again in recent years. In May of 2020, the events that started in the region turned into an armed conflict on June 15, and dozens of soldiers lost their lives. After the war in 1962, the Line of Actual Control (LAC) was drawn up between the two countries, and the two countries acted accordingly. The tensions that increased in 1987 and 2013 were also eliminated within the LAC framework. Another border conflict between China and India is at the McMahon Line. In 1914, an agreement was signed between British India and Tibet, which did not include China, which at that time the Qing Empire collapsed, the Republic of China was newly established. As per this agreement, India accepts the McMahon line as its border. The PRC, which keeps Tibet under occupation, opposes it. But Aksai Chin, where tensions are rising, and the Galwan Valley in the middle of Ladakh are signs of how sino-colonialist rule will pursue a policy in the new era. The People's Liberation Army (PLA) administration claimed that Indian soldiers had violated the region's border. However, it is seen here that the Indian Government is acting to protect its country and its allies against the new hegemonic ambitions of sino-colonialist China. Although Sino-colonialist China is one of India's largest trading partners, the Indian government recently banned 150 Chinese applications, including TikTok. [66]

Until today, India has kept a distance from the new BRI-centered order that the Neo-colonialist Chinese government wanted to establish. India's government has followed an attitude in favor of international cooperation since the 2000s, on the condition of protecting its national interests. From this point of view, India is expected to join the BRI. However, Prime Minister Narendra Modi found the huge infrastructure projects under BRI risky for their national security interests. India has a 7.5 percent share in AIIB. As it has a multilateral structure, AIIB is considered more secure by the Indian government. However, the Indian government is suspicious of BRI since sino-colonialist China completely dominates BRI. [67] When looking at the maps showing the BRI's plans, it will be clear why India abstained. The transformation of Pakistan, which is the interlocutor of India in the Kashmir problem that has been going on for years, into the satellite state of China, the Beijing government's expansion to the Indian Ocean via Pakistan, the BRI projects signed between China and Bangladesh show that India is being embraced from all sides by China's imperialist plans. Seeing the shrinking range of action in the Indian Ocean, India has to position itself against China in the security and economic fields. The Sino-colonialist Chinese regime wants to keep the line from Asia to Europe under its control alone. As China could not agree with India on these issues and the Indian government responded to Beijing's moves, the border disputes between the two countries, which had been dormant for years, came to the fore again. The Chinese regime, which has expanded its hinterland with the artificial islands built in the South China Sea, is now testing similar steps on India over the land borders. And China is trying to grab land from India piece by piece.

The Soviet Union, the superpower of Asia, has not seen the PRC as a rival since the Yalta Conference when they shared the land with western states. However, the relations between the Central Asian countries and Russia on the map that emerged after the collapse of the Soviet Union continue in the old order, even if they are not publicly described like this. For the states in Central Asia, although sino-colonialist Chinese rule comes to their door with investments, Russia is still the Big Boss. Russia sees Xi's BRI plans as investments in regions in its hinterland but does not rule out that these investments can harm its national interests. Despite this, Russia, which has been subjected to sanctions by western states, especially America, in recent years, redefined and supported BRI in 2015. This is because BRI will support Russia in international politics and that Russia will be able to access products and commodities that it cannot obtain from the western market via China. The two countries act jointly in the renewal of the routes that will provide logistics to Europe and the Northern Arctic region. Liquefied gas, LNG, especially in the Arctic Circle, is critical for both countries. China has partnered with a $12 billion investment in Yamal LNG here. Because America sanctions Yamal LNG, sino-colonialist Chinese rule is an important opportunity for Russia. [68] The Putin Regime, which is warm to BRI due to the Soviet Bloc and investments' economic development, develops models to protect its national security. The Putin government constantly gives the message that they have equal power with sino-colonialist China.

Conclusion

DESCRIBING the authoritarian regime turning the world into a hell with his iconic book 1984, George Orwell wrote that "Journalism is publishing what someone else does not want to publish, the rest is public relations", which is a quote that is at least as famous as his book. First of all, it should be highlighted that a journalist did not write this book. Rather, to shed light on the realities that the world does not want to see today, it was written to explain that the authoritarian Chinese Communist regime and the Islamic world and the Western world that entered its orbit did not want to be written. That is why our starting point is to examine China from the genocide in East Turkistan, which was systematically denied by the Beijing Government, which is aiming to govern the world with its own "public relations" program. It draws attention to the danger of the colonial order that China wants to establish in the new period and its threat to the world, that is, the situation that is also a clear and present menace.

It should be emphasized once again that East Turkistan is the place where the Chinese Communist Regime's desire to rule the world has been piloted, and if it succeeds in the homeland of Uighurs, Kazakhs, and Kyrgyz, the next step will be to do the same in Pakistan. The Chinese colonial system, whose signs are visible in Pakistan today, is about to turn into a disaster that will take everything before it. The most critical wall that will stop this disaster is East Turkistan. Whenever East Turkistan is completely Sinicized, then Beijing will quickly expand its colonial policies to other countries.

The concentration camps established in East Turkistan, the millions of people being forced to work in factories like slaves, forced sterilization of women, separation of children from their families, and other violations of human rights all show that the Chinese government commits all of the crimes defined in the UN's Genocide Convention. For this reason, the US State Department has defined these acts against the Uyghurs as a systematic genocide. In Western countries, especially in the USA, essential steps are being taken to reach a public consensus that the monster they raised with their own hands is now a threat from the east. Hundreds of studies have been carried out by relevant government departments, universities, and think tanks, revealing this threat's extent. Unfortunately, it is a bitter fact that neither the Organization of Islamic Cooperation nor the Islamic countries have performed any remarkable work today to address the growing danger. With the propaganda mechanism that the Beijing government has spent billions of dollars on, we are facing the reality that governments that do not feel the pain of their coreligionists who are subjected to genocide, do not see the destruction of their religion, and remain silent in the face of the new veil of the persecution of humanity, in short, resemble the three monkeys. It is impossible to see anything other than the advertisement of Xi's imperialist goals on every channel, from televisions, newspapers, internet broadcasts, social media accounts, which are under the control of Beijing's communist regime with the propaganda mechanism of China. Explaining the future dangers of the communist order established by China for sino-colonialism, not ' in East Turkistan but also in their own countries, is censored. On the other hand, China is growing its sino-colonial empire while pushing forth the propaganda line that "we invest in you" to the countries it has handled. Beijing turns them into its satellite state. This work aims to fill an important gap in explaining both the Islamic World and the colonial threat from the East to Turkic World. The aim is to keep people alert to the threat and to create a swift consensus against Chinese cruelty with the information to be used.

As Communications Coordinator of Campaign for Uyghurs Julie Millsap stated, a step has been taken towards fulfilling responsibilities towards humanity by explaining the facts that a significant part of the world does not want to see. Distinguished readers will also play a role in the proliferation of these steps and oppose the hegemonic plans of the Chinese Communist regime, starting from the genocide in East Turkestan and extending to the exploitation of the world.

APPENDIX - I

On the Way Back to East Turkistan

"The responsibility of publicizing Red China's persecution in East Turkistan falls on us, the East Turkistanis who live abroad as migrants. We, the delegates who took part in the Hejaz Congress, appointed Mehmet Emin Buğra and İsa Yusuf Alptekin, two of our national leaders, as our deputies on behalf of eight million people in East Turkistan and 10 thousand living abroad to force Nationalist China to recognize our independence by taking our cause to the United Nations in case they fail to do so through negotiations."

THE PEOPLE OF EAST TURKISTAN living in various countries came together on September 1, 1954, in Taif, Saudi Arabia, and held a congress where also Mehmet Emin Buğra and İsa Yusuf Alptekin attended from Turkey. With one of the decisions taken in this 4-day congress on East Turkistan Mehmet Emin Buğra and İsa Yusuf Alptekin were, as stated above, declared representatives of this struggle.

Buğra, Alptekin, and Mesut Sabri Baykozi, known as "Three Effendis" were the names that marked East Turkistan's struggle for independence. 35 years after the two leaders were declared representatives of the East Turkistan cause, friends fighting for Uyghurs, including me, met in 1989 in the holy Arafat. Our concern was again how we would defend the just cause of the Muslim Uyghur people. After consultations, we decided to appeal to European and other Western countries and mobilize the world against Colonial China. After this decision in Arafat, a path of struggle lied ahead of us until the just cause of East Turkistan was accepted in all countries.

This difficult path started in East Turkistan's Hotan city in May 1968, where I was born to Abdulkarim Hajim and Habibehan Hajim as their first son, at a time when the Cultural Revolution, declared by the Chinese Communist regime under Mao's leadership was raging hard. It was a time when oppression and persecution were felt in every corner of our country. People were even afraid of greeting each other. As all schools and madrasahs of Muslim Uyghurs teaching in their native language were closed with the Cultural Revolution, the first five years of our education were spent in schools established by the Chinese Communist Party (CCP). For five years, we have been educated in line with the CCP's communist doctrine, which deemed religion opium and adherence thereto sickness.

At such a time when the Communist regime was pressing hard to destroy the religious and national identity of the Muslim Uyghurs, our religious leaders immediately found an alternative method: "Underground Madrasas." They began to give lessons in small groups, in secluded, outbuildings, or unused back rooms of the houses. In these small places that housed both dormitories and classrooms together, pupils had the opportunity to see their families only once a week or every two weeks.

Our teachers walked for miles every day to give lessons to us. Each day they used different routes to avoid being detected by the Communist Party police. Those who gave lessons to us had been persecuted in prisons for years during the Cultural Revolution after the Communist regime came to the power in 1966. Those teachers who, like Prophet Joseph, converted their dungeons to madrassahs to increase their knowledge and speed up their spiritual progress set up a secret madrasah system as soon as they left the dungeons where they stayed for 18 years. They sacrificed their lives to raise the Muslim Uyghur generation. In 1982, I had the opportunity to study for five years in one of these madrasas, about 8 km from our home in Hotan. I took lessons first from Abdulahad Han Mahsum Hajim and then from Master Muhammedali Akhun Helpitim. Since these madrasahs were run secretly, we did not use the words "Akhunum" to refer to our teachers so as not to be detected by the communist dictatorship police. When we talked among ourselves outside, it was safe to refer to them as "ustam" as if we were talking about a shopkeeper/craftsman.

When my education neared the end, I got the opportunity to emigrate by means of one of my masters, Muhammedali Akhun Helpitim. At that time, getting a passport under the communist party regime was like trying to herd cats. You were required, among others, to get an invitation from outside or to have your name on an invitation list. As fate would have it, my name and those of a few of my friends were added to a list of invitees of Mohammed Qasim Hajim, one of our elders living in Saudi Arabia. At the age of 18, I embarked on a challenging journey from Hotan in 1986 with students and businesspeople. My parents Abdulkarim Hajim and Habibehan Hajim gave all the money they had saved to me, whom they would never see again since they wanted me to follow the suit of scholars who raised me.

We had a heavy burden on our shoulders from then on, a heavy burden flowing forth from the responsibility concerning the future of our country and our teachers who wore their fingers to the bone for us as well as our families who sacrificed whatever they had for us...

We arrived from Hotan to Urumqi by bus in six days and from there to Beijing with a four-day train journey. It is not an exaggeration to say that we had never seen an airplane in our life, which was dominated by poverty and destitution. Another eight-day train journey to Moscow across Siberia and from there to Istanbul was waiting for us.

We arrived in Istanbul by mid-April in 1986. Here, we were to join the pilgrim convoys heading Saudi Arabia. Over three months, we got to know this historical city and met İsa Yusuf Alptekin, one of the pioneers of the East Turkistan cause. Visiting him we got his advice to Muslim Uyghur youth. At that time Turkish pilgrims traveled mostly by bus to Mecca. Together with the people of East Turkistan who came together in Istanbul for the pilgrimage, we set out to fulfill the sacred duty. We arrived in the holy places and performed the pilgrimage. The next goal was to go to Egypt and study at Al-Azhar University. Mohammed Shah, a prominent personage from Turkistan in Saudi Arabia, and Master Rahmetullah Turkistani took care of us. Thanks to these two people, we were able to fly to Egypt, whereby a 4-year period that lasted from 1986 to 1990 started.

Al-Azhar University, whose foundation dates back to the Fatimid era, received us with open arms. The administrators of this ancient university knew East Turkistan and the Muslim Uyghur youth very well. Many years before us, since the 1900s, Uyghurs had been educated in this ancient university of the Islamic world. Abdulaziz Chingizhan Damollam, who studied at Al-Azhar and then returned to his homeland, was one of them. This pundit was first thrown into jail and then martyred by a firing squad after the occupation of the communist regime.

While studying in Azhar, we decided to join forces with our fellow countrymen and spend our time more fruitful and useful. To meet some of our needs and get support from the university administration, we got in touch with Ahmed Shalaby, the Deputy of Al-Azhar. Following our suit, dozens of students came to study at Al-Azhar every year. However, this flow did not take place under the agreement made with the Chinese government in the 1930s. Not being happy about the agreement the Chinese had put all kinds of obstacles to prevent Muslim Uyghurs from benefiting from this opportunity. Those who were able to go to Al-Azhar were mostly those who could go abroad through their efforts or with the help of their acquaintances. Particularly after the Chinese Communist Party's occupation of East Turkistan, it became even more difficult to go to Egypt.

Having this said, Al-Azhar has gradually lost its attraction as a study center for Muslim Uyghurs in recent years. That is because the Egyptian government started to treat Muslim Uyghur students as criminals. Undoubtedly, the Egyptian administration's need for Chinese money, which is stained with Muslim Uyghurs' blood was influential in the change.

In 1989, in the third year of my study in Cairo, Allah granted me the opportunity to visit the holy places once again and to perform the pilgrimage. This biggest gathering of Muslims from all around the world proved to be an occasion for us to come together with our fellow students from Pakistan and other countries, allowing us to reflect on where we see ourselves in the future of the East Turkistan cause. One of the most important decisions in the lives of East Turkistan leaders was to go abroad to defend the Muslim Uyghurs' idea of independence.

We faced the same decision process. After a few years, the study was to end and we were either to return to East Turkistan or take refuge in a western country. In neither case would the struggle end. We had to decide which one would be beneficial both personally and for our homeland. The elders we knew from the period we studied in secret madrasahs in our homeland also came for pilgrimage. The following words of one of them were influential in our decision: "In hindsight, the idea of sending you outside only for religious education was wrong. This is because you will not be of much use to your people when you return to your homeland after getting religious education. After your return, you will face two options: One is speaking up in line with what you have learned and walking along that righteous path, in which case you would be put behind bars immediately from where you cannot get out again. The other is abiding by Chinese policies and living accordingly, in which case you will deviate from God's way. In either case, you will not be of any use to the country."

After long and tough consultations, we decided to further emigrate. Since the Soviet Union has not yet collapsed at that time and East Turkistan's neighbors Kazakhstan or Kyrgyzstan were not yet independent, going to these countries did not seem to be the way out. We had to also consider also the following fact about whether to continue to stay abroad or return to East Turkistan. If the East Turkistan cause got publicity in European capitals today, it is thanks to the struggle initiated by our leaders in exile such as İsa Yusuf Alptekin and Mehmet Emin Buğra. It was our duty to follow their suit. To this end, we decided to go to Europe after Egypt, with our families waiting for us at home in our thoughts. In order not to upset them, we decided to keep the decision we made in Arafat in 1989 secret from them. We completed the pilgrimage and returned to Egypt.

We had to stay in Egypt for a while. Meanwhile, we realized that thanks to the five-year intensive training we had received in secret madrasas in the homeland, our level was more advanced than that of many other students. Hence, we helped freshmen in their lessons. The biggest advantage of this was that it allowed us to meet not only Uyghurs but also people from other countries, such as the Maldives, Senegal, Turkey. We guided them.

Every person we met helped us to get to know the Muslim world better. These useful occasions provided us with a broader perspective in analyzing the problems facing Islamic countries nowadays. At that time, the growing love for the homeland combined with the sorrow of not being able to see our families for a long while. Having this said, they were the first steps of a long journey after all. Although our final goal was the victory, as we were responsible for the campaign and not for the victory, all we had to do for the time being was not to lose our determination to fight.

The education that started in Cairo ended when I set foot in Germany on September 9, 1990. Abdulcelil Karakash, who was helping the people of East Turkistan to settle in the west welcomed me when I landed at Munich Airport. After following Islamic studies and Arabic in East Turkistan and Egypt, I began to study German as well as Industrial Management in Germany.

In the meantime, the situation of the Uyghur people started to deteriorate in the homeland. After the Tiananmen massacre of 1989, the so-called "opening up and freedom" policy initiated by Deng Xiaoping was ended with his instructions. The "pro-freedom" image of Deng was shattered. The Chinese people started to put broken glass bottles in front of their doors to protest Deng, whose last name Xiaoping means small bottle.

The oppression and persecution that had been going on for years in East Turkistan gained momentum. I informed my family of my moving to Germany. Naturally, my parents Abdulkarim and Habibehan were a little upset about it. As the first youth who emigrated, we had a lot to do. While the Beijing government was busy with new genocide plans against East Turkistan, we had to fight to stop it. We took one of the first steps in 1991 by establishing the East Turkistan Union in Europe, together with İsa Yusuf Alptekin's son Erkin Alptekin, Ömer Kanat, and other Uyghurs. Joining forces with Turkish expatriates in Europe, we started activities aimed at informing the public about the Muslim Uyghurs and the situation in East Turkistan.

Turkey was as important for us then as it is today. Before us, in 1992 another congress held in Istanbul. This gathering was the second biggest event after the congress in Taif. Representatives from countries under the yoke of the Soviet Union, Turkey, and Saudi Arabia took part in the congress. Among them were also those who left the homeland before the Communist occupation in 1949. We established the World Uyghur Youth Congress in 1996 with Dolkun İsa and other friends in Germany. Two years later, we decided to hold the second Uyghur Youth Congress in Turkey. To this end, those who were involved in the convening of the first congress scattered across the world to convoke Uyghurs living in other countries to the forthcoming Congress in Ankara.

Kyrgyzstan, Kazakhstan, and Saudi Arabia fell to my lot. When I went on this occasion to Kazakhstan in 1998, I had the opportunity to visit Ziya Same-di, one of the leaders of the Second Republic established in East Turkistan in 1944, Abduruf Makhsum, who served as the Secretary-General in this govern-ment, Dolqun Yasin, a famous author, and Abdurrahman Sabit, an opinion leader. We visited Nigmet Haji Busaqof, who was the head of the Uyghur Al-liance Organization (Uyghur Ittipaq) in Bishkek, Kyrgyzstan. In Saudi Arabia, we came together with Husein Qari Islami and Dr. Abdul Qader Tash.

The second congress in Ankara was productive. With the help of Dr. Erkin Ekrem, the congress getting the attention of government and political lea-ders with Government representatives, who followed the developments in the Central Asian Republics and who participated in the congress made an impor-tant proposal that would guide us in our just cause. They advised us to move the East Turkistan cause's center of gravity to Europe to keep it nonpartizan and away from political strife in Turkey, believing that the Uyghur cause would be better communicated to the world if it was based in Europe.

One year after I returned to Germany, a team including Perhat Muhammed and me held the East Turkistan (Uyghuristan) National Congress in 1999. In this process, we met such valuable people as Haji Yakup Anat, an Uyghur leader, who struggled side by side with İsa Yusuf Alptekin and Mehmet Emin Buğra before 1949, retired General Mehmet Rıza Bekin, the President of the Turkey-based East Turkistan Foundation, and Qahriman Ghojamberdi, a famous Uyghur historian.

In September 2000, it was decided the third World Uyghur Youth Congress be held in Tallinn, Estonia. I went to Kazakhstan and Kyrgyzstan to invite new delegates to this congress. We planted the seeds of the Uyghur Youth Union from 1998 onwards in Kazakhstan together with Abdurashit Turdiyev and other pro-minent friends. Later on, this organization started its activities under the name of "Kazakhstan Uyghur Youth Union". While we were carrying out organizatio-nal activities, we constantly followed the developments in East Turkistan.

The Beijing regime also closely watched our work. They tried to dispara-ge the representatives of the Uyghur people both in East Turkistan and the diaspora, branding them Pan-Turkist and Pan-Islamist. They continued to re-settle the Han Chinese in East Turkistan to destroy the language, religion, and culture of the Uyghur people. The proportion of Uyghurs in the population has decreased with each passing day.

Although the People's Republic of China (PRC) was communist in its ruling philosophy, it began to transform into a wild capitalist of the global system by becoming a member of the World Trade Organization (WTO) in 2000. Posing as a capitalist – even more capitalist than Adam Smith himself – to the outside world, it was and still is sheer communist and authoritarian in its acts and actions against its own people and the people of East Turkistan and Tibet, which it holds under occupation.

The terrorist attack on the twin towers of the World Trade Center in New York, the financial heart of America, on September 11, 2001, constitutes one of the most important milestones in history. Then-US President George W. Bush's doctrine of "all-out war on terrorism" proved to be a windfall for the authoritarian regime at the other end of the world, whereby it got another handy tool to crack down on Muslim Uighurs. Thus, the name of the new round of persecution became "war on terror!". These people on whom the war was being waged were Muslim Uighurs, Kazakhs and Kyrgyz, and other peoples, who have been living in East Turkistan for centuries and who have never accepted the Chinese occupation. They preserved their language, religion, culture and were not assimilated despite the resettlement of millions of Han Chinese in their country. The Chinese regime, which equates resistance against its persecution in the lands it occupied with the attack on the twin towers, tried to terrorize every protest against its party and government. Non-retroactivity of laws, which is one of the most basic principles of law, was destroyed by the Beijing regime.

Even anti-government protests of the 1990s were sought to be assessed under the new doctrine. The need for the people of East Turkistan to carry out their struggle under one roof against this unfair and unjust mentality of the Chinese regime became more and more evident. Therefore, we decided in 2004 to merge the World Uyghur Youth Congress and the East Turkistan (Uyghuristan) National Congress. Led by Erkin Alptekin we established the World Uyghur Congress of which he became the first president. After a few years, I had to move once again. A new chapter opened in my life of immigration that started in 1986 when I emigrated to my new destination, the US, in 2009. We continued the fight for the cause of the Muslim Uighurs in Washington DC, the US capital, where I started to work in 2013 as Public Relations Coordinator of the Uyghur American Association, of which my brother-in-law Dr. Rishat Abbas, was one of the founders and first elected president.

In the meantime, the Chinese regime started to employ new oppression methods in our homeland, the occupied East Turkistan. Xi Jinping took office as the Secretary-General of the Chinese Communist Party and the President of China in 2012. He wanted to break East Turkistan's resistance against Sinification and achieve what Mao could not. Upon seeing a big gathering in a mosque during his first visit to Uyghurs' motherland in 2014, he rebuked the officials accompanying him.

He fully lived up to his remarks "Absolutely, no mercy", which he made at a closed-door meeting, by committing genocide against Uyghurs like that of Nazis against Jews. Like Mao's Red Guards, he resorted to a wide variety of persecution methods such as destroying mosques, sending people to concentration camps, forcibly sterilizing women, punishing those who grow beards, forcibly removing headscarves of women, separating children from their families, trespassing our privacy by introducing Han Chinese into our families' home, and forcibly marrying our daughters. To make the matters worse, he amended the law so that he would remain on the throne of persecution forever.

He announced the "community of common destiny" farce to the world, which, in fact, was the neo-colonialism of Xi and the CCP, and with which they targeted the Islamic and African countries with a weak economy. These countries started to "share a common destiny" with East Turkistan. Under the guise of "one belt, one road", motto they advertised as "equal development for all" they established a brutal neo-colonial order.

The actions of the Xi rule went beyond those of the British East India Company, the notorious symbol of colonialism. Every penny earned went to Chinese coffers. He invited Western companies to his country to benefit from cheap labor and forcing Muslim Uyghurs into slave labor in those factories.

When this cruel system started to pick up everyone from the streets, children and elderly alike, they also knocked on my parents' door. When I called my mother on April 25, 2017, she said in a sad voice, "My son, don't call us again." Is it conceivable? Where else in the world could a mother tell her son not to call him? The persecution was so intense. When I called them, the Chinese had already seized their home. My brother, his wife, their children, and all my relatives were taken away. They were all sent to a concentration camp of the Sino-colonial system. Whether they are alive or not nobody knows. They have not been heard from since.

Not contenting itself with this, the Chinese Communist regime kidnapped my wife's sister Dr. Gulshan Abbas because my wife Rushan Abbas talked about this persecution in a think tank in the US. For more than two years, no news has been received from my family, or my sister-in-law, or other relatives, or those sent to the camps. The Communist regime called Uyghurs who live abroad and demanded them to return to China threatening them with their families.

The Chinese regime cut the hairs of women who were kept in the concentration camps and forced into slave labor, producing wigs with them. Some of those wigs were captured at the US customs.

What the inmates of the camps said was shocking. But the sino-colonialist Xi and his regime, intent on turning the earth around their own orbit, continued to do as they please, turning a deaf ear to what others say. When asked they said that they are fighting extremism and educating people. What kind of education is this? They took away even the most educated people such as my wife's sister who is a doctor, film director Hursan Hasan, Professor Rehila Dawut, Professor of economics İlham Tohti, and writers Yalqun Rozi and Abdulqadir Jelaleddin. Moreover, since Xi regards adhering to Islam as a disease, he did not hesitate to persecute religious scholars, imams, madrasah teachers, and those who taught the Quran to their children.

But their persecution could not stop our just struggle. In my capacity as the Chief Inspector of the World Uyghur Congress, my wife Rushan Abbas and I established the Campaign for Uyghurs (CFU) in September 2017, and with this non-governmental organization, we strived to be the voice of the oppressed East Turkistan.

In this, we have been motivated by a hadith of our Prophet (pbuh), which declared: "He who remains silent in the face of injustice is a tongueless devil." Per the decision we made in Arafat in 1989, we intend to publicize the genocide of Muslim Uyghurs with the means within our reach. It might seem a formidable task to resist the colonial system with which the Chinese Communist regime wrapped up the world like an octopus. Yet it is our duty to make it clear with whom we are siding, as the ant carrying a tiny drop of water to put out Nimrod's fire did, given that it is our own family and our nation that are being subjected to one of the most horrible genocides in history. Therefore, it is our responsibility to announce this to humanity fully and to warn other people about the imminent danger. This book is written with this very intention.

Before giving some information about the outline of the book I have to clarify one more point and answer a question that might occur to the reader. Why could East Turkistan not gain the independence it deserved as opposed to Central Asian countries? This topic is enlarged upon in the relevant chapters of the book. At this stage, I will suffice to say that even though East Turkistan is under Chinese occupation today, it is the land where Muslim Uyghurs, Kazakhs, and Kyrgyz have been living for centuries. Being China's gateway to the West and outlet of the former Soviet Union or today's Russia to Asia, East Turkistan is situated in a unique geopolitical location like Turkey. Moreover, it is the transit zone connecting India and Pakistan to Russia and China.

In addition to its geopolitical importance, it had precious mineral deposits such as oil and natural gas, which every developed and industrialized country needed. Similar to what happened in the Middle East it has been coveted by colonialist countries as a matter of course. No wonder the power play involving the British and Russian Empires as well as China in the 19th century was called "the Great Game".

The British seemed to support Yakub Beg, who resisted the Qing Dynasty and founded the Kashgaria. But the same British weakened Yakub Beg by providing weaponry to the Chinese so that these lands would not be ruled by Muslims. It is also a fact that the first Eastern Turkistan Islamic Republic was destroyed in 1933 by the machinations of the Soviet Union and China. Likewise, the Second Republic succumbed to the intrigues of the Soviet Union in 1944.

The colonial powers, destroying the East Turkistani leadership with treacherous ambushes whenever they attempted to get independence, employed all kinds of manipulations in line with their imperialist ambitions to prevent the establishment of an independent state in those lands. They even resorted to purchasing people from East Turkistan if needed. In short, Uyghurs were never allowed to establish an independent state. Finally, the superpowers of the time, who shared the world among themselves at the Yalta Conference, gifted East Turkistan to China.

The Chinese Communist regime maintains that East Turkistan, which did not and will never belong to China, has been part of China for centuries based on its fabricated historical sources. However, just like this work, other books to be written in the future will continue to tell that the sino-colonial Beijing regime forcibly occupied East Turkistan, and reveal the Chinese imperialist lies. East Turkistan is not only the cause of the Uyghur Turks but also of all humanity.

In writing these lines, I do not claim that I have explained everything in the best and most comprehensive manner given that every chapter of this book can easily be the subject matter of a separate book. In this book, I tried to warn both the world and Islamic countries even if in limited pages. We are facing a big scourge, an evil or a cruelty and I intended to draw attention to the magnitude of the danger, hoping to help defuse it as our beloved prophet Muhammad (pbuh), whose ummah we are proud to be, ordered us to do in the following Hadith-i Sharif: "Whosoever of you sees an evil, let him change it with his hand; and if he is not able to do so, then [let him change it] with his tongue; and if he is not able to do so, then with his heart — and that is the weakest of faith."

It goes without saying that I do not possess the power and means owned by the Chinese Communist regime. Yet it lies within my ability to help stop this persecution with my pen and tongue. The cruel system established by Beijing certainly will not exist forever. One day it will collapse like Goliath defeated by David. It is our duty to talk on every occasion about the damages the sino-colonial system caused to the world. With this in mind, we established with a group of academics the Center for Uygur Studies as a think tank. This education and research center took the field and joined the just cause of the Muslim Uyghurs.

APPENDIX - II

A Uyghur Man's Letter to His Lost Mother

Dear Mother,

It was April 25, 2017, when I last heard your voice.

Today, it has been 1095 days. 3 years since our last phone conversation. I remember your trembling voice when you told me not to call you anymore.

When we met in Germany in 2001, you told me several times, "My son, we have seen all that we could see, and we are getting on in years. We fear no one but God. You should follow the path you have chosen for yourself." I know you, mother. I know your courage. What could have happened that so frightened you the way it did that day? What could have forced a mother to tell her own son not to call?

Since I arrived in the United States in 2010, I would call you daily. I left home in 1982, when I was still too young to understand many things. When I went to the underground religious school in Hotan, it meant that I could not help you with the household chores or fulfill my responsibilities to my family as a young adult.

When I left to go study abroad in 1986, you gave me all your life savings to take with me. Unbeknownst to you, my dear mother, in 1989, during our Hajj in Arafat we had a discussion with other Uyghur students studying abroad about the next steps after graduation. We were seeking answers about what we might do for our motherland: what might be the most beneficial? The decision was made to migrate to the Western democratic countries. Without your permission, I came to Germany with my friends on September 9, 1990 and settled there. I took the first practical step in the line of "departing the homeland for the sake of it." Even though I was getting further away from you physically, spiritually I was so close to you, mother.

I still live with the painful reminiscence of the day that you said not to call. It had already been over a year since my relationship with my siblings was cut off to protect them. And now I had lost contact with you as well. I still remember, after you hung up the phone, how I just stood still. My head hung low and tears welled up in my eyes. I was surrounded by a strange feeling of sorrow as a mixture of grief and eternal separation was taking over my soul.

I already knew that as a result of this continuing oppression my brother, Abdurehim, was enslaved by an unwelcome Han Chinese family. They were blatant impostors who had come forcibly into your home as "relatives" under the government's "double relative" program. I had asked you once, "Are those shameless guests still there?" You would ' deeply sigh and say nothing.

Ever since our homeland was occupied in 1949 by the Communist regime, the Chinese government had always attempted to break the prestige and pride of our family. They confiscated the horses and property of my grandfather, and continued with demolishing our palatial courtyards and destroying our garden paradise. You did not react then the way you did this time. Now this viciousness, shame, and honor has broken into our nest, our home, our last stronghold. Is it this that has broken you, mother? Has it made you miserable that my hard-working and patient father is so helpless? Have the abuses my sisters are facing and my altruistic brother Abdurehim's slave-like torment made you despair? Did the unknown fate of your innocent grandchildren scare you to such an extent as to cut off contact with me?

I know that you know very well how to endure hardships and calamities, mother. What kind of cruelty is it that has caused my angelic mother to be forced to refrain from screaming? East Turkistan, a cradle of civilization, has fallen into darkness.

Since the day that I lost contact with you, I have been devastated and astounded by the pain. Shortly after, I started to become quiet. While I was in one place, my mind was in another. Sometimes, I was overwhelmed by frustration and annoyance. There have been times that I have lost my senses. My spirits began to drop.

After more than a hundred days, a relative sent me a message and informed me that my brother Abdurehim had been sentenced to 21 years in prison and that all my sisters had been thrown into the concentration camps. They continued and told me that the fate of my parents was unknown. At the end of the message, I was informed that the door to your house was locked and sealed. When I asked about your grandchildren, I was told that no one knew where they were. I still remember how I felt at that moment. It was as if I were on the verge of my own demise, and this news felt as if it would rob me of my last breath. I was overwhelmed by feelings of helplessness and vulnerability. News began to circulate that many of my friends' relatives were also taken to the camps.

I remember that once you said to me: "My son, if one day in the future, the borders are closed and if we lose contact, you can rest assured of our situation. You take care of your own family and do not worry about us." I did not understand why you said that at that time, but now I have grasped the meaning of your words, mother. How wise of you to foresee what was coming for our homeland.

During all this time, the ' thing that I could do each day was to think about you: you were constantly in my deepest thoughts and in my heart. Your memories, your voice, and your face were always with me, no matter where I was or what I was doing. The worry and despair were taking over my life. The feeling of being unable to know where you were, what sort of horror that you and dad might be living through, and the feeling of helplessness... all of this was leaving me with extreme emotional distress.

The evil communist Chinese government has deprived you and millions of innocent Uyghur brothers and sisters of human dignity. They have forced lives to be spent in prisons and concentration camps. We have tried to the best of our ability to tell the world. We cooperated with the World Uyghur Congress and the Campaign for Uyghurs was recently established by us, as the platforms to end this evil.

On September 5, 2018, nearly 500 days after our last phone conversation, your daughter-in-law participated in a panel discussion at one of America's prestigious think tanks. She talked about the disappearance of our family while pointing out the horrific conditions of the camps and the Orwellian-style complete police state that East Turkistan had become. She called on the United States government and the international community to act. Six days later, the Chinese government abducted her sister Gulshan Abbas, who is a retired medical doctor in Urumchi. They also abducted her 60-year-old aunt in Artush to retaliate for Rushan's activism.

During these difficult times, my devoted, courageous wife Rushan has been by my side. She has been not merely a soulmate to me; she has also become a best friend and companion in the journey of activism. We, as husband and wife, have continued to explore the path of salvation for our people while we try to be a voice for the voiceless and advocate for the defenseless, innocent Uyghurs. However, at the point when I lost contact with you, millions of people were being thrown into prisons and concentration camps, and the international community in this free world was mute, while the press was not reporting on it. It seemed as if it had all been swept under the rug.

Your daughter-in-law has been busy sitting in front of a computer day and night sending messages to reporters. She has been trying to bring attention to these unprecedented atrocities and has been advocating for you and millions of others. The "One Voice, One Step" women's initiative generated simultaneous global protests in all four corners of the world, lasting for 22 hours,

When I would tell people around me who are not Uyghur that China was not allowing me to have any contact or information from my parents and my family, it was so difficult for them to believe. How could such a thing happen in this information era of the 21st Century?

Mother, if you could have ' witnessed my wife, with a personality in many ways like yours: the same hatred and love that is as clearly defined as can be. She is never unfair to anyone, she is never afraid of anything, and she will never give up her rights. If ' you could have known how she has been constantly confronting the Chinese government using every platform of social media. She constantly grants interviews with journalists and is constantly asking:

"Where is my sister? Where are my in-laws? Where are my relatives? Where are millions of my people?" I can imagine how proud you would be, and the love and respect and praise you would have for her as you would encourage her to work harder and be stronger.

I miss hearing your voice and listening to your words so much, Mom. I miss talking to you. I want to tell you my thoughts and share my contentment with you. I want to tell you that your daughter-in-law was recognized for her hard work advocating for the Uyghurs on a stage prepared for the U.S. President Trump, in the presence of the Vice President Pence, Speaker Pelosi, Secretary of State Pompeo, and other high-ranking politicians, statesmen, foreign diplomats, members of the press, and economists. I wanted to see your satisfied, proud look when you would raise your head slightly and show a kind smile when I spoke of her achievements.

Rushan and I, as a couple, will spend our entire lives advocating for you and the Uyghur people. In every opportunity, in every waking hour, we are working hard. We will continue to be a voice for you, Uyghurs, and all the people of East Turkistan in every place that we can reach—in forums, in Islamic organizations, mosques, and universities. We must reach audiences and platforms from Japan to Australia, from Turkey to Canada, from Europe to the different states in America, and we must continue to raise awareness.

We must advocate, in order that the call to prayer would not be halted in our motherland, that our noble nation would never cease to exist, that the prisons would be closed, the walls of the concentration camps be broken down, and that the chains of oppression would be cut off and the whole of East Turkistan's liberty be restored. For the sake of our people and their right to live in peace and prosperity, we are fighting to the best of our ability to contribute to regain the independence of East Turkistan!

This was part of our vision of emigrating to the West when we were young, and I am grateful for the current establishments and for the existence of the Uyghur community in every corner of the world, as well as for the formation of organizations that are devoted to the Uyghur cause.

Earlier this year, during our trip to Canada, we met with Mr. Shawn Zhang, who lives in Vancouver. He was the first person to identify and prove by satellite imagery that the camps in East Turkistan existed, and he is internationally known as a camp expert. He showed me the Bostan neighborhood with the tomb of Beg Tugman next to it, and then our house—the house which I had not been to for 34 years since I left. I felt like breaking through the screen in front of me. I felt my soul leave me in defiance of my control and open those gates to run inside to see you, mother! My heart was beating so fast as I searched for you there, but I could not find you.

I asked Shawn, "Where is the closest camp to my parents' house?" He immediately took us through the reservoir in our neighborhood, pointing to a large-scale camp built in the New Awat Desert, which is located at the North of Khan Erik, West of New Erik, and the northwest section of Laskuy. He told us that the camps were being expanded in the area. Then, he showed us the part of the camp that was added on December 29, 2019. I imagined that most of my siblings were in this camp. I avoided imagining what kind of horrors my sisters were being subjected to, both emotionally and physically, inside this camp. But I did not know what to imagine about the fate of you and dad. I hurriedly asked about the orphanages nearby our house. Shawn showed us and I felt myself trembling until I could not bear anymore to imagine my nieces and nephews being subject to brainwashing there, forsaking their ethnic identity, their mother language, and their religion.

Shawn also showed us my wife's house in Urumqi, across from the Noghay mosque, in 3D. However, our gentle sister Dr. Gulshan Abbas was not in this house anymore. We do not know where she is, Mother. My wife was clearly heartbroken. From the big screen in front of us we saw that our homeland was filled with countless camps and prisons. We were also shown that the camp in Dawanqing was bigger than the entire town and that the prison in Urumqi was probably one of the largest in the world.

I am so worried, mother. What has this Coronavirus from Wuhan brought you? What added difficulties and hardship have you faced? Has there been enough bread to eat and water to drink? How many of my sisters and brothers-in-law are among those who are being forced to go and work in the factories in China proper as a part of this slavery? Where are my little nieces and nephews who are being treated as orphans? Which of my siblings have lost their lives for forced organ transplants? Has my brother Abdurehim been transferred to one of the prisons in China proper? To be honest, my mother, I do not know which of you is still alive or who is lost forever. But my hope is that you all are fine somehow. I pray to God, for you, for all Uyghurs, and for the universe, that this Ramadan will bring blessings, forgiveness, mercy, and salvation.

I believe that God will answer millions of mothers' cries while they are praying every morning before dawn. I believe our people must be saved. After darkness, the light will most definitely come. The truth must prevail. We will win against this evil.

We shall meet again, my beloved mother. Either in this world, or in the next!

Abdulhakim Idris
Washington
April 25, 2020

Source: Bitter Winter

Bibliography

INTRODUCTION
1-Özgüdenli, Osman G. "Moğollar" Türkiye Diyanet Vakfı Ansiklopedisi https://islamansiklopedi-si.org.tr/mogollar (accessed December 31, 2020)
2- Ibid.
3- London, Miriam, "China: The Romance of Realpolitik" Freedom at Issue, September-October 1989 https://www.carnegiecouncil.org/publications/articles_papers_reports/0080/_res/id=Atta-chments/index=0/China_The_Romance_of_Realpolitik.pdf (accessed December 31, 2020)
4- Ibid.
5- Ibid.
6- BBC, "China's Xi allowed to remain 'president for life' as term limits removed", March 11, 2018, https://www.bbc.com/news/world-asia-china-43361276 (Accessed at January 6, 2020)
7- McGreal, Chris, "Thanks China, now go home: buy-up of Zambia revives old colonial fears" The Guardian, February 5, 2007
https://www.theguardian.com/world/2007/feb/05/china.chrismcgreal (Accessed at January 6, 2020)
8- PBS, "China: Power and Prosperity -- Watch the full documentary" November 22, 2019 https://www.youtube.com/watch?v=JovtmKFxi3c&feature=youtu.be (Accessed at January 6, 2020)
9- U.S Department of State, "Communist China and the Free World's Future" July 23, 2020 htt-ps://www.state.gov/communist-china-and-the-free-worlds-future/ (Accessed at January 6, 2020)
10- O'Brien Robert C, "The Chinese Communist Party's Ideology and Global Ambitions" Foreign Policy, June 24, 2020 https://www.whitehouse.gov/briefings-statements/chinese-com-munist-partys-ideology-global-ambitions/
11- Reuters, "House to consider bills on Chinese goods made with forced labor, Pelosi says" CNBC, September 18, 2020 https://www.cnbc.com/2020/09/18/house-to-consider-bills-on-chinese-go-ods-made-with-forced-labor-pelosi-says.html (Accessed at January 4, 2020)
12- Basu, Zachary, "Biden campaign says China's treatment of Uighur Muslims is "genocide", Axios, August 25, 2020 https://www.axios.com/biden-campaign-china-uighur-genocide-3a-d857a7-abfe-4b16-813d-7f074a8a04ba.html (Accessed at December 4, 2020)
13- Buckley, Chris "China's Combative Nationalists See a World Turning Their Way" The New York Times, December 14, 2020 https://www.nytimes.com/2020/12/14/world/asia/china-natio-nalists-covid.html (Accessed at January 4, 2020)

CHAPTER 1
1- Steinmetz, George – The Sociology of Empires, Colonies, and Postcolonialism P.79-80
2- Ibid. P: 79
3- Webster, Richard A. "Western Colonialism" - https://www.britannica.com/topic/Western-colo-nialism, (accessed October 31, 2020)
4- Blakemore, Erin – "The history of colonialism is one of brutal subjugation of indigenous peoples." https://www.nationalgeographic.com/culture/topics/reference/colonialism/ (accessed November 01, 2020)
5- Webster, Richard "A. Western Colonialism" - https://www.britannica.com/topic/Western-colo-nialism (accessed October 31, 2020)
6- Blakemore, Erin – "The history of colonialism is one of brutal subjugation of indigenous peoples" National Geographic https://www.nationalgeographic.com/culture/topics/reference/colonialism/ (accessed October 31, 2020)
8- Efe, Mustafa "Afrika'da Fransa Kâbusu -1 Tarihsel Arka Plan" , May 5, 2020 https://www.aa.com.tr/tr/analiz/afrika-da-fransa-k%C3%A2busu-i-tarihsel-arkaplan/1725259 (accessed October 31, 2020)
9- Gates, Henry Louis, Jr – "How Many Slaves Landed in the U.S.?" https://www.pbs.org/wnet/african-americans-many-rivers-to-cross/history/how-many-slaves-landed-in-the-us/ (accessed October 31, 202010- Webster Richard A. "Western Colonialism" - https://www.britannica.com/

topic/Western-colonialism (accessed November 01, 2020)

11- Ibid.

12- Ibid.

13- Fuchs, Christian - Global Communication and Imperialism P.266

14- Ibid, P: 266

15- Ibid, P: 269

15- Ibid, P: 269

16- Ibid, P: 271

17- Ibid, P: 286

18- Harvey, David, "Spaces of Global Capitalism. A theory of Georaphical Development" London, Verso, 2009 S.98

CHAPTER 2

1- Bilge Khagan Inscriptions

2- Rossabi, Morris. History of China, John Wiley & Sons, Incorporated, 2013. P.6

3- Ibid, P: 16

4- Ibid, P: 32

5- Lambert, Tim "A History of China" http://www.localhistories.org/china.html (accessed October 31, 2020)

6- Rhoads Murphey, Kristin Stapleton, "A History of Asia" P. 209 – 210

7- Ibid, P: 209-210

8- Rossabi, Morris. "A history of China", John Wiley & Sons, Incorporated, 2013. P.369-370

9- Ibid, P. 281-282

10- Ibid, P. 294-295

11- Ibid, P. 295

12- Nowell, Charles, E "Western Colonialism" 2020 https://www.britannica.com/topic/Western-colonialism/Economic-imperialism (accessed November 2, 2020)

13- Rhoads, Murphey and Kristin, Stapleton, "A History of Asia" P. 313

14- Asia for educators, "China and the West: Imperialism, Opium, and Self-Strengthening. 1800-1921" http://afe.easia.columbia.edu/main_pop/kpct/kp_imperialism.htm (accessed November 1, 2020)

15- Wang, Yi Chu, "Sun Yat-sen" Britannica https://www.britannica.com/biography/Sun-Yat-sen (accessed November 03, 2020)

16- Rossabi, Morris. "A History of China", John Wiley & Sons, Incorporated, 2013. P.345

17- Ibid, P.347

18- Lambert, Tim "A History of China" http://www.localhistories.org/china.html (accessed October 31, 2020)

19- Rossabi, Morris. "A history of China", John Wiley & Sons, Incorporated, 2013. P.362

20- Ibid, P.364

21- Lambert, Tim "A History of China" http://www.localhistories.org/china.html (accessed October 31, 2020)

22- Rossabi, Morris. "A History of China", John Wiley & Sons, Incorporated, 2013. P.369-370

23- Ibid, P.369-370

24- Ibid, P.369-370

25- Lambert, Tim "A History of China" http://www.localhistories.org/china.html

26- Rossabi, Morris. "A history of China", John Wiley & Sons, Incorporated, 2013. P.369-370

27- Rhoads Murphey, Kristin Stapleton, "A History of Asia" P. 377-379

28- Ibid, P.377-379

29- Rossabi, Morris. "Çin Tarihi", John Wiley & Sons, Incorporated, 2013. P.392

30- Ibid, P.392

31- Rhoads Murphey, Kristin Stapleton, "A History of Asia" P. 385

32- Fitzgerald, Josep, "Mind your tongue" ASPI, October 2, 2019 https://www.aspi.org.au/report/mind-your-tongue (accessed November 03, 2020)

33- Ibid,

34- Searight, Amy, "Countering China's Influence Operations: Lessons from Australia" CSIS, May 8, 2020 https://www.csis.org/analysis/countering-chinas-influence-operations-lessons-australia (accessed November 03, 2020)

35- Newlin, Cyrus, et al. Chinese Influence Operations. Center for Strategic and International Studies (CSIS), 2020, pp. 13–22, Countering Russian and Chinese Influence Activities: Examining Democratic Vulnerabilities and Building Resiliency, www.jstor.org/stable/resrep25322.6.

36- The Economist, "China is spending billions to make the world love it" March 23, 2017 Edition, https://www.economist.com/china/2017/03/23/china-is-spending-billions-to-make-the-world-love-it (accessed November 04, 2020)

37- Scott, David, China's Soft Power and International Relations, P-45

38- Allen-Ebrahimian, Bethany, "Meet the U.S. Officials now in China's Sphere of Influence" The Daily Beast, November 21, 2018 https://www.thedailybeast.com/meet-the-us-officials-who-now-lobby-for-china (accessed November 03, 2020)

39- Cave, Damien, "Australian Politician's Home Raided in Chinese Influence Inquiry," The New York Times, June 26, 2020 https://www.nytimes.com/2020/06/26/world/australia/politician-home-raid-china-influence.html (accessed November 03, 2020)

40- Šimalčík, Matej & Turcsanyi, Richard & Matura, Dr. jur, Tamas & Karásková, Ivana. Central Europe for Sale: The Politics of China's Influence, 2018

41- Chinese Influence Activities in Select Countries https://www.hoover.org/sites/default/files/research/docs/13_diamond-schell_app2_web.pdf P.145 (accessed November 04, 2020)

42- Wuthnow, Joel. Chinese Diplomacy and the un Security Council : Beyond the Veto P-7

43- Ibid, P.8

44- Ibid, P.45

45- Feltman, Jeffrey, "China's expanding influence at the United Nations — and how the United States should react" P.2

46- Ibid, P.2

47-Tung Cheng-Chia and Alan H. Yang, "How China Is Remaking the UN In Its Own Image" https://thediplomat.com/2020/04/how-china-is-remaking-the-un-in-its-own-image/ (accessed November 03, 2020)

48- https://unwatch.org/wp-content/uploads/2012/01/CompositionCGNew2020_2021.pdf (accessed November 03, 2020)

49- Piccone, Ted – "China's Long Game On Human Rights at the United Nations" https://www.brookings.edu/wp-content/uploads/2018/09/FP_20181009_china_human_rights.pdf (accessed November 3, 2020)

50- Ibid.

51- Ibid.

52- Military and Security Developments Involving the People's Republic of China 2020 P.II

53- Ibid, P.V, VI

54- Ibid, P.X

55- Ibid, P.7

56- Ibid, P.127

57- Open Arms Evaluating Global Exposure to China's Defense-Industrial Base – C4ADS

58- Ibid.

59- "Ne ihlali, Uygurların insan hakkı yok ki ihlal olsun" https://campaignforuyghurs.org/tr/ne-ihlali-uygurlarin-insan-hakki-yok-ki-ihlal-olsun/ (accessed November 04, 2020)

60- Allen, Gregory C - Understanding China's AI Strategy: Clues to Chinese Strategic Thinking on Artificial Intelligence and National Security P-4

61- Ibid, P.4

62- Buckley, Chris – Meyers, Steven Lee – "As New Coronavirus Spread, China's Old Habits Delayed Fight" February 1, 2020, The New York Times, https://www.nytimes.com/2020/02/01/world/asia/china-coronavirus.html?action=click&module=Top%20Stories&pgtype=Homepage (accessed November 04, 2020)

63- The U.S. Coronavirus Data, https://www.nytimes.com/interactive/2020/us/coronavirus-us-cases.html (accessed November 04, 2020)

64- Reuters, "Pompeo says 'significant' evidence that new coronavirus emerged from Chinese lab" May 3, 2020 https://www.reuters.com/article/us-health-coronavirus-usa-pompeo/pompeo-says-significant-evidence-that-new-coronavirus-emerged-from-chinese-lab-idUSKBN22F-0SC (accessed November 04, 2020)

65- Pfluke, Corey – "Biohazard: A Look at China's Biological Capabilities and the Recent Coronavirus Outbreak" Air University, March 2, 2020 https://www.airuniversity.af.edu/Wild-Blue-Yonder/Article-Display/Article/2094603/biohazard-a-look-at-chinas-biological-capabilities-and-the-recent-coronavirus-o/ (accessed November 04, 2020)

66- Sagev, Hiddai – Lavi, Galia – "China's Donation Diplomacy" – Institute for National Studies.

67- Chen, Alicia – Molter, Vanessa – "Mask Diplomacy: Chinese Narratives in the COVID Era" Stanford University" June 16, 2020 https://fsi.stanford.edu/news/covid-mask-diplomacy (accessed November 04, 2020)

68- World Economic Outlook, October 2020: A Long and Difficult Ascent - https://www.imf.org/en/Publications/WEO/Issues/2020/09/30/world-economic-outlook-october-2020 (accessed November 04, 2020)

69- Mauldin John – "China's Grand Plan To Take Over The World," Forbes, November 12, 2020 https://www.forbes.com/sites/johnmauldin/2019/11/12/chinas-grand-plan-to-take-over-the-world/#4d4c04d85ab5 (accessed November 04, 2020)

70- Ibid.

71- Brands, Hal – "What does China really want? To dominate the World" Bloomberg, May 20, 2020, https://www.bloomberg.com/opinion/articles/2020-05-20/xi-jinping-makes-clear-that-china-s-goal-is-to-dominate-the-world (accessed November 04, 2020)

72- Asia Times, "China +1.9%, India -10.3% headline IMF forecasts" October 14, 2020, https://asiatimes.com/2020/10/china-1-9-india-10-3-headline-imf-forecasts/- (accessed November 04, 2020)

73- Morgan, Pippa – Zheng, Yu : "Tracing the Legacy: China's Historical Aid and Contemporary Investment in Africa" - International Studies Quarterly (2019) 63, 558–573

74- China Africa Research Initiative - http://www.sais-cari.org/chinese-investment-in-africa (accessed November 05, 2020)

75 – Maverick, J.B – "The 3 Reasons Why Chinese Invest in Africa", Investopedia, April 9, 2020 https://www.investopedia.com/articles/active-trading/081315/3-reasons-why-chinese-invest-africa.asp (accessed November 05, 2020)

76- Akol Nyok Akol Dok - Bradley A. Thayer – "Takeover Trap: Why Imperialist China Is Invading Africa" National Interest, June 10, 2019 https://nationalinterest.org/feature/takeover-trap-why-imperialist-china-invading-africa-66421 (accessed November 05, 2020)

77- Ibid.

78- 2020 China Africa Research Initiative at Johns Hopkins University's School of Advanced International Studies

79- Lawler, Dave – "The 53 countries supporting China's crackdown on Hong Kong" Axios, July 3, 2020 https://www.axios.com/countries-supporting-china-hong-kong-law-0ec9bc6c-3a-eb-4af0-8031-aa0f01a46a7c.html (accessed November 05, 2020)

80- Gopalds, Ronak - Lessons from Sri Lanka on China's 'debt-trap diplomacy' https://issafrica.org/amp/iss-today/lessons-from-sri-lanka-on-chinas-debt-trap-diplomacy (accessed November 05, 2020)

81- Chellaney, Brahma – "China'sa Creditor Imperialism", Project Sydicate, December 20, 2017 https://www.project-syndicate.org/commentary/china-sri-lanka-hambantota-port-debt-by-brahma-chellaney-2017-12 (accessed November 05, 2020)

82- Ibid.

83- Strangio, Sebastian - "Laos Stumbles Under Rising Chinese Debt Burden" The Diplomat, September 7, 2020 https://thediplomat.com/2020/09/laos-stumbles-under-rising-chinese-debt-burden/ (accessed November 05, 2020)

84- Chellaney, Brahma – "China'sa Creditor Imperialism", Project Sydicate, December 20, 2017 https://www.project-syndicate.org/commentary/china-sri-lanka-hambantota-port-debt-by-brahma-chellaney-2017-12 (accessed November 03, 2020)

85- Brautigam, Deborah, Jyhjong Hwang, Jordan Link, and Kevin Acker (2020) - "Chinese Loans to Africa Database," Washington, DC: China Africa - Research Initiative, Johns Hopkins University School of Advance - International Studies

86- Le Miere, Christian – "Increasing mutual dependence in Sino-Gulf relations is changing the strategic landscape," Atlantic Council May 11, 2020 https://www.atlanticcouncil.org/blogs/energysource/increasing-mutual-dependence-in-sino-gulf-relations-is-changing-the-strategic-landscape/ (accessed November 05, 2020)

87- Lons, Camille – China's Great Game in the Middle East. "Europian Council on Foreign Relations" October 2019 https://www.ecfr.eu/page/-/china_great_game_middle_east.pdf (accessed November 4, 2020)

88- Fulton, Jonathan - China's Great Game in the Middle East. "Europian Council on Foreign Relations" October 2019 https://www.ecfr.eu/page/-/china_great_game_middle_east.pdf (accessed November 4, 2020)

89- Al Tamimi, Naser - China's Great Game in the Middle East. "Europian Council on Foreign Relations" October 2019 https://www.ecfr.eu/page/-/china_great_game_middle_east.pdf (accessed November 4, 2020))

90- The Economist, "The battle for the Middle Eastern arms market is heating up" February 13, 2020 Edition https://www.economist.com/business/2020/02/13/the-battle-for-the-middle-eastern-arms-market-is-heating-up (accessed November 05, 2020)

91- Le Miere, Christian - Increasing mutual dependence in Sino-Gulf relations is changing the strategic landscape - https://www.atlanticcouncil.org/blogs/energysource/increasing-mutual-dependence-in-sino-gulf-relations-is-changing-the-strategic-landscape/ (accessed November 05, 2020)

CHAPTER 3

1-Radio Free Aisa – "Uyghurs Under 65 Now Banned From Daily Prayers Required by Their Faith" https://www.rfa.org/english/news/uyghur/prayers-09242020194025.html (accessed November 06, 2020)

2- Ibid.

3-Tsonchev, T.S. – Religion and Communism in Modern China – The Montreal Review, April 2011 https://www.themontrealreview.com/2009/Religion-and-Communism-in-Modern-China.php (accessed November 06, 2020)

4- Ibid.

5- Ibid.

6- Brady, Maddi – "Religion and State in Communist China" - http://blogs.bu.edu/guidedhistory/law-and-religion/maddi-b/ (accessed November 06, 2020)

7- Tsonchev, T.S. – "Religion and Communism in Modern China" - The Montreal Review, April 2011 https://www.themontrealreview.com/2009/Religion-and-Communism-in-Modern-China.php (accessed November 06, 2020)

8- Brady, Maddi – "Religion and State in Communist China" - http://blogs.bu.edu/guidedhistory/law-and-religion/maddi-b/ (accessed November 06, 2020)

9- Alber, Elenor –" Maizland Lindsay – Religion in China, Council on Foreign Relations, Last Updated September 25, 2020 (accessed November 06, 2020)

10- Brady, Maddi – "Religion and State in Communist China" - http://blogs.bu.edu/guidedhistory/law-and-religion/maddi-b/ (accessed November 06, 2020

11- Tsonchev, T.S. – "Religion and Communism in Modern China" - The Montreal Review, April 2011 https://www.themontrealreview.com/2009/Religion-and-Communism-in-Modern-China.php (accessed November 6, 2020)

12- Ibid.

13- Ibid.

14- ChinaAid – "Chinese Government Persecution of Churches and Christians in Mainland China," 2019 Annual Report, Feb. 28, 2020 https://drive.google.com/file/d/1OE9Y3_JzPW5Kofjo-aaQiD72Zbv2BPnsm/view (accessed November 06, 2020)

15- Tsonchev, T.S. – "Religion and Communism in Modern China" - The Montreal Review, April 2011 https://www.themontrealreview.com/2009/Religion-and-Communism-in-Modern-China.php (accessed November 06, 2020)

16- Alber, Elenor – "Maizland Lindsay – Religion in China, Council on Foreign Relations", Last Updated September 25, 2020 (accessed November 07, 2020)

17- Ibid.

18- (accessed November 07, 2020)

19- ChinaAid "2018 Annual Report Chinese Government Persecution of Churches and Christians in Mainland China" - January-December 2018 – P.59 https://drive.google.com/file/d/1deR-6dkQpidTsJ0RheaZ2Y8Q-C4XVvEWZ/view (accessed November 07, 2020)

20- Koh, Lyndey – "Early Rain Covenant Church pastor slapped with new charges", Mission Network News, July 23, 2019 https://www.mnnonline.org/news/early-rain-covenant-church-pastor-still-in-prison-wife-released/ (accessed November 07, 2020)

21- Lowry, Lindy – "Will the World's Largest Church Survive Amid Growing Hostility and Oppression?" Nations, Jun 1, 2020 - https://nationsmedia.org/will-worlds-largest-church-survive-amid-growing-hostility-and-oppression/ (accessed November 07, 2020)

22- Winfeld, Nicole – "Vatican: Pope Benedict XVI approved bishop accord with China" AP News, Oct. 3, 2020 (accessed November 07, 2020)

23- Hua, Shen – China is stepping up its control over religion - https://www.voanews.com/east-asia-pacific/voa-news-china/china-stepping-its-control-over-religion (accessed November 07, 2020)

24- Smith, Saphora – "China forcefully harvests organs from detainees, tribunal concludes" NBC News, June 18, 2019 https://www.nbcnews.com/news/world/china-forcefully-harvests-organs-detainees-tribunal-concludes-n1018646 (accessed November 07, 2020)

25- Auslin, R. Michael – "The Long Encounter: China and Islam's irreconcilable tensions" Hoover Institution, October 9, 2018 https://www.hoover.org/research/long-encounter-china-and-islams-irreconcilable-tensions (accessed November 07, 2020)

26- Ma, Haiyun – "The Anti-Islamic Movement in China," Hudson Institute, June 13, 2019 https://www.hudson.org/research/15095-the-anti-islamic-movement-in-china (accessed November 07, 2020)

27- Atwill, The Chinese Sultanate: Islam, Ethnicity, And The Panthay Rebellion In Southwest China, 1856-1873, 2005 https://china.usc.edu/atwill-chinese-sultanate-islam-ethnicity-and-panthay-rebellion-southwest-china-1856-1873-2005 (accessed November 07, 2020)

28- Ma, Haiyun – "The Anti-Islamic Movement in China" Hudson Institute, June 13, 2019 (accessed November 07, 2020)

29- Greer, Lucille – Bradley Jardine – "The Chinese Islamic Association in the Arab World: The Use of Islamic Soft Power in Promoting Silence on Xinjiang", July 14, 2020 https://www.mei.edu/publications/chinese-islamic-association-arab-world-use-islamic-soft-power-promoting-silence (accessed November 07, 2020)

30- Ibid.

31- Sandsedt, Melinda - The Impact Of The U.S.' War On Terror On China's Muslim Population https://theowp.org/the-impact-of-the-u-s-war-on-terror-on-chinas-muslim-population/ (accessed November 08, 2020)

32- Ibid.

33- Ma, Haiyun – "The Anti-Islamic Movement in China" Hudson Institute, June 13, 2019 (accessed November 08, 2020)

34- Ibid.

35- 2019 Report on International Religious Freedom - https://www.state.gov/reports/2019-report-on-international-religious-freedom/china/ (accessed November 08, 2020)

36- Yang William – "What does China want to achieve by 'modifying' Islam?" August 1, 2019 https://www.dw.com/en/what-does-china-want-to-achieve-by-modifying-islam/a-46995813 (accessed November 08, 2020)

37- The Week, "Xi Jinping says 'Sinicizing Islam' should continue in Xinjiang" September 28, 2020 https://www.theweek.in/news/world/2020/09/28/xi-jinping-says-sinicizing-islam-should-continue-xinjiang.html (accessed November 08, 2020)

38- Xi, Gu – "Imams Indoctrinated, Forced to Spread Communist Ideology" Bitter Winter, September 28, 2019 https://bitterwinter.org/imams-indoctrinated-forced-to-spread-communist-ideology/ (accessed November 08, 2020)

39- Minxguan, Li – "Sinicization of Islam: Xi Jinping Thought Instead of Quran" Bitter Winter, February 25, 2020 (accessed November 08, 2020)

40- Greer, Lucille – Bradley Jardine, "The Chinese Islamic Association in the Arab World: The Use of Islamic Soft Power in Promoting Silence on Xinjiang" July 14,2020 https://www.mei.edu/publications/chinese-islamic-association-arab-world-use-islamic-soft-power-promoting-silence (accessed November 08, 2020)

41- Minxguan, Li – "Sinicization of Islam: Xi Jinping Thought Instead of Quran" Bitter Winter, February 25, 2020 https://bitterwinter.org/xi-jinping-thought-instead-of-quran/ (accessed November 08, 2020)

42- Ibid.

43- Hua, Shen – "China is stepping up its control over religion" Voice of America, October 19, 2020 https://www.voanews.com/east-asia-pacific/voa-news-china/china-stepping-its-control-over-religion (accessed November 09, 2020)

44- Shin, Gerry – "'Boiling us like frogs': China's clampdown on Muslims creeps into the heartland, finds new targets" September 20, 2019 (accessed November 09, 2020)

45- 2019 Report on International Religious Freedom - https://www.state.gov/reports/2019-report-on-international-religious-freedom/china/

46- https://kuran.diyanet.gov.tr/tefsir/Hicr-suresi/1811/9-ayet-tefsiri

47- Hafez, Farid – "China's Attempt to Change to Quran", Brigde, Jan 14, 2020, https://bridge.georgetown.edu/research/how-chinese-is-western-islamophobia-2/ (accessed November 09, 2020)

48- Deif, Farida – "A missed Opportunity to Protect Muslims in China", Human Rights Watch March 21, 2019, (accessed November 09, 2020)

49- Ma, Alexandra – "A wave of Islamic countries started to stand up to China over its persecution of its Muslim minority. But then they all got spooked." Business Insider, April 6, 2019 (accessed November 09, 2020)

50- Xinhua, "Xi sends congratulatory message to 14th OIC summit", Xinhua.net June 01, 2019 -http://www.xinhuanet.com/english/2019-06/01/c_138107122.htm (accessed November 09, 2020)

51- Al Jazeera, "Pakistan's PM: Our economic future is now linked to China" September 2, 2020 https://www.aljazeera.com/program/talk-to-al-jazeera/2020/9/3/pakistans-pm-our-economic-future-is-now-linked-to-china/ (accessed November 09, 2020)

52- Chaudry, Dipanjan R. "Imran Khan remains mum on Uyghur plight even as he targets OIC on Kashmir" The Economic Times, February 6, 2020 https://economictimes.indiatimes.com/news/international/world-news/imran-khan-remains-mum-on-uyghur-plight-even-as-he-targets-oic-on-kashmir/articleshow/73978122.cms?from=mdr (accessed November 09, 2020)

53- Dhume, Sadanad – "Pakistan Gives a Pass to China's Oppression of Muslims" Wall Street Journal, October 3, 2019 (accessed November 09, 2020)

54- Chaudry, Dipanjan R. "ET analysis: China's trade concessions to Bangladesh a 'dual-deficit and debt trap" The Economic Times, July 11, 2020 https://economictimes.indiatimes.com/news/international/world-news/et-analysis-chinas-trade-concessions-to-bangladesh-a-dual-deficit-and-debt-trap/articleshow/76907291.cms?utm_source=contentofinterest&utm_medium=text&utm_campaign=cppst (accessed November 09, 2020)

55- London School of Economics, "Bangladesh-China relations have metamorphosed into a strategic partnership" June 20, 2019 (accessed November 09, 2020)

56- Ani News, "Massive protest held in Dhaka against China's repression of Uyghur Muslims", August 20, 2020 https://www.aninews.in/news/world/asia/massive-protest-held-in-dhaka-against-chinas-repression-of-uyghur-muslims20200828180846/ (accessed November 09, 2020)

57- Lwin, Nan - "Megaprojects a Double-Edged Sword for Myanmar" The Irrawaddy, August 9, 2019 (accessed November 10, 2020)

58- Asrar, Shakeeb "Rohingya crisis explained in maps" Al Jazeera, October 28, 2017 (accessed November 10, 2020)

59- Jamestown Foundation, Rohingya Crisis: Will China's Mediation Succeed?, 22 November 2017, China Brief Volume: 17 Issue: 15, available at: https://www.refworld.org/docid/5a168ac04.html (accessed November 10, 2020)

60- Time Türk, "İslam İşbirliği Teşkilatından Myanmar kararı" March 4, 2019 (accessed November 10, 2020)

61- Grassi, Sergio – "The Belt And Road Initiative in Malaysia" February 2020 – P.5 - http://library.fes.de/pdf-files/iez/16766.pdf (accessed November 10, 2020)

62- CIMB ASEAN Research Institute – "China's Belt and Road Initiative (BRI) and Southeast Asia" October 2018
https://www.lse.ac.uk/ideas/Assets/Documents/reports/LSE-IDEAS-China-SEA-BRI.pdf (accessed November 10, 2020)

63- Reuter, "Malaysia PM says can't provoke Beijing on South China Sea, Uighur issue" September 28, 2019 (accessed November 10, 2020)

64- RFA, "Indonesia Deports 4 Uyghur Terrorism Suspects to China, Experts Say" October 23, 2010 (accessed November 10, 2020)

65- CIMB ASEAN Research Institute – "China's Belt and Road Initiative (BRI) and Southeast Asia" October 2018
https://www.lse.ac.uk/ideas/Assets/Documents/reports/LSE-IDEAS-China-SEA-BRI.pdf (accessed November 10, 2020)

66- Wang, Maya and Harsono, Andreas, "Indonesia Silence over Xinjiang" Human Rights Watch, January 31, 2020 (accessed November 10, 2020)

67- Brautigam, Deborah, Jyhjong Hwang, Jordan Link, and Kevin Acker (2020) "Chinese Loans to Africa Database," Washington, DC: China Africa / Research Initiative, Johns Hopkins University School of Advanced International Studies.

68- Putz, Catherine – "Which Countries Are For or Against China's Xinjiang Policies?" The Diplomat, June 14,2020 (accessed November 10, 2020)

69- Brautigam, Deborah, Jyhjong Hwang, Jordan Link, and Kevin Acker (2020) "Chinese Loans to Africa Database," Washington, DC: China Africa / Research Initiative, Johns Hopkins University School of Advanced International Studies.

70- Xinhua, "Algeria, China bound by excellent relations presidency spokesperson" Xinhua.net May 14, 2020 (accessed November 10, 2020)

71- Mahalingam, V Brig, "Will China's Military Presence and Economic Involvement in Tajikistan Undermine Russia's Influence in the Region?" Indian Defence Review, August 15,2020
www.indiandefencereview.com/spotlights/will-chinas-military-presence-and-economic-involvement-in-tajikistan-undermine-russias-influence-in-the-region/ (accessed November 10, 2020)

72- Kaura, Vinay, "What does China's growing engagement in Afghanistan mean for the US?" Middle East Institute, August 7, 2020 (accessed November 10, 2020)

CHAPTER 4

1-From The Memoirs of İsa Yusuf Alptekin for Captive East Turkistan (P: 26)

2- Bakır Abdullah, Doğu Türkistan Milli İstiklal Hareketi ve Mehmet Emin Buğra – P. 2-3

3- Uyghurlar - Turghun Almas

4- Millward, James A - China, Xinjiang, and Central Asia : History, Transition and Crossborder Interaction into the 21st Century, edited by Colin Mackerras, and Michael Clarke, Taylor & Francis Group, 2009. P-56

5- Ibid P-57

6- Ibid. P-58

7- Embassy of the People of Republic of China in India "Xinjiang Natural Resources" http://in.china-embassy.org/eng/ssygd/xbdkf/Xinjiang/t166811.htm#:~:text=Oil%2C%20natural%20gas%2C%20and%20nonferrous,third%20of%20the%20nation's%20totals. (accessed November 12, 2020)

8-Doğu Türkistan Milli İstiklal Hareketi ve Mehmet Emin Buğra, Doğu Türkistan Vakfı Yayınları İstanbul 2005

9- Buğra, Mehmet Emin – Şarki Türkistan Tarihi (1940)

10- Buğra, Mehmet Emin – Şarki Türkistan Tarihi (1940)

11- Kurban, Nur Ahmet - Mehmet Emin Buğra https://islamansiklopedisi.org.tr/bugra-mehmet-emin

12- Kul, Ömer – İsa Yusuf Alptekin - https://islamansiklopedisi.org.tr/alptekin-isa-yusuf

14- Oğuz, Abdullah – "Şarki Türkistan Tarihi: Metin Tenkidi, Türkiye Türkçesi ve İnceleme" İstanbul Üniversitesi, Sosyal Bilimler Enstitüsü Türkiyat Araştırmaları Anabilim Dalı – İstanbul 2020

15- Doğu Türkistan Milli İstiklal Hareketi ve Mehmet Emin Buğra, Doğu Türkistan Vakfı Yayınları İstanbul 2005

16- Dillon, Michael 'Ethnic, Religious and Political Conflict on China's Northwestern Borders: The Background to the Violence in Xinjiang' IBRU Boundary and Security Bulletin Spring 1997

17- Roberts, Sean R. "The War on the Uyghurs" – Princeton Studies in Muslim Politics – 2020

18- Moneyhon, Matthew "Controlling Xinjiang: Autonomy on China's 'New Frontier'" Asian – Pasific Law & Policy Journal – 2002

19- "Doğu Türkistan davasını Çin'in iç meselesi görenler yanılıyor!" Campaign For Uyghurs, April 20, 2020 (accessed November 13, 2020)

20- Roberts, Sean R. "The War on the Uyghurs" – Princeton Studies in Muslim Politics – 2020

21- Esir Doğu Türkistan İçin, İsa Yusuf Alptekin'in Hatıraları – Doğu Türkistan Neşriyat Merkezi – 1985 P. 550

22- Roberts, Sean R. "The War on the Uyghurs" (Princeton Studies in Muslim Politics) (p. 47). Princeton University Press.

23- Ibid.

24- Political History Of The Uyghurs - Qahriman Ghojamberdi

25- Kayaoğlu, Arzu, "Çin Kültür Devrimi: Toplu Cinayetlerin 50. Yıl dönümü", Euronews, May 16, 2016 https://tr.euronews.com/2016/05/16/cin-kultur-devrimi-toplu-cinayetlerin-50-yil-donumu (accessed November 13, 2020)

26- Ibid.

27- Roberts, Sean R. "The War on the Uyghurs" (Princeton Studies in Muslim Politics) (p. 48). Princeton University Press.

28- Roberts, Sean R. "The War on the Uyghurs" (Princeton Studies in Muslim Politics) (p. 48). Princeton University Press.

29- Bovingdon, Gardner. Autonomy in Xinjiang: Han Nationalist Imperatives and Uyghur Discontent. Edited by Muthiah Alagappa, East-West Center, 2004, www.jstor.org/stable/resrep06498

30- Kayaoğlu, Arzu, "Çin Kültür Devrimi: Toplu Cinayetlerin 50. Yıl dönümü", Euronews May16, 2016 https://tr.euronews.com/2016/05/16/cin-kultur-devrimi-toplu-cinayetlerin-50-yil-donumu (accessed November 12, 2020)

31- Ibid.

32- Roberts, Sean R. "The War on the Uyghurs" (Princeton Studies in Muslim Politics) (p. 49). Princeton University Press.

33- İsa Dolkun , "Before the Tiananmen Massacre, Uyghurs Led Their Own Protest", The Diplomat, June 16, 202

34- Roberts, Sean R. "The War on the Uyghurs" (Princeton Studies in Muslim Politics) (p. 49). Princeton University Press.

35- Ibid, P: 49

36- Ibid, P: 29

37- Uygurların Siyasi Tarihi - Qahriman Ghojamberdi

38- Roberts, Sean R. "The War on the Uyghurs" (Princeton Studies in Muslim Politics) (p. 54-55). Princeton University Press.

39- Ibid, P: 54-55.

40- Gutmann, Ethan. "BITTER HARVEST: China's 'Organ Donation' Nightmare." World Affairs, vol. 175, no. 2, 2012, pp. 49–56. JSTOR, www.jstor.org/stable/41639005.
41- Roberts, Sean R. "The War on the Uyghurs" (Princeton Studies in Muslim Politics) (p. 54-55). Princeton University Press.
42- Arkın, Tuhti Ahun - "Turkistanu'l-Muslime ve'l-Kadiyyetu'l-Mensiyye (Müslüman Türkistan ve Unutulan Dava)
43- Dwyer, Arianne M. – The Xinjiang Conflict – East West Center – 2005 http://www.jstor.com/stable/resrep06543.1
44- US removes separatist group condemned by China from terror list - https://www.dw.com/en/us-removes-separatist-group-condemned-by-china-from-terror-list/a-55527586 (accessed November 17, 2020)
45- Dillon, Michael – "Ethnic, Religious and Political Conflict on China's Northwestern Borders: The Background to the Violence in Xinjiang" - IBRU Boundary and Security Bulletin, Spring 1997
46- İsa Yusuf Alptekin Doğu Türkistan Davası Seha Neşriyat 1992 .
77- Uygurların siyasi tarihi Qahriman Ghojamberdi
48- İsa Yusuf Alptekin Doğu Türkistan Davası Seha Neşriyat 1992 .
49- Uygurların siyasi tarihi - Qahriman Ghojamberdi
50- İsa Yusuf Alptekin Doğu Türkistan Davası Seha Neşriyat 1992 .
51- The Bingtuan, China's Paramilitary Colonizing Force in East Türkistan - UHRP - Nisan 2018
52- Howell Anthony, and Fan, C. Cindy "Migration and Inequality in Xinjiang:
A Survey of Han and Uyghur Migrants in Urumqi" - Department of Geography, University of California, Los Angeles - https://geog.ucla.edu/sites/default/files/users/fan/403.pdf (accessed November 17, 2020)
53- Roberts, Sean R. "The War on the Uyghurs" (Princeton Studies in Muslim Politics) (p. 46). Princeton University Press.
54- Joniak-Lüthi, Agnieszka. "Han Migration to Xinjiang Uyghur Autonomous Region: Between State Schemes and Migrants' Strategies." Zeitschrift Für Ethnologie, vol. 138, no. 2, 2013, pp. 155–174. JSTOR, www.jstor.org/stable/24364952. Accessed 10 Nov. 2020.
55- Howell Anthony, and Fan, C. Cindy "Migration and Inequality in Xinjiang:
A Survey of Han and Uyghur Migrants in Urumqi" - Department of Geography, University of California, Los Angeles - https://geog.ucla.edu/sites/default/files/users/fan/403.pdf
56- Bovingdon, Gardner. Autonomy in Xinjiang: Han Nationalist Imperatives and Uyghur Discontent. Edited by Muthiah Alagappa, East-West Center, 2004, www.jstor.org/stable/resrep06498.
57- Ibid.
58- Howell Anthony, and Fan, C. Cindy "Migration and Inequality in Xinjiang:
A Survey of Han and Uyghur Migrants in Urumqi" - Department of Geography, University of California, Los Angeles - https://geog.ucla.edu/sites/default/files/users/fan/403.pdf
www.jstor.org/stable/resrep06498.
59- Ibid.
60- Bovingdon, Gardner. Autonomy in Xinjiang: Han Nationalist Imperatives and Uyghur Discontent. Edited by Muthiah Alagappa, East-West Center, 2004, www.jstor.org/stable/resrep06498
61- Esir Doğu Türkistan İçin, İsa Yusuf Alptekin'in Hatıraları – Doğu Türkistan Neşriyat Merkezi – 1985 P. 35
62- Emet, Erkin – Doğu Türkistan'da Çift Dilli Eğitim, Atatürk Kültür ve Dil Tarih Kurumu Yayınları 2015 – P. 537
63- Esir Doğu Türkistan İçin, İsa Yusuf Alptekin'in Hatıraları – Doğu Türkistan Neşriyat Merkezi – 1985 P. 35
64- Emet, Erkin – Doğu Türkistan'da Çift Dilli Eğitim, Atatürk Kültür ve Dil Tarih Kurumu Yayınları 2015 – P. 537
65- Bovingdon, Gardner. Autonomy in Xinjiang: Han Nationalist Imperatives and Uyghur Discontent. Edited by Muthiah Alagappa, East-West Center, 2004, www.jstor.org/stable/resrep06498.

66- Wei, Cuiyi. "An Historical Survey of Modern Uyghur Writing since the 1950s in Xinjiang, China." Central Asiatic Journal, vol. 37, no. 3/4, 1993, pp. 249–322. JSTOR, www.jstor.org/stable/24467845.

67- Emet, Erkin – Doğu Türkistan'da Çift Dilli Eğitim, Atatürk Kültür ve Dil Tarih Kurumu Yayınları
2015 – S. 537

68- Roberts, Sean R. "The War on the Uyghurs" (Princeton Studies in Muslim Politics) (P. 139). Princeton University Press.

69- Emet, Erkin – Doğu Türkistan'da Çift Dilli Eğitim, Atatürk Kültür ve Dil Tarih Kurumu Yayınları
2015 – S. 537

70- Roberts, Sean R. "The War on the Uyghurs" (Princeton Studies in Muslim Politics) (P. 139). Princeton University Press.

71- Ibid, P: 139

72- Bovingdon, Gardner. Autonomy in Xinjiang: Han Nationalist Imperatives and Uyghur Discontent. Edited by Muthiah Alagappa, East-West Center, 2004, www.jstor.org/stable/resrep06498

73- Roberts, Sean R. "The War on the Uyghurs" (Princeton Studies in Muslim Politics) (P. 139). Princeton University Press.

74- Uyghur Girls Forced into Labor Far from Home By Local Chinese Officials | Uyghur Human Rights Project. 27.07.2020, from https://uhrp.org/news/uyghur-girls-forced-labor-far-home-local-chinese-officials (accessed November 17, 2020)

75- Roberts, Sean R. "The War on the Uyghurs" (Princeton Studies in Muslim Politics) (P. 139). Princeton University Press

76- Ibid, P: 139

77- Uygurları Siyasi Tarihi - Qahriman Ghojamberdi

78- Ibid.

79- Ibid.

80- Roberts, Sean R. "The War on the Uyghurs" (Princeton Studies in Muslim Politics) (P. 146). Princeton University Press.

81- Uygurların Siyasi tarihi - Qahriman Ghojamberdi

82- Ibid.

83- Roberts, Sean R. "The War on the Uyghurs" (Princeton Studies in Muslim Politics) (P. 154). Princeton University Press.

84-Uygurların siyasi tarihi - Qahriman Ghojamberdi

85- Cliff Thomas – "The Partnership of Stability in Xinjiang: State–Society Interactions Following the July 2009 - The China Journal , No. 68 (July 2012), pp. 79-105 https://www.jstor.org/stable/10.1086/666581

86- Roberts, Sean R. "The War on the Uyghurs" (Princeton Studies in Muslim Politics) (P. 150). Princeton University Press.

87- Ibid, P: 151

88- Ibid, P: 151

CHAPTER 5

1- Qelbinur Sidik – A Twisted Life, Dutch Uyghur Human Rights Foundation, July 28, 2020 https://www.duhrf.org/project/qelbinur-sidik-a-twisted-life/ (accessed November 22, 2020)

2- Albert, Melissa, "Xi Jinping" – Britannica https://www.britannica.com/biography/Xi-Jinping

3- O'Brien, Robert C, "The Chinese Communist Party's Ideology and Global, Ambitions" White House, June 24, 2020 https://www.whitehouse.gov/briefings-statements/chinese-communist-partys-ideology-global-ambitions/ (accessed November 18, 2020)

4- Doubek, James – "China Removes Presidential Term Limits, Enabling Xi Jinping To Rule Indefinitely" – NPR – March 11, 2018 https://www.npr.org/sections/thetwo-way/2018/03/11/592694991/china-removes-presidential-term-limits-enabling-xi-jinping-to-rule-indefinitely (accessed November 18, 2020)

5- Roberts, Sean R. "The War on the Uyghurs" (Princeton Studies in Muslim Politics) (P. 161).

Princeton University Press

6- Ibid, P: 164

7- Ibid, P: 171

8- Singh, Gunjan – "Xi Jinping Continues China's Repressive Policies in Xinjiang" Vivekenanda International Foundation, June 2028 (accessed November 18, 2020)

9- Roberts, Sean R. "The War on the Uyghurs" (Princeton Studies in Muslim Politics) (P. 172). Princeton University Press

10- Blanchette, Jude, "Xi Jinping's Vision for Xinjiang", CSIS, September 30, 2020 (accessed November 18, 2020)

11- Ibid.

12- Ibid.

13- Torigan, Joseph – "What Xi Jinping Learned—And Didn't Learn—From His Father About Xinjiang" – The Diplomat, November 26, 2019 , https://thediplomat.com/2019/11/what-xi-jin-ping-learned-and-didnt-learn-from-his-father-about-xinjiang/

14- Singh, Gunjan – "Xi Jinping Continues China's Repressive Policies in Xinjiang" Vivekenanda International Foundation, (accessed November 18, 2020)

15- Nazi döneminin kurbanları: Nazi Irkçı İdeolojisi. – Holokost Ansiklopedisi https://encyc-lopedia.ushmm.org/content/tr/article/victims-of-the-nazi-era-nazi-racial-ideology (accessed November 18, 2020)

16- 'Soykırım Suçunun Önlenmesine ve Cezalandırılmasına Dair Sözleşmesini'

17- "China's Genocide in East Turkistan", Campain for Uyghurs – Washigton DC, 2020

18- Maizland, Lindasy – "China's Repression of Uyghurs in Xinjiang" – Council Foreign Relations (CFR), June 30, 2020 - https://www.cfr.org/backgrounder/chinas-repression-Uyghurs-xinjiang (accessed November 18, 2020)

19- Shepherd, Christian – "Fear and opressession in Xinjiang: China's war on Uyghur Culture" Financial Times, September, 12 2019 https://www.ft.com/content/48508182-d426-11e9-8367-807ebd53ab77 (accessed November 19, 2020)

20- Maizland, Lindasy – "China's Repression of Uyghurs in Xinjiang" – Council Foreign Relati-ons (CFR), June 30, 2020 - https://www.cfr.org/backgrounder/chinas-repression-Uyghurs-xinji-ang (accessed November 19, 2020)

21- Reuters / ABC "Chinese President Xi Jinping defends Xinjiang detention network, claiming 'happiness' is on the rise", September 27, 2020 https://www.abc.net.au/news/2020-09-28/chine-se-president-xi-jinping-uyghur-xinjiang-correct-happiness/12708930

22- Maizland, Lindasy – "China's Repression of Uyghurs in Xinjiang" – Council Foreign Relations (CFR), June 30, 2020 - https://www.cfr.org/backgrounder/chinas-repression-Uyghurs-xinjiang (accessed November 19, 2020)

23- UHRP – "Qarakash Document Report" https://docs.uhrp.org/pdf/UHRP_QaraqashDocument.pdf

24- https://www.washingtonpost.com/politics/2020/06/17/bolton-says-trump-didnt-just-igno-re-human-rights-encouraged-chinas-concentration-camps/

25- Ramz, Austin – Buckley, Chris – "Absolutely No Mercy': Leaked Files Expose How China Or-ganized Mass Detentions of Muslims" New York Times November 16, 2019 https://www.nytimes.com/interactive/2019/11/16/world/asia/china-xinjiang-documents.html

26- Ibid.

27- Maizland, Lindasy – "China's Repression of Uyghurs in Xinjiang" – Council Foreign Relations (CFR), June 30, 2020 - https://www.cfr.org/backgrounder/chinas-repression-Uyghurs-xinjiang (accessed November 19, 2020)

28- Ramz, Austin – Buckley, Chris – "Absolutely No Mercy': Leaked Files Expose How China Or-ganized Mass Detentions of Muslims" New York Times November 16, 2019 https://www.nytimes.com/interactive/2019/11/16/world/asia/china-xinjiang-documents.html (accessed November 19, 2020)

29- Qarakash Document - Uygur Human Right Project, February 2020 https://docs.uhrp.org/pdf/UHRP_QaraqashDocument.pdf (accessed November 20, 2020)

30- Maizland, Lindasy – "China's Repression of Uyghurs in Xinjiang" – Council Foreign Relations

(CFR), June 30, 2020 - https://www.cfr.org/backgrounder/chinas-repression-Uyghurs-xinjiang (accessed November 20, 2020)

31- Zenz, Adrian – ""Thoroughly Reforming Them Towards a Healthy Heart Attitude" - China's Political Re-Education Campaign in Xinjiang" Central Asian Survey – September 6, 2018 -

32- Ibid.

33- Ibid.

35- Maizland, Lindasy – "China's Repression of Uyghurs in Xinjiang" Council Foreign Relations (CFR), June 30, 2020 - https://www.cfr.org/backgrounder/chinas-repression-Uyghurs-xinjiang

35- "China Uyghurs: Detainees 'free' after 'graduating', official says" BBC News, December 9, 2019 https://www.bbc.com/news/world-asia-china-50712126 (accessed November 20, 2020)

36- Ruser Nathan "Exploring Xinjiang detention system" – Xinjiang Data Project – ASPI 2020 https://xjdp.aspi.org.au/explainers/exploring-xinjiangs-detention-facilities/ (accessed November 20, 2020)

37- Ibid.

38- Ibid.

39- Çin Komünist Parti, Doğu Türkistan'da milyonlarca Uyguru kamplara gönderdiğini itiraf ediyor – Campaign for Uyghurs - https://campaignforuyghurs.org/tr/cin-komunist-parti-dogu-turkistanda-milyonlarca-uyguru-kamplara-gonderdigini-itiraf-ediyor/ (accessed November 20, 2020)

40- "Kanadalı gazeteci Çin kampını anlattı: Uygurlara kimlik soykırımı yapılıyor" Karar Gazetesi – September 6, 2019 https://www.karar.com/kanadali-gazeteci-cin-kampini-anlatti-uygurlara-kimlik-soykirimi-yapiliyor-1316858 (accessed November 22, 2020)

41- "Kanadalı Akademisyen: Çinliler, Hitlerin yaptığından daha beterini Uygurlara yapıyor" – Uygur Hareketi, https://www.referansmedya.com/kanadali-akademisyen-cinliler-hitlerin-yaptigindan-daha-beterini-uygurlara-yapiyor-3811h.htm (accessed November 22, 2020)

42- Qelbinur Sidik – A Twisted Life, Dutch Uyghur Human Rights Foundation, July 28, 2020 https://www.duhrf.org/project/qelbinur-sidik-a-twisted-life/ (accessed November 22, 2020)

43- Rauhala, Emily – Fifield Anna, "She survived a Chinese internment camp and made it to Virginia. Will the U.S. let her stay?" Washington Post, November 17, 2019 https://www.washingtonpost.com/world/2019/11/17/she-survived-chinese-internment-camp-made-it-virginia-will-us-let-her-stay/?arc404=true

44- Abou-Sabe Kenzi - Lehran, Andrew W – Martinez, Didi – Snow, Kate – "Secret Chinese documents reveal inner workings of Muslim detention camps" NBC News, November 24, 2019 https://www.nbcnews.com/news/all/secret-chinese-documents-reveal-inner-workings-muslim-detention-camps-n1089941 (accessed November 22, 2020)

45- Rauhala, Emily – Fifield Anna, "She survived a Chinese internment camp and made it to Virginia. Will the U.S. let her stay?" Washington Post – November 17, 2019 https://www.washingtonpost.com/world/2019/11/17/she-survived-chinese-internment-camp-made-it-virginia-will-us-let-her-stay/?arc404=true (accessed November 22, 2020)

46- "The Independent Tribunal ino Forced Organ Harvesting from Prisoners of Conscience in China" March 1, 2020

47- Wojcik, Nadine, "Sayragul Sauytbay: How China is destroying Kazakh culture" DW, May 8, 2020 https://www.dw.com/en/how-china-is-destroying-kazakh-culture/a-54434930 (accessed November 22, 2020)

48- Conrad, Naomi and Bayer, Julia and Chan, Cherie "China convicts Uyghurs in sham trials at Xinjiang camps" DW, May 8, 2020 - https://www.dw.com/en/china-convicts-Uyghurs-in-sham-trials-at-xinjiang-camps/a- 53699982?fbclid=IwAR2BOWUmS6Ub1mKLrgsG-zXbniq552Pn1c5XZNEpaBXndFgPSVi2bj2a2lCA

49- Ibid

50- Xu, Vicky Xiuzhong - Cave, Danielle - Leibold, Dr James – Munro, Kelsey – Ruser, Nathan – "Uyghurs for Sale" ASPI, March 1, 2020 - https://www.aspi.org.au/report/uyghurs-sale (accessed November 22, 2020)

51- Ibid.

52- Ibid.

53- H.R 6210 – Uyghur Forced Labor Prevention Act - https://www.congress.gov/bill-l/116th-congress/house-bill/6210 (accessed November 23, 2020)

54- Albergotti, Reed, "Apple is lobbying against a bill aimed at stopping forced labor in China" The Washington Post, November 20, 2020 https://www.washingtonpost.com/technology/2020/11/20/apple-uighur/ (accessed November 27, 2020)

55- Cuma, Mamatjan, and Seytoff Alim "Xinjiang Authorities Sending Uyghurs to Work in China's Factories, Despite Coronavirus Risks", RFA, February 2, 2020 (accessed November 23, 2020)

56- Xiao, Muyi and Willis, Halley and Koetti, Christoph and Reneau, Natalie and Jordan, Drew "China Is Using Uyghur Labor to Produce Face Masks" – The New York Times, July 19, 2020 (accessed November 23, 2020)

57- "China cuts Uyghur births with IUDs, abortion, sterilization" The Associated Press June 29, 2020 https://apnews.com/article/269b3de1af34e17c1941a514f78d764c (accessed November 23, 2020)

58- Ibid

59- Qin Amy – "In China's Crackdown on Muslims, Children Have Not Been Spared" The New York Times, December 28, 2019 - https://www.nytimes.com/2019/12/28/world/asia/china-xinjiang-children-boarding-schools.html (accessed November 28, 2020)

60- "500 bin Çocuk Üzerinde Oynanan Kültürel Mühendislik" – Uygur Hareketi, March 27, 2020 https://campaignforuyghurs.org/tr/500-bin-cocuk-uzerinde-oynanan-kulturel-muhendislik/ (accessed November 28, 2020)

61- Zenz, Adrian, "Parent-Child Separation in Yarkand County, Kashgar", October 13, 2020 https://adrianzenz.medium.com/story-45d07b25bcad

62- Referans Medya, "Çocuk haklarını savunanlar konu Uygur olunca neden susuyor?" August 18, 2020 (accessed November 28, 2020)

63- Ruser, Nathan and Leibold, Dr. James and Munro, Kelsey and Hoja Tilla – "Cultural erasure: Tracing the destruction of Uyghur and Islamic Spaces in Xinjiang, July 24, 2020 https://xjdp.aspi.org.au/explainers/cultural-erasure/ (accessed November 28, 2020)

64- Ibid.

65- China's Algorithms of Repression, Reverse Engineering a Xinjiang Police Mass Surveillance APP. Human Rights Wacth – May 1, 2019 https://www.hrw.org/report/2019/05/01/chinas-algorithms-repression/reverse-engineering-xinjiang-police-mass# (accessed November 28, 2020)

66- China Undercover, Frontline, April 7, 2020, https://www.pbs.org/wgbh/frontline/film/china-undercover/ (accessed November 28, 2020)

67- Cyranoski, David - China's massive effort to collect its people's DNA concerns scientists – Nature.com July 7, 2020 https://www.nature.com/articles/d41586-020-01984-4 (accessed November 28, 2020)

68- Dirks, Emile – Leibold, - China Is Harvesting the DNA of Its People. Is This the Future of Policing? – The New York Times, July 24, 2020 - https://www.nytimes.com/2020/07/24/opinion/china-dna-police.html (accessed November 28, 2020)

69- Islam, Imrul – "Xinjiang: Colleteral Damage of China's Belligerent Nationalism", Bridge, Georgetown University Initiative , May 3, 2019 https://bridge.georgetown.edu/research/xinjiang-colleteral-damage-of-chinas-nationalism/ (accessed November 28, 2020)

70- Kocaoğlu, Arsen – "Milliyetçilikten Faşizme giden yol" – Agos, September 2, 2016 http://www.agos.com.tr/tr/yazi/16439/milliyetcilikten-fasizme-giden-yol (accessed November 28, 2020)

71- "Çin zulmüne ilk elden tanık olan Afrikalının acil yardım çağrısı, lütfen arkadaşımı kurtarın!" Uygur Hareketi, July 22, 2020 https://campaignforuyghurs.org/tr/cin-zulmune-ilk-elden-tanik-olan-afrikalinin-acil-yardim-cagrisi-lutfen-arkadasimi-kurtarin/ (accessed November 28, 2020)

CHAPTER 6

1-Ilham Tohti – "Present-Day Ethnic Problems in Xinjiang Uyghur Autonomous Region: Overview and Recommendations"- (Translated by Cindy Carter) - https://ilhamtohtisite.files.wordpress.com/2016/09/ilham-tohti_present-day-ethnic-problems-in-xinjiang-Uyghur-autonomous-regionoverview-and-recommendations_complete-translation3.pdf.

2-Blakemore Erin, "How the East India Company became the world's most powerful business

– National Geographic", September, 2019 https://www.nationalgeographic.com/culture/topics/reference/british-east-india-trading-company-most-powerful-business/ (accessed December 01, 2020)

3- Cliff, Thomas Matthew James (2009) "Neo Oasis: The Xinjiang Bingtuan in the Twenty-first Century', Asian Studies Review" 33:1,83 — 106

4- Seymour, James D "Xinjiang's Production and Construction Corps, and the Sinification of Eastern Turkestan", Inner Asia, 2000 Vol. 2. No. 2 Special Issue: Xinjiang, P. 171-193 JSTOR https://www.jstor.org/stable/23615556

5- Cliff, Thomas Matthew James (2009) "Neo Oasis: The Xinjiang Bingtuan in the Twenty-first Century", Asian Studies Review, 33:1, 83 — 106

6- Seymour, James D "Xinjiang's Production and Construction Corps, and the Sinification of Eastern Turkestan", Inner Asia, 2000 Vol. 2. No. 2 Special Issue: Xinjiang, P. 171-193 JSTOR https://www.jstor.org/stable/23615556

7- Ibid, P: 171-193

8- Ibid, P: 171-193

9- Holdstock, Nick – "China's Forgotten People Xinjiang, Terror and The Chinese State" Published By L.B Tauris, 2015 – P: 37

10- Seymour, James D "Xinjiang's Production and Construction Corps, and the Sinification of Eastern Turkestan", Inner Asia, 2000 Vol. 2. No. 2 Special Issue: Xinjiang, P. 171-193

11- Ibid, P: 171-193

12- The Bingtuan – "China's Paramilitary Colonizing Force in East Turkistan" – Uyghur Human Rights Project, 26 April 2018 https://docs.uhrp.org/pdf/bingtuan.pdf

13- Seymour, James D "Xinjiang's Production and Construction Corps, and the Sinification of Eastern Turkestan", Inner Asia, 2000 Vol. 2. No. 2 Special Issue: Xinjiang, P. 171-193

14- Ibid, P: 171-193

15- Cliff, Thomas Matthew James (2009) "Neo Oasis: The Xinjiang Bingtuan in the Twenty-first Century", Asian Studies Review, 33:1,83 — 106

16- The Bingtuan – "China's Paramilitary Colonizing Force in East Turkistan" – Uyghur Human Rights Project, April 26, 2018 https://docs.uhrp.org/pdf/bingtuan.pdf

17-Seymour, James D "Xinjiang's Production and Construction Corps, and the Sinification of Eastern Turkestan", Inner Asia, 2000 Vol. 2. No. 2 Special Issue: Xinjiang, P. 171-193

18- Ibid, P: 171-193

19- The Bingtuan – "China's Paramilitary Colonizing Force in East Turkistan" – Uyghur Human Rights Project, April 26, 2018

20- Bate, Alex – "U.S.-Sanctioned Xinjiang Paramilitary Has Over 800,000 Holdings Worldwide" Sayari.com August 4, 2020 https://sayari.com/blog/u-s-sanctioned-xinjiang-paramilitary-has-over-800000-holdings-worldwide/ (accessed December 02, 2020)

21- Lehr, Amy K. – "Xinjiang Uyghur Autonomous Region: Toward a Shared Agenda" CSIS Briefs July 30, 2020 - https://www.csis.org/analysis/addressing-forced-labor-xinjiang-uyghur-autonomous-region-toward-shared-agenda

22- Cliff, Thomas Matthew James (2009) "Neo Oasis: The Xinjiang Bingtuan in the Twenty-first Century", Asian Studies Review, 33:1,83 — 106

23- Qian Wang, "Xinjiang Production and Construction Corps to Build 38 Townships" China.org.cn, April 15, 2004 http://www.china.org.cn/english/2004/Apr/93048.htm

24- " China's Paramilitary Colonizing Force in East Turkestan" – Uyghur Human Rights Project, April 26, 2018 https://docs.uhrp.org/pdf/bingtuan.pdf

25- Cliff, Thomas Matthew James (2009) "'Neo Oasis: The Xinjiang Bingtuan in the Twenty-first Century", Asian Studies Review, 33:1,83 — 106

26- "The Bingtuan, China's Paramilitary Colonizing Force in East Turkistan" – Uyghur Human Rights Project, 26 April 2018 https://docs.uhrp.org/pdf/bingtuan.pdf

27- Ibid.

28- Seymour, James D "Xinjiang's Production and Construction Corps, and the Sinification of Eastern Turkestan", Inner Asia, 2000 Vol. 2. No. 2 Special Issue: Xinjiang, P. 171-193

29- Lehr, Amy K. "Xinjiang Uyghur Autonomous Region: Toward a Shared Agenda" CSIS Briefs

September 30, 2020 - https://www.csis.org/analysis/addressing-forced-labor-xinjiang-uyghur-autonomous-region-toward-shared-agenda (accessed December 02, 2020)

30- "The Bingtuan, China's Paramilitary Colonizing Force in East Turkestan" – Uyghur Human Rights Project, April 26, 2018 https://docs.uhrp.org/pdf/bingtuan.pdf

31- Lehr, Amy K. – "Xinjiang Uyghur Autonomous Region: Toward a Shared Agenda" CSIS Briefs September 30, 2020 - https://www.csis.org/analysis/addressing-forced-labor-xinjiang-uyghur-autonomous-region-toward-shared-agenda (accessed December 02, 2020)

32- The Bingtuan – "China's Paramilitary Colonizing Force in East Turkestan" – Uyghur Human Rights Project, April 26, 2018 https://docs.uhrp.org/pdf/bingtuan.pdf

33- Lehr, Amy K. – "Xinjiang Uyghur Autonomous Region: Toward a Shared Agenda" CSIS Briefs September 30, 2020 - https://www.csis.org/analysis/addressing-forced-labor-xinjiang-uyghur-autonomous-region-toward-shared-agenda

CHAPTER 7

1- "President Xi Jinping proposes to build a Silk Road Economic Belt with Central Asian countries" China.org.cn – November 1, 2013 http://www.china.org.cn/travel/revitalize_the_silk_road_in_Shaanxi/2013-11/01/content_30468580.htm (accessed December 03, 2020)

2- Ibid.

3- İnayet, Prof. Dr. Alimcan, "Doğu Türkistan Örneğinden 'Bir Kuşak Bir Yol' Projesine Bakış, - 'Çin'in 'Bir Kuşak Bir Yol' Gerçeği ve Türk Dünyası - Ferhat Kurban Tanrıdağlı' İstanbul 2020

4- Chronology of China's Belt and Road Initiative – Xinhua, March 28, 2015 http://english.www.gov.cn/news/top_news/2015/04/20/content_281475092566326.htm (accessed December 01, 2020)

5- Baogang He (2019) The Domestic Politics of the Belt and Road Initiative and its Implications, Journal of Contemporary China, 28:116, 180-195, DOI: 10.1080/10670564.2018.1511391

6- "The Belt and Road Initiative Progress, Contributions and Prospects" – Belt and Road Portal – April 4, 2019 https://eng.yidaiyilu.gov.cn/zchj/qwfb/86739.htm (accessed December 05, 2020)

7- "The Belt and Road Initiative Progress, Contributions and Prospects" – Belt and Road Portal – April 4, 2019 https://eng.yidaiyilu.gov.cn/zchj/qwfb/86739.htm (accessed December 05, 2020)

8- Chatzky, Andrew and Mcbride James, "China's Massive Belt and Road Initiative" Council of Foreing Relations, January 28, 2020 - https://www.cfr.org/backgrounder/chinas-massive-belt-and-road-initiative (accessed December 05, 2020)

9- Ibid.

10- Zhao, Suisheng, "The Belt and Road Initiative and Xi Jinping's foreign and domestic policy agenda" The Asia Dialogue, October 2019 https://theasiadialogue.com/2019/10/29/the-belt-and-road-initiative-and-xi-jinpings-foreign-and-domestic-policy-agenda/ (accessed December 05, 2020)

11- Baogang He (2019) The Domestic Politics of the Belt and Road Initiative and its Implications, Journal of Contemporary China, 28:116, 180-195, DOI: 10.1080/10670564.2018.1511391

12- Chronology of China's Belt and Road Initiative – Xinhua, March 28, 2015 http://english.www.gov.cn/news/top_news/2015/04/20/content_281475092566326.htm (accessed December 05, 2020)

13- Zhao, Suisheng, "The Belt and Road Initiative and Xi Jinping's foreign and domestic policy agenda", The Asia Dialogue, October 2019 https://theasiadialogue.com/2019/10/29/the-belt-and-road-initiative-and-xi-jinpings-foreign-and-domestic-policy-agenda/ (accessed December 06, 2020)

14- Fabricius, Peter, "Taiwan has lost all its friends in Africa – except eSwatini", Institute for Security Studies, May 31, 2018 https://issafrica.org/iss-today/taiwan-has-lost-all-its-friends-in-africa-except-eswatini (accessed December 06, 2020)

15- Johnson, Christopher K. "President Xi Jinping's "Belt and Road" Initiative" - A Report of the CSIS Freeman Chair in China Studies, March 2016

16- Kleven, Anthony – "Belt and Road: colonialism with Chinese Characteristics" – Lowy Institute, May 6, 2019 https://www.lowyinstitute.org/the-interpreter/belt-and-road-colonialism-chinese-characteristics (accessed December 07, 2020)

17- Zhao, Suisheng – "The Belt and Road Initiative and Xi Jinping's foreign and domestic policy agenda" The Asia Dialoge, October 29, 2019 https://theasiadialogue.com/2019/10/29/the-belt-and-road-initiative-and-xi-jinpings-foreign-and-domestic-policy-agenda/ (accessed December 08, 2020)

18- Kleven, Anthony – "Belt and Road: Colonialism with Chinese Characteristics" – Lowy Institute, May 6 2019 https://www.lowyinstitute.org/the-interpreter/belt-and-road-colonialism-chinese-characteristics (accessed December 06, 2020)

19- "Six Years of Belt and Road" – Belt and Road Portal, October 11, 2019 https://eng.yidaiyilu.gov.cn/qwyw/rdxw/105854.htm

20- Kleven, Anthony – "Belt and Road: Colonialism with Chinese Characteristics" – Lowy Institute, 6 May 2019 https://www.lowyinstitute.org/the-interpreter/belt-and-road-colonialism-chinese-characteristics

21- Deborah, Brautigam, Hawng, Jyhjong, Link, and Acker, Kevin (2020), "Chinese Loans to Africa Database," Washington, DC: China Africa - Research Initiative, Johns Hopkins University School of Advance - International Studies, Database last updated: July 1, 2020.

22- Ibid.

23- Kleven, Anthony – "Belt and Road: Colonialism with Chinese Characteristics" – Lowy Institute, May 6, 2019 https://www.lowyinstitute.org/the-interpreter/belt-and-road-colonialism-chinese-characteristics (accessed December 08, 2020)

24- Guinea GDP, Trading Economics https://tradingeconomics.com/guinea/gdp

25- Kleven, Anthony – "Belt and Road: Colonialism with Chinese Characteristics" – Lowy Institute, May 6, 2019 https://www.lowyinstitute.org/the-interpreter/belt-and-road-colonialism-chinese-characteristics (accessed December 08, 2020)

26- Zambia GDP , Trading Economics - https://tradingeconomics.com/zambia/gdp (accessed December 08, 2020)

27- Deborah, Brautigam, Hawng, Jyhjong, Link, and Acker, Kevin (2020), "Chinese Loans to Africa Database," Washington, DC: China Africa - Research Initiative, Johns Hopkins University School of Advance - International Studies, Database last updated: July 1, 2020.

28- Kleven, Anthony, "Belt and Road: colonialism with Chinese characteristics", Lowy Institute, May 6, 2019 https://www.lowyinstitute.org/the-interpreter/belt-and-road-colonialism-chinese-characteristics (accessed December 10, 2020)

29-Zhao, Suisheng, "The Belt and Road Initiative and Xi Jinping's foreign and domestic policy agenda" The Asia Dialogue, October, 29 2019 https://theasiadialogue.com/2019/10/29/the-belt-and-road-initiative-and-xi-jinpings-foreign-and-domestic-policy-agenda/ (accessed December 10, 2020)

30- Ibid

31- Ibid

32- "Six Years of Belt and Road", Belt and Road Portal, October 11, 2019 https://eng.yidaiyilu.gov.cn/qwyw/rdxw/105854.htm

33- Ibid.

34 Jin, Jianmin, "The True Intent Behind China's AIIB Strategy" Fujitsu Research Institute, 25 August 2015, https://www.fujitsu.com/jp/group/fri/en/column/message/2015/2015-08-25.html

35- Ibid.

36- Keck, Zachary "China's Growing Hegemonic Bent", The Diplomat, June 26, 2014, https://thediplomat.com/2014/06/chinas-growing-hegemonic-bent/ (accessed December 10, 2020)

37- Cabestean, Jean-Pierre, "China's Djibouti naval base increasing its power", East Asia Forum, May 16, 2020. https://www.eastasiaforum.org/2020/05/16/chinas-djibouti-naval-base-increasing-its-power/ (accessed December 11, 2020)

38- U.S.-China Economic and Security Review Commission's Report, December 2020
https://www.uscc.gov/sites/default/files/2020-12/2020_Annual_Report_to_Congress.pdf (accessed December 11, 2020)

39- Meyers, Steven Lee, "Beijing takes its South China Sea Strategy to the Himalayas" The New York Times, November 27, 2020 https://www.nytimes.com/2020/11/27/world/asia/china-bhutan-india-border.html (accessed December 11, 2020)

40- Putz, Catherine, "Why did Tajikistan make an appearance in the China Military Power Report;" The Diplomat, September 3, 2020 https://thediplomat.com/2020/09/why-did-tajikis-tan-make-an-appearance-in-the-china-military-power-report/

41- Milliward, James A, "Is China a Colonial Power", The New York Times, May 4, 2018 https://www.nytimes.com/2018/05/04/opinion/sunday/china-colonial-power-jinping.html (accessed December 11, 2020)

42- Kurbandağlı, Ferhat - 'Çin'in 'Bir Kuşak Bir Yol' Gerçeği ve Türk Dünyası - Ferhat Kurban Tanrıdağlı' İstanbul 2020 P.21-22

CHAPTER 8

1- The Belt and Road Initiative Progress, Contributions and Prospects – Belt And Road Portal, April 22, 2019 https://eng.yidaiyilu.gov.cn/zchj/qwfb/86739.htm (accessed December 14, 2020)

2- Afridi Jamal – Bajoria, Jayshree – China – Pakistan Relations, Council on Foreign Relations, June 6, 2010

3-Awan, Zamir Ahmed, "China-Pakistan; A Journey of friendship – (1950-2020), Global Times, May 5, 2020, https://www.globaltimes.cn/content/1189007.shtml (accessed December 11, 2020)

4- Pakistan – China Diplomatic Relations, Ministry of Foreign Affairs, Government of Pakistan, http://mofa.gov.pk/pakistan-and-china-diplomatic-relations/ (accessed December 11, 2020)

5- Afzal, Madiha – "At All Costs": How Pakistan and China Control the Narrative on the China-Pakistan Economic Corridor, the Brookings Institute, June 2020,

6- Pakistan, https://datacommons.org/place/country/PAK (accessed December 11, 2020)

7- "General Qamar Javed Bajwa, Chief of Army Staff (COAS) called on Chinese President Xi Jinping on special invitation," Inter Services Public Relations, September 19, 2018, https://www.ispr.gov.pk/press-release-detail.php?id=4940.

8- Afzal, Madiha – "At All Costs": How Pakistan and China Control the Narrative on the China-Pakistan Economic Corridor, the Brookings Institute, June 2020,

9- Notezai, Muhammad Akbar, "CPEC 2.00: Full Speed Ahead" The Diplomat, September 10, 2020 https://thediplomat.com/2020/09/cpec-2-0-full-speed-ahead/ (accessed December 13, 2020)

10- "CPEC: Business, security headache for China, Pak", Business Standard, April 23, 2018 https://www.business-standard.com/article/news-ani/cpec-business-security-headache-for-china-pak-118042300083_1.html (accessed December 13, 2020)

11- "Pakistan says to support China on South China Sea, Taiwan, Xinjiang, and Tibet", CGTN, December 1, 2020 https://news.cgtn.com/news/2020-12-01/Pakistan-to-support-China-on-South-China-Sea-Taiwan-Xinjiang-Tibet-VS4tonaaTC/index.html (accessed December 13, 2020)

12- Notezai, Muhammad Akbar, "CPEC 2.00: Full Speed Ahead" The Diplomat, September 10, 2020 https://thediplomat.com/2020/09/cpec-2-0-full-speed-ahead/ (accessed December 13, 2020)

13- Hussain, Khurram, "Exclusive: CPEC Master Plan Revealed" Dawn, 21 Haziran 2017 https://www.dawn.com/news/1333101/exclusive-cpec-master-plan-revealed

14- Agriculture Report - http://www.finance.gov.pk/survey/chapters_18/02-Agriculture.pdf Ryan Shaffer, China-Pakistan relations: a historical analysis, International Affairs, Volume 94, Issue 4, July 2018, Pages 963–964, https://doi.org/10.1093/ia/iiy111 (accessed December 13, 2020)

15- Hussain, Khurram, "Exclusive: CPEC Master Plan Revealed" Dawn, June 21, 2017 https://www.dawn.com/news/1333101/exclusive-cpec-master-plan-revealed (accessed December 13, 2020)

16- "CPEC designed to bring profit to China, not Pakistan, say experts on Balochistan", ANI, July 20, 2017 https://www.business-standard.com/article/news-ani/cpec-designed-to-bring-profit-to-china-not-pakistan-say-experts-on-balochistan-117072000170_1.html

17- "Ne İhlali, Uyguların insan hakkı yok ki ihlal olsun" Campaign for Uyghurs, April 17, 2020 - https://campaignforuyghurs.org/tr/ne-ihlali-uygurlarin-insan-hakki-yok-ki-ihlal-olsun/ (accessed December 13, 2020)

18- Hussain, Khurram, "Exclusive: CPEC Master Plan Revealed" Dawn, June 21, 2017 https://www.dawn.com/news/1333101/exclusive-cpec-master-plan-revealed

19- Raza, Syed Irfan, 'CPEC could become another East India Company' Dawn, June 21, 2017

20- Long Term Plan for China-Pakistan Economic Corridor – www.cpek.gov.pk P. 5

21- Mahbubani, Rhea – "Pakistani leader Imran Khan admitted he refuses to criticize China's treatment of its Uighur minority because they 'helped us when we were at rock bottom", Business Insider, January 22, 2020 https://www.businessinsider.com/imran-khan-pakistan-wont-criticize-china-on-uighurs-2020-1 (accessed December 13, 2020)

22- Afzal, Madiha – "At All Costs": How Pakistan and China Control the Narrative on the China-Pakistan Economic Corridor, the Brookings Institute, June 2020,

23- Giuseppe Gabusi (2020) "China's Structural Power and the Fate of the BCIM Economic Corridor", The International Spectator, 55:3, 17-34, DOI: 10.1080/03932729.2020.1782071

24- Khan, Shadiuzzaman – "A thriving economic belt the making" The Financial Express, November 2, 2020, Published at https://www.globaltimes.cn/content/1205407.shtml (accessed December 13, 2020)

25- Brewster David, "Bangladesh's road to the BRI", The Interpreter, May 30, 2019 https://www.lowyinstitute.org/the-interpreter/bangladesh-road-bri (accessed December 14, 2020)

26- Chaudhury, Dipanjan R. "Analysis: China's trade concessions to Bangladesh a 'dual-deficit and debt trap" The Economic Times,

https://economictimes.indiatimes.com/news/international/world-news/et-analysis-chinas-trade-concessions-to-bangladesh-a-dual-deficit-and-debt-trap/articleshow/76907291.cms?utm_source=contentofinterest&utm_medium=text&utm_campaign=cppst (accessed December 15, 2020)

27- Meyers, Steven Lee, "Beijing takes its South China Sea Strategy to the Himalayas" The New York Times, November 27, 2020 https://www.nytimes.com/2020/11/27/world/asia/china-bhutan-india-border.html (accessed December 15, 2020)

28- Report to Congress 2020, "US-China Economic and Security Review Commission", (accessed December 15, 2020)

29- Myanmar Policy Briefing, "Selling the Silk Road Spirit", Transitional Institute, November 2019 https://www.tni.org/en/selling-the-silk-road-spirit (accessed December 15, 2020)

30- Myers, Lucas – "The China-Myanmar Economic Corridor and China's Determination to see it Through", Wilson Center, May 26, 2020 https://www.wilsoncenter.org/blog-post/china-myanmar-economic-corridor-and-chinas-determination-see-it-through (accessed December 15, 2020)

31- Jenn-Jaw Soong & Kyaw Htet Aung (2020) "Myanmar's Perception and Strategy toward China's BRI Expansion on Three Major Projects Development: Hedging Strategic Framework with State-Market-Society Analysis", The Chinese Economy, DOI: 10.1080/10971475.2020.1809815

32- Ibid.

33- Luce, Dan de and Romo, Christine, "Myanmar soldiers confess to Rohingya massacre: 'Shoot all that you see'", NBC News, September 8, 2020 https://www.nbcnews.com/news/world/myanmar-soldiers-confess-rohingya-massacre-shoot-all-you-see-n1239563 (accessed December 17, 2020)

34- Myanmar Policy Briefing, "Selling the Silk Road Spirit", Transitional Institute, November 2019 https://www.tni.org/en/selling-the-silk-road-spirit (accessed December 17, 2020)

35- Rajah, Ronald – Dayant, Alexandra – Pnyke Jonathan, "Ocean of Debt? Belt and Road and Dept Diplomacy in the Pasific" Lowy Institute, October 21, 2019 https://www.lowyinstitute.org/publications/ocean-debt-belt-and-road-and-debt-diplomacy-pacific (accessed December 17, 2020)

36- "Thailand will pay heavy price for over-reliance on China" November 6, 2018 https://www.nationthailand.com/opinion/30358048 (accessed December 17, 2020)

37- Kha, Sok, "The Belt and Road in Cambodia: Successes and Challenges" The Diplomat August 30, 2019 https://thediplomat.com/2019/04/the-belt-and-road-in-cambodia-successes-and-challenges/ (accessed December 17, 2020)

38- Chheang Vannarith – Pkeakdey Heng, "Cambodian Perspective on the Belt and Road Initiative" National Institute for Defense Studies, http://www.nids.mod.go.jp/english/publication/joint_research/series17/pdf/chapter01.pdf

39- Mingjiang Li, "The Belt and Road Initiative: geo-economics and Indo-Pacific security competition", International Affairs, Volume 96, Issue 1, January 2020, Pages 169–187,

40- Global Conflict Tracker, "Territorial Disputes in the South China Sea" Council on Foreign Relations. https://www.cfr.org/global-conflict-tracker/conflict/territorial-disputes-south-china-sea

41- Hiep, Hong Le, "The Belt and Road Initiative in Vietnam: challenges and prospects" International Institute for Asian Studies, Fall 2018 https://www.iseas.edu.sg/articles-commentaries/iseas-perspective (accessed December 17, 2020)

42- Rowedder, Dr. Simon "Understanding China's BRI in Laos" Business Times, January 13, 2020 https://www.businesstimes.com.sg/asean-business/understanding-chinas-bri-in-laos (accessed December 17, 2020)

43- "Speech by Chinese President Xi Jinping to Indonesian Parliament", Asian-China Centre, October 2, 2013, http://www.asean-china-center.org/english/2013-10/03/c_133062675.htm (accessed December 17, 2020)

44- Mulyonto, Randy, "After 70 years of ties, China and Indonesia have a fruitful, complicated relationship", This Week in Asia, https://www.scmp.com/week-asia/politics/article/3079446/after-70-years-ties-china-and-indonesia-have-fruitful (accessed December 17, 2020)

45- Qian, Xiao, "Insight: Work hand-in-hand for a new era of China-Indonesia friendship", The Jakarta Post, April 14, 2020 https://www.thejakartapost.com/academia/2020/04/14/insight-work-hand-in-hand-for-a-new-era-of-china-indonesia-friendship.html. (accessed December 20, 2020)

46- "Colonial Period of Indonesia" Indonesia – Investmenst https://www.indonesia-investments.com/culture/politics/colonial-history/item178#:~:text=The%20colonial%20period%20of%20Indonesia,end%20of%20the%2016th%20century.&text=In%201796%20the%20VOC%20went,the%20Dutch%20crown%20in%201800. (accessed December 20, 2020)

47- Asmarini, Wilda – Jefriando Maikel – "Indonesia asks China for special fund under Belt and Road: ministers", Reuters July 3, 2019 https://www.reuters.com/article/us-indonesia-china-beltandroad/indonesia-asks-china-for-special-fund-under-belt-and-road-ministers-idUSKCN1TY-1DU (accessed December 20, 2020)

48- Wang, Maya – Harsano, Andreas , "Indonesia's Silence over Xinjiang" Human Rights Watch, October 31, 2020 https://www.hrw.org/news/2020/01/31/indonesias-silence-over-xinjiang (accessed December 20, 2020)

49- Chang, Felix K, "The Next Front: China and Indonesia in the South China" Foreign Policy Research Institute, January 27, 2020, https://www.fpri.org/article/2020/01/the-next-front-china-and-indonesia-in-the-south-china-sea/ (accessed December 20, 2020)

50- CIMB ASEAN Research Institute - China's Belt and Road Initiative (BRI) and Southeast Asia https://www.lse.ac.uk/ideas/Assets/Documents/reports/LSE-IDEAS-China-SEA-BRI.pdf (accessed December 20, 2020)

51- Foon, Ho Wah – "China factor looms ahead of election" The Star, May 25, 2018 https://www.thestar.com.my/news/nation/2018/03/25/china-factor-looms-ahead-of-election-the-china-card-was-flashed-in-almost-every-general-election-in (accessed December 20, 2020)

52- Kuo, Mercy A "Malaysia in China's Belt and Road" The Diplomat, November 23, 2020 https://thediplomat.com/2020/11/malaysia-in-chinas-belt-and-road/ (accessed December 20, 2020)

53- Sipalan, Joseph "China, Malaysia restart massive 'Belt and Road' Project after hiccups" Reuters, July 25, 2019 https://www.reuters.com/article/us-china-silkroad-malaysia/china-malaysia-restart-massive-belt-and-road-project-after-hiccups-idUSKCN1UK0DG

54- Casarini, Nicola "Southeast Asia's security dilemma – How West is responding" - CIMB ASEAN Research Institute - China's Belt and Road Initiative (BRI) and Southeast Asia https://www.lse.ac.uk/ideas/Assets/Documents/reports/LSE-IDEAS-China-SEA-BRI.pdf (accessed December 20, 2020)

55- Chang, Felix K – "A Faint Breeze of Change: Malaysia's Relations with China" Foreign Policy Research Institute, January 8, 2020 - https://www.fpri.org/article/2020/01/a-faint-breeze-of-change-malaysias-relations-with-china/ (accessed December 20, 2020)

56- Frayer, Lauren – "In Sri Lanka, China's Building Spree Is Raising Questions About Sovereignty" NPR, December 13, 2019 https://www.npr.org/2019/12/13/784084567/in-sri-lanka-chinas-building-spree-is-raising-questions-about-sovereignty (accessed December 20, 2020)

57- Ibid.

58- Ethirajan, Anbarasan – "China debt dogs Maldives 'bride to prosperity'" BBC News, September 17, 2020 https://www.bbc.com/news/world-asia-52743072 (accessed December 20, 2020)

CHAPTER 9

2- "Concept of Neither nor West" – Government and Politics of Iran, US Library of Congress http://countrystudies.us/iran/101.htm

3- Geranmayeh, Ellie – "A Pragmatic partnership: Why China and Iran try to collaborate", European Council on Foreign Relations, July 17, 2020 https://ecfr.eu/article/commentary_a_pragmatic_partnership_why_china_and_iran_try_to_collaborate/ (accessed December 17, 2020)

4- Ibid.

5- Ibid.

6- Wintour, Patrick, "Iranian official backtracks after calling Chinese Covid-19 figures a 'joke'" The Guardian, April 6, 2020, https://www.theguardian.com/world/2020/apr/06/iranian-official-backtracks-after-calling-chinese-covid-19-figures-a-joke (accessed December 17, 2020)

7- Fassihi, Farnaz – Myers, Steven Lee – "Defying U.S China and Iran Near Trade and Military Partnership" The New York Times, July 11, 2020 https://www.nytimes.com/2020/07/11/world/asia/china-iran-trade-military-deal.html (accessed December 17, 2020)

8- Cohen, Ariel – "China and Iran Approach Massive $400 Billion Deal" Forbes, July 17, 2020 https://www.forbes.com/sites/arielcohen/2020/07/17/china-and-iran-approach-massive-400-billion-deal/?sh=75d61b132a16 (accessed December 17, 2020)

9- Fassihi, Farnaz – Myers, Steven Lee – "Defying U.S China and Iran Near Trade and Military Partnership" The New York Times, July 11, 2020 https://www.nytimes.com/2020/07/11/world/asia/china-iran-trade-military-deal.html (accessed December 17, 2020)

10- Cohen, Ariel – "China and Iran Approach Massive $400 Billion Deal" Forbes, 17 Temmuz 2020 https://www.forbes.com/sites/arielcohen/2020/07/17/china-and-iran-approach-massive-400-billion-deal/?sh=75d61b132a16 (accessed December 17, 2020)

11- Ibid.

12- Khorrami, Nima – "The Pitfalls of the China-Iran Agreement" The Diplomat, July 15, 2020, https://thediplomat.com/2020/07/the-pitfalls-of-the-china-iran-agreement/ (accessed December 17, 2020)

13-Ruser Nathan – Leibold, Dr. James – Munro, Kelsey – Hoja Tilla – "Cultural erasure: Tracing the destruction of Uyghur and Islamic Spaces in Xinjiang, September 24, 2020 https://xjdp.aspi.org.au/explainers/cultural-erasure/ (accessed December 17, 2020)

14- Gallagher, Delia – Jiang, Steven, "Pope Francis refers to China's Uyghurs as 'persecuted' for the first time" CNN.com, November 24, 2020 https://www.cnn.com/2020/11/24/europe/pope-francis-china-uyghur-intl-hnk/index.html (accessed December 17, 2020)

15- "Salman Ruşdi için fetva çıkaran İran, şeytana şapka çıkartan Çin'e ses çıkarmıyor!" – Campaign For Uyghurs, August 18, 2020 https://campaignforuyghurs.org/tr/salman-rusdi-icin-fetva-cikaran-iran-seytana-sapka-cikartan-cine-ses-cikarmiyor/ (accessed December 17, 2020)

16- Fulton, Jonathan, "The Gulf Cooperation Council's "Visions" of Maritime Silk Road Initiative Cooperation. China's Maritime Silk Road Initiative, Africa, and the Middle East, pages 227-254.

17- Bridge Sam, "UAE-China trade rises 6% to $34.7bn, says, top diplomat" Arabian Business. 20 February 2020 - https://www.arabianbusiness.com/politics-economics/440772-uae-china-trade-rises-6-to-347bn-says-top-diplomat#:~:text=Of%20the%20total%20bilateral%20trade,-lower%20oil%20prices%20in%202019 (accessed December 13, 2020)

18- Fulton, Jonathan, "The Gulf Cooperation Council's "Visions" of Maritime Silk Road Initiative Cooperation." China's Maritime Silk Road Initiative, Africa, and the Middle East, pages 227-254.

19- Bridge Sam, "UAE-China trade rises 6% to $34.7bn, says, top diplomat" Arabian Business. February 20, 2020 - https://www.arabianbusiness.com/politics-economics/440772-uae-china-trade-rises-6-to-347bn-says-top-diplomat#:~:text=Of%20the%20total%20bilateral%20trade,lower%20oil%20prices%20in%202019 (accessed December 13, 2020)

20-Girard, Bonnie "China and the UAE: Birds of a Father?" The Diplomat, November 23, 2019 https://

thediplomat.com/2019/11/china-and-the-uae-birds-of-a-feather/ (accessed December 13, 2020)

21- Mohamed, Sidi – "Qatar and China are strategic partners: Ambassadors" The Peninsula, September 23, 2020 https://thepeninsulaqatar.com/article/23/09/2020/Qatar-and-China-are-strategic-partners-Ambassador (accessed December 13, 2020)

22- Chaziza M. China–Qatar Strategic Partnership and the Realization of One Belt, One Road Initiative. China Report. 2020;56(1):78-102. doi:10.1177/0009445519895612

23- Fulton, Jonathan – "China's Changing Role in the Middle East" Atlantic Council, June 2019 https://www.atlanticcouncil.org/wp-content/uploads/2019/06/Chinas_Changing_Role_in_the_Middle_East.pdf (accessed December 13, 2020)

24- Chaziza M. China–Qatar Strategic Partnership and the Realization of One Belt, One Road Initiative. China Report. 2020;56(1):78-102. doi:10.1177/0009445519895612

25- Chaziza, Mordechai "China-Bahrain Relations in the Age of the Belt and Road Initiative" The Institute for National Security Studies, October 4, 2020 https://www.inss.org.il/publication/china-bahrain-relations-in-the-age-of-the-belt-and-road-initiative/ (accessed December 15, 2020)

26- Workman, Daniel – "Top 15 Crude Oil Suppliers to China." World Exports, March 18, 2020 http://www.worldstopexports.com/top-15-crude-oil-suppliers-to-china/ (accessed December 15, 2020)

27- Chaziza, Mordechai "The Significant Role of Oman in China's Maritime Silk Road Initiative" the Arab Gulf States Institute in Washington July 21, 2020 https://agsiw.org/omans-bittersweet-economic-relations-with-china/ (accessed December 15, 2020)

28- Mogielnicki, Robert – "Oman's Bittersweet Economic Relations With China" 2019 https://journals.sagepub.com/doi/pdf/10.1177/2347798918812285

29- Tekgündüz, Alican, "What is China doing in Yemen" TRT World, December 12, 2019 https://www.trtworld.com/middle-east/what-is-china-doing-in-yemen-32183 (accessed December 15, 2020)

30- Chang, Jennifer I-Wei, "China and Yemen's Forgotten War" United States Institute of Peace, June 16, 2018, https://www.usip.org/publications/2018/01/china-and-yemens-forgotten-war# (accessed December 15, 2020)

31- Workman, Daniel, "Top 15 Crude Oil Suppliers to China." Worldexport.com March 2020, http://www.worldstopexports.com/top-15-crude-oil-suppliers-to-china/ (accessed December 15, 2020)

32- Zambelis, Chris, "China and Saudi Arabia Solidify Strategic Partnership Amid Looming Risks" The Jamestown Foundation, March 2, 2017 https://jamestown.org/program/china-saudi-arabia-solidify-strategic-partnership-amid-looming-risks/ (accessed December 15, 2020)

33- Juan, Chen and Meng, Shu and Shaobiao, Wen – "Aligning China's Belt and Road Initiative with Saudi Arabia's 2030 Vision" 2018 World Century Publishing Corporation and Shanghai Institutes for International Studies China Quarterly of International Strategic Studies, Vol. 4, No. 3, 363–379 DOI: 10.1142/S2377740018500203

34- Fulton Jonathan, "Thirty Years of Sino-Saudi Relations" Atlantic Council, Ağustos 2020 https://www.atlanticcouncil.org/wp-content/uploads/2020/08/Sino-Saudi-Relations_WEB.pdf (accessed December 20, 2020)

35- Ibid

36- Juan, Chen and Meng, Shu and Shaobiao, Wen, "Aligning China's Belt and Road Initiative with Saudi Arabia's 2030 Vision" 2018 World Century Publishing Corporation and Shanghai Institutes for International Studies China Quarterly of International Strategic Studies, Vol. 4, No. 3, 363–379 DOI: 10.1142/S2377740018500203

37- Fulton Jonathan, "Thirty Years of Sino-Saudi Relations" Atlantic Council, August 2020 https://www.atlanticcouncil.org/wp-content/uploads/2020/08/Sino-Saudi-Relations_WEB.pdf (accessed December 20, 2020)

38- Haber Ajansları, "Saudi crown prince defends China's right to fight 'terrorism' Al Jazeera, February 23, 2019 https://www.aljazeera.com/news/2019/2/23/saudi-crown-prince-defends-chinas-right-to-fight-terrorism (accessed December 20, 2020)

39- "China-Israel relations enjoy sound momentum of growth: Chinese ambassador" Xinhua, September 26, 2019 http://www.xinhuanet.com/english/2019-09/26/c_138425793.htm (accessed December 20, 2020)

40- Abrams, Elliot, "What's Behind Israel's Growing Ties With China" Council on Foreign Relations, June 21, 2018 https://www.cfr.org/expert-brief/whats-behind-israels-growing-ties-china (accessed December 20, 2020)

41- Ibid.

42- "Chinese Investment in Israeli Technology and Infrastructure: Security Implications for Israel and the United States". Santa Monica, CA: RAND Corporation, 2020. https://www.rand.org/pubs/research_reports/RR3176.html

43- Chaziza M. "Israel–China Relations Enter a New Stage: Limited Strategic Hedging." Contemporary Review of the Middle East. 2018;5(1):30-45. doi:10.1177/2347798917744293

44- Su, Alice, "Jordan: China's Gateway to the Middle East." The Atlantic, September 25, 2013 https://www.theatlantic.com/china/archive/2013/09/jordan-chinas-gateway-to-the-middle-east/279988/ (accessed December 20, 2020)

45- Tran, Edwin – "China's Ambitions in The Kingdom of Jordan" Encyplopediageopolitica.com September 23, 2020 https://encyclopediageopolitica.com/2020/09/23/chinas-ambitions-in-the-kingdom-of-jordan/ (accessed December 18, 2020)

46- Mroue, Bassem, "Lebanon Looks to China as US, Arabs Refuse to Help in Crisis" The Diplomat, July 16, 2020 https://thediplomat.com/2020/07/lebanon-looks-to-china-as-us-arabs-refuse-to-help-in-crisis/ (accessed December 16, 2020)

47- "Lebanon's Hezbollah chief calls French cartoons "an aggression," Middle East Monitor, October 20, 2020, https://www.middleeastmonitor.com/20201030-lebanons-hezbollah-chief-calls-french-cartoons-an-aggression/ (accessed December 18, 2020)

48- Global Conflict Tracker, "Civil War in Syria" Council on Foreign Relations" December 4, (accessed December 16, 2020)

49- Caferio, Giorgio, "China plays the long game on Syria" Middle East Institute, February 10, 2020 https://www.mei.edu/publications/china-plays-long-game-syria (accessed December 17, 2020)

50- Ibid.

51- Ibid.

52- Ibid.

53- Hafizullah Emadi. "China and Iraq: Patterns of Interaction, 1960-1992." Economic and Political Weekly, vol. 29, no. 53, 1994, pp. 3315–3318. JSTOR, www.jstor.org/stable/4402191. Accessed 7 Dec. 2020.

54- Calabrese, John, "China-Iraq Relations: Poised for a "Quantum Leap"? "Middle East Institute" October 8, 2019, https://www.mei.edu/publications/china-iraq-relations-poised-quantum-leap (accessed December 14, 2020)

55- Workman, Daniel – "Top 15 Crude Oil Suppliers to China" World Exports, March 18, 2020 http://www.worldstopexports.com/top-15-crude-oil-suppliers-to-china/ (accessed December 18, 2020)

56- Xinhua, "China-Iraq trade exceeds 30 bln USD in 2018 amid increasing cooperation: Chinese ambassador." Xinhuanet.com May 5, 2019 http://www.xinhuanet.com/english/2019-05/06/c_138036250.htm (accessed December 13, 2020)

57- Samet, Daniel J. "China, Not Iran, Is the Power to Watch in Iraq" The Diplomat, October 30, 2019, https://thediplomat.com/2019/10/china-not-iran-is-the-power-to-watch-in-iraq/ (accessed December 18, 2020)

58- Dana, Joseph, "China, Russia exploit 'Covid diplomacy' in Iraq" Asia Times, September 21, 2020 https://asiatimes.com/2020/09/china-russia-exploit-covid-diplomacy-in-iraq/ (accessed December 15, 2020)

59- Calabrese, John, "China-Iraq Relations: Poised for a "Quantum Leap"? "Middle East Institute" October 8, 2019, https://www.mei.edu/publications/china-iraq-relations-poised-quantum-leap (accessed December 13, 2020)

60- Watkins, Simon, "Iraq Considers a String of Massive Oil Deals with China" Oilprice.com, June 24, 2020, https://oilprice.com/Energy/Energy-General/Iraq-Considers-A-String-Of-Massive-Oil-Deals-With-China.html (accessed November 18, 2020

CHAPTER 10

1-Bocharo, Ivan "Egypt-China Relations at the Present Stage" Russian Council. March 3, 2020 https://russiancouncil.ru/en/analytics-and-comments/columns/middle-east-policy/egypt-china-relations-at-the-present-stage/

2- Ibid.

3- Hassanein, Haisam, "Egypt Takes Another Step Toward China" Washington Institute, August 19, 2019 https://www.washingtoninstitute.org/policy-analysis/view/egypt-takes-another-step-toward-china (accessed November 18, 2020)

4- Bocharo, Ivan "Egypt-China Relations at the Present Stage" Russian Council. March 3, 2020 https://russiancouncil.ru/en/analytics-and-comments/columns/middle-east-policy/egypt-china-relations-at-the-present-stage/ (accessed October 18, 2020)

5- Calabrese, John, "Towering Ambitions: Egypt and China Building for the Future" Middle East Institute, October 6, 2020 https://www.mei.edu/publications/towering-ambitions-egypt-and-china-building-future#_ftn10 (accessed December 18, 2020)

6- Fouly, Mahmoud, "China largest investor in Egypt's Suez Canal region with earnest, win-win partnership: official" Xinhuanet.com March 16, 2017 http://www.xinhuanet.com//english/2017-03/16/c_136134254.htm (accessed November 18, 2020)

7- Al Youm, Al Masry, "Head of Suez Canal Economic Zone, Chinese officials discuss TEDA projects" Egyptian Independent, December 9, 2019 https://egyptindependent.com/head-of-suez-canal-economic-zone-chinese-official-discuss-teda-projects/ (accessed December 18, 2020)

8- Hassanein, Haisam – "Egypt Takes Another Step Toward China" Washington Institute, August 19, 2019 https://www.washingtoninstitute.org/policy-analysis/view/egypt-takes-another-step-toward-china (accessed December 18, 2020)

9- Fouly, Mahoud, "Feature: Chinese construction projects in Egypt's new capital city model for BRI-based cooperation" Xinhuanet.com March 18, 2019 http://www.xinhuanet.com/english/2019-03/18/c_137902708.htm (accessed November 13, 2020)

10-Radcliffe, Damian "Egypt's building a new capital: Inside the smart city in the desert" ZDnet.com January 28, 2020, https://www.zdnet.com/article/egypts-building-a-new-capital-inside-the-smart-city-in-the-desert/ (accessed December 18, 2020)

11- Ibid.

12- Ibid.

13- TIMEP Brief: "China's Role in Egypt's Economy" The Tahrir Institute for Middle East Policy, November 21, 2019 https://timep.org/reports-briefings/timep-brief-chinas-role-in-egypts-economy/ (accessed December 18, 2020)

14- Brautigam, Deborah, Jyhjong Hwang, Jordan Link, and Kevin Acker (2020) "Chinese Loans to Africa Database," Washington, DC: China Africa Research Initiative, Johns Hopkins University School of Advanced International Studies.

15- Calabrese, John – "Towering Ambitions: Egypt and China Building for the Future" Middle East Institute, Octeber 6, 2020 https://www.mei.edu/publications/towering-ambitions-egypt-and-china-building-future#_ftn10 (accessed December 18, 2020)

16- Bocharo, Ivan "Egypt-China Relations at the Present Stage" Russian Council. March 3, 2020 https://russiancouncil.ru/en/analytics-and-comments/columns/middle-east-policy/egypt-china-relations-at-the-present-stage/ (accessed December 16, 2020)

17- Cairo AFP, "'Nightmare' as Egypt aided China to detain Uighurs" France24, August 18, 2019 https://www.france24.com/en/20190818-nightmare-as-egypt-aided-china-to-detain-uighurs (accessed December 16, 2020)

18- Napolean, François "A Stark Choice for Cairo's Chinese Muslims" The Diplomat, August 2, 2017, https://thediplomat.com/2017/08/a-stark-choice-for-cairos-chinese-muslims/ (accessed December 16, 2020)

19-Large, Daniel. "China's Sudan Engagement: Changing Northern and Southern Political Trajectories in Peace and War." The China Quarterly, no. 199, 2009, pp. 610–626. JSTOR, www.jstor.org/stable/27756493. Accessed 8 Dec. 2020.

20- Hammond, Joseph, "Sudan: China's Original Foothold in Africa" The Diplomat, June 14, 2017 https://thediplomat.com/2017/06/sudan-chinas-original-foothold-in-africa/

21- Barber, Laura "China's Response to Sudan's Political Transition" United States Institute of

Peace, May 2020 https://www.usip.org/publications/2020/05/chinas-response-sudans-political-transition#

22- Projects, "Belt and Road Initiative" https://www.beltroad-initiative.com/projects/ (accessed December 15, 2020)

23- Barber, Laura "China's Response to Sudan's Political Transition" United States Institute of Peace, May 2020 https://www.usip.org/publications/2020/05/chinas-response-sudans-political-transition# (accessed December 15, 2020)

24- Brautigam, Deborah, Jyhjong Hwang, Jordan Link, and Kevin Acker (2020) "Chinese Loans to Africa Database," Washington, DC: China Africa Research Initiative, Johns Hopkins University School of Advanced International Studies.

25- Tesfaye, Aaron, "China-Ethiopia Relations and Horn of Africa" Italian Institute for International Political Studies, September 20, 2019 https://www.ispionline.it/en/publication/china-ethiopia-relations-and-horn-africa-23968 (accessed December 15, 2020)

26- Marks, Simon, "How an African state learned to play the West off China for billions" Politico, February 2, 2020 https://www.politico.com/news/2020/02/07/ethiopia-china-west-power-competition-110766 (accessed December 15, 2020)

27- Maini, Tridivesh Singh – Lingala, Mahitha "BRI and China-Ethiopia Relationship" The Geopolitics, December 10, 2019 https://thegeopolitics.com/bri-and-the-deepening-china-ethiopia-ties/ (accessed December 16, 2020)

28- Yalew MT, Changgang G. China's 'Belt and Road Initiative': Implication for Land Locked Ethiopia. Insight on Africa. 2020;12(2):175-193. doi:10.1177/0975087819891538

29- Blanchard, Lauren P – Collins, Sarah R. – "China's Engagement in Djibouti" Congressional Research Service" September 4, 2019 https://fas.org/sgp/crs/row/IF11304.pdf (accessed December 16, 2020)

30- Ibid.

31- Hill, Sam, "Black China: Africa's First Superpower is Coming Sooner Than You Think" Newsweek Magazine, January 15, 2020 https://www.newsweek.com/2020/01/31/nigeria-next-superpower-1481949.html (accessed December 16, 2020)

32 Akeredolu, Fikayo – "Why is China interested in Nigeria?" Stear Business, October 11, 2019 https://www.stearsng.com/article/why-is-china-interested-in-nigeria (accessed December 18, 2020)

33- Ibid.

34- Brautigam, Deborah, Jyhjong Hwang, Jordan Link, and Kevin Acker (2020) "Chinese Loans to Africa Database," Washington, DC: China Africa Research Initiative, Johns Hopkins University School of Advanced International Studies.

35- "Eradicating Ideological Viruses", Human Rights Watch, September 9, 2018 https://www.hrw.org/report/2018/09/09/eradicating-ideological-viruses/chinas-campaign-repression-against-xinjiangs# (accessed December 14, 2020)

36- Fulton Jonathan, "China's Changing Role in the Middle East" Atlantic Council, June 2019

37- Hodman, Samuel, "China vs. the West: A New Cold War on Morocco's Doorstep" Morocco World News, June 5, 2020, https://www.moroccoworldnews.com/2020/07/307627/china-vs-the-west-a-new-cold-war-on-moroccos-doorstep/ (accessed December 18, 2020)

38- Ghafar, Adel Abdel – Jacobs, Anna "Beijing Calling: Assessing China's Growing Footprint in North Africa" Brookings Doha Center, September 2019 https://www.brookings.edu/wp-content/uploads/2019/09/Beijing-Calling-Assessing-China%E2%80%99s-Growing-Footprint-in-North-Africa_English-1.pdf

39- Brautigam, Deborah, Jyhjong Hwang, Jordan Link, and Kevin Acker (2020) "Chinese Loans to Africa Database," Washington, DC: China Africa Research Initiative, Johns Hopkins University School of Advanced International Studies.

40- Hodman, Samuel, "China vs. the West: A New Cold War on Morocco's Doorstep" Morocco World News, June 5, 2020, https://www.moroccoworldnews.com/2020/07/307627/china-vs-the-west-a-new-cold-war-on-moroccos-doorstep/ (accessed December 18, 2020)

41-"Partnership between Algeria and China accelerates economic growth and infrastructure expansion" Oxford Business Group, https://oxfordbusinessgroup.com/analysis/historic-ties-algeria-and-china%E2%80%99s-mutually-beneficial-partnership-accelerates-economic-growth-an-

d#:~:text=Chinese%20foreign%20direct%20investment%20(FDI,of%20Nigeria%2C%20Zam-
bia%20and%20Zimbabwe.

42- Ghafar, Adel Abdel – Jacobs, Anna "Beijing Calling: Assessing China's Growing Footprint in North Africa" Brookings Doha Center, September 2019 https://www.brookings.edu/
wp-content/uploads/2019/09/Beijing-Calling-Assessing-China%E2%80%99s-Growing-Footp-
rint-in-North-Africa_English-1.pdf (accessed December 20, 2020)

43- "Partnership between Algeria and China accelerates economic growth and infrastructure
expansion" Oxford Business Group, https://oxfordbusinessgroup.com/analysis/historic-ties-alge-
ria-and-china%E2%80%99s-mutually-beneficial-partnership-accelerates-economic-growth-an-
d#:~:text=Chinese%20foreign%20direct%20investment%20(FDI,of%20Nigeria%2C%20Zam-
bia%20and%20Zimbabwe. (accessed December 20, 2020)

44- Zhang, Chuchu, "Potential to Leap Forward? Interrogating the Relations betwe-
en China and Tunisia, Asian Journal of Middle Eastern and Islamic" Studies, DOI:
10.1080/25765949.2020.1847853

45- Ibid

46- Ibid.

47- Ghafar, Adel Abdel – Jacobs, Anna "Beijing Calling: Assessing China's Growing Footprint in North Africa" Brookings Doha Center, September 2019 https://www.brookings.edu/
wp-content/uploads/2019/09/Beijing-Calling-Assessing-China%E2%80%99s-Growing-Footp-
rint-in-North-Africa_English-1.pdf (accessed December 20, 2020)

48- Zoubir, Yahia H "Expanding Sino–Maghreb Relations." Chatham House, February 26, 2020,
https://www.chathamhouse.org/2020/02/expanding-sino-maghreb-relations/4-tunisia-and-chi-
na-evolution-relations#block-mainnavigation (accessed December 20, 2020)

49- Ghafar, Adel Abdel – Jacobs, Anna "Beijing Calling: Assessing China's Growing Footprint in North Africa" Brookings Doha Center, September 2019 https://www.brookings.edu/
wp-content/uploads/2019/09/Beijing-Calling-Assessing-China%E2%80%99s-Growing-Footp-
rint-in-North-Africa_English-1.pdf

50- Brautigam, Deborah, Jyhjong Hwang, Jordan Link, and Kevin Acker (2020) "Chinese Loans
to Africa Database," Washington, DC: China Africa Research Initiative, Johns Hopkins University
School of Advanced International Studies.

51- Ibid.

52- Pandley, Erica "Angola's Chinese oil debt-trap" Axios, May 13, 2018

53- Brautigam, Deborah, Jyhjong Hwang, Jordan Link, and Kevin Acker (2020) "Chinese Loans
to Africa Database," Washington, DC: China Africa Research Initiative, Johns Hopkins University
School of Advanced International Studies.

54- Olender, Eric, "Kenya: China faces a critical test in train debt" The Africa Report, September
30, 2020 https://www.theafricareport.com/43367/kenya-china-faces-a-critical-test-in-train-de-
bt/ (accessed December 20, 2020)

55- Hairsine, Kate "Kenya struggles to manage debt for railway" DW, October 18, 2019 https://
www.dw.com/en/kenya-struggles-to-manage-debt-for-railway-to-nowhere/a-50887431 (accessed December 20, 2020)

56-Brautigam, Deborah, Jyhjong Hwang, Jordan Link, and Kevin Acker (2020) "Chinese Loans
to Africa Database," Washington, DC: China Africa Research Initiative, Johns Hopkins University
School of Advanced International Studies.

57- "Zambia on the brink of defaulting on foreign debt" BBC News November 13, 2020 https://
www.bbc.com/news/world-africa-54928836?xtor=AL-72-%5Bpartner%5D-%5Binforadi-
o%5D-%5Bheadline%5D-%5Bnews%5D-%5Bbizdev%5D-%5Bisapi%5D (accessed December 20,
2020)

58- Brautigam, Deborah, Jyhjong Hwang, Jordan Link, and Kevin Acker (2020) "Chinese Loans
to Africa Database," Washington, DC: China Africa Research Initiative, Johns Hopkins University
School of Advanced International Studies.

59- "Reality Check: Is China burdening Africa with debt," BBC News November 5, 2018 https://
www.bbc.com/news/world-africa-45916060 (accessed December 20, 2020)

60- Dok Akol, A.N and Thayer, Bradley A "Takeover Trap: Why Imperialist China Is Invading Africa" The National Interest, June 10, 2019 https://nationalinterest.org/feature/takeo-ver-trap-why-imperialist-china-invading-africa-66421 (accessed December 20, 2020)

CHAPTER 11
1- "Türkiye – Çin Halk Cumhuriyeti Siyasi İlişkileri" – Türkiye Dışişleri Bakanlığı http://www.mfa.gov.tr/turkiye-cin-halk-cumhuriyeti-siyasi-iliskileri.tr.mfa (accessed December 23, 2020)
2- Ibid.
3-"Türkiye – Çin Halk Cumhuriyeti Ekonomik İlişkileri" – Türkiye Dışişleri Bakanlığı http://www.mfa.gov.tr/turkiye-cin-halk-cumhuriyeti-ekonomik-iliskileri.tr.mfa (accessed December 23, 2020)
4- Tanrıdağlı, Ferhat K. "Çin'in Bir Kuşak Bir Yol Gerçeği ve Türk Dünyası." İstanbul 2020
5-Çolakoğlu, Selçuk – "China's Belt and Road Initiative and Turkey's Middle Corridor: A Question of Compatibility" Middle East Institute, January 29, 2019 https://www.mei.edu/publications/chinas-belt-and-road-initiative-and-turkeys-middle-corridor-question-compatibility-
6- Ibid.
7- Ibid.
8- White, Maddy, "Turkey inks US$5bn BRI agreement with Sinosure", Global Trade Review, March 31, 2020. https://www.gtreview.com/news/asia/turkey-inks-us5bn-bri-agreement-with-si-nosure/ (accessed December 23, 2020)
9- Kulaksız, Sıla "Financial Integration via Belt and Road Initiative: China – Turkey Cooperation" 2019 Emerging Markets Institute, Beijing Normal University - in.sagepub.com/journals-permis-sions-india DOI: 10.1177/0974910119874632 journals.sagepub.com/home/eme
10- "Üçüncü köprü Çinlilere satılıyor" – Sözcü Gazetesi, December 23, 2019 https://www.sozcu.com.tr/2019/ekonomi/cinli-devler-turkiyede-insaat-sirketi-alacak- (accessed December 20, 2020)
11- Kulaksız, Sıla "Financial Integration via Belt and Road Initiative: China – Turkey Cooperati-on" 2019 Emerging Markets Institute, Beijing Normal University - in.sagepub.com/journals-per-missions-india DOI: 10.1177/0974910119874632 journals.sagepub.com/home/eme
12- Tanrıdağlı, Ferhat K. "Çin'in Bir Kuşak Bir Yol Gerçeği ve Türk Dünyası" İstanbul 2020 P.119
12- Ibid, P.131-132
13- Ibid, P.131-132
14-Kavalski, Emilian "China's "16+1" Is Dead? Long Live the "17+1." The Diplomat, March 29, 2019 (accessed December 23, 2020)
15- Brinza, Andreea "How a Greek Port Became a Chinese 'Dragon Head'", The Diplomat, April 25, 2016 (accessed December 23, 2020)
16- Zeneli, Valbona "The Western Balkans: Low Hanging Fruit for China?" Belt And Road News, February 20, 2020 https://www.beltandroad.news/2020/02/25/the-western-balkans-low-lang-ging-fruit-for-china/ (accessed December 23, 2020)
17- Ibid
18- Ibid.
19- Crawford, Nicholas "Growing public debt isn't the only problem with Chinese lending to the Balkans" International Institute for Strategic Studies, March 18, 2020 https://www.iiss.org/blogs/analysis/2020/03/gstrat-bri-in-the-balkans (accessed December 25, 2020)
20- Jafarli, Shahin "Azerbaijan – China relations" Baku Research Institute, September 22, 2020 https://bakuresearchinstitute.org/azerbaijan-china-relations/ (accessed December 25, 2020)
21- Tan, Su-Lin "China working with Azerbaijan on belt and road transport route even as Baku restricts investment" South China Morning Post, August 24, 2020 https://www.scmp.com/eco-nomy/global-economy/article/3098600/china-working-azerbaijan-belt-and-road-transport-rou-te-even (accessed December 25, 2020)
22- Jafarli, Shahin "Azerbaijan – China relations" Baku Research Institute, September 22, 2020 https://bakuresearchinstitute.org/azerbaijan-china-relations/ (accessed December 25, 2020)
23- Kuchins, Andrew C – Mankoff, Jeffrey – Backes, Oliver "Central Asia in a Reconnecting Eurasia" Center for Strategic & International Studies, June 2015 https://csis-website-prod.s3.ama-zonaws.com/s3fs-public/legacy_files/files/publication/150513_Kunchins_CentralAsiaTurkme-nistan_Web.pdf (accessed December 20, 2020)

24- Hess, Maximilian "Central Asian Gas Exports to China: Beijing's Latest Bargaining Chip?" Foreign Policy Research Institute, June 16, 2020 https://www.fpri.org/article/2020/06/central-a-sian-gas-exports-to-china-beijings-latest-bargaining-chip/ (accessed December 25, 2020)

25- Kuchins, Andrew C – Mankoff, Jeffrey – Backes, Oliver "Central Asia in a Reconnecting Eurasia" Center for Strategic & International Studies, Haziran 2015 https://csis-website-prod.s3.amazonaws.com/s3fs-public/legacy_files/files/publication/150513_Kunchins_CentralAsia-Turkmenistan_Web.pdf

26- Jawari, Naweed, "Can China be a peacemaker in Afghanistan?" Lovy Institute, October 20, 2020 https://www.lowyinstitute.org/the-interpreter/can-china-be-peacemaker-afghanistan (accessed December 24, 2020)

27- Sadat, Sayed K. "Sovyet işgali Afganistan'da derin izler bıraktı" Anadolu Ajansı, February 14, 2019 https://www.aa.com.tr/tr/dunya/sovyet-isgali-afganistanda-derin-izler-birakti/1392109# (accessed December 24, 2020)

28- Brown, Vanda F, "A BRI(DGE) Too Far: The Unfulfilled Promise anda Limitations of China's Involvement in Afganistan" Brookings Insitute, June 2020 https://www.brookings.edu/wp-con-tent/uploads/2020/06/FP_20200615_china_afghanistan_felbab_brown.pdf (accessed December 24, 2020)

29- Jawari, Naweed, "Can China be a peacemaker in Afghanistan?" Lovy Institute, October 20, 2020 https://www.lowyinstitute.org/the-interpreter/can-china-be-peacemaker-afghanistan (accessed December 24, 2020)

30- Kaura, Vinay, "What does China's growing engagement in Afghanistan mean for the US" Middle East Institute, August 7, 2020 https://www.mei.edu/publications/what-does-chi-nas-growing-engagement-afghanistan-mean-us (accessed December 24, 2020)

31- Jawari, Naweed, "Can China be a peacemaker in Afghanistan?" Lovy Institute, October 20, 2020 https://www.lowyinstitute.org/the-interpreter/can-china-be-peacemaker-afghanistan (accessed December 24, 2020)

32- Brown, Vanda F, "A BRI(DGE) Too Far: The Unfulfilled Promise and Limitations of China's Involvement in Afganistan" Brookings Insitute, June 2020 https://www.brookings.edu/wp-con-tent/uploads/2020/06/FP_20200615_china_afghanistan_felbab_brown.pdf

33- Alice Wells, " A Conversation with Ambassador Alice Wells on the China-Pakistan Economic Corridor" (speech, Washington, DC, November 21, 2019), https://www.state.gov/a-conversati-on-with-ambassador-alicewells-on-the-china-pakistan-economic-corridor/ (accessed December 26, 2020)

34- Cavanough, Edward "Tajikistan: An opportunity for great power cooperation" The Diplomat, May 10, 2015 https://thediplomat.com/2015/05/tajikistan-an-opportunity-for-great-power-coo-peration/ (accessed December 26, 2020)

35- Shahbazov, Fuad, "China's economic and military expansion in Tajikistan" The Diplomat November 23, 2016 https://thediplomat.com/2016/11/chinas-economic-and-military-expansi-on-in-tajikistan/ (accessed December 20, 2020)

36- Ibid.

37- Putz, Catherine "Why did Tajikistan make an appearance in the China Military Power Report" The Diplomat, September 3, 2020 https://thediplomat.com/2020/09/why-did-tajikis-tan-make-an-appearance-in-the-china-military-power-report/ (accessed December 26, 2020)

38- Shih, Gerry, "In Central Asia's forbidding highlands, a quiet newcomer: Chinese troops" The Washington Post, February 18, 2019 https://www.washingtonpost.com/world/asia_pa-cific/in-central-asias-forbidding-highlands-a-quiet-newcomer-chinese-troops/2019/02/18/78d4a8d0-1e62-11e9-a759-2b8541bbbe20_story.html?noredirect=on (accessed December 26, 2020)

39- Xinhua, "Factbox: China's economic cooperation with Tajikistan, Kyrgyzstan re-aps fruitful results" Xinhuahet.com June 11, 2019 http://www.xinhuanet.com/englis-h/2019-06/11/c_138134440.htm (accessed December 26, 2020)

40- Qi, Ren "Tajik leader, hails broad benefits of Belt, Road" China Daily, April 26, 2019 https://www.chinadaily.com.cn/a/201904/26/WS5cc26932a3104842260b8863.html (accessed December 26, 2020)

41- Eurasian Times Desk, "China-Tajikistan Relations Deepen; Has Beijing Debt-Trapped Another Country?" The Eurasian Times, November 4, 2019 https://eurasiantimes.com/china-tajikis-tan-relations-deepen-has-beijing-debt-trapped-another-country/ (accessed December 26, 2020)

42- Tan, Amorith "China and Russia: Competition in Kyrgyzstan" Future Directions Internatio-nal, January 30, 2020, https://www.futuredirections.org.au/publication/china-and-russia-compe-tition-in-kyrgyzstan/ (accessed December 26, 2020)

43- Silk Road Briefing, "Kyrgyzstan Cancels China Logistics Super-Hub Investment After At-Bashy Protests" February 28, 2020 https://www.silkroadbriefing.com/news/2020/02/28/ky-rgyzstan-cancels-china-logistics-super-hub-investment-al-bashy-protests/ (accessed December 26, 2020)

44- Sukhankin, Sergey, "The Security Component of the BRI in Central Asia, Part Two: China's (Para)Military Efforts to Promote Security in Tajikistan and Kyrgyzstan" The Ja-mestown Foundation, August 12, 2020 https://jamestown.org/program/the-security-compo-nent-of-the-bri-in-central-asia-part-two-chinas-paramilitary-efforts-to-promote-security-in-ta-jikistan-and-kyrgyzstan/

45-Perris, Rainer M. "Uzbekistan Is The Hidden Gem In China's New Silk Road" Forbes, Septem-ber 9, 2019

46- Limanov, Oleg, "Uzbekistan-China Relations During the COVID-19 Pandemic" Central Asian Bureau for Analytical Reporting, January 6, 2020 https://cabar.asia/en/uzbekistan-china-relati-ons-during-the-covid-19-pandemic (accessed December 24, 2020)

47-Putz, Catherine "What's Next for the Belt and Road in Central Asia?" The Diplomat, May 17 2017 https://thediplomat.com/2017/05/whats-next-for-the-belt-and-road-in-central-asia/ (accessed December 24, 2020)

48- Limanov, Oleg, "Uzbekistan-China Relations During the COVID-19 Pandemic" Central Asian Bureau for Analytical Reporting, January 6, 2020 https://cabar.asia/en/uzbekistan-china-relati-ons-during-the-covid-19-pandemic (accessed December 24, 2020)

49- "Kazakhstan and Uzbekistan spurn US call to confront China" Nikkei Asia, February 13, 2020 https://asia.nikkei.com/Politics/International-relations/Kazakhstan-and-Uzbekis-tan-spurn-US-call-to-confront-China (accessed December 24, 2020)

50- Reuters Staff, "Kazakhstan summons Chinese ambassador in protest over article" April 14, 2020 https://www.reuters.com/article/us-kazakhstan-china/kazakhstan-summons-chinese-am-bassador-in-protest-over-article-idUSKCN21W1AH (accessed December 22, 2020)

51- Ibid.

52- China Org – "Past, present and future Sino-Kazakhstan Relations" http://www.china.org.cn/english/2003/Jun/65983.htm (accessed December 22, 2020)

53- Jamali, Ahmed B. "China's Silk Road diplomacy in Kazakhstan" Asia Times June 5, 2020 https://asiatimes.com/2020/06/chinas-silk-road-diplomacy-in-kazakhstan/ (accessed December 22, 2020)

54- Yau, Niva – "Tracing the Chinese Footprints in Kazakhstan's Oil and Gas Industry" The Diplomat, December 12, 2020 https://thediplomat.com/2020/12/tracing-the-chinese-footp-rints-in-kazakhstans-oil-and-gas-industry/ (accessed December 22, 2020)

55-Lin, Leo "A State Visit by Kazakhstan's President Demonstrates China's Increasing Influence in Central Asia" The Jamestown, November 19, 2019 https://jamestown.org/program/a-sta-te-visit-by-kazakhstans-president-demonstrates-chinas-increasing-influence-in-central-asia/ (accessed December 22, 2020)

56- Ibid.

57- Jamali, Ahmed B. "China's Silk Road diplomacy in Kazakhstan" Asia Times June 5, 2020 https://asiatimes.com/2020/06/chinas-silk-road-diplomacy-in-kazakhstan/ (accessed December 22, 2020)

58- Reid, Standish "China's Path Forward Is Getting Bumpy" The Atlantic, https://www.theatlan-tic.com/international/archive/2019/10/china-belt-road-initiative-problems-kazakhstan/597853 (accessed December 27, 2020)

59- Jamali, Ahmed B. "China's Silk Road diplomacy in Kazakhstan" Asia Times June 5, 2020 https://asiatimes.com/2020/06/chinas-silk-road-diplomacy-in-kazakhstan/ (accessed December 27, 2020)

60- Magistad, Mary K "China's new Silk Road traverses Kazakhstan. But some Kazakhs are skeptical of Chinese influence." The World, September 14, 2020 https://www.pri.org/stories/2020-09-14/chinas-new-silk-road-traverses-kazakhstan-some-kazakhs-are-skeptical-chinese (accessed December 27, 2020)

61- Shukhankin, Sergey "The Security Component of the BRI in Central Asia, Part Three: China's (Para)Military Efforts to Promote Security in Kazakhstan, Uzbekistan and Turkmenistan", The Jamestown Foundation, October 19, 2020 https://jamestown.org/program/the-security-component-of-the-bri-in-central-asia-part-three-chinas-paramilitary-efforts-to-promote-security-in-kazakhstan-uzbekistan-and-turkmenistan/ (accessed December 20, 2020)

62- Teizzi, Shannon "Xi in Mongolia: Trade, Security, and Neighborhood Diplomacy" The Diplomat, August 22, 2014 https://thediplomat.com/2014/08/xi-in-mongolia-trade-security-and-neighborhood-diplomacy/ (accessed December 22, 2020)

63- Gill, Rob "Balancing Mongolia's Growth and Sovereignty: Up, Down, or Out?" Center for Strategic & International Studies https://www.csis.org/npfp/balancing-mongolias-growth-and-sovereignty-down-or-out (accessed December 22, 2020)

64- DemDigest "From 'Chinese influence' to 'Beijing interference': Time to aid Mongolia" September 27, 2019 https://www.demdigest.org/from-chinese-influence-to-beijing-interference-time-to-aid-mongolia/ (accessed December 22, 2020)

65- Teizzi, Shannon "As Mongolia Welcomes China's Foreign Minister, Citizens Protest" The Diplomat, September 16, 2020 https://thediplomat.com/2020/09/as-mongolia-welcomes-chinas-foreign-minister-citizens-protest/ (accessed December 22, 2020)

66- BBC News: "India-China dispute: The border row explained in 400 words" https://www.bbc.com/news/world-asia-53062484 (accessed December 22, 2020)

67- Neagle, Kai "Why Is China's Belt and Road Initiative Being Questioned by Japan and India" May 2, 2020, https://www.e-ir.info/2020/05/02/why-is-chinas-belt-and-road-initiative-being-questioned-by-japan-and-india/ (accessed December 20, 2020)

68- Yujun, Feng – Gabuev, Alexander - Haenele, Paul – Bin, Ma – Trenin, Dimitri "The Belt and Road Initiative: Views from Washington, Moscow, and Beijing" Carnegie – Tsinghua Center for Global Policy, April 8, 2019 https://carnegietsinghua.org/2019/04/08/belt-and-road-initiative-views-from-washington-moscow-and-beijing-pub-78774 (accessed December 18, 2020)